Women, Power and Policy

Second Edition

Pergamon Titles of Related Interest

Arnot RACE AND GENDER: Equal Opportunities Policies in Education
Brock-Utne EDUCATING FOR PEACE: A Feminist Perspective
Bryner BUREAUCRATIC DISCRETION: Law and Policy in Federal
Regulatory Agencies
Levin/Ferman THE POLITICAL HAND: Policy Implementation and Youth
Employment Programs
Radin/Hawley THE POLITICS OF FEDERAL REORGANIZATION: Creating
the Department of Education
Slipman HELPING OURSELVES TO POWER: A Training Handbook for
Women on the Skills of Public Life

Related Journal*

WOMEN'S STUDIES INTERNATIONAL FORUM

*Free sample copies available upon request.

Women, Power and Policy

Toward the Year 2000

Second Edition

Edited by

Ellen Boneparth
United States Department of State

Emily Stoper
California State University, Hayward

PERGAMON PRESS
New York   Oxford   Beijing   Frankfurt
São Paulo   Sydney   Tokyo   Toronto

U.S.A.	Pergamon Press, Maxwell House, Fairview Park, Elmsford, New York 10523, U.S.A.
U.K.	Pergamon Press, Headington Hill Hall, Oxford OX3 0BW, England
PEOPLE'S REPUBLIC OF CHINA	Pergamon Press, Room 4037, Qianmen Hotel, Beijing, People's Republic of China
FEDERAL REPUBLIC OF GERMANY	Pergamon Press, Hammerweg 6, D-6242 Kronberg, Federal Republic of Germany
BRAZIL	Pergamon Editora, Rua Eça de Queiros, 346, CEP 04011, Paraiso, São Paulo, Brazil
AUSTRALIA	Pergamon Press Australia, P.O. Box 544, Potts Point, N.S.W. 2011, Australia
JAPAN	Pergamon Press, 8th Floor, Matsuoka Central Building, 1-7-1 Nishishinjuku, Shinjuku-ku, Tokyo 160, Japan
CANADA	Pergamon Press Canada, Suite No. 271, 253 College Street, Toronto, Ontario, Canada M5T 1R5

Copyright © 1988 Pergamon Books Inc.

First edition 1982
Second edition 1988

Library of Congress Cataloguing in Publication Data

Women, power, and policy.
Includes index.
1. Feminism--United States. 2. Women in politics--United States. 3. Women--Employment--United States.
4. Motherhood--United States. I. Boneparth, Ellen, 1945- . II. Stoper, Emily.
HQ1426.W647   1988   305.4'2'0973   87-16051

British Library Cataloguing in Publication Data

Women, power and policy: toward the year 2000.——2nd ed.
1. Women—Social conditions
I. Boneparth, Ellen II. Stoper, Emily
305.4'2   HQ1154

ISBN 0–08–034486–0 Hardcover
ISBN 0–08–034485–2 Flexicover

Printed in Great Britain by A. Wheaton & Co. Ltd., Exeter

This book is dedicated
with our deepest affection and gratitude
to our parents,
Marjorie and Joseph Boneparth
and
George Schottenfeld and Adele Kampf

Contents

Acknowledgements

This book would have been impossible without the generous assistance of people too numerous to mention. Our very special thanks go to our editor, Lynn Rosen; to Lily Cincone for so ably managing our communications to the contributors; to Roberta Johnson and Arnold Stoper for their sharp ideas and warm encouragement; and to Sissy Hristodoulakis, Peggy Backlund and Betty Perry for secretarial help above and beyond the call of duty.

WPP—A*

Foreword
Feminism and Political Power: Some Thoughts on a Strategy for the Future

Margarita Papandreou

If we define politics as involvement in the public sphere for social, economic or political purposes, whether for creating change or for preservation of the status quo, then women have been involved in politics informally for many years. Most recently, women have been working for change through the large political movement called women's liberation. All through history, however, they have been excluded from the formal political bodies where they could participate in making decisions in pursuit of their goals.

Only recently, in the past few years, a small number of women have become legislators and heads of state in many countries. Despite this involvement in the public sphere, we observe that the system of every country still reflects almost exclusively the male vision of how the members of its society should function. This can be said without exception because there is no society in the world which is not patriarchal, or male-dominated.

In tests on sex differences in values and interests (the same basic results are seen in almost all cultures) women score high on scales for esthetic, social, and religious values. Men receive high marks for politics, economics, and technology. These *socially induced* characteristics make a difference in male and female culture. How would society be if it developed a culture that had the *value system* of a women's world—that of non-violence, of caring and nurturing, of non-oppressive personal and institutional relations? The answer is necessarily hypothetical. These values would be most likely the basis for governing by women, and we have not had enough women in positions of power to give us a glimpse of such a society. However, in Scandinavian countries where there is a high feminist consciousness and a commitment to social justice, the priorities on issues are different, less militaristic and more humanistic. These so-called feminine values are sorely needed in giving birth to a new ethos—a new era.

Now I come to a key question for feminists. How do we manage from a position of relative powerlessness to change our societies? To realize this vision of the world? How do we manage to make those changes when we are not in positions of power to do so? And, if we need to get into decision-making centers, how do we do that without compromising our own value systems?

Let me start by making a distinction among three terms: *sisterhood*, the *women's movement* and *feminism*. Worldwide or global *sisterhood* can be defined simply as a universal concern and individual caring for women as a group everywhere—a compassion, an understanding, an empathy. It is a way in which women relate to each other. We offer each other the love and support that we have been socialized to lavish primarily on husband and children. It is a consciousness that in spite of all things that divide women—class, religion, color, cultural traditions—we do share things *in common* as a gender group. We are the least educated, the lowest on the economic pyramid, responsible for child-raising and the household, and we have little political and decision-making power in the public sphere.

These similarities are the grounds then for *sisterhood*. The *worldwide women's movement* can be considered the organized arm of sisterhood, a loosely knit federation of women's organizations, working in resistance to humiliation, inequality, and injustice. Developing *strategy* for this women's movement is where *feminism* comes in. Feminism embodies the awareness of the special oppression and exploitation that all women face as a gender group. Feminism is the willingness to organize and fight against women's subjugation in society and for the elimination of *sex-based injustice*. Feminists must decide what exactly is wrong, whose fault it is, and what should be done to make matters right. Difficult decisions have to be made, a political-ideological framework developed, and priorities decided. Above all, *we must have a vision*, an image of the kind of world we would like to live in if we had the power to mold it, with a new social organization that would create a different kind of society.

The reason I make these distinctions is that the support of women in general under sisterhood does not translate necessarily to the support of all women running for or elected to political office. In the case of politics, it is not sufficient that the candidate be a woman; she must be a woman with feminist goals, demands, and principles. Women in political positions will be deciding issues that concern our lives, our children's lives, and the life of society; their *political orientation* is critical.

When discussing feminism at the global level, it is important to understand that feminism is suspect in many countries, particularly in Eastern Europe, the Soviet Union, the Arab countries of the Middle East, and dictatorial Latin American countries. Politically empowered women are seen as a threat to a patriarchal system of power. Feminism is rejected in some socialist countries because it is perceived as a reform movement in capitalist societies; that is, it does not challenge the political-economic system on which inequality is based, but merely tries to improve the status of women within the existing capitalist order. With the exception of socialist feminists, feminism does not have a class consciousness. But no matter how you couch the objections to feminism, in political-philosophical terms, in fancy or plain language, it is the feminists' insistence on the right of women to develop their full human potential and to have control over their reproductive functions that has offended the patriarchal mentality, not to mention economic interests that may be hurt by losing women's poorly paid or unpaid labor.

Feminism is the most powerful revolutionary force in the world today. And feminism is urgently needed in a world that is not working, is dangerously out of control, and is losing a sense of what it means to be human. In getting at the heart of sex bias, feminism is challenging the social fabric of society, its political orientation, and the decisions of its political authority. And, it is challenging *all* political and social systems.

What *does* feminism have to say about the burning political, economic, social issues of today? How do feminists look at the armaments race, nuclear power, international relations, development in the third world, value of women's work, and the budget allocations of our respective countries? Do we have *a new, a different perspective*? An enlarged vision of the human experience?

As far as political power is concerned, I wish to focus on mainstream politics and particularly about those societies where electoral politics are possible, where the individual is free to organize to achieve power. I am also going to discuss the power of a mass movement which may ultimately, if used effectively, be the most important force for change. Already women have accomplished much in terms of global consciousness-raising. The women's movement can be credited with changing laws, eliminating barriers to upward mobility in careers, achieving higher levels of education, breaking into "male" fields, and eliminating some sexual stereotyping.

Yet, significant numbers of women have not yet been able to break into that bastion of male power, the traditional political arena—electoral politics. Nor have they, in fact, in one-party states captured important posts in the party or governmental hierarchy. In order to complete the social revolution begun by women, we must develop a strategy that is concerned with the acquisition of political power. Generally, feminists have a negative reaction to such terms. The word power sounds too male. Power for feminists, however, represents the capacity to change—the individual and the environment—without the use of force. In other words, this is not exploitative power, but power that is mutually strengthening. In addition to the lobbying effort, which must continue, women must achieve positions where they can be an integral part of the decision-making process, to decide equally with men on the direction of their societies and of the world. Obtaining these positions can only be done by a strengthening of the women's movement.

A problem in gaining power is that the very thing we want to transform—the relation of men and women to political power and reproductive labor—is one of the major obstacles to gaining power. It is very difficult to organize a campaign, attend meetings, write brochures, and read political theory while washing diapers, dispensing cough syrup, cooking meals, nursing sick relatives, cleaning house, and providing the emotional needs of family members, to mention just a few tasks of women.

And yet this must be done if feminist principles are to become a way of life. If the women's movement is to increase its power, both as a lobbying force and an organization backing and electing its spokespersons to traditional political positions, then it must become more of a *mass movement*, more of a *grass-roots movement*. It means not only getting in touch with the average woman, the truly dispossessed woman, the racially discriminated-against woman, the factory worker, but also incorporating *her* into the movement. It means learning from *her* how she perceives changes that would make her oppression less, and her life more decent; and how *she* looks at the struggle for equality—what she likes about it, what she finds threatening about it.

This would be a second stage of consciousness-raising, but at a more sophisticated level. The first stage created an awareness that women had problems in common. The next stage is to discuss priorities in attacking these problems by letting *those speak who previously had the least opportunity to participate in the struggle for equality*. This involves community organization, which will broaden our concept of "women's issues" and propel us into a social reform platform to suit the needs of more and more women. And, it will bring greater numbers of women into the movement.

A key issue for women today in the western world is full employment; that is, an expansion of the economy. At the same time that we want to be able to make a decent living and have our economic independence, we want to balance this with the demands of child-raising. If we are to be practical and objective about gaining elected positions, then we must recognize that in all western democracies, in fact, in all societies, economic issues are of enormous importance to women. We have come to accept too readily that a certain percentage of people will be unemployed, that the right to work is not also a human right. We forget that the percentage of nonworking people represents human beings, individual lives, and increasingly with the feminization of poverty, women's lives.

Fighting for alternative economic policies while simultaneously focusing specifically on jobs for women would join women's issues with the broader social issue of unemployment; men and youth are also unemployed. This would give new meaning to feminism. In Greece, our women's organization has been encouraging women to engage in self-help projects, particularly cooperatives, as one way of subverting the effects of female unemployment during the international economic crisis, but also as a means of achieving a form of collective power that can be turned to political advantage.

The strategy in the early stages of the contemporary women's movement, to fight for equality—equal rights and opportunities with men—was a good, specific, understandable goal, one that immediately delineated a line of action, a series of targets that we could all work for. Perhaps we didn't always clarify that equality encompasses values of inter-relatedness, cooperation, and reciprocity, rather than tough competition and self-interest. Perhaps we didn't clarify that the present system has allowed violence and oppression to enter the family in male–female and child–parent relationships, and that we are not anti-family when that unit, in whatever form it may take, provides the environment for the expression of feelings of warmth and tenderness, of closeness and mutuality. Perhaps we didn't make clear that feminists are not against biological motherhood, nor against mothering. I believe *feminists make the best mothers*, but we stand against the use of motherhood to keep us powerless.

Perhaps we didn't pay enough attention during our struggle for equal rights to that heavy sack, that sandbag, which we carried on our backs—the disproportional responsibility for the house, the children, and the elderly. So when the doors were finally opened to us (and they have been to a considerable extent) for education, for entry into traditionally male jobs and professions, and for political participation, there we were, standing at the door, with a man next to us, and we were still carrying a staggering weight as we moved ahead to take advantage of our new opportunities.

If these are criticisms of the women's movement, then that is a sign of basic robustness of the movement. If we are in a period of criticism it is because while working to hold on to our successes (and successes there were as the U.N. Women's Conference in Nairobi confirmed) we are also searching for new directions and appropriate strategies. We are not dogmatic; we are not rigid. *Change is integral to the feminine experience.*

How, then, do we now equalize our burdens, our responsibilities? One possibility is to divide that burden of responsibilities and spread its weight evenly between man and woman. In Sweden, considerable progress has been made in this direction, as in other Nordic countries. We know, of course, that a man considers reproductive labor too time-consuming and, furthermore, if he is doing it while the woman is out politicking, he considers it a serious threat to his masculinity. The two most difficult changes to make in terms of equalizing our responsibilities are relations within the family and role delegations, and entry into the structured political arena. The entry into politics is not only a right, but also a responsibility.

A possible solution for equalizing that responsibility is for the community to take over some of our traditional burden, through child-care centers, old age homes, or government aid for housing for disabled children. A division of domestic work is still essential, because even with community help, no public employee is going to come in at 3 a.m. and calm a baby with an acute earache. To accomplish this sharing requires more work on changing of attitudes and improving the economic independence of the women, so that not only does she earn *something*, but her financial status is comparable to a man's. It requires also that those countries in the western world that haven't already done so develop *a national child care plan*, with paid maternity leave and job protection, so that there is truly a balance among demands of child-raising, work, and politics. Women will mobilize around this issue, a necessary concomitant of opportunity for good jobs outside the home.

In order to get our spokespeople into decision-making political positions, we have to have a strong and dynamic movement and an ever-growing organization. That is why I emphasize the Second Phase—the community organization/grass-roots phase. In electoral politics today in most democracies, organizational support is a key factor to victory. Charismatic leadership is another, and money, still another. The importance of *organization* for women is primary—both before an election and after. The women's movement is a means for both achieving political office and raising the *conscience* of those who reach office. This answers the earlier question of how do we not compromise our value system in the struggle for power? A broadly based movement will be our candidates' super-ego. It will give the woman who achieves a position in a male-dominated environment the strength and courage to stick to her feminist agenda. We don't have money, and we are not enchanted by the notion of charismatic personality leadership roles. When I say women don't have money, this is not entirely true; women just are not accustomed to putting that money to political purpose. We have not yet learned to support ourselves, at least on any grand scale. Where are the campaign funds for feminist candidates? Where are the foundations, originated by a woman or women, for furthering women's studies, research on women or scholarships? Where is a feminist strategy board, a think tank or a feminist Institute on Foreign Affairs?

While I have been dwelling on a strategy for action within our countries that seem to be of more immediate domestic concern, all actions of feminist organizations have *international meaning*. Feminists throughout the world watch, study, learn, and get ideas from feminist actions in other countries. On international goals, feminists must work to form coalitions with the peace movement, the ecological movement, the movement against hunger in the world, and others. The peace movement especially is a natural home for feminists. Our history confirms this: the Pankhursts, the Ashtons, the Schwimmers, the Jane Addams's in the past; recently the Greenham Common women of Great Britain, women of the Nordic countries, and women in Greece as well have set the example. The looming threat of nuclear devastation demands our participation in peace activities, activities for survival. The connection between militarism and sexism is of great concern to us. Patriarchy is a system of values of competition, aggression, emotional denial, and violence. These values are *particularly* prevalent in war, in which the competition is through force, and there are victors and victims, losers and winners. It is a *Weltanschauung*, a belief which tries to smother the human capacity to care. We must press the peace movement into asking the question of whether peace is possible in a patriarchal world. This will force peace educators to explore the links between denial of women's rights and the war system, and the dependence that both sexism and militarism have on violence.

We must understand how and why violence has become so much a part of our lives: violence in the home, muggings, rapes in the streets, terrorism throughout the world, confrontation between nations. We are really a world at war. The huge international arms traffic, the immense budgets of defense departments, the fleets traveling the world through international waters, the 40 or more local wars that are raging now: *we are on a war system*. A new mode of thinking, one that feminism is in the process of developing, is essential to a world where conflict can be solved by non-violent means. Feminists are trying to transcend the dichotomous thinking that has produced the we–they syndrome that divides and factionalizes the world, polarizing the world and feeding the war system. Human beings make distinctions between good and evil: *we* being virtuous and noble, *they* being incapable, unreliable, corrupt. In the feminist world of tomorrow, all people would be looked at alike and all people would have the responsibility to nurture, build trust, enhance life, and to participate in political and community affairs.

Women are not at the negotiating table where our commitment to peace, our capacities to find solutions through dialogue and debate, and our sensitivities to human needs and human rights *are sorely needed*. Therefore, we still must pressure from the outside for considerable improvement in relations between the superpowers, and for a process of international confidence-building and trust. Feminists can make clear that one does not have to agree with the political or economic system of a country in order to like and understand its people. One does not have to assume that one must blast a population off the face of the earth because it has different cultural values, or different political and societal organizations.

The movement must get involved in issues of development at the international level. For those of us in the privileged western world (and I use that term to mean that we are better off in both our economic and human rights, being aware, of course, of the economically disadvantaged *within* our advanced cultures) we have an obligation, a moral duty, if you like, to explore what can be done to reduce the enormous gap in wealth between rich and poor nations. We as concerned women must give serious attention to the special needs and situations of women in these countries and determine whether development has improved or worsened their lot. If development continues along the lines of the present world order, women will continue to have a subordinate position in the development. The economic gap between men and women will widen. Development in the third world has actually *reduced* the power of women and made them more dependent on the system, less self-reliant as the structure of agriculture has changed and most economies have moved from agrarian-based to industrial-based. We must ask the question: What are the development policies of our countries toward the less-advantaged nations? Have we taken into consideration the plight of women and what happens to them under certain development programs? Do we finance projects that worsen the status of women? (This seems often to be the case.)

We are entering a new phase of feminism—call it Grass Roots Feminism, call it Feminism 2000, call it Global Feminism, call it Life-Preserving Feminism, call it simply New Phase Feminism—whatever it may be, it will make history, as did the first phase of modern feminism. Its horizons are unlimited. Never before have women become possibly the *only* salvation for the survival of humanity.

Not so long ago on a flight from Dallas to Chicago, I sat next to a young woman, not very politically aware, but very appealing, and as so often happens with passing acquaintances, people you never expect to see again, we told each other our life histories. At some point she turned to me and said, "You know, I would like to be an activist; I would like to fight for a cause, but I'm not that type."

"What type would you say you are?" I inquired.

"A dreamer," was her response.

"My dear young friend," I said, "The very first condition for being an activist is that you be a dreamer. Without dreams, without a vision, there can be no hope, and hope is the essence and motivating force in the struggle for social change."

I told her that the feminist movement has a vision. We understand, first of all, that we have but one earth, shared by one human race. This globe is home to all—all people, all life, all laughter, all love, all music, all art. We will make it a woman's world, not in the sense of control, power, or dominance, but in the sense of the revolutionary vision that we have, a revolution of the human spirit. Those values that we call women-centered values—caring, gentleness, equality, justice, dignity, compassion—will be diffused throughout societies worldwide.

Perhaps my young friend will join the movement; I would welcome that. The stronger we become, the more certain that we will succeed. We will use that strength to plumb the depths of the human capacity to reach beyond ourselves, to accomplish the "impossible." We will move into positions of power to make a difference, to be a humanizing force with life preservation as our goal.

1
Introduction: A Framework for Policy Analysis

Ellen Boneparth and Emily Stoper

In the late 1960s the women's movement profoundly changed the agenda of American politics by raising a series of new issues that ranged over the areas of economics, reproduction, family relations and sexuality. The women's movement took what had been considered "private" concerns and turned them into public issues — a process called *politicizing the personal*. By the end of the 1970s, issues previously relegated to the private sphere, such as sex-stereotyping, pregnancy, contraception, child care, displaced homemakers, sexual harassment, rape, pornography and domestic violence, were not only matters for public discussion but also matters meriting at least some governmental attention.

The challenge for the women's movement in the 1970s was to convert those issues into actual changes in public policies in the form of new laws, judicial decisions and executive implementation. By giving birth to a series of interest groups, and by expanding its base, the movement met that challenge quite successfully. In the 1980s the movement faced a new challenge: sustaining its gains of the previous decade in a far less friendly climate than it had experienced in the 1970s.

The very speed of the changes wrought in the 1960s and 1970s had aroused the fears and harmed the interests of groups and individuals who had never subscribed to the feminist message in the first place. In 1964 even the idea of passing a law against sex discrimination in employment had seemed laughable to some members of Congress. To such people, feminist positions evolving later, for example, that a man could be legally charged with raping his own wife, must have seemed extremely threatening. Opposition to the kinds of changes sought by the women's movement had begun in the early 1970s with the formation of organized groups opposed to the Equal Rights Amendment (ERA) and the legalization of abortion. Sympathizers with anti-feminist movements won positions in the

1

Reagan administration, and were more vocal and active politically on the national political scene in the 1980s. Now it was their turn to attempt to rewrite the agenda of American politics.

What became of the policy innovations made in the 1960s and 1970s? How did the women's movement shift its strategies to deal with the new environment it faced? What will happen in the future? The Reagan administration and the religious right now both appear to be weakened by scandal. As the political pendulum swings in a more liberal direction, the women's movement has an opportunity to regain the initiative. What new public policy contributions might it offer? To answer these questions, this book offers a series of case studies, providing in-depth examinations of particular issue areas. The case studies shed light on women's issues that have already become public policy, as well as on issues that have yet to appear on the national policy agenda.

An important element of the analysis is a framework for understanding why some efforts at influencing policy are more successful than others. Policy analysis involves examining a wide range of policy characteristics and other variables, including environmental, systemic, and political variables, in order to assess the prospects for policy change. In this introductory chapter, we will chart the course of various women's policies that have appeared on the national agenda over the last decade in order to lay a framework for analysis in the years to come.

ENVIRONMENTAL VARIABLES

Social Climate

The contemporary women's movement was born in the 1960s climate of social change, benefiting in particular from the civil rights movement of that era. By borrowing many of the strategies and much of the rhetoric of the civil rights movement and by piggybacking on some of its legislative victories, such as the Civil Rights Act of 1964 and affirmative action, women achieved notable policy successes in the areas of employment, education, and legal equality. They were able to do this because of the idealistic mood that the civil rights movement had contributed so much to creating. The passage of the Equal Pay Act of 1963 and Title VII of the 1964 Civil Rights Act, the signing of Executive Order 11375 extending affirmative action to women in 1967, the passage of Title IX of the Education Amendments in 1972 and the passage by Congress (its first hurdle) of the Equal Rights Amendment in 1972 may, in part, be attributed to a social climate in which women became recognized as an oppressed group whose needs were a legitimate concern of the policy-making process.

The most striking change of the period, however, did not involve legal or economic issues, but, rather, a uniquely women's issue: reproductive rights. The reform of abortion laws by numerous states in the late 1960s, culminating with the landmark Supreme Court decision in *Roe v. Wade* in 1973, which declared abortion a constitutional right, held out the hope that women could press their policy demands beyond a call for economic and legal equality to questions of social justice.

The social climate changed dramatically between the early 1970s and the early 1980s. The U.S. defeat in Vietnam, the shocking Watergate revelations, the shifting economy, the rising crime rate, and rapidly changing family patterns — all contributed to a mood of insecurity and to an increasing distrust during the 1970s of social change, particularly change brought about by governmental solutions to social problems. While the women's movement expanded during this period, pressing a whole new set of policy demands, the popular mood shifted from social movements and toward looking for answers from a more traditional direction.

In the early 1980s, the fundamentalist churches, led by preachers such as Jerry Falwell and Pat Robertson, and utilizing the mass media and political organizing, popularized a social philosophy that emphasized paternal authority and maternal subordination within the family, the infusion of religion and traditional values into public education, an end to legal abortion, and a hostility to homosexuals and, for that matter, to anyone who did not live in a traditional nuclear family. Although few if any of the goals of this traditional revival have been achieved, the women's movement had to divert resources from such areas as the struggle for more child care to prevent the passage of laws like the Family Protection Act and to resist attempts to censor feminist materials in public libraries and school curricula. The "Born Again" Christians claimed millions of faithful followers, including all three of the 1980 presidential candidates: Reagan, Carter and Anderson.

At the same time, the 1980s have been a period in which many of the social changes of the 1970s were extended and consolidated. Women's labor force participation continued to rise; women doctors, lawyers and business executives became an increasingly normal and accepted part of the American scene; increasing numbers of mothers entered the labor force and placed their children in child care. Whereas 15 years earlier, such mothers would have been vulnerable to criticism as selfish and neglectful, by the 1980s, the shoe was on the other foot: mothers who were not employed, particularly after their youngest child entered school, often felt apologetic and defensive. This rapid change in social attitudes caused some women (both feminist and traditionalist) to take an increasingly confrontational stance, while it caused many others to see themselves as groping for a decent way to live in a world with seriously competing demands on their time and with fewer reliable social guidelines. Neither of these attitudes was conducive to the development of clear new lines of policy on women's issues.

Economic Climate

The economic climate also helps set the stage for policy making. In an expanding economy, new programs, especially programs involving substantial government expenditure, are more favorably received than in an economy beset by recession and/or inflation. Just as the general social climate of the 1960s supported new policy initiatives, so did the healthy economic climate. Economic arguments were not a powerful deterrent in the late 1960s and early 1970s to the passage of new programs. Even so, the policy achievements of the women's movement in this period were primarily in the form of anti-discrimination policies, which are far less costly than programs providing economic benefits.

By the end of the 1970s, the economic situation in the United States had worsened to the point where the economy was suffering the effects of "stagflation," simultaneous inflation and recession. The prevailing mood of both the executive branch and the Congress was one of fiscal conservatism. Economic concerns were a significant but not determining source of opposition to women's policy demands in the early 1970s; however, by the end of the decade economic arguments against new programs became paramount for many policymakers.

A good example is the issue of child care. Although government-subsidized day care was recognized as expensive in the early 1970s, liberals and moderates in Congress weighed the social advantages of child-care programs against the costs and passed a substantial child-care package in 1971, only to have it vetoed by President Nixon. In contrast, by the end of the 1970s, child-care programs failed even to move out of congressional committees as supporters concluded that it would be impossible to obtain a national child-care program in a climate of extreme fiscal constraints.

Under the Reagan administration, the terms of the debate became ideological again. Ronald Reagan entered office with a strong, ideologically conservative commitment to cut domestic spending and balance the budget. He did indeed sharply cut domestic spending, including many of the programs the women's movement had fought for. However, the initial effect of his much-touted "supply-side economics," when combined with the policies of the Federal Reserve Board, was to plunge the country into the worst recession since the 1930s and to triple the size of the budget deficit. In 1983, the country embarked on a long, slow recovery from the recession. Reagan continued to adhere to his ideological belief that the government should pay for fewer social programs; at the same time, the enormous deficit and Reagan's continued desire to greatly increase weapons spending made the restoration of the slashed programs seem impractical.

Ironically, one of Reagan's other ideological commitments — tax cutting — resulted in salvaging some feminist gains. While child-care programs for the poor were cut, the generous child-care tax credit that largely benefited the middle class was retained, even when tax reform closed many other "loopholes." Apparently, in the conservative climate of the 1980s, permitting millions of middle-class parents to pay somewhat lower taxes did not seem as distasteful as appropriating money for programs to provide child care that would largely have benefited the working poor. In future years, the budget deficit will probably spell doom for any new social programs that require substantial amounts of money. And if Congress and the president are at all serious about cutting the deficit, there are likely to be more cuts in programs that benefit primarily women and children.

Public opinion in the middle 1980s seems to be shifting again, this time against military spending and in favor of some social spending. For example, the Gramm–Rudman–Hollings approach (the law mandating a balanced budget by the year 1991) probably means that the budget will not be balanced on the backs of women alone, but rather will require automatic reductions across the board, including cuts in military programs. However, the looming deficit probably means that the situation will get worse before it gets better for social programs. The fact that so many of the women's programs, such as assistance for battered women and displaced homemakers, were innovations of the 1970s does not bode well for them. They have not been in existence long enough for the public to think of them as an essential part of the "safety net." Moreover, they were funded by a combination of state and local moneys and federal block grants to state and local governments under revenue sharing. All these sources of funding have proved much more vulnerable to cuts than federal entitlement programs such as social security.

Political Climate

The political climate is perhaps the hardest to assess as a variable. With respect to policy change, it determines the extent to which a social movement's goals are recognized as legitimate and deserving of a political response. In the 1960s, the greatest problem the women's movement faced was being taken seriously. More devastating than political opposition was the ridicule heaped on the movement by opinion leaders in government, in the arts, in universities, and most significantly, in the media. Women's issues were noted mostly for their entertainment value. "Bra burning," not employment discrimination, was the identifying tag for the women's movement.

Then, beginning in 1969, the movement began to be taken more seriously by the media. The 1970s saw a dual process: the spreading and legitimation of feminist ideas throughout the population and the rise of a well organized movement in opposition to these ideas. The view that sex discrimination in employment was unjust became almost universally accepted by the American people. Other feminist ideas also gained widespread acceptance: that rape victims deserved far more respectful and caring treatment by the police and courts, that the battering of women was a widespread problem and merited public concern, that women should not be discriminated against in education, that female athletes should be given full opportunities for training, and so on.

Simultaneously, however, there arose significant opposition to the women's movement. That opposition is today firmly established in a wide variety of organizations with considerable financial backing and grass-roots support. While the rallying cries of these groups vary (anti-abortion, anti-ERA, morality, and preservation of the family), they have a common rationale, namely, to keep women in their traditional roles of wife, mother, and homemaker. Support for these organizations comes from the Catholic, Mormon, and fundamentalist Christian churches and from political organizations of the far right.

The greatest political victory of the anti-feminists was the defeat of the Equal Rights Amendment, which failed in 1982 to achieve ratification by the necessary 38 state legislatures. Even with a Democrat-controlled House of Representatives and Senate, the ERA appears unlikely in the near future to gain the two-thirds vote necessary in both houses of Congress, the necessary first step in a second attempt at passage. Perhaps even more important than particular legislative defeats was the psychological victory won by the anti-feminists, who managed to put the women's movement on the defensive. The resulting angry confrontations and sour rhetoric — on both sides — created a climate in which many women did not wish to identify themselves as either feminists or anti-feminists. Furthermore, by managing to identify their cause with that of the family, anti-feminists created doubts in the minds of a great many women about accepting the world view of feminism, no matter how much they might agree with its particular program (and they did continue to do so in public opinion polls).

In the 1980s the women's movement continued to identify new problems that called for public policy responses, such as sexual harassment of tenants, marital rape and pornography, but none of these had the power and broad appeal of the issues generated in the 1960s and 1970s. And there were other new urgent social issues on the public agenda, such as teen pregnancy, child sexual abuse and drug abuse, which, at least in the popular mind, had little connection with feminism. Finally, a new cohort of young women behaved as if the women's movement had already achieved equal status for them, allowing them to either direct their attention to other issues or simply get on with the work of building their careers and their families.

SYSTEMIC VARIABLES

Decentralized Government

Our decentralized political system has been both a blessing and a curse for the policies proposed by the women's movement. Decentralized policy making brought the women's movement a great defeat in the last decade—the loss of the Equal Rights Amendment (ERA)—but it has kept alive many other programs in the dark days of the Reagan administration.

The failure to ratify the ERA was a direct result of the decentralized process of ratification of a constitutional amendment, requiring approval not only by two-thirds of both houses of Congress but also by three-quarters of the state legislatures. Opposition to the ERA was regionally based: of the 15 states that failed to ratify, all but two are in, or border on, the South or Southwest. Thus, the majority national will was thwarted by a regional minority.

Ironically, on another key women's issue, abortion, the complexities of the constitutional amending process have thus far prevented the banning of abortion. While there is support for such an amendment, as evidenced by the 19 states where there have been calls for a constitutional convention on abortion, pro-choice forces in Congress have been able to forestall any such move.

On the thorny issue of the financing of abortion for poor women, decentralized government has worked in favor of the feminist position. In 1976 when Congress passed the Hyde Amendment, eliminating federal funding under Medicaid for abortion except in very limited circumstances, access to abortion for most low-income women was placed in jeopardy. But feminists were able to use their influence in several states to secure state funding for Medicaid abortions (though as of 1986, the number of such states had decreased from a peak of 15 to nine plus the District of Columbia).

Feminists have also been able to secure state and local funding to compensate for some of the spending cuts of the Reagan years in areas such as child care, battered women's shelters, rape crisis centers, and displaced homemakers' centers. Much of the federal funding for these programs had come in the form of block grants for social services under revenue sharing, and it was state and local governments that had made the original choices to spend a good deal of this money on services for women. When federal revenue sharing was cut, some state and local governments restored, or partially restored, the funds from their own budgets.

This illustrates an important point, namely, that states may serve as laboratories in which new social policies are tried. Two good examples from the 1980s are marital rape and enforcement of women's custody rights. Ten years ago, no state had a law against a man raping his wife; today 24 states have such a law, although it would have been impossible to pass such legislation at the federal level. Similarly, when a few states began to take seriously the complaints of divorced women whose former husbands had abducted their children or, more commmonly, were simply not making their child support payments, the issue was eventually brought to national attention and a major new federal law was passed in 1984, requiring all states to set up programs that would deduct child support payments from the paychecks of delinquent fathers. Thus, the decentralized system of government, by providing "multiple cracks," can both help and obstruct policy change.

The Role of the Courts

Another kind of "multiple crack" is through the courts, which operate in this country with an almost unique degree of independence of and power over the other branches, reflecting the principle of separation of powers. The Supreme Court dealt a serious blow to the women's movement in the 1984 case of *Grove City College v. Bell*, when it interpreted Title IX of the Education Amendments of 1972, which forbids sex discrimination in education, in such a way as to greatly weaken enforcement. An entire educational institution could no longer be threatened with denial of federal funding because of discrimination in one program; only the discriminating program was subject to the penalty. Congress could pass legislation restoring the stronger enforcement rule for Title IX but has so far failed to do so.

The Grove City College case represented the courts acting in opposition to the goals of the women's movement. However, in other important areas of the law, the Supreme Court has protected women's rights during a politically hostile Reagan period. It has twice struck down local legislation designed to make it more difficult to obtain an abortion by requiring waiting periods, the provision of specific misleading information supposedly needed for "informed consent," and the need for the presence of a second physician and other arbitrary policies that cause delay and expense. (The cases involved were *City of Akron v. Akron Center for*

Reproductive Health, 1983, and *Thornburgh v. American College of Obstetricians and Gynecologists*, 1986.)

The Court has also upheld and strengthened the principle of affirmative action. In 1987 it decided its first case concerning affirmative action for women (earlier cases had involved minority group members). In the case of *Johnson v. Transit Agency, Santa Clara County, California*, the Court upheld the legality of an affirmative action program that was not based on proven past or present discrimination, thus going beyond precedent in a significant way.

Incremental Policymaking

An additional systemic variable, different from but related to decentralization and separation of powers, is a policy-making process characterized by incrementalism. In a system of divided government it is easier to obtain agreement to move in new policy directions in increments than to fashion major policy out of "whole cloth." Thus, initiatives that expand the coverage of existing policies, which take the form of amendments to existing legislation, or which are introduced as "pilot" programs, are more likely to succeed than initiatives that are presented as highly visible, large-scale new programs, moving in directions different from existing policy.

The major governmental responses to the demands of the women's movement over the past 20 years have occurred through incremental policymaking. Progress in equal employment opportunity has been made by extending to women the same protections afforded racial minorities. Thanks largely to the long struggle of Black people, anti-discrimination policy fits with accepted notions, at least for liberals and moderates, of the proper exercise of governmental power. Having made an incremental step by obtaining legislation against sex discrimination in employment in 1964, women were then able to add other incremental anti-discrimination legislation: in education in 1972, in the granting of credit in 1973, for pregnant women in 1978, and in pensions in 1984.

Women have been less successful in achieving policy goals in areas that have no history of government involvement. Although the principle of anti-discrimination is well recognized, the idea of correcting discrimination not on an individual basis but by requiring employers to change their policies toward whole groups of employees is without direct precedent in American policy. Therefore, it has been more difficult to win support for affirmative action and pay equity policies. (The latter issue, incidentally, represents an excellent example of policy initiative at the state and local level.)

Where major new government programs are sought, there has also been strong resistance to change. For example, the new issues of aid to displaced homemakers, violence against women, and rape prevention have received government support in the form of small pilot programs but have not yet been recognized as widespread social needs deserving of major funding. Even child care, which is a policy demand with a long history, has never been recognized as a fundamental right for working women, but rather has been provided relunctantly and often temporarily as a solution to other problems such as labor shortages or welfare dependency. Thus, the style of incremental policymaking, while permitting social change in established policy areas, inhibits the process of change when the demand is for policy in new realms.

POLITICAL VARIABLES

Lobbying

While environmental and systemic variables set the broader stage for policymaking, political variables determine the immediate prospects for effective policy change. In the past 20 years, the women's movement has evolved from a diffuse social movement to an increasingly organized political interest. New women's groups such as the National Organization for Women (NOW), the National Women's Political Caucus (NWPC) and the Women's Equity Action League (WEAL) have established themselves as general lobbying organizations. Many other lobbies have been established in specialized issue areas such as employment, health, education, reproductive rights, and violence against women.

The success of a lobbying organization depends on many factors. Financial resources are critical to support the functions of information gathering, communicating with group members and the general public, making political contacts, and establishing a presence in the many institutional arenas where policymaking occurs. All these functions require personnel who have substantive expertise and who are highly knowledgeable about the intricacies of the policy-making process. While the women's movement has had since its inception some leaders with extensive political experience, lobbying efforts have rarely kept pace with the growth of new issues, in part because of insufficient financial resources and in part because of a dearth of experienced personnel.

Today, the list of organized interest groups in Washington dealing with women's concerns is impressive. Moreover, women's organizations are learning the techniques of fund raising, such as utilizing direct mail solicitations, tax-exempt legal and defense funds, and appeals to large financial interests such as corporations and foundations that have not traditionally supported women's programs. While scarce resources will remain a problem for women, the principal concern for women's lobbies today is less one of organizational survival than of channeling resources into areas where their efforts will yield the most tangible results.

Political Coalitions

Rarely is an organized interest so influential that it can achieve its policy goals without the help of allies. In the case of the women's movement, political allies have been difficult to find. Some likely allies are competing for their own share of government benefits and others such as labor unions, liberal religious groups, and civil rights groups, may covertly be defending themselves against challenges by women.

A good example of the competition between likely allies is the tension between women and minorities in the field of equal employment opportunity. Women's groups complain that enforcers of equal opportunity legislation put racial minorities before women; Blacks and Hispanics complain that affirmative action goals are met by the hiring of white women rather than minority women and men. While there is some justification for both of these positions, it is a shame that the tensions between women and minorities have made them antagonists in many situations where they could be allies.

The child-care issue illustrates the difficulty of forming coalitions with organizations that are on the liberal end of the spectrum but favor traditional responses to social problems. When national child-care legislation was a real possibility in the early 1970s, both women's groups and labor unions strongly agreed that child-care centers were urgently needed by working women. The unions, however, wanted child care incorporated into the public school system and administered by professional personnel, who of course would be organized into existing teachers' unions. Most women's groups, on the other hand, wanted child-care centers controlled by the local community, with parents setting policy and playing a major administrative role. Such disagreements have remained a major stumbling block in the formation of an effective child-care coalition.

With some groups, coalition-building has been quite successful. New women's movement groups have found allies among the older, more traditional women's organizations such as Business and Professional Women, the American Association of University Women, the League of Women Voters, the National Council of Negro Women, and so on. These groups were willing to set aside their differences on issues like abortion in order to form mutually beneficial coalitions on the ERA and various anti-discrimination policies.

In the 1980s, women's groups working for pay equity have succeeded in forming coalitions with labor unions, which are now more responsive to women, as the numbers of their female members grow. Some feminists who sought to pass legislation against pornography have found themselves in an uneasy and rather shaky coalition with groups on the religious right (a coalition that infuriates many other feminists).

Although many feminists are sympathetic to the peace and anti-nuclear causes, women's lobbies are only now slowly taking on these issues or forming coalitions with such groups. Feminist leaders are wary of the temptation to argue that peace is a special responsibility of women, fearing the implication that if women take care of peace, men can then feel free to make war.

Without coalitions, feminist groups are isolated and impotent in American politics, but the quest to form coalitions creates problems of its own.

Leadership

While public awareness of women's issues has increased dramatically over the past 20 years, most national policymakers still place a low priority on women's concerns as opposed to issues like the economy, foreign policy, and defense. Leadership on women's issues has rested with a small handful of women and men in federal, state and local legislatures and executive branches.

Women members of Congress have been too few and too often divided by political ideology, partisan allegiances, and regional loyalties, as well as their own attitudes regarding women's concerns. The Congressional Caucus for Women's Issues has been unable to achieve consensus on some issues and, initially, served mostly as a forum for discussion. Today the caucus, with 150 members, can count a number of legislative victories. However, leadership on women's issues, whether by women or men, has made officeholders vulnerable to negative campaigns, particularly by anti-abortion groups. Such campaigns contributed to the defeat of several liberal senators in the 1980 election, though they do not appear to have been as successful in more recent elections.

Leadership on women's issues has, if anything, been even less visible in the executive branch than in Congress. While more women were appointed to influential policy-making positions in the Carter administration than in earlier administrations, most served in positions that gave them little opportunity to voice their concerns over women's issues. Female Carter administration officials did speak out as a group against the administration's stand opposing abortion as a means of family planning.

Challenging administration policy proved dangerous, however, as President Carter's first presidential liaison for women's groups, Midge

Costanza, discovered when she was dismissed for her open criticism of the president. Costanza's successor, Sarah Weddington, while serving as an advocate for women within the administration, maintained a very low profile in her public role. Both of Carter's female cabinet appointees, Patricia Harris of the Department of Housing and Urban Development (HUD) and later Health Education and Welfare (HEW), Juanita Kreps of the Commerce Department, and Shirley Hufstedler of the Department of Education had the political support of women's groups, but none made women a particular constituency in their departments.

In the Reagan administration, women hold a number of senior administrative positions, but they are either not dealing with women's issues or have focused their efforts on matters like women in business, which have little relevance for the great majority of American women. President Reagan in the 1980 election used the slogan "Equal Rights, not Equal Rights Amendment." Yet the woman he appointed to search the federal statute books for provisions involving unequal treatment of women that should be corrected resigned in disgust, publicly proclaiming her belief that the Reagan administration was not serious about correcting inequities and admitting her powerlessness to do anything about it.

The failure of women in the executive branch to provide leadership on women's issues is based on two related conditions. First, most women administrators do not have an institutional mandate to address women's issues. Those few women who do work on women's issues have been political appointees confined to working within the administration's policy preferences. Thus, advocates for women in the executive branch must choose between quietly working from within, with the risk of losing credibility with groups outside, or openly challenging presidential policy-making with the risk of losing their jobs.

Ironically, the only individuals who have fully benefited from their association with women's issues may have been members of Congress leading the opposition. Beginning with the ERA and moving to the issues of abortion and the family, these politicians, secure in the support of their conservative constituencies, have gained national recognition and financial backing for their opposition campaigns. Moreover, given the fragmented nature of the political system, they have established firm footholds in Congress where, particularly on abortion, they have used every conceivable maneuver to obstruct the legislative process.

The gains of women's groups in lobbying expertise and proficiency in coalition-building in the 1970s must be balanced against the failure to develop strong support among political leaders. The shift in Congress to a more conservative cast during the years 1980–86, the low priority given to women's issues on the Reagan agenda, and the institutional weakness of women policymakers in either branch of government made it difficult to maintain or build momentum. Furthermore, the constant pressure during those years from opposition leaders seeking to chip away at established policies forced leaders on women's issues to devote so much energy to defending past gains that they had little reserve energy for new initiatives. However, the Democratic recapture of the Senate in 1986 and the weakening of the Reagan administration as a consequence of the Iran–Contra scandal have placed feminists in a far more promising position.

Meanwhile, women officeholders at the state and local levels have achieved some impressive victories during the past decade. Women in 1985 were 9.6 percent of mayors (not only of small towns but of some very large cities like San Francisco and Houston) and 14.8 percent of state legislators, up from 1.0 percent and 4.7 percent respectively in 1971.[1] In 1986 an all-time record of 26 out of 52 women candidates won statewide executive positions and the number of women state legislators increased to 1,120. These women in state and local offices have in many cases devoted themselves to women's issues, even when they were not ideologically predisposed to do so. In many states and municipalities, they have been effective in promoting funding for such vital social services as child care, battered women's shelters, rape crisis centers, and abortion, as well as marital rape legislation and more aggressive programs for the collection of child-support payments. These state and local officeholders are an ever-widening pool of potential candidates for higher office.

POLICY CHARACTERISTICS

Visibility, Degree of Controversy, and Scope

The characteristics of a particular policy also affect its chances for success. In many ways women's policies are no different from policies in other issue areas. If a policy has low visibility, fits with prevailing values, and involves narrow concerns, its chances for success are greater than if it is highly visible, controversial, and wide-ranging.

Two issues from the 1980s illustrate these points clearly. One of the few legislative successes women's groups had in 1980 was the passage of the Foreign Service Act, which (among other things) entitled divorced wives of foreign service officers to a share of their former husband's benefits. Passage of this legislation can in large part be attributed to the policy's characteristics. The issue had little visibility at the grass roots; women's groups rarely mentioned it in their communications and the media never gave it attention until final congressional passage. The low visibility of the issue is explained in part by its noncontroversial nature. Most people would agree that women who devote a portion of their lives to husbands and families, who live overseas and give up their own opportunities for independent careers, deserve upon divorce to share in benefits earned during the marriage. The low visibility of the issue was also attributable to its narrow scope: the new policy affects relatively few families although it has implications for much larger groups, namely, wives of men in the military and civil services.

Another good example is pension reform. This was an issue that was raised by the women's lobbies but received virtually no media coverage or public attention. Yet the Retirement Equity Act of 1984 provided significant new benefits and protections for women. Under its terms, spouses of employees who die after attaining eligibility for pensions are guaranteed a benefit beginning at age 55; a pension plan member may no longer waive the option of providing a survivorship benefit without the signed consent of the survivor; the divorced spouse of a plan member is entitled to a part of the pension, if this is stipulated in the separation papers or ordered by a judge; pension plan members may leave the work force for up to 5 consecutive years without losing pension credits; and plan members may take maternity or paternity leaves of up to one year without losing service credit for the period.[2] This was a significant—but very, very quiet—series of gains for women.

Policy on violence against abortion clinics provides a clear contrast. At least 29 incidents of bombings or arson at abortion clinics occurred in 1984. These incidents received substantial coverage in the local press wherever they occurred. The pattern of violence—really, a form of political terrorism—was loudly protested by the women's movement and by people concerned with family planning. Yet FBI Director William Webster refused to accord the clinic violence the high priority given to other acts of terrorism. He did not see the bombings as a threat to the government or its property; apparently, he was unconcerned that people were being inhibited in the exercise of their constitutional rights, even though such inhibition is a crime.[3] No amount of negative publicity on this well-publicized issue appears to have moved the Reagan administration—no doubt because the very visibility of the issue created countervailing pressures by the "pro-life" forces.

Policy Types: Distributive, Regulatory, and Redistributive

Another way of characterizing policy is to examine the policy's effect on society. Using such an approach, Theodore Lowi has differentiated three types of domestic policy: distributive, regulatory, and redistributive.[4] Distributive policies involve distributing benefits to individuals or groups, essentially in the form of a government subsidy. Regulatory policies involve governmental regulation of practices by individuals or groups, most frequently in the private sector. Redistributive policies involve the redistribution of benefits, tangible or intangible, from one broad group to another. Lowi argues that the amount of conflict generated by a policy can be predicted by its type, with distributive policies generating relatively little conflict, regulatory policies generating a moderate amount of conflict, and redistributive policies generating greater amounts of conflict.

Lowi's typology has been widely used by social scientists but has also come under some criticism. The distinctions among the three types of policy are not always clear; for example, a policy may be regulatory in the short run but have redistributive implications in the long run. While policy makers may view policies as having one kind of impact, the affected groups may perceive the policy differently. With these notes of caution, it is useful to examine women's policies within the Lowi classification scheme.

Considering the array of women's policies proposed in the 1970s and '80s, it is interesting that most policies fall into either regulatory or redistributive categories. The few policies that were distributive in nature, such as providing individual tax credits for child care or subsidies to businesses and labor unions for training programs for non-traditional jobs, did, in fact, generate relatively little controversy. Furthermore, while those policies that were primarily regulatory, such as anti-discrimination policies in the areas of credit or pregnancy benefits, generated some debate, they were also achieved with only moderate levels of conflict. Thus, the typology is useful in explaining why these particular women's policies met with little resistance in the policy-making process.

The typology is less useful, however, in examining other women's policies. On the face of it, the ERA, affirmative action, and Title IX are also regulatory policies in the sense that they regulate behavior by prohibiting sex discrimination in law, employment, and education, respectively. These policies, however, have generated high levels of conflict because they have been perceived by both policymakers and the general public as redistributive in nature, taking away benefits (legal rights, jobs, athletic appropriations) from men and conferring them on women. Indeed, these policies may be redistributive in the long run. While affirmative action regulations do not remove men from eligibility for jobs, if properly enforced, they should result in women obtaining some jobs that would otherwise have been obtained by men. And nondiscrimination in athletic appropriations has taken some financial support from male athletes and reallocated it to female athletes.

Thus, existing policy typologies are not always the most reliable means to predict outcomes in the policy-making process. In the case of women's policies, other distinctions may be necessary to understand why policy proposals meet more resistance in some areas than in others. Recent studies of public policy affecting women have begun to illuminate some of the underlying factors at work.

Role Equity Versus Role Change

A role is a pattern of behavior individuals adopt in response to social expectations. Roles are based on many different characteristics, including age, occupation, and marital status. Sex roles are behavioral patterns based on gender; sex roles prescribe appropriate behavior for males and females in social, economic, and political contexts. Sex roles are institutionalized in society by rules and practices established through public policy.

The public policies sought by the women's movement have affected sex roles. In some cases, the policies have had the goal of equalizing opportunity or increasing equity for men and women without changing sex roles. In other cases, the policies have had the goal of role change: opening up new roles for both sexes and assisting women to move into new roles.[5]

As with other typologies, this distinction is not clear-cut in all cases. Some policies may have equity as their short-term goal but may result in role change over the long term. For example, the policy barring sex discrimination in credit may merely provide equity for women as consumers in the short run, while in the long run it may result in some women becoming the principal economic decisionmakers in the family.[6] Likewise, certain policies may be perceived as effecting equity by some and role change by others. To illustrate, some individuals may perceive child care as an equity issue, equalizing the employment options of mothers and fathers, while others may perceive child care as an issue of role change, allowing women to move from the role of full-time mother to that of employed mother.

What is valuable about the equity/role change distinction is that it explains the relatively easy acceptance of some women's policies and the massive resistance to others. Equity fits with the American political tradition of fairness and equality before the law; equity issues rest on basic economic, social, and political values. In contrast, role change challenges traditional sex-role ideology. It involves the redefinition of sex roles in some areas, the elimination of sex roles in others. Most importantly, it changes the roles of men as well as women. Thus, for example, opening up combat roles to women in the military is far more threatening than equalizing benefits for male and female military personnel.

Sometimes role change seems so threatening and equity seems so expensive that a third alternative approach to policy may be used: special treatment for women. The best historical example is protective labor legislation for women, which for 60 years until the 1960s established special rules for women workers affecting minimum wages, night work, weight-lifting limits, rest periods, and so on. In the 1970s special treatment became unpopular, as it became clear that most protective laws had actually limited women's access to better-paying jobs.

In the 1980s, however, the issue of special treatment arose again. Nine states passed laws giving pregnant women, and not other workers, the right to take unpaid leave without loss of job rights in jobs that did not otherwise permit any time off. These laws were challenged in the courts as a violation of equality before the law for non-pregnant workers but were upheld by the U.S. Supreme Court in *California Federal Savings and Loan Association v. Guerra* (1987). Feminist opinion on the case was divided. The issue of maternity leave raises similar questions. Is it equitable to permit female but not male employees to take time off, with or without pay, after the birth of a child? A similar issue concerns toxic work environments: should pregnant women be permitted and/or required to transfer out of such environments? Should the work environments of all women of child-bearing age (any of whom might have an early, as yet undetected pregnancy) be kept more free from toxics than those of males?

In each of these cases (unpaid time off from work, maternity leave, toxic-free work environment), the best and most obvious solution would be to follow the principle of equity and extend the benefit to males as well as females, but this more costly solution might deter policy change for all affected groups. Moreover, while the special treatment approach is likely to block role change by making women less desirable employees, it may be the most popular approach for employers attempting to reduce female labor turnover and avoid lawsuits while keeping costs down. Feminists must ask themselves whether they wish to accept the short-term benefit, possibly at the long-term expense of role change.

A framework for analyzing policy change must include both long-range and short-term variables. Environmental and systemic variables influence the long-range prospects for policy change. Political variables and policy characteristics influence the short-term prospects. In the studies in this volume, the effects of long-range and short-term variables are discussed across the range of issues. Because policymaking is complex, no single variable or set of variables explains the dynamics at work across the spectrum of policies included. Rather, different variables come into play on different issues and at different stages of policy development.

One recurring theme in this volume is the interplay between power and policy. Power has been a thorny problem for the women's movement. As an oppressed group, women have suffered from powerlessness. Yet the simple solution of gaining more power in the context of existing power structures has been rejected by many feminists as perpetuating patterns of oppression. Much feminist thought, therefore, has gone into seeking ways to restructure power relations, in both the public and private spheres, so that they are more democratic, participatory, and just.

At the same time it is clear that policy change occurs only when groups seeking change have sufficient power to influence the policy-making process. The women's movement has come to distinguish between power *over* and power *for*. The feminist critique of power has been directed at ways of reducing the power of one group *over* another. The goal of women's groups in the policy-making process has been to achieve and utilize power *for* both equity and role change.

No group can expect to revolutionize power relations in so short a time as 20 years, yet there are several examples in this volume of attempts by women to pursue policy goals while simultaneously expanding participation in the policy-making process. If this volume stimulates discussion not only about the ends of policymaking but also about the means, its purpose will have been accomplished.

NOTES AND REFERENCES

1. *National Directory of Women Elected Officials* (Washington, DC: National Women's Political Caucus, 1985), p. 10.

2. *Monthly Labor Review, 107* (October, 1984), p. 47.

3. *Ms.*, Vol. 13, No. 9 (March 1985), p. 19.

4. A good summary of Lowi's classification scheme may be found in Randall Ripley and Grace A. Franklin, *Congress, the Bureaucracy and Public Policy* (Homewood, III: Dorsey Press, 1970), pp. 16 18.

5. The distinction between role equity and role change was first made by Maren Lockwood Carden, *Feminism in the Mid 1970s* (New York: Ford Foundation, 1977), pp. 40 43.

6. The equity/role change distinction is well illustrated in a policy analysis of legislation on credit, education, abortion, and pregnancy benefits by Joyce Gelb and Marian Lief Palley, "Women and Interest Group Politics: A Comparative Analysis of Federal Decision-Making," *The Journal of Politics, 41* (May 1979), 361–392.

PART I

USING POWER TO INFLUENCE POLICY

Introduction

In the 1970s feminism evolved from a diffuse social movement into a number of organized political interest groups on the national, state, and local levels. Women acting on behalf of women achieved some major successes: a wide range of anti-discrimination legislation in employment and education, a powerful tool for enforcing this legislation (affirmative action), a new public awareness and some innovative new policies in the area of violence against women (rape and battering), a limited government commitment to subsidize child care, and a major breakthrough in the area of reproductive freedom (the legalization of abortion).

With the election of Ronald Reagan to the presidency in 1980, these gains were placed in jeopardy by the hostility of the new administration, by the seemingly more conservative and anti-government-spending climate of public opinion and, before long, by the ballooning federal budget deficit, puffed up by the recession, the huge tax cuts and the escalation of the arms race that all took place in the early 1980s. The prospects for further gains for women in the area of public policy looked bleak indeed.

At the same time, the ever-rising tide of women entering the labor force created a greater need than ever before for effective policies. Feminists began to see that public policies need not be created only by government and that in fact the most effective policies would involve an interplay between government and the private sector. This would prove true in such diverse areas as equal pay for work of comparable value, maternity leaves, employer-provided child care, alternative work patterns such as flexitime and part-time employment, affirmative action, and sexual harassment in the work-place. As the proportion of women in the work force approached 50 percent, many employers began for the first time to ask themselves how their personnel policies could be changed to increase the productivity of women workers. Some new policies were so obviously in management's self-interest that they were introduced voluntarily, with little or no external pressure; examples include flexitime, an increase in part-time employment along with a strengthening of the rights of part-time workers, and the offering by a few firms of paid maternity leave and by many other firms of unpaid maternity leaves.

Other policies, such as affirmative action and protection against sexual harassment on the job, were initiated by government but were accepted by employers (if not by the general public) with lessening resistance over time. Ironically, when the Reagan administration in 1986 began actively to attempt to weaken affirmative action, it found that most employers supported the policy, taking the position that they would continue it even if no longer required to by the federal government. Still other policies, such as pay equity (or comparable worth), employer-provided child care, and requirements to free the workplace of toxic chemicals were resisted by employers.

Whatever the source of the policy, women employees often found that it was useful to have the protection of legislation or unions or both. Flexitime, for example, although generally very popular with women employees, had the potential for being abused. For example, management might pressure employees to work longer hours at the times when management rather than the employees preferred, thus reducing management's bill for overtime pay at premium rates. Unions could prove very useful in preventing this sort of abuse, especially if backed up by legislation specifically prohibiting it.

Another excellent example is 'equal pay for work of comparable value' (sometimes called 'comparable worth'). Unions that were willing and able to strike proved a very effective pressure tool for elimination of sex bias, particularly when they appealed to the courts or to sympathetic state and local officeholders. Beginning in the 1960s, unions for the first time began organizing significant numbers of women employees and, like the corporations, they found themselves reexamining their policies and priorities to meet the needs of their new members.

Meanwhile, in the 1970s, feminism was evolving from a diffuse social movement to an organized political interest on the national, state and local levels. This evolution was not always an easy process. Tensions developed within and among women's groups regarding the directions women should follow in trying to improve the status of women.

Some activists continued to concentrate their energies on the grass roots level, developing alternative institutions and lifestyles to meet women's social needs and generating new issues from the realities of women's lives. Their efforts yielded a wide variety of local activities for women ranging from women's centers, health and counseling services, and women's shelters to women's theaters, coffee houses, businesses, and communes.

These tensions among women's groups have not been fully resolved and, in all likelihood, never will be. Why not? One reason is that as long as women are competing for limited political resources, there will never be enough time, money, or organizational talent available to accomplish all the goals of either the lobbyists or the grass-roots organizers. A second, more fundamental reason for these tensions is that there are basic ideological differences between the professional lobbyists and grass-roots organizers. The lobbyists, in becoming part of the policy-making process, must adapt to the rules of the game, which include decisionmaking by elites, the need to develop allies among other groups, the use of traditional political rewards for supporters, and most significantly, the need to compromise. The grass-roots organizers, in rejecting politics as usual, consciously subscribe to different political principles: participatory democracy, self-determination, occasionally separatism, and the rejection of compromise politics in favour of ideological purity.

Because this volume focuses on policymaking, it does not treat the grass-roots organization of the women's movement in any detail. This lack of attention does not reflect any judgment concerning its importance. Rather, the work of the activists at the grass roots levels is recognized as critical in expanding the reach of the movement, putting pressure on the system, and generating a variety of perspectives on issues. While there is a tension between the grass-roots organizers outside the established political system and the lobbyists inside, the inside/outside strategy provides the movement with a continuing momentum. Moreover, the grass-roots organizers indirectly benefit the lobbyists by providing a more radical image that contrast with the more traditional image of the lobbyists, thereby giving the lobbyists the aura of respectability.

Women's groups have had to confront numerous obstacles in moving into the political system. Once they embraced the need to become lobbyists, they encountered various developmental problems: how to gain access to policymakers, how to build coalitions with other interests, how to persuade office-holders to represent women's interests, and how to build credibility. Costain's chapter 2 describes the first and second stages of interest group organization for the women's movement at the national level.

Diane Franklin and Joan Sweeney in chapter 3 examine the problems of women as both managers and clerical workers in participating in and affecting corporate policymaking. They explore the myths and realities of progress and analyze the impediments to transforming the corporation.

In chapter 4, Sara E. Rix describes the impact of the Reagan administration's budget cuts on programs for women and children, as well as its attempts to weaken the enforcement of anti-discrimination legislation.

The general conclusion one can draw from this overview of the interplay of power and policy is that while the women's movement has grown tremendously in professionalism and effectiveness in the past 20 years, the contemporary social, political and economic climate necessitates powerful defensive strategies at the federal level, and creative new strategies at lower levels of government and in the private sector.

2
Representing Women: The Transition from Social Movement to Interest Group

Anne N. Costain

In recent decades social movements have pressured the political system to change existing public policies and try new approaches to solving social problems.[1] The civil rights movement stimulated government to integrate public schools, to require that federal contractors adopt affirmative action programs and to legislate a halt to racial discrimination in housing sales and rentals. These were not just new laws; each one represented a broadening of the scope of federal responsibility. Similarly, the women's movement successfully pushed government to prohibit sexual harassment in the workplace, to insist that sex not be a factor in the granting or denial of financial credit and to open federally supported educational programs to men *and* women. These moves, like those in response to the civil rights movement, broadened the agenda of government, involving it in areas of social policy that it had earlier avoided. It is possible to compile similar lists of public policy breakthroughs for most of the politically oriented social movements of the 1960s and 1970s, but not much is understood about the strategies these movements used to achieved influence.[2]

This chapter examines the women's movement and its efforts to engage in the most visible and direct form of pressuring government — legislative lobbying. We look first at the early years of the "women's lobby" — the cooperative lobby formed in the mid-1970s to demand that government respond to the public outcry against sex discrimination. Several factors stand out as contributing to the organization and success of this lobbying effort in its early years. Among these are a major change in the external political environment, making it more amenable to women as an interest group; the aid and assistance of pre-existing organized groups willing to join with the women's movement groups in common endeavors; and

26

congressional sponsors who played leading roles in involving the lobby in legislative work.

Next we examine the women's lobby 10 years later, in the mid-1980s. It is a continuing presence in Washington. The lobby has influenced a broad range of public policies, yet it operates in a conservative and even hostile environment. The movement that gave it birth is in decline as an active force in politics, and the lobby has become part of the interest group establishment, with existing programs to defend and past actions to justify. A new set of conditions appears to have preserved much of the lobby's influence and interests it represents despite the current unfavorable external environment — the perceived impact of gender in electoral politics, favorable public opinion, and the routinization and professionalizing of the lobby.

A lobby seeking to represent the interests of American women faces a number of inherent difficulties that have changed little during the last decade. Although attempting to speak for the large and varied constituency of American women, it will never represent more than a fraction of all women. It has the potential to exercise political influence based on its size and the geographic dispersion of its constituency, yet must face the reality of serious organizational problems in reaching and attempting to bring together the diverse needs and priorities of its members. These difficulties are similar to other diffuse interests, but the evolving relationship between this lobby and the women's movement has also shaped the strategy and tactics of representing women's interests in Washington. The pattern of representation that has evolved is one example of the way social movements influence the political system.

The following material about the founding of the women's lobby is drawn from 65 interviews with lobbyists active in women's rights issues and members of Congress whom they lobbied in the mid-to-late 1970s. Great emphasis is placed on information gathered in structured interviews with 17 individuals representing 14 organizations who were actively involved in starting a cooperative lobby to represent women's interests in Washington.[3] Second, 36 members of Congress and congressional staff who worked on legislation lobbied by women's interests were questioned in a somewhat less structured format concerning their contacts with and impressions of the women's lobby.[4] These interviews were supplemented by less formal discussions with 12 lobbyists who were allies of the new women's lobby on these issues.[5]

Evaluations of the lobby in the 1980s is drawn from two smaller waves of interviews. The first was conducted in 1981; the second in 1984.[6] Both sets of interviews concentrated on representatives of groups that were consistently identified by other lobbyists as part of the core of the Washington women's lobby. These interviews were supplemented by information drawn from published material concerning the women's lobby.[7]

PROBLEMS SOCIAL MOVEMENTS CONFRONT IN ORGANIZING TO LOBBY

Like most new interests, the first problem social movements must over-come when starting a national lobby is organization. To lobby, decisions must be made rapidly about which issues to pursue, how to allocate scarce resources, and when to compromise or hold firm on pending legislation. Social movements, which are only partially organized interests, cannot undertake such efforts without substantial transformation. Consequently, the most organized parts of social movements are those that first become active in lobbying. Without an initial involvement by groups within a social movement, it is unlikely that a movement will channel major effort into conventional interest group politics.

Although the emphasis on change of social movement organizations might suggest that they would move naturally into lobbying activity, several critical components of their organizational makeup exert pressure in the opposite direction. First, movement groups tend to rely primarily on purposive incentives to maintain and expand their memberships.[8] Members are attracted to the group because of its purposes and goals; through their participation, they believe they can contribute to attaining valued outcomes. Yet this may create a variety of problems when the groups begins to lobby. By lobbying, a group creates a situation in which specific tactical priorities must be set, risking factional splits within the movement, as the purposes that attracted some individuals to the movement are modified to achieve legislative success. The National Organization for Women (NOW) has withdrawn support from several lobbying coalitions, including those pushing the Pregnancy Disability Act of 1979 and the Fair Insurance Practices Act of 1984, out of concern for the compromises that had been made to win legislative passage. Women were an unorganized interest for so long that factional splits were of particular concern to many of its groups. Women are similar to other minority groups in their reluctance to adopt collective consciousness, but different in their more intense resistance to developing a sense of unity.[9] Since women's groups had experienced both the difficulty of educating women to view themselves as possessing shared interests and the factionalizing which often resulted from policy disputes in the movement in their first years of existence, lobbying was initially unappealing to most movement groups.[10]

The organizational transformation necessary for effective lobbying also threatened a key feminist value: commitment to nonhierarchical organization.[11] No successful lobby can function without centralized direction. The dependence of women's movement organizations on the goodwill and trust of their members made the development of hierarchical organizational structures risky because many movement members thought that such structures betrayed the purpose of the organization. As Jo Freeman suggests:

> These problems reflect the classic dilemma of social movement organizations; the fact that the tightly organized hierarchical structures necessary to change social institutions conflict directly with the participatory style necessary to maintain membership support and the democratic nature of the movement's goals.[12]

A second general characteristic of social movement organizations also creates pressure not to lobby. Movement groups are more likely than most formal organizations to utilize unorthodox or noninstitutionalized means to achieve their objectives.[13] This tendency is partly a function of the difficulty of initiating major changes in policy by traditional means, and partly a reflection of the goal of most movements to change institutional structures as well as policy. By lobbying, an organization chooses to direct a major effort through established political channels. This choice, in effect, acknowledges the legitimacy of existing structures and may jeopardize the movement's ability to continue using protest tactics to push for change.[14] Since much of the attention focused on the women's movement in the 1960s had been the product of what Theodore Lowi refers to as "disorderly" politics — picketing, sit-ins, demonstrations, civil disobedience, and even national strikes — the fear was that the thrust of the women's movement could well be blunted by its becoming just another interest group.[15]

These difficulties associated with purposive incentives for membership and commitment to unorthodox political tactics quickly came to the fore when the two largest women's movement organizations began national lobbying in 1973. NOW and the National Women's Political Caucus (NWPC) were particularly hard hit by membership anger over developments associated with lobbying in each organization. Conflict in both NOW and NWPC centered on the relationship between the national offices of the organizations and the state and local chapters. Since lobbying requires a uniform organizational posture on specific issues and centralized decision making, the initiation of lobbying was a factor in mobilizing membership opposition to leadership and central direction within both groups.

Dissent within the NWPC centered on the funding of the national office, of which the lobbying staff was a part. Although state and local caucuses were supposed to pay the national caucus at least one dollar per member in dues each year, many refused to pay. In 1973, 14 state organizations paid no dues to the national while ten others paid 50 dollars or less.[16] This nonpayment of national dues was the method used by state and local organizations to protest what they viewed as the unnecessary concentration of power in the national office.[17] Far from bringing the national office and the grass-roots members together, national lobbying emphasized the divisions between them. Thus the caucus, after initiating congressional lobbying in 1973, did little in the next few years to expand its efforts. Although members of the national staff of NWPC expressed their belief that it was important to follow up the election campaign work of the caucus with political pressure to ensure that individuals elected to office with help from caucus voted correctly once they got there, this side of NWPC's work was allowed to stagnate at the national level.[18] Instead, the caucus focused its energy on activities that could be decentralized more easily, like supporting women candidates.

NOW's problems in initiating lobbying in 1973 were more severe. NOW was also plagued by the refusal of state organizations to pay dues to the national headquarters during this period. Although NOW's national office was in Chicago and its legislative office in Washington, this non-monolithic national organization did not adequately allay membership mistrust. In 1974, several of the largest state organizations placed their national dues in escrow to protest actions of the national leadership. The thrust of criticism directed toward leadership and staff was that NOW was becoming too reformist under the domination of a small elite.[19] The culmination of criticism of the national legislative staff came at NOW's 1975 convention when the entire staff was fired in response to pressure from more politically and organizationally radical NOW members. In an interview several months prior to this convention, a member of the Washington legislative staff described the pressure she saw building in the organization: "A number of crazies are trying to end the legislative activity of NOW. Rather than lobbying against abortion laws they want to teach self-abortion."[20]

As these experiences suggest, movements' reliance on purposive incentives for membership and their use of noninstitutionalized political channels make it difficult for them to initiate congressional lobbying. Without strong outside motivation, it is unlikely that the women's movement organizations would have begun national lobbying.

NEW PRESSURES TO ENTER THE LEGISLATIVE ARENA

The first significant factor pushing the women's movement to begin lobbying was substantial change occurring outside the movements in the early 1970s, including positive change in public attitudes towards the goals of the movement and passage of favorable legislation by Congress in several areas of great concern to the movement. These related changes are closely tied to aspects of a movement organization's environment that have been shown to be particularly important to groups: the attitude of society as a whole toward the movement and the number of potential movement supporters in society.[21] Although pluralist theory stresses the importance of negative external stimuli for the emergence of new interest groups,[22] the case of the women's movement suggests that positive events may also provide powerful incentives to break down resistance to lobbying activity. Taken together, these factors are influential in determining the ability of a movement group to recruit new members and to achieve its goals.

Increased support for the goals of women's liberation coupled with public opposition to many of the tactics used by the women's movement to achieve these goals pushed the movement toward conventional lobbying activity. From a sizable minority of men (44 percent) and women (40 percent) who favored efforts to strengthen women's status in society in 1970, by 1974 a solid majority of men (63 percent) and women (57 percent) favored this change according to a Virginia Slims poll.[23] An earlier Virginia Slims poll showed, however, that despite substantial agreement by both sexes with the statement, "If women don't speak up for themselves and confront men on their real problems, nothing will be done about these problems" (women, 71 percent agree; men, 67 percent agree), widespread uneasiness existed about some of the tactics used by women's movement groups.[24] The politics of disorder practiced by women's groups engendered strong disapproval among some segments of the population.

At the same time, the Ninety-Second Congress passed an unprecedented amount of legislation strengthening the status of women.[25] The ERA in particular seemed to provide the single most important catalyst for groups to accomplish the transition to legislative politics. The amendment itself had the advantage of addressing the central issue of the denial of women's rights under the law. In addition to the legal advantages of passing such an amendment, which would put sex discrimination on an equal footing with racial discrimination as a suspect classification, the ERA proved an important rallying point for a variety of groups which had previously shunned the feminist label.[26]

In Washington the fight for congressional passage of the ERA was largely orchestrated by members of Congress, particularly Representative Martha Griffiths, but a number of individuals and organizations joined together to support this legislation. An ad hoc committee formed to coordinate lobbying for the ERA began patterns of cooperation and resource sharing that would prove invaluable in later lobbying efforts. Several of the women within this committee recognized the need for continued congressional lobbying and founded Women's Lobby Inc. in 1972.[27] Other women affiliated with existing movement organizations encouraged those groups to commit resources to continuing pressure on Congress after the passage of the ERA. In 1972 the Women's Equity Action League (WEAL) moved its headquarters from Ohio to Washington. In 1973, as noted previously, NOW and NWPC opened Washington legislative offices.

⸍ Passage of the Equal Rights Amendment by Congress provided a stimulus for further lobbying efforts. First, it demonstrated the receptiveness of Congress to women's movement goals. Second, it showed skeptical social movement groups the potential of legislation for initiating far-reaching social and political change. Third, it showed both social movement and more traditional voluntary organizations that they could work together to achieve common goals. Finally, since the ERA was a constitutional amendment and had to go to the states for ratification, (and even if ratified would not have been implemented for several years), this long process highlighted the continued need for interim legislation to end the most blatant cases of legal discrimination⸍ These positive changes in political and social conditions broke down the resistance of movement group members to organized political lobbying.

The failure to add the Equal Rights Amendment to the Constitution after more than a decade of effort was less devastating to the women's lobby in Washington than one might expect. In the 1981 and 1984 interviews with active women's lobbyists, only the lobbyist for NOW spoke at any length about the ERA. This is not surprising since NOW played a major role in working for state ratification. NOW's efforts fit in with its continuing preference for grass-roots activism. The other group representatives viewed the stalling and subsequent defeat of the ERA as a mandate for a piece-by-piece or incremental legislative approach to equality, rather than sweeping constitutional reform. Although it is wrong to draw the inference that any of those interviewed opposed the ERA, one representative noted, that women's issues were no longer restricted to the ERA and abortion. The defeat of ERA seemed to make legislative work for women's rights even more necessary.

ORGANIZED GROUPS ASSIST THE WOMEN'S LOBBY

In starting a new lobby, three capabilities must be developed rapidly: (a) an ability to obtain reliable information on pending legislation; (b) a network of contacts on Capitol Hill to get this information circulated; and (c) links to congressional constituencies to mobilize pressure through the district, and to assure that the lobbyist is reflecting the interests of these constituents. When NOW, NWPC, and WEAL came to Washington in 1972 and 1973, they had neither the resources nor the network of congressional contacts to begin full-fledged lobbying activity. What they did have was a number of groups, primarily women's voluntary organizations, that were sympathetic to the goals of the women's movement and available to help develop a women's rights lobby. The availability of groups willing to assist the women's movement is the second important factor in enabling a successful women's lobby to organize. (The development of this lobby suggests a pattern of social movement growth similar to that described by Maurice Pinard in his study of the Social Credit Party in Quebec. Pinard found that intermediate social organizations, such as voluntary associations, can facilitate the spread of social movements. According to Pinard, when "pre-existing primary and secondary groupings possess or develop an ideology or simply subjective interest congruent with that of a new movement, they will act as mobilizing rather than restraining agents toward that movement."[28] This assistance is essential in the case of social movements because most movement groups lack resources and have difficulty getting access to the political system without a sponsor.[29])

Why did relatively traditional organizations like the National Federation of Business and Professional Women (BPW) and the American Association of University Women (AAUW) become involved in joint lobbying efforts with women's movement groups? Why were they so receptive to feminism? Part of the answer lies in the origins of these women's groups. The AAUW, BPW, and League of Women Voters were all founded out of concern for participation by women in society.[30] Other traditional women's groups like the National Council of Jewish Women and the United Methodist Women began out of feminist protest.[31] Feminism was not new to many of these organizations, although it may, in some cases, have been dormant for a number of years.

The membership characteristics (with the exception of age) of the traditional women's groups are similar to those of the women's movement groups. As Carden[32] and Freeman[33] both discover in their data on women's movement followers, these women are predominantly white, middle class, and well educated. These are similar characteristics of membership in voluntary organizations generally, according to studies.[34]

The rising age and lack of new members in many traditional women's associations caused some concern.[35] Involving themselves with feminist causes had the additional benefit of attracting younger members to organizations such as the AAUW and BPW.[36] Cooperation between traditional women's groups and women's movement groups may have been easier because many of their members were already working together in the states on ERA coalitions.[37]

Why the women's movement needed voluntary organizations is equally clear. Many of the traditional groups such as the AAUW, the National Council of Jewish Women, and the League of Women Voters have long engaged in legislative activity. These groups provided training and contacts on Capitol Hill to the new movement organizations. Many of the older organizations had memberships that dwarfed the combined figures of all the social movement groups. A large active membership in the districts together with the legitimacy and experience of the voluntary groups provided sufficient incentive for the movement organizations to seek cooperation. The availability of associations with interests congruent to the new movement made it possible for the women's movement to develop a Washington lobby in a relatively short period of time.

The legislative successes of the women's lobby are impressive, particularly for such a new lobby. In 1974, the lobby persuaded Congress to add a minimum wage for domestic workers to the Fair Labor Standards Amendments and to pass bills providing educational equity for women and granting women equal access to credit.[38] In 1975, the lobby's effort gained admittance for women to American military academies, established a National Commission on the Observance of International Women's Year and directed it to convene a National Women's Conference, and defeated congressional attempts to weaken Title IX of the 1972 Education Amendments Act, which prohibits most forms of sex discrimination in federally funded educational programs.[39] The women's lobby also met with defeats, chiefly in its efforts to continue federal funding for abortions and to pass comprehensive day-care legislation. Yet, on balance, for a new and untested interest, the lobby accomplished a great deal.

The help of traditional voluntary groups was crucial because of the movement's early inability to attract support from economic interests, particularly labor unions. Highly sought after by women's movement groups, labor unions were rarely willing to work with them in the early 1970s. Their disinterest seemed to stem from the conditions William Gamson described as leading to the "stable unrepresentation" of interests in America.[40] Women's rights lobbyists in the early 1970s had little to offer economic interests but much that they wanted in return. Interviews revealed that only rarely did the interests of both sides coincide sufficiently for joint action to be feasible. Although unions sometimes endorsed a women's issue on the national level, the endorsement was rarely backed by any action. One women's movement lobbyist said, "The AFL-CIO really has not done a damn thing for the Equal Rights Amendment on the national level. They have had very little involvement with any feminist issue."[41]

The women's movement highlights the importance of non-economic voluntary organizations. Without this type of secondary group, sympathetic to the goals of the new interest group and willing to provide resources and expertise to help it develop, it is less likely that a new interest will succeed in becoming a national lobby. Other recent social movements found similar benefactors. Church organizations and liberal groups such as the Americans for Democratic Action and the American Civil Liberties Union aided the development of a civil rights lobby. The environmental movement gained from the political expertise of conservation and nature groups such as the Audubon Society, the Sierra Club, and the National Wildlife Federation. The pattern of existing voluntary associations facilitating the entry of social movements into the policymaking process seems well established in American politics.

MEMBERS OF CONGRESS SUPPORT THE LOBBY

The third factor affecting the ability of social movements to gain access to the system is the necessity of having allies in Congress willing to help direct and organize early lobbying by the interest. This factor also helps assure that lobbying by movement groups will produce some rapid successes. Given the aforementioned likely opposition to lobbying by some vocal movement members, such early success is almost essential to formation of a national lobby.

In the case of the women's movement, the passage of the ERA by Congress put the spotlight on several members of Congress who would welcome and work with an organized women's lobby. Most notable among these early supporters were Representative Martha Griffiths (D-Mich.) and Senator Birch Bayh (D-Ind.). In addition, the women's movement had a readily identifiable additional source of help in the persons of the other women members of Congress. Although the representatives of women's organizations who were interviewed reported little face-to-face contact with most members of Congress, the overwhelming exception was in the case of congresswomen.[42] There appeared to be a high level of contact, trust and cooperation between those seeking to form a women's lobby and the women in Congress.

Women members of Congress were the chief sponsors and floor managers of most of the legislation supported by the women's lobby in its first years. Representative Patsy Mink (D-Hawaii) steered the Women's Educational Equity Act through the House of Representatives. The Equal Credit Opportunity Act was a product of the combined work of Representatives Leonor Sullivan (D-Mo.), Margaret Heckler (R-Mass.), and Edward Koch (D-N.Y.).[43] Pressure to extend the minimum wage to domestic workers, an early legislative priority of the women's movement, was coordinated by Representative Shirley Chisholm (D-N.Y.). Women as a new interest and as outsiders in the legislative process needed this congressional direction to employ their scarce resources as effectively as possible.

The existence of at least a minority of members of Congress who feel intensely enough about a social movement to coordinate and guide its early lobbying is necessary both for the movement to get a hearing before the legislative body, and more importantly, for its overall chances for success.

The recent influential social movements—civils rights, environmental, and women's movements—have had identifiable groups of supporters within Congress who championed, publicized, and led earlier legislative battles.

AN ESTABLISHED LOBBY FIGHTS FOR INFLUENCE

The established women's movement in the mid-1980s drew strength from its allies in the interest group and congressional communities and from the record of legislative successes it had accumulated in earlier years. At the same time, the high expectations of its supporters and the mobilization of its adversaries posed problems for the lobby. Conservatives viewed the women's lobby as part of the left. The lobby had worked repeatedly with civil rights, public interest, labor union, and educational groups. Although there were several campaigns in which business and even Rights-to-Life groups cooperated with the women's lobby, these were anomalies.[44] With a conservative president, Republican control of the Senate, and an increasingly conservative mood in the country as a whole, these former associations limited future access to conservative politicians and business groups.

By winning as many legislative victories as it did in the 1970s, the women's lobby established credibility, and created a record that would be difficult to surpass in the future. Women's rights advocates had been instrumental in winning passage of laws prohibiting discrimination against pregnant workers, opening U.S. military academies to women and guiding the Equal Rights Amendment through Congress and close to ratification by the states. They had also applied pressure to stiffen enforcement of existing anti-discrimination laws, such as Title VII of the 1964 Civil Rights Act and Title IX of the Educational Amendments Act of 1972. With all this legislation to defend from repeal and non-enforcement, some feminists felt that it was not worth the effort to work hard on new bills.

Others saw the record of past successes as a yardstick to measure current achievements and lamented the lack of comparable gains in the 1980s. Many of the issues of the 1980s, such as protecting the pension rights of divorced spouses of State Department and military personnel, had less mass appeal than the older issues of opening jobs and education programs to all.

Within today's generally hostile political environment, the women's lobby has more influence over legislation than one might expect. The first factor that has preserved this influence is the "gender gap" in voting behavior. Although the gender gap that emerged with the 1980 election is still largely a mystery to scholars of voting behavior,[46] it has unquestionably had an impact on the political work of the women's lobby. Both Democratic and Republican candidates have become eager to position themselves correctly with respect to the women's vote. For Democrats this often means championing causes that are particularly popular with women, such as support for the Equal Rights Amendment or for an arms control agreement with the Soviet Union. For Republicans, it frequently entails an effort to downplay or neutralize the gender gap. President Reagan has appointed women to high-profile positions, including naming the first woman justice to the Supreme Court. He has stressed family issues, including a war on drugs, in an apparent effort to counteract the negative image he has with women due, in part, to his bellicose stands on foreign policy and his opposition to the Equal Rights Amendment and to many social services and transfer programs that benefit largely women and children.

The representatives of women's groups interviewed in the mid-1980s saw great tactical importance in the gender gap. The two lobbyists for the National Women's Political Caucus (NWPC) linked success in influencing policy to the gender gap. Catherine East observed, "We [the women's lobby] are likely to get a number of pieces of legislation through [the 98th Congress]. None is earth-shattering. We probably could not have gotten any of them if it were not for the gender gap." Linda Anderson added, "members of Congress who voted wrong on Medicaid funding for abortion [opposing it] are lining up eager to sponsor other pieces of [women's rights] legislation."[47] Patricia Reuss, lobbyist for the Women's Equity Action League (WEAL), added that:

> [Representative] Ed Markey (D-Mass.) has been a long-time anti-abortion advocate. After Senator Paul Tsongas [D-Mass.] announced his retirement from the Senate, Markey declared his candidacy for the Senate and changed his position on abortion. That is the gender gap.[48]

The lobbyists working with Congress on women's issues saw the gender gap as increasing the importance of women as a constituency. As a result, they felt that their own access to and influence with members of Congress was greater.

The appearance of the gender gap also opened the door for a new category of public policy issues: those appealing to women as a special interest. Arguably, most of the successful policy issues of the 1960s and 1970s were "equality" issues that attempted to make women equal to men through the law (the Equal Rights Amendment Title VII, and the 1963 Equal Pay Act). By contrast, the dominant women's issues by the end of the 1970s and early 1980s were "special needs" issues: legislation tailored to the particular requirements of women, including pregnancy, financial problems following divorce, medical problems and victimization from spousal abuse or rape. This opens a new and largely untapped legislative

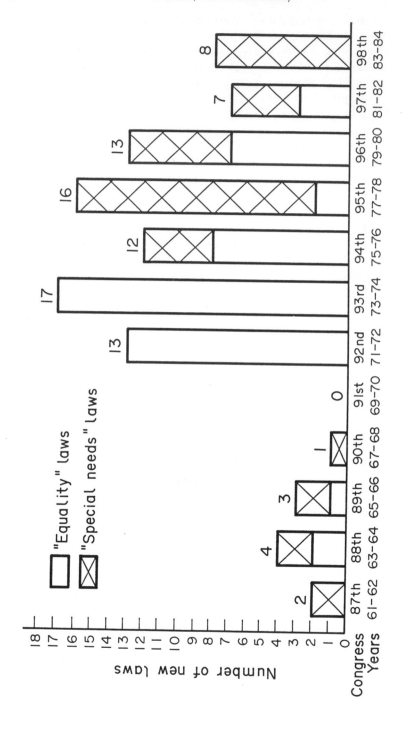

Figure 2.1 From data in Costain, "The gender gap and women's lobbying: equality v. special needs", in *The Politics of the Gender Gap*, Carol Mueller (ed.), Beverly Mills, Sage.

agenda that seems somewhat more acceptable than equality to conservative legislators.

A second factor is increasingly favorable public opinion concerning women's issues, with the noteworthy exception of abortion. Egalitarian attitudes about women's roles have become more common throughout the population during the last ten years. Men and women in the 1980s are more likely to support equal opportunity for women in jobs, education and politics.[49] By contrast, the levels of support for and opposition to abortion have changed very little during this period.[50] This broad public approval of an active governmental role in improving the position of women unquestionably confers legitimacy on demands by the women's lobby, as long as they are unrelated to the abortion issue.

A third factor is the routinized and smoothly functioning cooperative network of groups supporting women's issues. The conflicts and missed opportunities that afflicted the women's lobby in the 1970s were no longer a problem by the 1980s.[51] Both the 1981 and 1984 series of interviews showed virtual unanimity that there was an efficient lobbying effort that could be mobilized on short notice in support of important women's issues. Carol Bros, lobbyist for the NWPC, noted:

> We [NWPC] work with a network of coalitions: pro-choice; health-oriented groups. . . . There are unstructured lobbyist meetings on the Hill. There is a trend toward more cooperation after the last [1980] election. We realize how bad things could be. People recognise that the only chance is to work together and set priorities.[52]

Pat Reuss of WEAL echoed these sentiments in 1981: "For the first time women's groups are really working together well. I sometimes think that the [1980] election is the best thing that happened to us."[53]

The 1984 interviews, in general, continued this new cooperative spirit. Catherine East and Linda Anderson of NWPC explained:

> There is a really friendly cooperative relationship among the organizations working in the women's area. WEAL and BPW [Business and Professional Women] share all kinds of information with us. WEAL's year-end newsletter on Congress is the best thing I've seen summing up the last legislative session. . . . We have to depend on other organizations to keep us informed on a number of these issues. We depend on a pension rights organization with 501-C-3 tax status [tax exempt] to give us information on that issue. WEAL has a marvelous group on women and the military. There is expertise [in organizations] all over town.[54]

Ann Smith, director of the Congressional Caucus for Women's Issues, explained her group's role in helping to coordinate those interested in women's rights issues:

> We [the Congressional Caucus for Women's Issues] have now succeeded in institutionalizing information on women's issues. This makes lobbyists and legislators a lot more effective of these issues. . . . We can give help to small women's organizations that may not have the organization to collect all the facts and data that they need to be effective on issues. . . . We circulate a legislative agenda and a "Weekly Report on Women's Issues" to the press. If they [the press] have particular questions we refer them to other women's groups—groups that we know are working and are knowledgeable in the area they are interested in.[55]

The one apparent exception to this well-oiled machine is NOW. In a 1981 interview, NOW's legislative representative explained that they were widely involved in lobbying coalitions; most of the other lobbyists interviewed noted that NOW cooperated with other lobbying efforts, but rarely played a very active role in them. NOW has never been especially committed to legislative lobbying; the majority of its resources are devoted to building a mass membership, working on ERA ratification in the states and influencing electoral politics. In 1984, this theme sounded even more strongly in all the interviews.[56] One lobbyist explained:

> NOW has not been lobbying on a lot of [women's] issues. They released a statement saying that they supported insurance reform, but disapproved of the compromises that had been made in that legislation. They [NOW] said that they are devoting all their time to the election and ERA. NOW is so closely linked to the Democratic Party that it creates problems in lobbying.

The existence of a smoothly functioning, well-informed lobby on women's rights issues reinforced the leverage women's groups picked up with the emergence of the gender gap in 1980. Since the gender gap coincided with a keenly felt election loss, women's groups seemed to react to this negative outcome by building up their organizations and increasing their active support of women's issues.

CONCLUSIONS

The early, largely unheralded days when social movements or other emerging interests are trying to organize and gain the ear of government decisionmakers are often ignored by those describing the policy process.[57] Yet the ability of government to design policy responsive to new, as well as old, interests, hinges critically on the ease with which new interests seeking change in existing policies gain an initial hearing from government decisionmakers.

The case of the women's movement suggests three factors that appear necessary for social movements to gain initial access to the policy system. An external stimulus must have an impact on the movement with sufficient force to break down the resistance of movement members to lobbying. Second, outside groups must be available and willing to help develop such lobbying. Third, at least a minority of members of Congress must be willing to provide direction for early lobbying efforts.

These linkages between societal conditions and the organization of social movements as new interests have several implications for the ability of the system to respond to new interests. First, there is no guarantee within this framework that new change-oriented interests appearing initially as social movements will gain access to the political system. Many of the organizational characteristics of the most developed segments of social movements indicate exactly the opposite. It appears that the transition from social movement to represented interest will not occur without significant sources of external pressure on the movement. The stimulating effect of positive governmental action in this regard suggests that governmental intervention is useful and sometimes even necessary for maintaining the openness of the system to this type of interest.

Second, these links also indicate the need to examine further the role of voluntary organizations within American society. Existing groups have an important role in determining which social movements will be integrated into the policy system. If organizations such as the League of Women Voters and the National Council of Jewish Women play as major a part in the transition from unrepresented to represented interests as is suggested by the experience of the women's movement, their organizational goals establish a kind of value parameter determining which new interests in fact gain acceptance within the American system and which are excluded. Analysis of existing groups could provide a kind of rough prediction concerning future directions of policy change within the system.

Third, these factors suggest a more significant role for Congress in maintaining the openness of the system to new interests than many modern scholars have assigned it.[58] The importance of having representatives of unrepresented groups in Congress is also underscored in the case of the civil rights and women's movements; these representatives were influential in allowing social movement groups to gain access to the legislative body.

The contrast between the new women's lobby in the early 1970s and its position as an established interest in the 1980s has likewise received little attention. The mature women's lobby has had to cope with some of the negative consequences of its beginnings. It has used the gender gap, favorable public opinion, and an increasingly professional lobbying style to maintain its position in Washington and to continue exercising influence over policy toward women.

There is also a less optimistic side to this transition. By adjusting to political realities in its legislative work, the women's lobby has been "domesticated" to a degree. Most of the group representatives interviewed in 1984 were somewhat uncomfortably talking about *feminist* issues. They preferred the term *women's issues*, which they felt tied in more directly to the concerns of congressional constituencies. They did not shy away from controversial issues such as comparable worth or abortion, but they clearly paid a great deal of attention to what was feasible politically. Priority issues were those that did not cost much and drew bi-partisan support.

A more complete assessment of the achievements of the women's lobby in the 1980s may depend on an economic evaluation of its major legislative efforts. If insurance and pension reform, tougher enforcement of child support provisions of divorce settlements, improved status of women in the military, tax reform, and comparable worth studies leave women in a stronger position economically by the end of the decade, the lobby will have accomplished significant achievements. If women are relatively worse off than men economically by the 1990s, the lobby may be considered ineffective despite tactics that seemed well-adapted to the political climate.

The case of the women's lobby suggests that a social movement-linked lobby can make great progress legislatively by emphasizing civil rights issues in its early years. The mature women's lobby has subsequently shifted its focus from equal rights to economic issues with a more uncertain payoff. This progression looks like standard interest group politics. Its success or failure is one measure of the benefits for a social movement in sustaining a long-term lobbying presence in Washington.

NOTES AND REFERENCES

1. In this chapter, I limit consideration of social movements to those often labeled *socio-political* or *political* movements, or movements that "make changes in power arrangements, especially those structured through the state, a central part of their program." J. Craig Jenkins, "Socio-Political Movements." *The Handbook of Political Behavior*, Vol. 4, Samuel L. Long (ed.) (New York: Plenum Press, 1981), p. 83.

2. There are noteworthy exceptions, including: J. Craig Jenkins, "Interpreting the Stormy Sixties." Paper presented at the American Sociological Association Annual Meeting, New York, New York, September 1986; Paul Burstein, *Discrimination, Jobs and Politics* (Chicago, University of Chicago Press, 1985); Jo Freeman, "Who You Know Versus Who You Represent," paper presented at the American Sociology Association Annual Meeting, New York, New York, September 1986; Frances Piven and Richard Cloward, *Poor People's Movements* (New York: Vintage Books, 1979); and Frances Piven and Richard Cloward, "Electoral Demobilization and Movement Politics in Twentieth Century America," Paper presented at the American Sociological Association Annual Meeting, New York, September 1986.

3. Interviews were conducted with representatives of 14 organizations meeting the following criteria: (a) each has an ongoing interest in women's rights that is central to the organization's purpose; (2) each makes a systematic effort to influence congressional policy relating to women; and (3) each has offices in

Washington, D.C. Initial interviews, lasting from 45 minutes to $2\frac{1}{2}$ hours were conducted between September 1974 and January 1975. In most cases the director of the group's legislative office was interviewed. In a few of the organizations either a lobbyist or the president of the group was interviewed instead. Less structured follow-up interviews were held through March 1976 with selected organizations to check on current legislative activities. The groups whose representatives were interviewed are listed in: Anne N. Costain, "Representing Women," *Western Political Quarterly, 34* (March 1981), p. 101.

4. For a list of members of Congress who were interviewed about the impact of the women's lobby see Anne N. Costain, "Representing Women," p. 102.

5. Representatives of 12 other groups were also interviewed. These groups, which did not meet all of the criteria specified at the time of the initial interviews were conducted, but were active in joint lobbying on some women's issues, are listed in Anne N. Costain, "Representing Women," p. 102.

6. In 1981, the following group representatives were interviewed in Washington, D.C.: Patricia Reuss, WEAL, January 6; Carol Bros, NWPC, January 6; Jane Wells-Schooley, NOW, January 7; and Ann Smith, Congresswomen's Caucus, January 7. In 1984, I conducted the following interviews in Washington: Ann Smith, Congressional Caucus for Women's Issues (formerly named the Congresswomen's Caucus), January 20, Catherine East and Linda Anderson, NWPC, January 20; and Patricia Reuss, WEAL, January 18.

7. In addition to the sources that have already been mentioned, the following proved quite helpful: Joyce Gelb and Marian Palley, *Women and Public Policies* (Princeton: Princeton University Press, 1982); Myra Ferree and Beth Hess, *Controversy and Coalition* (Boston: Twayne Publishers, 1985); Pamela Conover and Virginia Gray, *Feminism and the New Right* (New York: Praeger, 1983); Gilbert Steiner, *Constitutional Inequality* (Washington, D.C.: Brookings, 1985); Nadine Cohadas, "More Service, Less Construction," *Congressional Quarterly Weekly Report, 41*, (February 19, 1983), pp. 415–416; Nadine Cohadas, "New Unity Evident," *Congressional Quarterly Weekly Report, 41* (April 23, 1983), pp. 782–783; and Dom Bonafede, "Women's Movement Broadens the Scope of its Role in American Politics," *National Journal, 14* (December 11, 1982), pp. 2108–2111.

8. Mayer Zald and Roberta Ash, "Social Movement Organizations: Growth, Decay and Change," *Social Forces, 44* (March 1966), pp. 327–340.

9. Helen Mayer Hacker, "Women as a Minority Group," in *This Great Argument: The Rights of Women*, ed. Hamida Bosmajian and Haig Bosmajian (Reading, MA: Addison-Wesley, 1972), pp. 127–145.

10. Jo Freeman, *The Politics of Women's Liberation* (New York: Longman, 1975), provides an excellent overview of the ambivalence felt by many members of movement groups toward direct lobbying.

11. Cellestine Ware, *Women Power: The Movement for Women's Liberation* (New York: Tower Publications, 1970), p. 26.

12. Freeman, *The Politics of Women's Liberation*, p. 100.

13. Roberta Ash, *Social Movements in America* (Chicago: Markham, 1972), p. 1; John Wilson, *Introduction to Social Movements* (New York: Basic Books, 1973), pp. 229–239.

14. Paul Wilkenson, *Social Movements* (New York: Praeger, 1971), p. 30.

15. William H. Chafe, *The American Woman* (New York: Oxford University Press, 1972), pp. 226–227.

16. Susan Carroll, *Women's Rights and Political Parties: Issue Development, the*

1972 Conventions and the NWPC (Master's thesis, University of Indiana, 1972), p. 62.

17. Ibid.

18. Ibid, p. 55. Also interview with a representative of the National Women's Political Caucus conducted on October 22, 1974, in Washington, D.C.

19. Interview with a representative of the National Organization for Women conducted on August 5, 1975, in Washington, D.C.

20. Ibid.

21. Zald and Ash, "Social Movement Organizations."

22. See for example, David B. Truman, *The Government Process* (New York: Knopf, 1951), pp. 104–105.

23. The Roper Organization, *Virginia Slims American Women's Opinion Poll*, 1974.

24. The following figures from the *Virginia Slims American Women's Opinion Poll*, Vol. 2, p. 6, conducted by Louis Harris and Associates in 1972 illustrate this dissatisfaction:

Statements About Activist Women's Groups

	WOMEN			MEN		
	Agree	Disagree	Not Sure	Agree	Disagree	Not Sure
Women who picket and participate in protests are setting a bad example for children. Their behavior is undignified and unwomanly . . .	60	32	8	57	35	8
Women are right to be unhappy with their role in American society but wrong in the way they are protesting . . .	51	34	15	44	40	16

25. Freeman, *The Politics of Women's Liberation*, pp. 202–205.

26. The following are dates when some of the leading women's voluntary organizations first endorsed the ERA in either its present version or a slightly different pre-1943 version: American Association for University Women, 1971; Business and Professional Women, 1937; General Federation of Women's Clubs, 1944; League of Women Voters, 1972; National Council of Jewish Women, 1923.

27. Flora Crater, "Women Lobbyists Incorporate for Full Scale Action for Women," *The Woman Activist 2* (November 1972): 1.

28. Maurice Pinard, *The Rise of a Third Party* (Englewood Cliffs, NJ: Prentice-Hall, 1971), p. 186.

29. John E. Sinclair, *Interest Groups in America* (Morristown, NJ: General Learning Corp., 1976), p. 45.

30. The AAUW was started in 1882 to expand educational opportunities for women. BPW was established in 1919 to improve women's role in the business world. The League, founded in 1920, the year women's suffrage was written into

the Constitution, sought to teach the newly enfranchised women how to use their vote.

31. The National Council of Jewish Women was founded in 1894 after Jewish women had asked to participate in the Columbia Exposition's Parliament of Religions, to celebrate the four-hundredth anniversary of the New World, and were admitted only as hostesses. (Bernice Grazian, *Where There is a Woman, 75 Years of History as Lived by the National Council of Jewish Women*, McCall Corporation, 1967). The National Women's Party, originally named the Congressional Union for Women Suffrage, was started by Alice Paul in 1913. The Congressional Union organized White House demonstrations, mass marches, and hunger strikes in support of women's suffrage. Miss Paul and several of her followers were jailed in 1917, producing angry public response over their harsh treatment in jail. (Elizabeth Chittick, "Biographic Material — Miss Alice Paul." Mimeographed. National Women's Party. 144 Constitution Avenue, N.E., Washington, D.C. 20002.) The United Methodist Women began as part of the missionary movement in the Methodist Church. After the male leadership of the church refused to allow single women to become missionaries, a women's missionary division was established to sponsor the women. (Interview with a representative of the United Methodist Women conducted on November 4, 1974, in Washington, D.C.).

32. Maren Lockwood Carden, *The New Feminist Movement* (New York: Russell Sage, 1974), pp. 19–21.

33. Freeman, *The Politics of Women's Liberation*, pp. 36–38.

34. Sidney Verba and Norman H. Nie, *Participation in America* (New York: Harper and Row, 1972), pp. 200–205. James Q. Wilson, *Political Organizations* (New York: Basic Books, 1973), p. 56.

35. As data from Abbott L. Ferris, *Indicators of Trends in the Status of American Women* (New York: Russell Sage, 1971), p. 404, and from interviews with representatives of the League of Women Voters (October 8, 1974), the Business and Professional Women (October 1, 1974) indicate, all of these organizations have reason to be concerned about their future levels of membership. The League of Women Voters had 156,800 members in 1968 and 17,000 members in 1974. Forty percent of the League's 1974 membership was 50 or older. The Business and Professional Women declined from a membership of 178,300 in 1968 to 168,000 in 1974. The American Association of University Women is one of the few traditional organizations experiencing a period of growth, from 173,200 members in 1968 to 182,000 members in 1974, but the average age of AAUW members in 1974 was 49.

36. Interview with a representative of the American Association of University Women conducted on November 19, 1974, in Washington, D.C. Interview with a representative of the Business and Professional Women conducted on October 1, 1974, in Washington, D.C.

37. Groups that were reported working actively in state ERA coalitions in nine unratified states include the AAUW; American Nurses Association; BPW; Common Cause; League of Women Voters; NOW; and NWPC. These results are taken from a telephone poll conducted by Common Cause during June 1974, covering the states of Utah, Arizona, Georgia, Alabama, Arkansas, Florida, North Carolina, South Carolina, and Indiana. Only organizations mentioned in four or more of these states are included in the list.

38. Fair Labor Standards Amendments of 1974, Public Law 93–259, Section 7, April 8, 1974; Women's Educational Equity Act, Public Law 93–380, Title IV, Section 408, August 21, 1974; and Equal Credit Opportunity Act, Public Law

93–495, Title VII, October 28, 1974. For descriptions of some of the lobbying for this legislation, see Joyce Gelb and Marian Lief Palley, "Women and Interest Group Politics," *American Politics Quarterly 5* (July 1977): 331–352 and Anne N. Costain, "Lobbying for Equal Credit," in *Women Organizing*, Bernice Cummings and Victoria Schuck (eds.), (Metuchen, NJ: Scarecrow Press, 1979), pp. 82–110.

39. Department of Defense Appropriation Authorization Act, 1976, Public Law 94–106, Title VIII, October 7, 1975; and Public Law 94–167, December 23, 1975 (To organize and convene a National Women's Conference). For a description of efforts to combat congressional moves to weaken or amend Title IX of the 1972 Education Amendments Act, see Anne N. Costain, "Eliminating Sex Discrimination in Education: Lobbying for Implementation of Title 9." *Policy Studies Journal,* 7 (Winter 1978): 189–195.

40. William A. Gamson, "Stable Unrepresentation in American Society," *Group Politics, A New Emphasis*, E. J. Malecki and H. R. Mahood (eds.), (New York: Charles Scribner's Sons, 1972) pp. 60–75.

41. Although several of the lobbyists interviewed suggested that the Coalition of Labor Union Women (CLUW) established in 1974 might either pressure organized labor to lobby on women's issues, or might lobby these issues itself, these expectations do not seem to be realistic. In interviews with two activists from CLUW, it was clear that the thrust of CLUW's activity is to increase representation of women in union leadership, not to push for action on specific legislation. This preference is confirmed by the absence of any CLUW presence in Congress during the period of this research.

42. For a list of contacts between the women's lobby and women members of Congress see Anne N. Costain, "Representing Women," p. 111.

43. Anne N. Costain, "Lobbying for Equal Credit," *Women Organizing*, Bernice Cummings and Victoria Schuck (eds.) (Metuchen, NJ: Scarecrow Press, 1979), 82–110.

44. The most broad-gauged was the coalition supporting the Pregnancy Disability Act of 1979, which included civil rights, labor, Right-to-Life, civil liberties, and women's groups.

45. Carol Mueller (ed.), *The Politics of the Gender Gap*, Vol. 12, Sage Yearbooks in Women's Policy Studies (Beverly Hills, CA: Sage, 1987) provides a good overview of the controversies surrounding the gender gap.

46. Interview, January 20, 1984.

47. Interview, January 18, 1984.

48. Interview with Patricia Reuss, January 18, 1984.

49. Keith Poole and Harmon Zeigler, *Women, Public Opinion, and Politics* (New York: Longman, 1985). See also the *Gallup Public Opinion Indices*, 1972 to 1985.

50. *The Gallup Poll: Public Opinion, 1983* (Wilmington, DE: Scholarly Resources, 1983) p. 140.

51. For the contrast, see Anne Costain, "The Struggle for a National Women's Lobby," *Western Political Quarterly, 33* (December 1980): 476–491.

52. Interview, January 6, 1981.

53. Interview, January 6, 1981.

54. Interview, January 20, 1984.

55. Interview, January 20, 1984.

56. I was unable to schedule an interview with the NOW lobbyist in 1984. I was first told that she was attending a lesbian–gay rights conference in Madison, Wisconsin and later that she had gone from Wisconsin to California. A national

staff member of NOW told me off the record that these were stock reasons given when NOW officials preferred not to grant an interview.

57. Exceptions to this generalization include Walker, "A Critique of the Elitist Theory of Democracy"; John Kingdon's discussion of the predecision stage of congressional policy making in *Congressmen's Voting Decisions* (New York: Harper and Row, 1973), pp. 242–260; and Roger W. Cobb and Charles D. Elder, *Participation in American Politics: The Dynamics of Agenda-Building* (Baltimore: Johns Hopkins University Press 1972).

58. Once again there are exceptions, including Gary Orfield, *Congressional Power: Congress and Social Change* (New York: Harcourt, Brace, Jovanovich, 1975); and Jack L. Walker, "Setting the Agenda in the U.S. Senate: A Theory of Problem Selection," *British Journal of Political Science, 4* (October 1977): 423–446.

3
Women and Corporate Power

Diane W. Franklin and Joan L. Sweeney

Lauren Townsend is bright, ambitious, well-educated—and angry! A successful account manager in a Wall Street investment banking firm, Townsend has recently hit hard against the "glass ceiling," an invisible barrier aptly named by the *Wall Street Journal*,[1] which in innumerable cases stands between women and top executive posts. Though numbed by the blow and slightly bewildered, since she is young enough not to have had to fight for her current position the way her older female colleagues had, Townsend quickly contemplated her alternatives. Her first reaction was just to sit tight and wait for the pressures "in the pipeline" to build to their inevitable conclusion: the promotion of some female account managers to partnerships. As she thought about this option, however, she realized that it might not occur as fast as she would like for her career development. She then thought about taking on her firm in a legal fight, a battle she was counseled would probably be successful, though at great personal cost. Finally, she began mulling over the idea of leaving "The Street" altogether and starting an entrepreneurial venture she had been toying with since business school. Groomed for the "fast track," Townsend was extremely frustrated by the barrier she encountered just as she had almost reached the top. Both her training and her personal ambitions make it unlikely that she will sit and wait for a possible promotion that might be years in coming.

In comparison to most working women, Townsend has little to complain about. She has never known the monotonous work or the stifling of initiative and creativity that typifies the daily lives of most of her employed sisters. A member of a financial elite, she earns far more money than all but a handful of working women or working men. But, like most people, Townsend compares herself not to the average person but to her immediate reference group, the colleagues with whom she works and socializes. In comparison to this group, 75 percent of whom are men, she earns less money and has less likelihood of advancement than if she were male.[2]

Townsend's experience is not unique to Wall Street. Despite having made great strides in achieving middle management positions, in every geographical region and in many industries, women in the corporate world are less likely than their male counterparts to reach the top.[3] Awareness of this phenomenon is now new. Since the mid-1970s there have been numerous books and articles in both the academic and business press that purport to explain why women invariably fall short of achieving the corporate pinnacle. These explanations usually fall into one of two paradigms,[4] each of which has implications for what needs to change before women can achieve full equality in corporate life.

The first paradigm, which we will call the *person-centered* paradigm, suggests that women fail to achieve full corporate power because of their own characteristics, values, and behavior. Following the theory to its logical conclusions, women are counseled that if only they could think, dress, and behave like men, they, too, would succeed in the corporate world. The second paradigm, which we will call the *situation-centered* or *structural* paradigm, suggests that organizations are structured in ways that reinforce gender inequality. The opportunity structures, power structures, and female-to-male sex ratios that typify most organizations all contribute to women's disadvantaged position within organizations. Proponents of this view argue that if corporations would modify their organizational structures to provide women with the same opportunities for advancement and the same access to sources of organizational power as men have, eventually the inequalities between men and women in the corporate world would disappear. Individuals of both sexes would then have an equal chance of achieving success based on their own merits and work records.

It is our contention, however, that neither of these two paradigms, alone or together, constitutes a sufficient explanation for the gender inequities that currently exist in America's corporations. Neither view questions the value orientations of the typical corporation or looks at the primacy of the role of work in relation to other systems such as family life or individual interests. Both take for granted the idea that there is "one best way" of working, as embodied in current definitions of professionalism. Further, neither looks at these definitions from a multicultural perspective or in the context of the numerous challenges facing American businesses as the United States evolves from primarily a manufacturing to primarily a service and information economy.

In this chapter we summarize and critique the two main existing paradigms and then sketch a third paradigm that we call the *systems* paradigm. In discussing this paradigm, we document both the responses that individual women are making as they encounter the "glass ceiling" and changes that a small but growing number of forward-thinking corporations are making as they think about how businesses might be constituted in the future. A few companies are recognizing the crucial importance of protecting and developing their human assets in order to be competitive in the work world of tomorrow. Additionally, they have begun to realize that women are not only in the labor force on a permanent basis but also comprise a fast-growing pool of new talent that can help bring about the very changes that will ensure business survival in a service economy characterized by tight labor markets.[5]

Before examining these three paradigms, however, we need to see where women of the corporation are, how far they have come as a group, and how corporate realities and policies impact on their lives.

HOW FAR HAVE WOMEN COME?

In 1985, women constituted 33.6 percent of all executive, administrative, and managerial workers as compared with 21.9 percent in 1975.[6] While these figures indicated that women have made some strides in a relatively short time, a closer examination of the data is needed to understand what these changes mean.

Because government statistics lump together a variety of roles under the category of "executive, administrative, and managerial" workers, it becomes difficult to distinguish the types of managerial positions that women hold. The data do not differentiate, for example, between female office managers and chief executive officers of corporations. Moreover, although one-third of such executive and managerial positions were held by women in 1984, only 8.5 percent of all female workers were in this category (compared with 5.2 percent in 1975).

Other data suggest that the relatively few women who are managers, the majority are concentrated mainly in the low to middle management sectors. A 1982 *Time* magazine study, for example, reported that women held only 5 percent of executive positions in the 50 largest American companies. A more recent study conducted by the executive recruiting firm of Korn/Ferry International indicated that women held only 2 percent of top executive positions.[7] Only one company in the Fortune 500, the Washington Post Company, has a female CEO, and she has readily acknowledged that she got the job after her husband's death mainly because her family owned a controlling share of the company's equity.[8] Similarly, women hold few spots on corporate boards, comprising, for example, only 3 to 4 percent of Fortune 1000 dirctors.[9] Finally, only a handful are accepted into the prestigious Advanced Management Program at the Harvard Business School, a program considered to be the "finishing school" for executives being groomed for top positions.[10]

Salaries tell a similar story. Though corporate women are highly remunerated in comparison to most working people, their salaries still lag far behind those of their male counterparts. Government data suggest that, over all, women in executive, administrative, and managerial positions earn 63 percent of what men in similar positions earn, a ratio that is actually below that of the work force as a whole (64.8 percent).[11] Other studies, conducted by business school researchers, indicate that although men and women with MBAs begin their first jobs at roughly the same salary level, the salaries of women in middle management positions quickly fall behind those of men, sometimes by as much as $9,000 per year.[12] At the top levels, this disparity is considerably greater since women generally do not advance to the positions that are compensated by astronomical salaries.

ORGANIZATIONAL PRACTICES AND POLICIES

Within the corporate sector, managerial women are confronted with a set of organizational realities and policies with which they must cope in order to survive. Among these are definitions of professionalism that are based on the often tacit assumption of a wife in the background whose job it is to provide the support services that allow her husband to work 10- to 12-hour days without having to worry about shopping, cooking, or childcare. Most female executives must either do the job of a wife in addition to that of an executive, hire a substitute "wife," or, as many women have done, forego marriage and children altogether in order to achieve career success. A recent study of female executives suggests that a large number of women, and only a tiny fraction of men, have chosen the last option.[13]

Those women who decide to marry and especially those who choose to have children are often faced with agonizing decisions and time pressures beginning with a child's birth. Although some corporations have policies that allow up to 12 weeks of maternity leave, many women are pressured not to take the full amount of leave and acknowledge the costs to their careers that occur if they do so.[14] Despite these pressures, maternity leave is grudgingly allowed in many cases; in contrast, paternity leave is frowned upon and is certainly rarely incorporated into formal corporate policy. Men who wish to stay home with infants, even briefly, are generally the object of wonderment, if not open ridicule; and those few who choose to brave this censure may experience severe career setbacks as a consequence of their decision.[15]

In addition, the problems of balancing work and family life do not end shortly after the birth of a child. Day care and after-school care are difficult to find, even for people who can easily afford to pay for these, and few corporations have chosen to establish on-site day-care centers despite their evident success in the few places where they exist. Similarly, flexi-time, job-sharing, and working at home are formal options in only a handful of companies, though on an individual basis some women have been able to arrange "deals" with their bosses that allow them to work in non-conventional ways.[16] Thus, many women have to choose between career and loyalty to the company, and the needs of their children, or else become adept at coping surreptitiously with their dual lives; this choice is not without difficulties and costs.[17]

At another level, little is known about how pressures on parents are affecting children. While numerous studies have indicated that children of working mothers grow up to be as happy and able to cope as the children of mothers who are not in the labor force, *if* they are left in the care of loving and conscientious adults,[18] little research has yet been done to see whether children whose mothers have high-powered corporate careers feel that they are less important than their mothers' work and, if so, what the consequences are for their development.

WHY WOMEN ARE WHERE THEY ARE—THE COMPETING PARADIGMS

The Person-Centered Paradigm

The person-centered paradigm attributes women's lack of progress in the corporate sector to the fact that women are different from men—less competitive, less aggressive, less ambitious, and more nurturing—in what is still a man's world. Variants of the paradigm portray these unique female qualities as resulting from a number of factors working alone or in concert: differences in male/female socialization patterns that begin in infancy and continue throughout adult development,[19] different paths for forming gender identity,[20] and even different ways of comprehending the world and construing reality.[21] After discussing typical female characteristics and their possible origins, the paradigm then goes on to show a lack of congruence between these characteristics, value patterns, and behaviors and those needed for success and advancement in the corporate world.[22] If only women could learn to be more like men, the theory posits, they would be able to break through the "glass ceiling" with little difficulty.[23]

The person-centered paradigm involves several assumptions and implications. To begin with, this view assumes that women and men are in fact different in personality and temperament and that these differences determine their managerial behavior. While it is clear that men and women do behave differently in many situations and do not always share similar value orientations, several studies have demonstrated few differences in *management style* between the sexes. A study by Harlan and Weiss, for example, indicated that women had no trouble functioning on management teams, and performed as well as men on standardized tests measuring assertiveness and leadership ability.[24] Another study of more than 2,000 male and female managers, conducted by Hall and Donnell, yielded similar results and concluded that there were no significant differences in the ways men and women managed human and technical resources.[25] Despite the evidence of these studies, many men hang on to outmoded stereotypes about female behavior, asserting differences where none exist, and then use these alleged differences as justifications for the *status quo*.

Although there are few differences between the sexes regarding management style, women and men *do* behave differently with regard to their expression of feelings and their concern for relationships within the work environment. On those dimensions where gender differences do exist, the common pattern is to devalue the predominantly female value and behavior patterns and to assume the greater effectiveness of those that are male.[26] Implicit in this thought pattern is the notion that male values and behavior patterns are "normal" and "correct," whereas typically female values and behaviors are deviant and dysfunctional. It is common wisdom, for instance, that the business world is a rational sphere in which the nurturing behavior and intuition frequently associated with women have no place. But a number of recent books and research projects have challenged this view.[27] For example, from a study of 12 very senior executives in a number of successful corporations,[28] Isenberg concluded that the thinking processes of top executives involve not merely a series of rational decisions but rather combine both intuition and rationality in an interactive process. In addition, implementation rather than strategy formation is of prime importance to these executives, all of whom emphasize that successful implementation requires a focus on organizational and interpersonal processes as much as it does the analysis of hard data. The implications of these findings for male versus female behavior patterns should not be underestimated. Such studies challenge the belief that for successful managers, rationality and task-orientation are more important than intuition and relationship-building and suggest that the qualities frequently seen resulting from female socialization may be quite functional in the business world.

While the male model of behavior may work in the fast-paced, hard-driving environment that characterizes many of today's corporations, there is increasing evidence that such a style will be counterproductive in a service/information economy or for a workforce that is expected to include approximately 50 percent women by the 1990s.[29]

The Structural Paradigm

In contrast to the person-centered paradigm, the structural paradigm considers the organization rather than the individual as its unit of analysis. Its proponents assert that it is important to understand how women and men are distributed across structural positions and how this distribution affects behavior rather than to focus on how women differ from men. In its implications for change, this paradigm avoids a "blaming the victim" mentality and instead concentrates on structural changes that would increase women's opportunities in the corporate world.

Rosabeth Moss Kanter, a major proponent of the structural paradigm, describes three structural characteristics of organizations that influence the behavior of people within those organizations: (a) the structures of opportunity—the possibilities the organization offers for mobility, advancement, and growth, (b) the structures of power—the capacity to mobilize resources and to influence people within a wider organizational context, and (c) the degree of occupational segregation by sex, race, or class. She also documents that until relatively recently, women have had few opportunities for advancement within most organizations, little power or ability to influence others within or outside of the wider organizational context, and only token representation in management positions.[30]

Kanter also argues that the characteristic and frequently ineffective behaviors ascribed to women are a function of their unenviable structural position within organizations rather than their gender or patterns of upbringing.[31] She notes that complex organizations whose power and opportunity structures routinely disadvantage particular groups of people are likely to generate the behavioral consequences of such segregation. Such behaviors include authoritarian leadership styles, an inability to delegate responsibility, turf protection, and concentration on the petty details of interpersonal relations rather than on the task or the overall organizational goals. These behaviors are viewed by many as ineffective or dysfunctional, but from another perspective, they are quite functional for most women's situations. In many cases, they provide coping mechanisms that help protect women from the psychological stresses associated with having high aspirations in an environment where advancement opportunities are limited or blocked.

A recent study of female professionals and businesswomen looked at the linkages among structural variables, organizational positions, and respondents' attitudes and behaviors. Despite some methodological shortcomings, this study confirmed Kanter's assertions, concluding that "women in upper-level corporate positions gave greater precedence to their careers, shared more of their leadership functions, had higher levels of job satisfaction, and had a greater sense of organizational commitment than lower-level women. Additionally, upper-level women focused on the intrinsic features of their job over the extrinsic ones. The opposite was true for lower-management women."[32]

Like the person-centered paradigm, the structural paradigm also offers prescriptions for change. If women's lack of corporate success is based on their limited opportunity within power structures and their minimal representation at top levels of the corporate hierarchy, then the key to changing this situation is to make available to women more advancement opportunities, more access to influence within the organization, and greater representation at all levels of corporate structure. To do this, corporations must understand that apparent differences in behavior and attitudes are more a function of organizational position than of gender, and must recognize that such differences will disappear once the requisite structural changes are made and access to opportunities increased.

Though having greater explanatory value than the person-centered paradigm, the structural paradigm and change strategics based on it are inadequate to either explain or address the prejudice and discrimination many women feel are at the root of their current situation. In numerous corporations, discrimination against women still exists, sometimes in subtly disguised forms and sometimes not. Such prejudice may consist of untested assumptions about women: they "can't hack" the rough-and-tumble of corporate life at the top, they do not have enough drive, they will not come back to work after having a baby, or they make clients uncomfortable. On other occasions, it may be manifested by men at the top openly asserting that they themselves feel uncomfortable with women working beside them. In some instances women are presented with a "Catch-22": "the woman who is tough isn't womanly, while the woman who isn't tough isn't worth having around."[33] Such a view forces women to choose between being women or being successful, a choice men are not asked to make.

Whatever its form, prejudice is an irrational response, and the resulting discrimination will not be easily eradicated as a consequence of rational arguments about the need to restructure organizations to allow greater opportunities and power for women. Arguments that suggest organizational change, by either reorganizing or setting up mechanisms to punish those who discriminate against women and to reward those who sponsor and promote them, are of little value unless they also provide incentives for such changes and implementation plans for bringing them about. Such arguments and incentives will have to deal with the vested self-interest of those currently in power. These strategies will most likely be effective if they can convincingly delineate the benefits to everyone, including those presently in top positions, of a structure and set of work relationships where power, decisionmaking, and rewards are more broadly shared.

Another weakness of the structural paradigm, one that it shares with the person-centered paradigm, is that it accepts the status quo regarding the primacy of work in people's lives. Although proponents of this view call for restructuring organizations, they do not question the values that permeate such organizations, values that define professionalism and success as requiring total commitment to one's work to the virtual exclusion of other areas of life. Unfortunately, many women have come to adopt these values. In a recent article describing both the gains women have made over the past decade and the problems they still face, Betty Friedan notes that "there's a whole new generation of women today flogging themselves to compete for success according to the male model—in a work world structured for men with wives to handle the details of life."[34]

Thus, both the person-centered and the structural paradigms are limited in that each assumes work is and should be the paramount focus of women's lives. Neither paradigm offers other ways of thinking about work in relation to either the needs of those performing it or to the goals and objectives of employers. At the individual level, the way work is presently structured does not easily allow for variation in people's relationship to their work as they move through different stages of the life cycle. Further, the inflexibly structured 8-hour-a-day, 5-day work-week creates severe role strain for many people, especially working parents. At the organizational level, in a society characterized more by service and information delivery than by industrial production, it may be more functional to view and organize work differently from the way in which it has previously been conceived and structured. Our analysis contends that to increase women's power in corporate life and indeed in any organization, we must look at both work and organizational forms in new ways. Men as well as women will benefit from this fresh vision, as will the corporations that must learn to function in a post-industrial era whose rules are very different from those that have worked up to now.

TRANSITIONS AND TRANSFORMATIONS: ALTERNATIVE VIEWS AND AN EMERGING PARADIGM

Whether because of frustration at hitting a "glass ceiling" or the sense of having achieved corporate success by betraying their female identity and values, some of the best and the brightest women increasingly are resigning from the corporate world to take positions with smaller firms or to begin their own businesses. Most frequently, women cite the inhospitable corporate climate as the reason for this decision.[35]

The growing numbers of women leaving corporate environments for more entrepreneurial ventures represent one type of shift; at the same time, some corporations are realizing the benefits to both the organization and employees of various kinds of changes in the workplace. Many of these changes reflect both the attitudinal and structural shifts that contemporary experts believe are necessary to revitalize American corporate life. In some cases, these changes go beyond resuscitation to actually "re-inventing the corporation."[36] In that sense, they intend deeper transformations, going beyond the two prevailing paradigms previously discussed[37] to reflect an "open systems" or systemic view.

Partially to maintain or gain competitive advantage in an unstable global economy[38] and partially from realizing the benefits to both organizations and employees, changes are being made in growing numbers of U.S. corporations. There seem to be three primary thrusts to these changes which are already or potentially affecting women's corporate worklife. First, decisionmakers in corporations are instituting practices that may fundamentally alter the work experiences for both women and men. Second, growing numbers of women are creating their own employment opportunities in the form of entrepreneurial ventures. Third, conceptions of what is possible in designing organizations for both the people in them and for high performance are shifting. Each change will be briefly described.

Corporate Transitions

Although the new corporate practices take various company-specific forms, the overall pattern is already visible if, as one writer put it, "one knows where and how to look."[39] Some who *are* looking describe the shift underway as being a radically different way of managing. Whatever the innovations and interventions being used to facilitate the shift—participative management, quality of work life programs, employee involvement—the profound changes being made can be seen as reflecting the choice between a strategy based on imposing control versus one based on eliciting commitment.[40] The evidence is mounting that working together works.[41]

Under such new policies and conditions, stereotypically female values and skills, such as regard for others' needs and working cooperatively, could have a new currency. For example a highly touted book, *In Search of Excellence* by Thomas J. Peters and Robert H. Waterman, Jr. (New York: Warner, 1982), provided lessons for managers to absorb and emulate, lessons emphasizing productivity through people, to be accomplished through an appreciation of individual effort, recognition, nurturing, and the encouragement of creativity. It is ironic that all of these qualities, devalued when they were seen as feminine qualities, are now lauded when they are reframed and defined as indicators of excellence.

Such a climate of change also holds promise for revamping the straitjack-eted male definitions of success and professionalism, definitions which even the most successful corporate women increasingly report deny their authentically female expectations and values. As has been amply detailed elsewhere, the "corporate mystique" as defined by men has demanded that women deny and neglect their basic selves as much as did the "feminine mystique," albeit in a different way.[42]

While some attribute the transitions occurring in American corporations to interest in a different way of managing, Naisbitt and Aburdene see investing in human capital as the most important strategic focus for the emerging information economy. They and others also cite the anticipated labor shortages and sellers' market of the 1980s and 1990s as factors underscoring the wisdom of such a focus.[43]

As a consequence of either or both of these sets of forces, some companies are changing and becoming great places to work in the opinions of their employees. While the accounts of these companies are not solely those of women, the research that generated the *100 Best Companies to Work for in America* by Robert Levering (New York: Plume Books, 1986) queried women and men at all levels of the corporations considered. The portraits these people paint of their work experiences stand in sharp contrast to accounts offered elsewhere of the growing dissatisfaction of so many corporate women.[44] In addition to good pay and comprehensive benefits, work experiences in these firms were characterized by a feeling of team participation, a sense of opportunity because of a policy of promotion from within, stress on quality and pride, the reduction of status distinctions between top management and those holding entry-level jobs, provision of fitness centers and other supports for health and wellness, and the expansion of people's skills through access to training programs and reimbursement for outside courses.[45] Rather than being distinguished by a lack of opportunity for growth, "glass ceilings," and a sense of betrayal, these companies managed to engage and satisfy the women and men working there and were thus excellent from their employees' points of view. They also manage to satisfy the criteria some consider critical for companies that want to stay viable under changing economic and labor force conditions.

Although the "100 best" and other corporations engaged in creating similar work places may be part of a first wave of a major change that will profoundly affect the way all of us think of our jobs and conduct business, for some this change is not happening fast enough. Increasingly dissatisfied with expectations for deference and patience, yet at the same time aware of the unresponsiveness of corporate authorities to their values and needs, women are leaving the corporate world in record numbers.[46] Having decided it may be easier to reach the pinnacle of corporate success by jumping off the corporate ladder and pursuing entrepreneurial goals,[47] they are leaving *now*, in a female "brain drain" some analysts say American corporations can ill afford if they are to compete more successfully in the global market-place.[48]

Entrepreneurial Ventures

Whether dissatisfied corporate managers who experience their growth and advancement as limited, new MBAs, re-entrants to the labor force, or women creatively struggling their way off welfare, women are starting businesses and creating their own jobs in unprecedented numbers and at a historic rate.[49] Women now own about 25 percent of the nation's small businesses, up from 5 percent in 1976. It is estimated, according to the Small Business Administration, that by the year 2000, half of all small businesses will be owned or controlled by women. Also, according to the Bureau of Labor Statistics, in 1985, 2.8 million women were self-employed,[50] a 75 percent increase over the past 10 years. During the same period, the number of self-employed men rose by only 12.1 percent to 6.5 million.[51]

Many people believe that the 1980s and 1990s will see the rise of the woman entrepreneur, by choice rather than through inheritance. Women are making a conscious decision to create and build businesses as a way of exercising influence not only within their own lives but also on the economic as well as the social structure of the United States.[52] The significance of this trend can be better appreciated when understood in light of shifts in the U.S. economy, which is increasingly being viewed and described as "an entrpreneurial economy."[53] By some accounts, women leaving large corporate settings are making advantageous choices. The number of permanent jobs with Fortune 500 corporations has been shrinking steadily since around 1970, while, simultaneously, small and new businesses have produced most of the approximately 20 million new jobs generated from 1970 to 1980.[54]

From a policy perspective, an extensive and compelling case can be and has been made for the role of entrepreneurship and new enterprise development in the revitalization of America's economy. Such entrepreneurial job-generating activity is important in another respect. For those women blocked from advancement in existing workplaces or outside the economic mainstream, the opportunity to start and expand businesses represents one of the few alternatives for personal economic advancement.[55] Women are generating a new approach to economic development, or what one author refers to as "economic development as if women mattered."[56] By doing so, they are creating economic opportunities for themselves and, as they become successful in larger numbers, for more and more of their similarly disenchanted sisters.[57]

Transformations

Thus far, "knowing where to look" has allowed us to illuminate two of the kinds of changes that have already or are likely to have an impact on corporate women's experiences. But some CEOs, managers, and consultants are taking an even more dramatic step by examining and transforming our basic conceptions of what is possible in corporate worklife.

Much of the reconceptualizing is informed by earlier theoretical work on open or living systems, as well as by the view that corporations have operated for too long with a reliance on reductionist and authoritarian rather than expansionist thinking.[58] Such "revisioning" of the corporation has also been influenced by the belief that fundamental socio-economic problems cannot be solved by the very same mind set that generated those problems in the first place.[59]

Others cite the changing workforce and changing expectations as fueling the transformation of work. Increasingly, the labor force is a highly educated one, comprised of more women than ever before in history and thus embodying to a greater degree the different values women hold. Further, evidence exists of a growing desire for work that is personally meaningful. More people are seeking work that is intrinsically valuable beyond the need for financial security.[60] In addition to the desire for meaningful work, there have been fundamental shifts with regard to authority relationships and leadership patterns in the work setting. Observers see a growing unwillingness by individuals to defer decisions to traditional authority figures and institutions.[61]

An Emerging Organizational Paradigm

These reactions, re-examinations, and reconceptualizations have generated a new set of beliefs, which are forming an emerging paradigm that emphasizes an expanded sense of identity and an awareness of the interconnectedness of people within a single organizational culture and of corporate cultures. As a consequence of this mind shift, organizations are experimenting with and creating environments in which more effectively designed social systems support higher levels of personal and organizational excellence.

In response to a fusion of the various forces noted, a small but significant number of corporations are emerging as prototypes of a new kind of organization. Such organizations have been described as *metanoic*, meaning a fundamental shift of mind, a term used to denote the reawakening of intuition and vision. Simply put, a metanoic organization operates with the conviction that it can shape its own destiny. The corporate philosophy of metanoic organizations can generally be seen as having five primary dimensions: (1) a deep sense of vision or purposefulness; (2) alignment around that vision; (3) the empowerment of people; (4) structural integrity; and (5) a balance between reason and intuition. Metanoic organizations represent an ideal toward which a growing number of companies of diverse kinds appear to be moving.[62]

The climate created in such corporations can have a profound effect on the employees, particularly by nurturing a sense of empowerment and an understanding of and responsibility for the larger social systems within which the individual and the organization operates.[63] Most importantly for our purposes, these organizations exemplify characteristics that are familiar and comfortable to women such as the sense of "self in connection to others," which is so much a part of women's sense of identity.[64]

As a result of their work with innovative managers, some of those closely involved with the design and evolution of such transformed corporations believe that it is possible to achieve simultaneously both very high organizational performance and great human satisfaction. In such companies, employees energetically work with a clear sense of being part of the whole. As a consequence, instead of exchanging their personal identities for a corporate identity or feeling betrayed by corporate unresponsiveness, they report feeling that they have expanded their personal identities.[65]

Such organizations represent a radical alternative to our accepted methods of managing complex systems. They replace top-down control with decentralized control. They replace rules and regulations that stifle initiative with alignment around a common vision. They foster the assumptions that everyone can win and that each individual has a unique part to play in the company's success. Finally, they demonstrate that leaders who catalyze vision, alignment, and personal responsibility, and who can be compelling teachers, are far more effective in achieving corporate goals than those relying on traditional forms of management and authority relationships.[66]

Given their values and organizational design, these kinds of corporations are environments in which we could expect women and the skills they bring to management to thrive and develop. But because these bold new experiments are in their infancy, more in-depth as well as longitudinal research will be needed to determine whether such corporations are capable of utilizing the skills and capacities of all their employees, but especially those of their women employees whose values and abilities have been for so long ignored.

Many people working with "high performance" organizations caution that corporations that approach the challenge ahead with impoverished ways of thinking will be caught at the "shear line" of conflicting paradigms. They can anticipate increasing difficulties as the pace of change continues to accelerate and their habits of thought, policies, and practices fall further behind the realities of an increasingly complex world.[67] Corporations that choose to ignore the exodus of highly talented women, minimize the import of changing workforce demographics, ignore changing values, or continue to act as though we are still in a primarily industrial economy can expect, from the patterns emerging, to continue to lose talent and, ultimately, to jeopardize their overall viability. In the final analysis, the female "brain drain" is likely to hurt American corporations far more than it hurts American women.[68]

NOTES AND REFERENCES

1. Carol Hymowitz and Timothy D. Schellhardt, "The Glass Ceiling," *Wall Street Journal*, March 24, 1986, p. 1D.

2. Beth McGoldrick and Gregory Miller, "Wall Street Woman: You've Come a Short Way, Baby," *Institutional Investor* (June 1985), pp. 235–237, 239–240.

3. Susan Fraker, "Why Women Aren't Getting to the Top," *Fortune*, April 16, 1984, pp. 40–45; Helen Rogan, "Top Women Executives Find Path to Power is Strewn with Hurdles," *Wall Street Journal*, October 25, 1984, p. 35.

4. Ellen Fagenson, "Women's Work Orientations: Something Old, Something New," *Group and Organization Studies 11* (March-June 1986), pp. 75–100.

5. John Naisbitt and Patricia Auburdene, *Re-Inventing the Corporation* (New York: Warner, 1985), passim

6. "The United Nations Decade for Women, 1976–1985: Employment in the United States," U.S. Department of Labor, Women's Bureau, July 1985, p. 125.

7. Marilyn Loden, " A Machismo That Drives Women Out," *New York Times*, February 9, 1986.

8. Fraker, "Why Women Aren't Getting to the Top," p. 40

9. Claire Ansberry, "The Board Game," *Wall Street Journal*, March 24, 1986, p. 29D.

10. Fraker, "Why Women Aren't Getting to the Top," p. 40

11. "The United Nations Decade for Women, 1976–1985," p. 129.

12. Alex Taylor, "Why Women Managers Are Bailing Out," *Fortune*, August 18, 1986, pp. 16–23; Fraker, *op. cit.*; Mary Dingee Fillmore, *A Foot in the Door* (New York: G. K. Hall, 1987).

13. Fraker, "Why Women Aren't Getting to the Top," p. 40

14. Ibid., p. 44.

15. Joann S. Lublin, "Courting the Couple," *Wall Street Journal*, March 24, 1986, pp. 28D, 30D. This article refers to a study conducted by Catalyst, a New York research group, that documented the general unavailability of paternity leave and the lack of encouragement for taking it even when it formally existed.

16. Taylor, "Why Women Managers Are Bailing Out."

17. Barbara J. Berg, *The Crisis of the Working Mother* (New York: Summit Books, 1986), passim.

18. Ibid.

19. Jean Baker P. Miller, *Toward a New Psychology of Women* (Boston: Beacon Press, 1976), passim.

20. Nancy Chodorow, *The Reproduction of Mothering* (Berkeley: University of California Press, 1978), passim.

21. Carol Gilligan, *In a Different Voice* (Cambridge, MA: Harvard University Press, 1982), passim.

22. Margaret Hennig and Ann Jardim, *The Managerial Woman* (New York: Doubleday, 1977); Rosabeth Moss Kanter, *Men and Women of the Corporation* (New York: Basic Books, 1977); Matina Horner, "Toward an Understanding of

Achievement Related Conflicts in Women," *Journal of Social Issues 28* (1972): 157–176; Mark Lipton, "Successful Women in a Man's World: The Myth of Managerial Androgyny," in Lynda L. Moore (ed.), *Not as Far as You Think* (Lexington, MA: Lexington Books, 1986), pp. 163–180.

23. Betty Harrigan, *Games Mother Never Taught You* (New York: Warner, 1977), passim.

24. Fraker, "Why Women Aren't Getting to the Top," p. 41.

25. Ibid., p. 42.

26. Richard T. Pascale and Anthony G. Athos, *The Art of Japanese Management* (New York: Warner Books, 1981), pp. 202–205.

27. Thomas J. Peters and Robert H. Waterman, Jr., *In Search of Excellence* (New York: Warner, 1982); Daniel Yankelovich, *New Rules* (New York: Random House, 1981); Robert Levering and *The 100 Best Companies to Work for in America* (New York: Plume Books, Inc., 1986); Weston H. Agor, *Intuitive Management* (Englewood Cliffs, NJ: Prentice-Hall, 1984); Roy Rowan, *The Intuitive Manager* (Boston: Little, Brown, 1986).

28. Daniel Isenberg, "How Senior Managers Think," *Harvard Business Review* 6 (Nov-Dec, 1984), pp. 80–90.

29. Naisbitt and Auburdene, *Re-inventing the Corporation*.

30. Rosabeth Moss Kanter, *Men and Women of the Corporation* (New York: Basic Books, 1977), passim.

31. Rosabeth Moss Kanter, "The Impact of Hierarchical Structures on the Work Behavior of Women and Men," in Rachael Kahn-Hut (ed.), *Women and Work* (New York: Oxford University Press, 1982).

32. Fagenson, "Women's Work Orientations," p. 89.

33. Hymowitz and Schellhardt, "The Glass Ceiling," p. 1D.

34. Betty Friedan, "Where Do We Go From Here?," *Working Woman*, November 1986, p. 152.

35. Sarah Hardesty and Nehama Jacobs, *Success and Betrayal* (New York: Franklin Watts, 1986); Loden, "A Machismo that Drives Women Out," passim.

36. Naisbitt and Auburdene, *Reinventing the Corporation*, passim.

37. Susan Riger and Patricia Galligan, "Women in Management: An Exploration of Competing Paradigms," *American Psychologist 35* (1980): 902–910.

38. Michael E. Porter, *Competitive Advantage* (New York: Free Press, 1985), passim.

39. Richard Walton, "From Control to Commitment in the Work Place," *Harvard Business Review* (March-April 1985): 260–273.

40. Ibid.

41. John Simmons, *Working Together* (New York: Harcourt Brace Jovanovich, 1984), passim.

42. Hardesty and Jacobs, *Success and Betrayal*, passim.

43. Paul Hawken, *The Next Economy* (New York: Holt, Rinehart and Winston, 1983); Naisbitt and Auburdene, *Reinventing the Corporation*; Peter F. Drucker, *Innovation and Entrepreneurship* (New York: Harper and Row, 1985); Joan L. Sweeney, *Risk Taking as a Necessity for Growth: A Study of the Perceptions and Experiences of a Sample of Successful Contemporary Women Entrepreneurs*, Unpublished doctoral dissertation, University of Massachusetts, 1984.

44. Levering et al.; Hardesty and Jacobs.

45. Levering, Robert, et al.

46. Trudy Heller, "Authority: Changing Patterns, Changing Times," in John Adams (ed.), *Transforming Work* (Alexandria, VA: Miles River Press, 1984).

47. Hymowitz and Schellhardt, "The Glass Ceiling," p. 1D.

48. Loden, "A Machismo that Drives Women Out."

49. *The Bottom Line: Unequal Enterprise Development in America*, Report of the President's Interagency Task Force on Women Business Owners, Washington, D.C., 1978; Marilyn Bender, "More Women Becoming Owners of Business," *New York Times*, April 25, 1986; Frances J. Charboneau, "The Woman Entrepreneur," *American Demographics 3* (1981): 21–23; Sara Gould, "Report of the National Strategy Session on Women's Self-Employment" (Washington, D.C.: Corporation for Enterprise Development, 1986).

50. We cite *both* small business ownership and self-employment statistics because they represent two facets of women's entrepreneurial activity. For some women, self-employment becomes the first step in owning and developing a business which subsequently generates jobs for others. Other women use self-employment, in the form of freelance or consultant work of various kinds, to satisfy their desire for a less restrictive employment option and do not choose to develop a larger enterprise.

51. Eric Schmitt, "Women Entrepreneurs Thrive," *New York Times*, August 18, 1986.

52. "Women Rise as Entrepreneurs," *Business Week*, Month, Date, 1980, pp. 85–91; C. R. Riggs, "The Rise of Women Entrepreneurs," *Dun and Bradstreet Reports 29* (1981): 19–23; Terry Tepper and Nina Tepper, *The New Entrepreneurs: Women Working from Home* (New York: Universe Books, 1980).

53. Peter F. Drucker, "Our Entrepreneurial Economy," *Harvard Business Review 62* (1984): 58–64.

54. P. Drucker, *Innovation and Entrepreneurship*.

55. Robert Friedman and William Schweke (eds.), *Expanding the Opportunity to Produce: Revitalizing the American Economy through New Enterprise Development—A Policy Reader* (Washington, D.C.: Corporation for Enterprise Development, 1981); Ray Marshall, *Work and Women in the 1980s* (Washington, D.C.: Women's Research and Education Institute of the Congressional Caucus for Women's Issues, 1983).

56. Sara Gould, *Economic Development as if Women Mattered: Some Thoughts and Model Programs* (Washington, D.C.: Corporation for Enterprise Development, 1985).

57. Gould, "Report of the National Strategy Session on Women's Self-Employment"; Marilyn Sinetar, "SMR Forum: Entrepreneurs, Chaos, and Creativity—Can Creative People Really Survive Large Company Structure?" *Sloan Management Review* (Winter 1985): 57.

58. James G. Miller, *Living Systems* (New York: McGraw-Hill, 1978); Russel Ackoff, *Creating the Corporate Future* (New York: Wiley, 1981)

59. Charles Kiefer and Peter Senge, "Metanoic Organizations," in John Adams (ed.), *Transforming Work* (Alexandria, VA: Miles River Press, 1984).

60. John Adams, *Transforming Work*; Charles Keifer and Peter Stroh, "A New Paradigm for Developing Organizations," in J. Adams, *Transforming Work*; Yankelovich, *op. cit.*

61. Heller, Hardesty and Jacobs, *Success and Betrayal*; Fraker, "Why Women Aren't Getting to the Top."

62. These companies include, for example, Kollmorgan Corporation, a diversified manufacturing company; Cray Research, a manufacturer of the world's largest computers; Analog Devices, Inc. (ADI), a producer of analog-digital converters and related devices for computerized measurement and control systems;

Dayton Hudson, an extensive retailing operation; Tandem Computer, maker of computers that offer continuous, non-stop service; Steak and Ale, now a division of Pillsbury; and Hanover Insurance Company, W. L. Gore and Associates and Herman Miller Furniture Company. For further discussion about these companies, see Kiefer and Senge.

63. Ibid.

64. Miller; Gilligan.

65. Kiefer and Stroh.

66. Ibid.

67. Linda Nelson and Frank Burns, "High Performance Programming: A Framework for Transforming Organizations," in John Adams (ed.) *Transforming Work*.

68. Loden.

4

Women and the Reagan Years: Budgetary Backlash

Sara E. Rix

THE REAGAN MISSION

When Ronald Reagan was sworn into office on January 20, 1981, federal spending or outlays as a percentage of GNP exceeded income by over two percentage points per year; federal social welfare expenditures were more than twice what they had been in 1960, and the annual deficit hovered around $80 billion. In the opinion of the new president, government had "grown beyond the consent of the governed."[1]

President-elect Reagan arrived in Washington with a mission "to check and reverse the growth of government,"[2] and thereby reduce and ultimately eliminate the deficit. However, his vision for the future involved more than just narrowing the gap between federal income and expenditures. When he spoke of reducing federal spending, he was not being all-inclusive: it was social welfare programs—typically programs of considerable importance to women and children—on which the axe would ultimately fall. Mr. Reagan was clearly dissatisfied with the welfare system, and dismantling it was paramount on the agenda.[3] Eliminating from the welfare rolls those participants not in "real need" would become an initial objective of his administration.

Reagan and his advisors planned a major reversal in the trend toward ever-increasing federal responsibility for the well-being of the nation's citizens that had characterized every administration since the Social Security Act was passed in 1935. This responsibility began with protection against income lost as a result of retirement, disability, or death of a breadwinner, and was broadened, particularly during the 1960s, to include a range of means-tested benefits to assist persons who had been bypassed by the economic growth of the post-war years.

The longstanding "income security" programs, such as social security, are the largest component of the domestic budget, while the newer ones of the 1960s and early 1970s, have, with the exception of Medicare, "never accounted for more than one-fifth of total federal social program spending."[4] Thus, what was regarded by some as excessive spending on the poor was in reality not so very much, especially when compared to programs such as social security. Moreover, according to economist Sar Levitan, the United States devotes a smaller proportion of GNP to social programs than any other advanced industrial nation except Japan.[5] Still, some of the numbers argued in Reagan's favor: between 1960 and 1981, for example, defense spending as a percent of outlays dropped from 52 to 23 percent, while human resource spending on programs for education, training, employment and social services, health, medicare, income security, social security, and veterans' benefits and services had risen from 28 to 53 percent. As a percent of GNP, defense spending in 1981 was also well below its 1960 level, and human resource spending was sharply up (see Table 4.1).

Table 4.1 Federal Outlays for National Defense and Human Resources[1] as Percent of Total Outlays and as Percent of Gross National Product (GNP): Selected Fiscal Years, 1940–1987

	As percent of outlays		As percent of GNP	
	National Defense	Human Resources	National Defense	Human Resources
1940	17.5	43.7	1.7	4.3
1945	89.5	2.0	39.1	0.9
1950	32.2	33.4	5.1	5.3
1955	62.4	21.8	11.0	3.8
1960	52.2	28.4	9.5	5.2
1965	42.8	30.9	7.5	5.4
1970	41.8	38.5	8.2	7.6
1975	26.0	52.1	5.7	11.4
1976	24.1	54.8	5.3	12.0
1977	23.8	54.2	5.0	11.5
1978	22.8	52.8	4.8	11.1
1979	23.1	53.1	4.7	10.9
1980	22.7	53.0	5.0	11.2
1981	23.2	53.4	5.3	12.1
1982	24.9	52.1	5.9	12.4
1983	26.0	52.7	6.3	12.8
1984	26.7	50.7	6.2	11.7
1985	26.7	49.9	6.4	12.0
1986[2]	27.1	49.0	6.3	11.4
1987[2]	28.4	49.3	6.2	10.8

[1] These are programs for education, training, employment, and social services; health; medicare; income security; social security; and veterans' benefits and services.

[2] Estimated.

Source: Office of Management and Budget, *Historical Tables: Budget of the United States Government, Fiscal Year 1987* (Washington, D.C.: U.S. Government Printing Office, 1986), Table 3.2.

If responsibility for public welfare resided in government, Mr. Reagan contended, then it was state or local governments, rather than the federal government that should assume most of that responsibility. In the minds of members of the new administration, the states themselves could better assess their particular needs and channel resources effectively to the persons and programs deemed most deserving of those resources.[6]

The federal budget is the instrument that best reflects federal commitment to the welfare of its citizens; the budget became the new president's instrument for implementing policies. The budget reflected the president's plans to cut the growth of government spending, reduce tax rates, eliminate excessive government regulation, develop a more rational and reasonable monetary policy, and move toward a balanced budget.

In the words of Gregory Mills of the Urban Institute, Reagan, more than any other president, used the budget "to articulate and pursue his policies,"[7] but to succeed, he needed the cooperation of Congress. The president obtained that cooperation during his first year in office, which accounts in large measure for his remarkable success in achieving an almost revolutionary redirection of federal priorities, as discussed below. Though at the outset, a Republican-controlled Senate and a Democratic-controlled House of Representatives presaged stormy times ahead, the 97th Congress' belief that the country wanted change worked to Reagan's advantage during the budget debate for fiscal year (FY) 1982. Reagan was assisted by Republicans in both the House and the Senate who joined forces to support his policies. Abetted by conservative Democrats and further aided by demoralized Democrats who apparently lacked the will for or saw the futility of a fight, Republicans won support for many of Reagan's policy changes in his first year in office.[8]

But the following year, the honeymoon ended. When the proposed FY83 budget was up for debate in early 1982, the president confronted a less cooperative Congress. The fact that 1982 was an election year meant that Congress would be especially resistant to cuts in social programs that benefited constituents. A consensus emerged that certain social programs had borne a disproportionate share of the cuts the year before and that more should not be demanded of them. Furthermore, it was evident that the prospect of deficit reduction was more a dream than an impending reality, and that if substantial inroads into the deficit were to be made, the ever-popular social security, as well as defense programs, would require slashing. Support for the president's policies was also probably undermined by Budget Director David Stockman's candid *Atlantic Monthly* interview,[9] during which it became clear that Reagan's policy objectives were unlikely to be realized under the economic program envisaged by the president and his advisors. As the years passed, it became increasingly difficult for the president to achieve sufficient congressional support for his social policy aims. Nevertheless, the era of significant expansion of social programs was at least temporarily over, a development for which President Reagan can claim much of the credit. Under Reagan, liberal lawmakers were put on the defensive, and fiscal conservatism became the order of the day.

When Reagan took office, he was concerned with more than the budget. He also had ideas about reducing the federal government's involvement in a wide range of social issues known as the "social agenda," and for that, he sought help from the courts. However, the Reagan administration experienced both victory and defeat at the hands of the Supreme Court.

THE PRESIDENT'S APPEAL

Mr. Reagan wasted no time in getting his message to Congress and the American people. His inaugural address was blunt in its assertion that a transfer of responsibility from the federal government to the states and to individuals themselves was in order.[10]

Whether the president actually had a mandate for the type and scope of change envisaged is perhaps beside the point. He clearly thought he had one and was prepared to act on it: "I urge Members of Congress to remember that last November the American people's message was loud and clear. The mandate for change . . . was not my mandate. It was our mandate."[11] Public sentiment had, indeed, reflected both concern with the tax burden and a perceived need for greater defense spending. Individual income and social insurance taxes were a growing percentage of federal income, while the proportion paid by corporations was dropping. A larger percentage of the defense budget was going to personnel, at the expense of military hardware. President Carter himself had proposed a real increase in defense spending in his outgoing budget for FY82. Moreover, a general pessimism regarding the future was pervasive;[12] the public was ready for change. Support existed for lowering taxes and increasing defense spending, although the public did not necessarily approve of the social welfare cuts that would, barring a miracle, be necessary to offset both lower taxes and higher defense expenditures. It certainly did not support the idea of cuts to the truly needy.

President Reagan apparently sensed this reluctance and promised not to slash what he called the "safety net" programs—those providing benefits and services to persons who "through no fault of their own must depend on the rest of us, the poverty stricken, the disabled, the elderly, all those with true need, can rest assured that the social safety net of programs they depend on are exempt from any cuts."[13] His promises encompassed full benefits for Supplemental Security Income (SSI), as well as assurances that there would be no cuts in Medicare, the summer youth program, or social security.

What tended to distinguish the programs that would be exempt from cuts, observed James Storey, was a protection of those "for whom cutbacks would likely have aroused the strongest reaction in Congress."[14] Thus Reagan initially would wisely steer clear of proposing reductions in programs that benefited the middle class.[15] Rather, those most affected would be programs designed to assist the poor, notably the working poor, who lacked effective organization and advocates to argue on their behalf.

THE REAGAN BUDGET FOR FY82

On March 10, 1981, the president submitted his first budget to the Congress. In retrospect, it is hard to deny that from the outset a revolution was in the offing. The president requested a 9 percent real increase in defense spending and substantial tax cuts, the impact of which would, it was contended, ultimately "trickle down" to benefit those at the bottom of the income distribution. If, however, he were to achieve a defense build-up and lower taxes while balancing the federal budget—an early and vociferously proclaimed objective—it would be necessary to cut spending sharply in other components of the budget. But in view of the fact that a promise had been made not to tamper with safety net programs, and other cuts in middle-class programs would be politically untenable, the choices were narrow: the poor would bear the brunt of the reductions proposed in that first budget.

Overall, the president proposed a budget that would reduce spending by some $49 billion in FY82. Although programs for the poorest of the poor would generally be left intact, the first round of cuts was designed to ensure that those the administration felt were not truly deserving—persons who presumably could either go to work or work more hours—lost eligibility for public benefits. Bawden and Palmer suggest that it was "the element of choice [that] proved most galling to the administration,"[16] so choice would be eliminated.

The president's proposals were far-reaching: given his way, he would have (1) made major changes in the country's primary welfare program, Aid to Families with Dependent Children (AFDC), and in the food stamp program to reduce the number of beneficiaries of both programs; (2) capped future increases in outlays for Medicaid, which provides health care to the poor; (3) eliminated or substantially cut funding for most federal child nutrition programs; (4) reduced funding for housing assistance and increased rental payments required of tenants; (5) consolidated a large number of health and social service programs and the low income energy assistance program into block grants to the states and reduced overall funding substantially; (6) consolidated federal aid for elementary and secondary education into block grants; (7) phased out social security benefits to dependent students; (8) reduced or restricted eligibility for student loans and grants, and (9) eliminated the minimum social security benefit.[17] Moreover, his cabinet secretaries would "search out areas of waste, extravagance, and costly administrative overhead which could yield additional and substantial reductions."[18]

CONGRESSIONAL RESPONSE

One need only look at the Omnibus Budget Reconciliation Act (OBRA) of 1981 (PL 97-35) to determine how persuasive the new president was. Federal spending for FY82 was projected to be $35 billion less than it would have been without the OBRA changes approved by Congress. Accompanying OBRA was a 3-year tax relief package that would benefit the affluent; it quickly began to have a devastating impact on the federal deficit.

President Reagan was not successful in achieving all of his aims for FY82. Congress balked at some of the block grant proposals, and refused to "cap" federal contributions to states for Medicaid. Congress also refused to sanction the elimination of either Legal Services, the Work Incentive Program, or the minimum social security benefit to current recipients. Nonetheless, acquiescence was considerable, and Congress actually agreed to a greater reduction in the food stamp program than the administration had asked for. James R. Jones, Chairman of the Budget Committee of the House of Representatives, called congressional action "clearly the most monumental and historic turnaround in fiscal policy that [had] ever occurred."[19]

An early assessment of the president's proposed budget for FY82 concluded that "poor, near-poor, and minority women and their children will be the hardest hit. In fact, a disproportionate share of the budget reductions are directed at programs in which women have a heavy investment. Fully one-third of the [proposed] reduction in FY82 outlays comes from just two program areas—health and income security—that are largely designed to meet the needs of poor people."[20] Then, as now, women and children predominated among the poor. When President Reagan took office, 78 percent of the nation's 29 million poor were women and children.

A highlighting of just a few of the actual legislative changes enacted by Congress in 1981 reveals the extent of the scaling back of social programs of importance to women and children. Congress tightened eligibility for food stamps, thereby eliminating an estimated one million from the program and cutting benefits for most other recipients.[21] Federal Medicaid payments to states were reduced; however, as noted above, federal contributions to states were not capped. A variety of health and education programs were consolidated into block grants, although Congress rejected some of the president's requests for consolidation. The minimum social security benefit was eliminated for *new* beneficiaries, and the Medicare deductibles for hospitals and Part B coverage were increased. Funding for subsidized housing was reduced, as were subsidies for school lunch programs. The direction of the AFDC program was shifted by restricting eligibility to families with gross incomes below 150 percent (rather than 180 percent) of a state's need standard, reducing or limiting amounts that could be claimed for child care and other work-related expenses, and eliminating the "work incentive," or earnings disregard, after 4 months.[22]

THE CONTINUED ASSAULT

The president's first budget requests were designed to put the country on a course toward a lower deficit that would presumably yield a slight budgetary surplus by FY84. However, even before PL 97-35 was signed into law, the anticipated surplus had evaporated, and the president asked Congress for additional cuts. Reagan backed away from his pledge not to tamper with the safety net when on May 12, 1981, he proposed sharp reductions in benefits to early social security retirees and the disabled, ostensibly to restore solvency to a system teetering on the edge of insolvency. Public outrage at the proposals confirmed the difficulty the president would have in seeking a solution to the deficit problem in programs that primarily benefit the middle-class; Reagan hastily withdrew his social security proposals and proclaimed instead his intent to seek a bipartisan compromise to the social security crisis.

Over the next several years, the deficit rose, a situation the president blamed on Congress. If Congress would only continue to accede to his requests for program cuts, he reasoned, the deficit problem could be solved. However, a recession in the early 1980s pushed unemployment rates to their highest levels in 40 years; poverty rates increased sharply, resulting an an increased demand for benefits under many welfare programs. Savings from abuse and fraud were less than expected,[23] and had a negligible impact on a seemingly intractable deficit.

Persistence, however, is a hallmark of the Reagan administration. Subsequent administration budgets continued to propose program cuts that had or could have a disproportionate impact on the most economically vulnerable, but after the Omnibus Budget Reconciliation Act, Congress was less receptive to the president's requests. Public sentiment either shifted or began to express itself in opposition to further social program cuts. Most of what the president wanted in the way of social welfare program reductions was given to him in FY82. This did not, however, discourage the administration from proposing the same changes year after year, despite Congress's clear and repeated rejection of certain proposals. Lawmakers would not, at least as of FY87, abolish the Legal Services Corporation, eliminate the Work Incentive Program, or require mandatory workfare for all welfare recipients. For FY83, the president proposed returning full responsibility for AFDC and food stamps to the states, while the federal government would assume full responsibility for Medicaid, a proposal that met with little receptivity on the part of the states. In FY84, the president proposed a freeze on aggregate federal spending. Defense outlays would still increase, necessitating further cuts in domestic programs in order to achieve an overall "freeze." Budget requests for FY85, FY86, and FY87 were consistent with all of the administration's earlier requests, except that it became increasingly evident that what was left to cut from low-income programs would have little overall impact on the federal deficit.

As it debated the FY87 budget, Congress was faced with another problem. A new law (PL 99-177, better known as the Gramm–Rudman–Hollings amendment) required a balanced budget by FY91. If Congress were not able to achieve a balanced budget through the regular budget process, a presidential sequester order would automatically impose cuts on all non-exempt programs.[24]

WOMEN AND THE BUDGET

An assessment of the Republican record through FY86 prepared by Fiscal Planning Services for the American Federation of State, County and Municipal Employees (AFSCME) concluded that grants-in-aid to states and local governments were 15 percent below the levels that would have been required to maintain services at their 1981 levels. Individuals, according to this study, had "lost" $34.8 billion over the same period, as a result of budget cuts.[25] Moon and Sawhill point out that FY84 federal benefits payments, both cash (such as AFDC and social security) and in-kind (e.g., food stamps and Medicaid), were about 7 percent below what they would have been without the Reagan budget cuts.[26]

Early budget cuts had a much greater impact on means-tested low income programs than on social insurance programs such as social security that were left relatively, though not exclusively, unscathed. Storey presents data showing that while low-income assistance programs (AFDC, SSI, food stamps, and the like) were about 18 percent of baseline outlays (or money that would have been spent under previous policies) projected through FY84, they accounted for 59 percent of the estimated budget savings through that year. The social insurance programs, which are of greater importance to the middle class, were 82 percent of projected outlays, but sustained only 41 percent of the budget cuts.[27] In other words, low-income programs received more than their "fair share" of the outlay changes through FY84. One program, however, consistently escaped budget cutting. Perceived as effective by legislators in both parties, WIC—the supplemental feeding program for women, infants, and children—has seen its participant and funding levels grow since 1981.

The Reagan administration did not explicitly single out women and children for differential treatment in its budget proposals. But because women and families headed by women tend to be disproportionately represented among the recipients of means-tested programs (table 4.2),

Table 4.2 Families and Female-Headed Families: Total Number, Number in Poverty, and Recipients of Selected Non-Cash Benefits, 1980 and 1984 (in thousands)

	All Families	Female-Headed Families	Percentage Female-Headed Families
Total			
1980	60,309	9,082	15.1
1984	62,706	10,129	16.2
Percent change	4.0	11.5	
Poor Families			
1980	6,217	2,972	47.8
1984	7,277	3,498	48.1
Percent change	17.0	17.7	
Recipients of:			
Food stamps			
1980	5,194	2,755	53.0
1984	5,370	2,948	54.9
Percent change	3.4	7.0	
Free/reduced price school lunches			
1980	5,486	2,458	44.8
1984	5,575	2,670	47.9
Percent change	1.6	8.6	
Public/subsidized housing			
1980	1,622	1,029	63.4
1984	2,132	1,361	63.8
Percent change	31.4	32.3	
Medicaid			
1980	5,965	3,038	50.9
1984	5,980	3,232	54.0
Percent change	0.2	6.4	

Sources: U.S. Bureau of the Census, *Current Population Reports*, Series P-60, No. 131 (1982), Tables 5, 6, 7, 8; Series P-60, No. 133 (1982), Table 17; Series P-60, No. 150 (1985), Tables 5, 6, 7, 8; Series P-60, No. 152 (1986), Table 13.

they stand to be disproportionately affected by changes in those programs. The rate of increase in participation in means-tested cash benefits has generally not kept pace with the increase in poverty rates, which among families rose by 17 to 18 percent between 1980 and 1984. The result is that with the exception of public and/or subsidized housing, a smaller proportion of poor families is receiving such in-kind benefits than in the past. What appears to be a significant improvement in the number of families residing in public or subsidized housing cannot be attributed to President Reagan, who pushed for and received sharp reductions in public/subsidized housing funds. Instead, this increase is due to past commitments to public/subsidized housing that bore fruit during this period.

As of 1982, government programs succeeded in lifting out of poverty fewer than 38 percent of those who otherwise would have been poor, as compared with 44 percent in 1976.[28] Estimates for 1985 indicate that there may have been nearly one-half million more poor families with children that year than there would have been if cash benefits such as social security, unemployment compensation, and public assistance were removing families from poverty rolls at the rate they did in 1979.[29]

When it made its first proposals to cut AFDC benefits, the administration estimated that 400,000 families would lose all benefits, while another 283,000 would have their benefits reduced. (A family ineligible for AFDC benefits would become ineligible for Medicaid as well.) In its evaluation of OBRA changes to this program, the General Accounting Office reported that the monthly AFDC caseload had decreased by 442,000, a figure very close to the administration's estimate.[30] Although some AFDC families are two-parent families, approximately nine out of ten of the 3.7 million AFDC families in 1981 were headed by women. Some states, at least, acted to offset the OBRA changes in a number of ways, such as by changing the standard of need.[31] As was true of many of the first round of budget cuts, the initial AFDC cuts primarily affected families with some earnings.

Most families have been affected by Reagan policies and the performance of the economy since 1980. For example, real family income (corrected for inflation) dropped substantially during the recession in Reagan's first term, and although real incomes have been improving, they are still not up to 1979 levels.[32] Reagan's policies have, overall, tended to benefit the affluent and to take away from the lower and (to a lesser extent) the middle classes. During the first several years of the Reagan era, the rich did get richer and the poor lost some income. Between 1980 and 1984, for example, aggregate income going to families in the lowest one-fifth (quintile) of the income distribution dropped from 5.1 to 4.7 percent, while that of families in the upper fifth rose from 41.6 to 42.9 percent.[33] At the same time, real disposable income (after taxes and inflation-adjusted) for those at the bottom dropped by nearly 8 percent and that at the top increased by nearly 9 percent.[34] Clearly, the 1980s witnessed a widening of the income disparities between the top and the bottom.

Sawhill and Moon report that real disposable income rose by only 3.5 percent between 1980 and 1984, modest by 4-year comparisons for the 1970s and substantially below comparable averages for the 1960s. Variation by quintile and family group was marked.

It is important to remember that no president can be blamed or credited for everything that transpires during his administration, and that holds as true for the Reagan administration as for any of the preceding ones. For example, not all of the deterioration in family income can be explained by policies implemented under Reagan. Sawhill and Moon have attempted to determine how much could be attributable to Reagan and how much to changes that might have occurred regardless of who had become president.[35] Their findings indicate that Reagan policies can explain a 4 percent drop in real disposable family income between 1980 and 1984 for the bottom quintile and 3 percent for the second quintile; the middle quintile's (or middle class's) loss was 1.7 percent. Almost no 1980–84 change in income in the fourth quintile was due to changes implemented under Reagan, while the policies did have a favorable impact on the uppermost group. In translating the Sawhill and Moon figures into impacts on individuals, as opposed to quintiles, one finds that nonaged female family heads in the second quintile (where the working poor are concentrated) suffered most under Reagan.

To be fair, however, one must point out that women have not always been the losers in the Reagan years. Though they were not always so well off to begin with, elderly families and older persons living alone, who are predominantly female, typically have done better for a variety of reasons: they were less affected by the high unemployment of the early 1980s and the value of their social security benefits was protected through cost of living increases. Women in the most affluent families have benefited from policies initiated by Reagan, especially if they were members of two-earner families: they were better insulated against the recession, and the tax break for two-earner couples (since repealed) was to their advantage. As of 1984, however, poor two-earner couples had experienced a sharp drop in real disposable income that could be directly attributed to the president's policies.

The general conclusion from evaluations of the Reagan administration's tenure is that the working poor were especially hard hit by his policies. If, however, the administration's budget cuts were to encourage the poor to become employed or to work more, they were by no means a resounding success: in 1980, 50 percent of all poor householders were in the labor force; by 1984, that figure was still 50 percent. Among female family heads, the comparable figures were 38 and 39 percent for 1980 and 1984. respectively. On the other hand, the average number of weeks worked among both groups did increase slightly over this period.

At the same time that the administration was hoping to push what it felt were the scofflaws off welfare, it was proposing to eliminate and/or make severe cuts in programs for training those without marketable skills. The administration succeeded in eliminating public service employment under the Comprehensive Employment and Training Act (CETA), but failed in its consistent efforts to abolish the Work Incentive Program (WIN), a small program tailored to the special needs of welfare recipients.

With the cooperation of Congress, the Reagan administration replaced CETA with the Job Training Partnership Act (JTPA) designed to embody "some of the Reagan Administration's key approaches to dealing with social problems . . . involving the business community, enhancing the role of the states while reducing federal involvement, and using performance standards to ensure that funds are spent effectively."[36]

A two-year study of JTPA's job training programs for the economically disadvantaged found, as feared, some tendency among contractors to obtain only the more promising participants,[37] but the programs did, according to Grinker Associates, focus successfully on welfare recipients, one of the groups mandated by law for targeting. Because the new law placed restrictions on the payment of stipends, it seemed to be welfare recipients with their own means of support who could or would take advantage of training opportunities that those without any income may have been forced to pass up. Most service delivery programs apparently came close to meeting their training goals for women, although they did not seem particularly interested in enrolling teen-age parents.

While some of the JTPA news is encouraging, the fact is that available funds are sufficient to serve only 4 to 5 percent of the eligible population,[38] hardly likely to have much impact on the welfare population. Moreover, the 1980 budget for training under CETA had been $3.9 billion, while the 1984 budget for JTPA training was only $2.6 billion, a substantial drop that seemed to reflect a weak commitment to making the poor employable.

THE COMMITMENT TO EQUAL RIGHTS AND OPPORTUNITIES

The president's objective of reducing the federal role in the nondefense arena extended beyond budgetary considerations to some of the basic civil rights issues that Americans had perhaps begun to take for granted. If the administration worried about the potential consequences of a gender gap in voting, this did not manifest itself in a commitment to women's rights.

Even prior to the 1980 election, the Republican party had renounced its support of the Equal Rights Amendment, a decision not objectionable to candidate Reagan. With the wisdom of hindsight, it should not be surprising that the Reagan administration did not follow the previous administration's rather aggressive approach to combating sex discrimination and to promoting equal rights and affirmative action.

Bawden and Palmer argue that Reagan was "the first president in the post-World War II period to reverse [the] trend of an increasingly active government role in ensuring the rights and opportunities of its citizens and redressing the consequences of past discrimination." Just as Reagan wanted to reduce intrusions in the private domain and the trend of growing federal responsibility for economic well-being, so too he pushed for a shift toward less government responsibility for issues on the social agenda.[39]

Although the president appointed the first woman to the Supreme Court, he did not encourage aggressive efforts to combat sex discrimination. One of the early ominous signs was a 1981 move to achieve a Civil Rights Commission (which monitors both sex and race discrimination) with views more in line with his own by appointing as chairman a conservative black man, whose lack of enthusiasm for affirmative action equaled that of the president. More conservative commissioners followed. Another disturbing indicator was a push for only voluntary compliance in the office of Federal Contract Compliance (OFPCC), which was established to issue affirmative action guidelines to combat sex and race discrimination among recipients of federal contracts. Goals had become a part of OFPCC compliance in 1971, but Reagan rejected goals, as well as timetables and quotas; rather, he wanted to require proof of intent to discriminate. In 1983 more lenient rules for federal contractors were published, but "vigorous protest" from women's organizations and civil rights groups prevented their implementation.[40] Since the submission of his first budget for FY82, the president attempted repeatedly to get Congress to abolish the Women's Educational Equity Act (WEEA), which supports programs to eliminate sex discrimination in educational institutions; Congress has repeatedly rebuffed these requests. It has been through the courts that the administration had made its most concerted effort to turn back the civil rights clock. Perhaps the administration's greatest success was the February 1984 ruling in *Grove City College v. Bell*, which significantly narrowed the scope of Title IX of the 1972 Education Act amendments. Title IX reads that "no person in the United States shall, on the basis of sex, be excluded from participation in, be denied the benefits of, or be subjected to discrimination under any educational program or activity receiving Federal financial assistance." Grove City College argued that federal financial aid received by students was not financial aid to the college; thus the college was not obliged to certify that it did not discriminate on the basis of sex. The case went to court when the Department of Health, Education, and Welfare threatened to cut off federal student assistance. When the case reached the Supreme Court, the Justice Department filed a brief arguing that only certification of nondiscrimination in disbursing student aid, not in all programs was required. The Court, in a 6-3 decision, ruled that federal financial aid to students was indeed aid to the college. However, of greater significance was the decision that Title IX did not apply to all programs at a recipient institution, but only to the specific program receiving federal aid. At Grove City College, therefore, the provisions of Title IX would not extend beyond the financial aid office.

Fifty members of the House of Representatives had filed a friend-of-the-court brief opposing a narrow interpretation of Title IX. In March 1983, the House voted 414-8 against restricting the reach of Title IX, which prompted Congresswoman Patricia Schroeder to point out that Congress had sent a clear message that it wanted Title IX interpreted broadly, "but the Supreme Court must have had their earmuffs on."[41]

In a second case, *Firefighters Local Union #1784 v. Stotts*, the Supreme Court ruled that white firefighters had been unjustly laid off in favor of blacks with less seniority who had been hired under an affirmative action program. The Reagan administration joined this case with a friend-of-the-court brief, and the Attorney General hailed the decision as meaning that the federal courts cannot "impose quotas based upon racial considerations in employment relationships."[42] In fact, affirmative action requires goals and timetables, although administration sources persist in referring to quotas. Obviously if, under *Firefighters v. Stotts*, quotas (or more precisely, goals) based on race were against the law, so too would be quotas or goals based on sex. Assistant Attorney General William Bradford Reynolds signaled the administration's intention by saying that the Justice Department would immediately begin to review all affirmative action decrees and agreements involving the federal government.

But if the administration thought that it was on the high road with regard to the Supreme Court, it was sadly mistaken. In Court decisions both modest in scope and far-reaching, women—at least through 1986—generally fared well during the Reagan years. In a number of cases, decisions have run counter to the administration's position and have been applauded by women's groups. For example, the Court has ruled that:

- States may require the U.S. Jaycees to admit women as full members (*Roberts v. U.S. Jaycees*).
- Law firms are not exempt from bans of discrimination against employees on the basis of sex (or of race, religion, or national origin) in deciding whom to make partner (*Hishon v. King & Spalding*). Lower courts had previously accepted the argument that law partnerships

were beyond the reach of Title VII of the 1964 Civil Rights Act.

- The use of affirmative action to rectify past discrimination may be valid (*Wygant v. Jackson Board of Education; Local #28 of the Sheet Metal Workers' International Association v. Equal Employment Opportunity Commission; Local #93, International Association of Firefighters v. City of Cleveland*). The Court rejected the administration's claim that only identifiable victims of discrimination were entitled to remedies.
- Sexual harassment on the job constitutes unlawful employment discrimination (*Meritor Savings Bank v. Vinson*).
- Religious schools are not exempt from a state's investigations into sex discrimination charges (*Ohio Civil Rights Commission v. Dayton Christian County Schools*).
- Discrimination continuing after enactment of Title VII is against the law, even if the discriminatory system had been in place before 1965 (*Bazemore v. Friday*).

Of great significance to women's groups, in *Thornburgh v. American College of Obstetricians and Gynecologists*, the Court also upheld a woman's constitutional right to abortion, and restricted a state's rights to control abortions. It also rejected the administration's request to strike down *Roe v. Wade*, and reaffirmed the general principles laid down in that decision.

While there have been some legal setbacks, such as the *Grove City* decision, the Supreme Court, especially in its 1985–86 term, has generally strengthened the legal rights of women.[42] As a result of the Court's action on affirmative action, the Justice Department announced that it would review its order to municipal governments to modify their existing affirmative action plans.

Whether women will fare as well in the future is a matter of considerable concern to feminists, among others, who will follow closely the decision of the Court under its new chief justice, William Rehnquist, and new associate justice Antonin Scalia. In his decade and a half on the court, Rehnquist has been its most conservative member.[43] A fellow conservative, Scalia has opposed preferential affirmative action for minorities. His appointment tilts the Court further to the right.

ORGANIZED OPPOSITION TO REAGAN POLITICS

It is probably safe to say that the magnitude of the administration's proposed policy changes in 1981 caught many individuals and organizations by surprise. While Reagan had promised change during the campaign, the scope of the proposals and the rapidity with which they would be brought before Congress were clearly unanticipated. Few of the groups that became major adversaries in subsequent years had the ammunition to fight the president's first proposed federal budget. One exception was the Center for the Study of Social Welfare (now the Center for the Study of Social Policy), which was reporting on the potential social costs of the FY82 budget as early as March 1981. Another was the research arm of the Congresswomen's Caucus (now the Congressional Caucus for Women's Issues), which prepared one of the first assessments of the impact on women of Reagan's proposals in 1981.[45]

By Reagan's second year in office, organized groups were ready to do battle. For example, headed by representatives of some of the major women's organizations based in Washington, D.C. (e.g., the Women's Equity Action League, the National Women's Law Center, and the Older Women's League), a coalition of 40 women's, religious, education, and other organizations was formed to take a close look at what Reaganomics meant for women and families. The Coalition's first report concluded that the president's budget demanded an "inequality of sacrifice" from women of all ages, a position it reaffirmed in subsequent years. Designed to be used by lobbyists, women's advocates, and others to thwart administration efforts to tamper with social programs, the coalition's annual reports through FY86 represented major efforts to disseminate information on the Reagan impact to women and organizations at the grassroots level.

By 1982, other efforts were underway to document and assess what was referred to as the Reagan Revolution. The Urban Institute began a multi-year assessment of changing domestic priorities under Reagan that has resulted in some 25 books and conference proceedings. While none of the books deals exclusively with women, many of them focus on programs in which women have a vested interest. The Children's Defense Fund began its own evaluations on social programs, as did numerous other organizations.

It is almost impossible to ascertain the impact of any of these reports. Congress was not disposed to act against the president during his first year, and it is unlikely that organized early opposition could have changed this. By the time various groups began issuing their reports, Congress had already begun to consider damage wrought by the first round of budget cuts. The General Accounting Office's examination of the OBRA cuts in the AFDC program resulted in a restoration of some benefits, but that is one of the few instances where research on the impact of budget cuts had a clear policy impact. Nonetheless, the evaluations done by women's and other groups provided the president's opponents with facts and figures to support their arguments against further budget cuts and were used extensively by lobbyists working on behalf of women.

CONCLUSION

While many of Reagan's goals have proven elusive, particularly as Congress began to resist the president's demands, national priorities *have* been reordered. President Reagan has succeeded in scaling back the welfare state. This popular president[46] may not have accomplished all that he had set out to accomplish when he took office; nonetheless, funding levels for many social programs are far below what they would have been had the policies in effect when Reagan took office been maintained. Moreover, the terms of the debate about federal responsibility for individual well-being appear to have been altered. As long as the deficit remains at record highs—$221 billion in FY86—and as long as both Congress and the president remain reluctant to make substantial cuts in either defense or the major entitlement programs such as social security, there is little hope for substantial expansion of or improvement in those social welfare programs on which so many women have come to depend.

NOTES AND REFERENCES

1. "President Reagan's Inaugural Address," *1981 Congressional Quarterly Almanac*, Vol. 37 (Washington, DC: Congressional Quarterly, Inc.: 1982), p. 11-E.

2. *Ibid.*

3. James R. Storey, "Income Security," in John L. Palmer and Isabel V. Sawhill (editors), *The Reagan Experiment*, (Washington, DC: The Urban Institute Press, 1982), p. 363.

4. D. Lee Bawden and John L. Palmer, "Social Policy: Challenging the Welfare State," in John L. Palmer and Isabel V. Sawhill (editors), *The Reagan Record*, (Cambridge, MA: Ballinger, 1984), p. 181.

5. Sar A. Levitan, "Welfare and Economic Security," *Political Science Quarterly* (Fall 1985), p. 456.

6. Overlooked or ignored was the fact that many federal programs had been established because states were unwilling or unable to respond to the needs of their residents in the first place.

7. Gregory B. Mills, "The Budget: A Failure of Discipline," in Palmer and Sawhill, *The Reagan Record*, p. 107.

8. See Lester M. Salamon and Alan J. Abramson, "Governance: The Politics of Retrenchment," in Palmer and Sawhill, *The Reagan Record*, pp. 31–68 for a particularly cogent discussion of the early days of the Reagan administration.

9. William Grieder, "The Education of David Stockman," *The Atlantic Monthly* (December 1981), pp. 27–54.

10. In that address, the president stressed his "intention to curb the size and influence of the federal establishment and to demand recognition of the distinction between the powers granted to the Federal government and those reserved to the states or the people. . . . Government can and must provide opportunity, not smother it; foster productivity, not stifle it." ("President Reagan's Inaugural Address," p. 12-E).

11. "Test of Reagan FY '82 Budget Revisions," *1981 Congressional Quarterly Almanac*, Vol. 37 (Washington, DC: Congressional Quarterly, Inc.: 1982) p. 19-E.

12. See, for example, Marilyn Moon and Isabel V. Sawhill, "Family Incomes: Gainers and Losers," in Palmer and Sawhill, *The Reagan Record*, p. 317.

13. "President Reagan's Economic Proposals Text," *1981 Congressional Quarterly Almanac*, Vol. 37 (1982), p. 16-E.

14. James R. Storey, "Income Security," p. 383.

15. Reagan advisor Martin Anderson argued that safety net programs were the programs that "would not be closely examined *on the first round* of budget change" because rational discussion about cutting these programs would be impossible (emphasis added). This statement implies that it was the administration's intention ultimately to go after some of these other programs, when the time was politically acceptable. (Martin Anderson, "The Objectives of the Reagan Administration's Social Welfare Policy," in D. Lee Bawden (ed.), *The Social Contract Revisited* (Washington, DC: The Urban Institute Press, 1984, p. 17.)

16. Bawden and Palmer, "Social Policy," p. 190.

17. Prior to 1982, if a social security benefit computed according to the regular computation formula was less than a certain amount, an alternative minimum benefit would be provided. Although the benefit was intended to insure that social security retirement income would never fall below a certain level, many of the minimum beneficiaries were, in fact, recipients of other public pension benefits. They worked just long enough to qualify for social security but were not dependent on social security as their only source of income. The minimum benefit provided many less-than-needy retirees with more income than they were entitled to under the normal benefit computation formula. The benefit was eliminated for workers first eligible for social security after December 31, 1981.

This minimum benefit should not be confused with the special minimum benefit available to some long-term, low-wage workers. That benefit still exists.

18. "President Reagan's Economic Policy Address," *1981 Congressional Quarterly Almanac*, Vol. 37 (Washington DC: Congressional Quarterly, Inc.: 1982), p. 14-E.

19. "Fiscal 1982 Reconciliation Cuts: $35.2 Billion," *1981 Congressional Quarterly Almanac*, Vol. 37 (Washington DC: Congressional Quarterly, Inc.: 1982), p. 256.

20. Women's Research and Education Institute (WREI), *Assessment of the Impact on Women of the Administration's Proposed Budget* (Washington, DC: WREI, April 1981), p.1.

21. "Food Stamp Legislation," *1981 Congressional Quarterly Almanac*, Vol. 37 (Washington, DC: Congressional Quarterly, Inc.: 1982), p. 467.

22. The OBRA provisions discussed in the text are only a few of the changes in the law that had a potential impact on women and families. For example, changes to AFDC also include further limiting allowable assets, the counting of stepparents' income in establishing family eligibility for benefits, and the removal from the roles of families in which the youngest child was over 18.

23. Jack A. Meyer, "Social Programs and Social Policy," in John L. Palmer (ed.), *Perspectives on the Reagan Years* (Washington, DC: The Urban Institute Press, 1986), pp. 79–81.

24. Many programs were exempted from automatic sequestration, among them social security benefits, food stamps, AFDC, SSI, child nutrition, the earned income tax credit, and Medicaid, while the cuts in a number of other programs of importance to women were limited under the new law. There was nothing, however, that precluded Congress from slashing these programs during the budget process if it so chose.

25. American Federation of State, County and Municipal Employees (AFSC-ME), *The Republican Record: a 5-Year Analysis of State Losses of Federal Funding.* (Washington, DC: AFSCME, September 1986).

26. Moon and Sawhill, "Family Incomes," p. 324.

27. From data in Storey, "Income Security," Table 12-3, pp. 374–375.

28. John L. Palmer and Isabel V. Sawhill, "Overview," in Palmer and Sawhill, *The Reagan Record*, p. 14.

29. Center on Budget and Policy Priorities, *The Decreasing Effectiveness of Anti-Poverty Programs 1979–1985* (Washington, DC: Center on Budget and Policy Priorities, 1986).

30. U.S. General Accounting Office (GAO), *An Evaluation of the 1981 AFDC Changes: Final Report* (Washington, DC: GAO, July 2, 1985). GAO's preliminary evaluation of the impact of the changes encouraged Congress to ease the eligibility requirements.

31. The Center for the Study of Social Policy, *Effects of Federal AFDC Policy Changes: A Study of A Federal-State 'Partnership'* (Washington, DC: The Center for the Study of Social Policy, March 1983).

32. Timothy B. Clark and Richard Corrigan, "Ronald Reagan's Economy," *National Journal*, December 13, 1986, p. 2990.

33. U.S. Bureau of the Census, Current Population Reports, Series P-60, No. 151, *Money Income of Households, Families, and Persons in the United States: 1984,* (Washington, DC: U.S. Government Printing Office, 1986), Table 12.

34. Moon and Sawhill, "Family Incomes," p. 320.

35. *Ibid.*

36. Grinker Associates, Inc., *An Independent Sector Assessment of the Job Training Partnership Act, Final Report: Program Year 1985* (New York: Grinker Associates, 1986), p. i.

37. Creaming is not unique to JTPA programs. When successful job placement is a goal, it should not be surprising that program administrators opt for participants most likely to succeed. CETA prime sponsors experienced their share of creaming accusations.

38. Grinker Associates, *An Independent Sector Assessment* p. 2.

39. Bawden and Palmer, "Social Policy," p. 201.

40. Cynthia E. Harrison, "Politics and Law," in Sarah M. Pritchard (ed.), *The Women's Annual* (Boston: G. K. Hall & Co., 1984), p. 152.

41. Elder Witt and Janice Hook, "Court Adopts Narrow View of Sex Bias in Education," *Congressional Quarterly* (March 3, 1984), p. 513.

42. Elder Witt, "Administration Hails Ruling on Affirmative Action Case: Seniority Prevails in Layoffs," *Congressional Quarterly* (June 16, 1984), p. 1451.

43. Congressional Caucus for Women's Issues, "A Report on the October 1985 Supreme Court Term," (Washington, DC: Congressional Caucus for Women's Issues, n.d.), mimeo.

44. Elder Witt, "Rehnquist to be Chief Justice, Reagan Names Scalia to Court," *Congressional Quarterly* (June 21, 1986), p. 1402.

45. Women's Research and Education Institute, *Assessment of the Impact on Women*, p. 1.

46. Although Democrats pinned some of their hopes on a gender gap in 1984, which public opinion polls indicated did exist, Reagan's failure to support women's rights and his efforts to dismantle welfare and other social programs were not enough to cause him to lose. Women were less likely than men to cast their votes

for Reagan in 1984, but a majority of them still did so. Ethel Klein reports a gender gap of 8 percent in 1980 and, depending on the exit polls, a gap of 6 to 8 percent in 1984. ("The Gender Gap: Different Issues, Different Answers," *The Brookings Review*, Winter, 1985, p. 33.)

PART II

PUBLIC POLICY ON WOMEN AND PRODUCTION

Introduction

Since the end of World War II, revolutionary changes have occurred in the way in which American women combine work and family life. These changes, which began slowly, escalated dramatically in the 1970s. In terms of family life, women have been moving away from patterns of early marriage and childbearing to longer periods of "singleness." In 1970 the median age of women at first marriage was 20.8 years; by 1982 it had risen fully a year and a half to 22.3.[1] Another way of looking at this pattern is to compare the 1970 percentage of American women over age 18 who were married, which was 68.5, with the corresponding 1984 figure, which was only 60.8.[2] These patterns among younger women are associated with rising levels of education leading to the choice of a career as an alternative to early marriage.

Many younger women have also been delaying childbearing until they are in their thirties. While population experts are debating whether the delay of childbearing will result in a temporary or permanent lowering of fertility rates, recent studies have shown that the longer a woman postpones childbearing after marriage, the less inclined she is to have a child.[3]

Later marriage, rising divorce rates, and increasing widowhood have all created a rapidly expanding group of single women whose economic needs are different from those of single women 40 years ago. Most significantly, the rising divorce rate has greatly increased the number of female single heads of households; from 1970 to 1978 alone, the number of female heads of households increased by 46 percent; from 1980 to 1985 this figure rose by another 16.4 percent.[4] Over 90 percent of all single-parent households are headed by women. Knowledge of the high divorce rate has made it impossible for young women to plan their lives in the expectation of being permanently supported by a husband.

The revolution in women's family lives has been intertwined with a revolution in women's work lives. From the end of World War II until 1984, the participation rate of women in the work force doubled, from 27 percent to 54 percent. The largest increase was among married women with children under 18; from 1970 to 1985 alone, the number of women with children ages 6–17 who were employed rose from 49.2 to 67.8 percent; for mothers of children under 6, the increase was from 30.3 to 53.4

percent.[5] There is every reason to believe that this expansion of the female labor force will continue.

The movement of women into the work force has been occasioned by many factors: the necessity of supporting a family as a single head of household, the need to supplement a husband's income, increasing levels of education among women, and greater social acceptance of working women. Although most women work out of economic necessity, they generally have high levels of job satisfaction. Not unexpectedly, job satisfaction is highest among younger women, women at the higher occupational levels, women who perceive their husbands as supportive of their working, and women whose children are over 6 years of age.[6]

However, women in 1987 still earn only 64 percent of the earnings of men, no larger a percentage than in 1955.[7] One of the primary causes of the earnings gap is occupational segregation by sex in the U.S. labor force. While women have been entering the labor force at a rapid rate, almost 80 percent work in clerical, service, or unskilled industrial jobs that are low-paying and low-status. In recent years, the labor force has become more rather than less sex-segregated. As an example, in 1972 there were three female clerical workers to every one male; by 1978, female clerical workers outnumbered males by four to one. This same four-to-one ratio still prevailed in 1984. While there have been impressive percentage increases of women in some high-paying, predominantly male job categories such as craft workers and managers, the absolute numbers of women in these positions remains very small.[8]

What impact have these revolutionary changes in women's lives had on American economic policy? As seen earlier, women's economic status has become a growing public policy concern. The main thrust of public policy in the 1960s and 1970s was to ban sex discrimination in pay, hiring, training, and promotion. These policies have provided greater equity for a small number of women workers but they have done little to change the general condition of working women as a "secondary labor market."[9] The few programs that were initiated to educate, train, and recruit women for nontraditional jobs have done more to raise awareness about occupational segregation than to change the status quo.

Unless new policy directions are taken in the 1990s, the female work force of the future will have the same characteristics as today, except that it will be larger. The chapters in Part II describe new policy approaches to improving the economic status of women. One example is "pay equity." Since 1963, equal pay for equal work has been official government policy. While considerable effort has gone into enforcing this policy, it has not succeeded in decreasing the earnings gap between men and women because men and women are not typically in "equal" jobs. Because the work force is highly sex-segregated, women's groups are now seeking to achieve pay equity, a policy which states that when women's work is of comparable value to men's work, pay should be equivalent.[10]

Another relatively new policy approach involves alternative patterns of employment, enabling women to integrate their family and work roles better. For example, job sharing and flexitime have been introduced in both the public and private sector to allow individuals greater flexibility in arranging their work lives. While not aimed exclusively at women, these policies have profound implications for women attempting to manage dual roles as workers inside and outside the home. In chapter 5, after surveying the literature on experiments with these policies, Stoper assesses the prospects for their broader adoption and warns about their limitations.

Alternative work patterns can give women more flexibility in combining work lives with personal lives. But such flexibility is rarely sufficient for mothers of new babies. Patricia Huckle in chapter 7 documents the transition in the 1970s from an era when pregnant women were routinely discriminated against to the adoption of legislation against such discrimination and the development more recently of policies to ensure the right to time off from work to spend with infants.

All these policies are designed to assist healthy women in working for pay during all or most of their pregnancy. But women who do this sometimes face another problem: exposure to work environments that endanger the health of their fetuses. Louise Williams in chapter 6 reviews the research, litigation, and regulatory efforts to safeguard reproductive health in the workplace.

These policy approaches transcend issues of discrimination against women workers. They address fundamental concerns such as the need to make work and family roles more compatible and the protection of the health of women workers and their offspring. The policies described here are only a sample of the new thinking on women's employment issues. Other important issues include reform of the social security system to recognize the value of women's labor in the home and the provision of training and support services to improve the employment prospects of women on welfare and thus end the dependency of many low-income women.

Finally, women's needs as workers are integrally associated with their needs as mothers. Economic policies must be developed in conjunction with policies concerning poverty and welfare, housing, child care, and reproductive technology. These will be considered in Part III.

The early 1980s provided an environment hostile to policy innovation and government spending to assist employed women. Many in the Reagan administration were working with an outdated model: well-heeled husbands as the best solution to women's economic needs. At the same time, women's labor force participation continued to rise, and the women's lobby fought a rear-guard battle not only to preserve what it had struggled so hard to gain during the 1960s and 1970s, but also to generate new policies to meet new needs. Strategies to promote these new policies will be suggested in the conclusion of this volume.

NOTES AND REFERENCES

1. *Statistical Abstract of the United States: 1986* (Washington, DC: Bureau of the Census, U.S. Department of Commerce, 1986), p. 79.

2. Ibid., p. 35.

3. *San Jose Mercury News*, February 8, 1981.

4. *A Statistical Portrait of Women in the United States: 1978* (Washington DC: Bureau of the Census, 1978), p. 43.

5. *Women and Work*, (Washington, DC: U.S. Department of Labor, 1977) pp. 16–17.

6. *A Statistical Portrait of Women*, p. 70.

7. *Statistical Abstract*, p. 402.

8. Ibid., pp. 402–3.

9. *Women and Work*, p. 1.

10. See "Pay Equity: Beyond Equal Pay for Equal Work," by Wendy Kahn and Joy Ann Grune, in Ellen Boneparth (ed.), *Women, Power and Policy*, 1st ed. (New York: Pergamon, 1982).

5
Alternative Work Patterns and the Double Life

Emily Stoper

Every woman in America leads a double life. She is shaped by a double socialization; she is torn apart by a double pull; often she carries a double burden. One side of her duality turns inward to the world of the home, children, "inner feelings"—femininity, in a word. The other side faces outward to the world of work, achievement, power, money, abstract thought—the "man's world."

A few women yield wholly to the inward pull, immersing themselves in home life, only to find that they are powerless against the manifold and pervasive ways in which the rest of the world shapes their lives and their children's lives. A few other women yield wholly to the outward pull, engaging totally in money and power pursuits, but with an increasing sense of hollowness. For these opposite extremes, one side of the double life is lived fully, the other side is a shadow.

But the vast majority of women, whether they are called housewives or career women, traditionalists or feminists, have their lives shaped at least to some degree by both sides of the duality. The experience of doubleness is generally an unpleasant one. Whenever a woman turns to one side, she tends to feel alienated from the other; it is difficult for her to experience an integrated life. She constantly faces impossible choices—between heart and head, between love and work, between children and career. Worse, since she is relatively powerless in both realms, circumstances often make choices for her.

The powerlessness also leads to a combination of overwork and under-reward. Women are overworked because they are trying to serve both sides. They are underrewarded at home because their work at home is cut off from what is most valued in the rest of society. They are underrewarded at work because, being women, they are assumed not to be fully committed to the world of work and so are assigned a secondary place within it. And,

93

indeed, most women are unwilling to give as little of their lives as men have to the world of home and children or, more broadly, the world of interpersonal relations and emotional meaning. Our society would surely be a worse palce to live in if they did. And yet, women seem permanently relegated to second-class citizenship as long as they yield to the inward as well as the outward pull.

Feminists, seeking to deal with this dilemma, have looked at many aspects of women's lives, as discussed in the various chapters of this book. This chapter will examine an intriguing approach that emerged in the 1970s: alternative work patterns. This is a catchall phrase that includes such innovations in work patterns as flexitime, staggered hours, compact work week, job sharing, and flexiyear.

THE PROMISE OF ALTERNATIVE WORK PATTERNS

Most alternative work patterns were pioneered in Europe in the late 1960s and early 1970s as an attempt by management to make the best use of labor during a shortage. In the United States, with its perennial unemployment, the adoption of new work patterns has been more gradual. They have been seen by American management as ways of dealing with declining worker morale and a slowdown in the rise of productivity and of attracting special categories of workers, especially women.

From the point of view of women, the new patterns have been seen primarily as offering more flexibility and opportunity for self-management on the job. Easier integration of work and family life has been viewed as one of a list of incidental benefits that also includes easing traffic congestion and permitting weekday access by employees to shopping, creation, and education.

Alternative work patterns fall into three broad types: those that re-arrange the hours at which work is done, those that reduce the total number of hours worked, and those that alter the place of work in life.[1] All three types have the potential of helping women to combine the two sides of their lives more easily.

Rearranging the Hours of Work

The first type of alternative work pattern includes flexitime, staggered hours, and the "compact" or "compressed" workweek. All of these are still sufficiently unusual that they require definition. *Flexitime* (sometimes called flextime) means an extension to the employee of the right to choose, within certain limits, on a day-to-day basis, when the hours of work will begin and end. In the minimum form, it merely means that the employee can choose at what time to start work within a band of two or three hours in the morning and at what time to finish within a band of two or three hours in the afternoon; everyone has to work certain core hours in the middle of the day. For example, a flexitime day could look like this:

Flexible hours	7–9 A.M.
Core hours	9–11:30 A.M.
Flexible lunch period	11:30–1:30 P.M.
Core hours	1:30–4 P.M.
Flexible hours	4–6 P.M.[2]

In a more advanced form of flexitime, employees can "bank hours" from day to day, sometimes for an indefinite period of time, sometimes limited to a single week or a single month. Banking hours means working extra hours on one day and then taking time off on another day chosen by the employee.

In 1978, Congress passed the Federal Employees Flexible and Compressed Work Schedules Act sponsored by Representative Stephen J. Solarz (D-N.Y.) and Senator Gaylord Nelson (D-Wis.), temporarily (for 3 years) suspending obstacles in labor legislation to the banking of hours, so that experiments could be conducted with flexitime and compressed work weeks.

Staggered hours differ from flexitime in that, once chosen, they do not vary from day to day. If chosen by the employer, staggered hours can actually make it more difficult for an employee to combine work with family life—if, for example, a parent is assigned a late work schedule that overlaps after-school hours and dinner preparation time. In most workplaces where they are used, though, staggered hours are chosen by the employee, so that they have some of the advantages of flexitime.

The *"compact"* or *"compressed" work week* involves a full-time job done in fewer than five days, usually four 10-hour days but occasionally three 12-hour days, or, over a biweekly period, eight 9-hour days and one 8-hour day. One might have expected that women would dislike this schedule because neither child care nor housework can easily be postponed from day to day. Skinned knees and dirty dishes both have a way of crying out for immediate attention. Studies show, however, that at least some women on this schedule like it, sometimes even more than men do, perhaps because it gives them a day to catch up on home-related tasks like shopping and sewing.[3] One study[4] did find that people with children at home saw the compact week as having unfavorable consequences for home life, and increasingly so over time. But men complained about this more than women. In any case, the 4/40 (4 days, 40 hours) work week peaked in popularity around 1975 at 2.2 percent of the workforce and has been declining since them, for reasons that have little to do with the impact on family life and much to do with disappointed expectations about raising productivity and cutting costs, largely owing to worker fatigue and the increased complexity of scheduling and other management tasks.[5]

Flexitime, however, has been steadily increasing in use throughout the 1970s to the point where in 1980 about 17 percent of nongovernment organizations with 50 or more employees and 237 government agencies had flexible schedules.[6] Some 6 percent of all American employees were on flexitime in 1977. In 1985 the Administrative Management Society conducted two surveys, one of the Fortune 500 companies, the other of 4,732 smaller companies. Of the respondents to the Fortune 500 survey, 29 percent said they made flexitime available to some or all of their employees, as did 18 percent of the respondents in the survey of smaller companies. Thirty-five percent of the respondents to a 1985 survey done by the American Management Association of its 1,600 member companies were offering flexitime to at least some of their employees.[7]

Flexitime is difficult (but not impossible) to use in work situations like an assembly line that involve interdependent functions, a buildup of work that must be handled by another person or a high degree of specialization of functions.[8] Flexible schedules are nothing new for many self-employed, professional, managerial, and sales persons who are accustomed to setting their own hours. Office workers are the most important part of the workforce for whom flexitime is a genuine new benefit—and, of course, a highly disproportionate percentage of these are women. Some 40 percent of employed women are clerical workers and many others are in jobs such as supervisor or social worker that lend themselves easily to flexitime.

Flexitime and the Double Life

In a series of informal interviews with workers on flexitime, the author found that it offers a number of advantages to mothers—and, of course, to fathers who want to play their parental role more actively. By starting the workday very early, a parent can be home when the children return from school or soon after. This is an advantage especially if the other parent is able to take responsibility for getting them off to school in the morning. Parents can also take time off during the day without using personal leave. Not having to arrive at work at a specific time can also ease the morning rush at home. Even on a normal day the morning rush at home is often the highest-pressure work of the day, and the parent is lucky to arrive at work on time, though exhausted.

Some ways in which flexitime helps everybody are particularly crucial for mothers. For example, the fact that flexitime often cuts down on travel time by enabling people to avoid rush hours is particularly helpful to mothers who cannot squeeze in much commuting time in an already overloaded schedule. The greater choice of times for college classes often benefits mothers, since they are a disproportionate number of the adults in college, having dropped out earlier in order to have children.

Flexitime also encourages greater self-management in routine office jobs since it is incompatible with petty, moment-to-moment supervision, if only because supervisors cannot be there during the entire expanded workday. And it encourages "cross-training"—that is, learning aspects of other people's jobs because the other people will not always be there to do them. Thus, clerical work under flexitime tends to become more autonomous and varied.

In all these ways it would seem that flexitime could help many working parents. Yet the interviews reported here, like much of the research on flexitime, are subjective and unsystematic. A controlled study by Halcyone Bohen of 700 employees on flexitime in two federal agencies found that flexitime actually made little difference in assisting people who were trying to combine work and parental roles. (The study was done before the implementation of Public Law 95-390 permitting the banking of hours, so it refers only to the most limited form of flexitime.) Bohen found that the main beneficiaries of flexitime were not mothers (who experience equal amounts of stress on flexitime and on a standard schedule) but women without children, for whom flexitime meant less stress.

Since flexitime has been touted not only as a way of easing the load of employed mothers but also as a way of encouraging fathers to spend more time with their children, Bohen also compared fathers on flexitime with those on standard schedules. When she looked at fathers whose wives are employed, she found that those on flexitime do not spend significantly more time on family work than those on standard time. But when she turned to fathers whose wives are not employed, she found that those on flexitime do spend more time on family work than those on standard times, though not more than men with employed wives on both schedules.

Bohen found that there were three kinds of people for whom flexitime made a measurable difference in the ease with which they could take care of personal and family chores and activities: fathers with nonemployed wives, employed married women without children, and single people. All of these are people who do not have primary child-care responsibilities! Single mothers and employed parents with employed spouses did not find that flexitime made any measurable difference.[9]

Another study, however, found that workers who had young children were somewhat more likely to use flexitime and also that workers who changed their hours under flexitime increased their time with their children more than did workers who chose not to change their schedules.[10] Obviously, more research is needed but it appears that flexitime's impact on easing the double pull will be small at best.

Reducing the Hours of Work

An obvious shortcoming of flexitime and the other variant schedules mentioned above is that the total number of hours to be worked is not reduced. No matter how one juggles them, 35 to 40 hours a week are likely to be hard to combine with major child-care responsibilities.

Give the double pull, many mothers of children under 12 do not want to work full-time unless it is economically necessary.[11] The 1977 Quality of Employment Survey done by the Survey Research Center at the University of Michigan found that 51 percent of wives and 42 percent of husbands with children under 18 preferred to reduce their work time in order to spend more time with their families. About 35 percent of workers with children under 18 experience significant interference between their jobs and their family lives. This is especially true of families with preschool children. Both men and women complained of excessive work time; women also complained of scheduling incompatibilities, especially between work hours and child-care hours.[12]

Besides making scheduling easier, part-time work satisfies mothers' needs in many cases for a balance between home life and work life. Part-time work offers parents many hours a day with their children to establish a strong emotional relationship and to get fully acquainted with them—something which may be difficult for some parents working full-time. Moreover, parents who are part-timers can offset the weaknesses of the child-care facility; for example, offering stimulation if the child-care center is very quiet or quiet if it is very stimulating.[13] Part-time working parents also find it easier to participate as volunteer aides in cooperative nursery schools or grade schools, thus helping assure the quality of the institutions provided by the community to help raise their children.

Part-time employment is also often better for the parents as people. Full-time employment combined with child-rearing leaves many people perpetually frazzled and exhausted. Full-time parenting is also a strain on many people, especially those who feel the outward pull strongly. One study[14] of mothers of young children found the following pattern:

- Employed full-time: highest stress
- Not employed: medium stress
- Employed part-time: lowest stress and greatest satisfaction as worker *and* parent.

Only 42 percent of women (and about 66 percent of men) in the work force now work full-time all year round.[15] Nearly thirty percent of employed women are part-week, compared with 13 percent of employed men.[16] Close to half of the women part-timers give "home and family responsibilities" as the reason for not working full-time.[17]

There have always been plenty of part-time jobs in the sales, clerical and service fields, which have become pink-collar ghettoes. The effect has been to reinforce the sex segregation of the labor market. When women asked why managerial and professional jobs could not be part-time, they were told that the jobs did not lend themselves to being performed on a part-time basis. But what did this mean? There is no objective basis for defining 35–40 hours as "full time." The parameters of any job could be set so that it took one hour or 70 hours. Forty hours had merely been a comfortable average work week for men who did not assume major child-rearing responsibilities. Men held most of those jobs that were said to be unsuitable for part-timers.

In the 1980s this has begun to change. There has been a significant increase in the number of part-time professional jobs available. This trend was actually pioneered by the federal government. The Federal Part-Time Career Employment Act of 1978 opened up some 20,000 part-time professional and managerial positions in federal employment by 1982.[18] In addition, many states have established programs for experimenting with alternative work patterns for their employees. Today, one-fifth of *all* women working part-time are in professional or managerial jobs.[19]

This is a very important change because these responsible jobs are the ones that actually pay well enough to support some people, even with a child or two, on a part-time basis. Most part-time jobs are so low-paid that they are desirable only if they are supplements to a family income. Hence, they remain job ghettoes for women.

Making available better jobs on a part-time basis is, however, only half the battle. Not all working mothers can have managerial and professional jobs, just as not all working fathers can have such jobs. Women in part-time jobs have another disadvantage: their jobs are usually thought of as temporary and carry no job security. Part-time workers cannot usually get any kind of job tenure or seniority. This fact encourages the prejudice that part-timers are less than fully qualified. There is no inherent reason why the categories of part-time and temporary should be confounded in this way—except perhaps that it is convenient for employers to be able to "let go" part-timers easily during slack seasons, as a way of keeping their wage bill lower.

This practice goes far toward explaining why many women who have been in the work force all or most of their adult lives still think of themselves as working temporarily. But the psychological basis for long-term "temporary" work is eroding, as women see increasingly that given the realities of inflation and unstable marriage, they are likely to be in the work force most of their lives.

Along with lack of job security goes lack of fringe benefits—paid vacations, sick leave, health insurance, workers' compensation, a retire-ment plan, and so on. Almost half of all Americans working under 35 hours a week do not receive fringe benefits.[20] This lack of fringes means that many part-time workers are in effect not getting equal pay for equal work—even with other workers in the same job categories who are full-time. Personnel departments, orientated toward full-time workers, are often stymied by the complexities of prorating benefits or making up an equitable package of benefits for part-timers. These technical difficulties have often been used as a reason for not giving part-timers any fringe benefits at all. Actually, a major study shows that equitable fringe benefits need not cost more.[21]

So there are two main problems with part-time jobs as they exist today: better-paid jobs are often not available on a part-time basis, and many part-time jobs lack job security and fringe benefits. Improvements in these conditions will follow changes in the social norm that dictates that all serious, long-term work must be done on a full-time basis.

There is a social and political movement trying to effect just such a change in social norms. Organizations like New Ways to Work in San Francisco, Catalyst in New York, and the National Council for Alternative Work Patterns in Washington are trying to stimulate the creation of more and better part-time jobs and to match them to workers. Many workers want part-time jobs, especially if they offer responsibility, good pay, fringe benefits, and job security, than there are such jobs. Not only women (or men) attempting to combine child-rearing and work roles, but also students, older people who want to phase into retirement, disabled people, people considering midlife career changes, and so on, would like to work part-time. Since most of these population categories are increasing, the pressure to improve the status and increase the number of part-time jobs is also growing.

Some interesting variations on part-time jobs are being developed, of which the best known is job sharing. In job sharing, two people hold a job that was formerly a single full-time job. Job sharing is becoming increasingly common. Among the Fortune 500 companies, only 11 percent were permitting it for some of their employees in 1981, but this had risen to 17 percent in 1985. In the smaller companies surveyed, job sharing was being permitted in only 2.1 percent of companies in 1984–85 but in 3.2 percent in 1985–86. Job sharing is, of course, desirable only if it is voluntary and only if it includes fringe benefits for both workers. The two workers may "split" the job—by hours or days, by task, by area of responsibility—or they may "share" it, working collaboratively. The collaborative pattern is surprisingly common. In one study by Gretl Meier[22] of 238 job sharers, 70 percent considered their jobs to be shared rather than split. An even larger proportion saw their partner's skills as complementary to theirs. The same study found that over half the teams tended to become more collaborative over time.[23] The study covered a variety of occupations including teachers, administrators/program developers, secretaries/receptionists/clericals, counselors/social workers/psychiatrists, and researchers/technicians.[24]

Job Sharing: Pros and Cons

What are the advantages and disadvantages of job sharing? According to Meier's study, the greatest advantage—one which should apply to any part-time person—was more energy on the job. No fewer than 91 percent of the respondents reported that they had more energy for work.[25]

Advantages from the employer's point of view included the ability to call on job sharing workers for emergency or temporary jobs and to train new people without disrupting the flow of work. Employers, of course, also benefited from the higher energy and the lower incidence of "burn-out", especially among helping professionals.[26]

Permanent part-time employment has been found to reduce labor costs, improve job performance, and raise the quality of the work force.[27] Part-time employees have been found to have no less commitment and dedication than full-time ones.[28] Part-time work has also been touted as solving labor-recruitment[29] and scheduling[30] problems.

Employers of large numbers of women might be most willing to offer permanent part-time employment at all levels, as women seem to find job sharing particularly advantageous. Seventy-seven percent of the respondents in the Meier study were in teams of two women, 19 percent in teams of one man and one woman (which were rarely husband and wife, except in academia), the remaining 4 percent in all-male teams. Women's preference is probably best explained in terms of their mothering responsibilities. Fifty-five percent of all the respondents had children aged 1 to 11 at home, and 81 percent were married, many of them probably with older children at home. Respondents reported that of the time not devoted to their paid job, 32 per cent is spent caring for their family, and 25 percent on caring for their home.[31]

Women also seemed to like job sharing better than men did. Asked whether job sharing "enhanced the quality and success of their work," 68 percent of those on all-female teams said yes, whereas only 50 percent of mixed teams agreed. The figure was even lower among the small number of all-male teams.[32]

It is probable that the chief reason for dissatisfaction with job sharing was financial. Some people in the study had left their job sharing arrangements for full-time work; the main reason they gave was money. For only 6 percent of the sample was the shared job the only source of family income.[33]

Related reasons for dissatisfaction were the loss of job security and of opportunities for promotion, perceived by a little under half the sample.

Higher-level jobs were rarely available on a job sharing basis and the inability to claim full credit for one's work, as well as slower accrual of seniority, might also impede promotion.[34] For employers, also, the blurring of accountability and responsibility was sometimes unwelcome.[35]

A different kind of problem was that although the jobs were genuinely half-time, many people, especially professionals, had a strong commitment to them and felt frustrated by the lack of time to act fully on their commitment. They tended to work very hard during the time they had or to take work home.[36] This was advantageous from the employer's standpoint, but it poses a real danger that job sharing (or part-time jobs in general) may lead to exploitation of women even when the jobs are well paid and carry fringe benefits and job security. Another study in fact found strong feelings of economic exploitation among job sharing married couples.[37]

One final disadvantage of job sharing is that it may undercut the movement for part-time jobs in general by implicitly conceding that work naturally breaks down into 40-hour-a-week blocks (though there is no reason why two people could not share, say, one and a half jobs, as occasionally is done). Job sharing is not the only desirable form of part-time work, and there are some practical obstacles to it that do not exist for other part-time jobs. The most obvious of these is the need to find a compatible pair; this need could limit the expansion of job sharing. Nevertheless, a major study found that job sharing and work sharing (part-timing as a substitute for layoffs) are the most likely modes for career part-time employment in the future.[38]

Rethinking Work Time

It is extraordinarily difficult for Americans to break the mind-set that thinks of "full-time" (35–40 hours) as the normal work week and that sees two kinds of workers: full-time (serious) and part-time (temporary, just earning a few extra dollars). In West Germany, experiments are being done, primarily in the retail trade, with something called "flexiyear," a plan under which every employee contracts annually with management for a certain amount of work time (hours per day, days per week, months per year, or however they want to break it down).[39] Management can then plan to have a work force of appropriate size for slack and busy times, while workers can strike a continually changing balance between work time on the one hand and time for family, education, travel, starting a small business, and so on, on the other. The distinction between part-time and full-time workers then breaks down into a series of gradations. Workers need no longer forfeit any claim to "seriousness" if they want to work less than every day or even every month.

An even more radical idea along these lines, the "full cyclic plan," has been developed by Fred Best.[40] Under this plan, education, work, and leisure would be much more evenly distributed over the life span, instead of being concentrated in youth, the middle years, and old age respectively. Best did an informal survey of workers' preferences and found that 46 percent preferred the full cyclic plan, while only 20 percent preferred the traditional linear model. The third choice was a "moderate cyclic plan," concentrating education in the younger years but redistributing leisure and work over the middle and later years. One device for doing this would be sabbaticals (every seventh year off, usually at reduced pay), a benefit now available to few workers other than teachers.

One writer has proposed a national economic security fund, one percent of which would be set aside to pay for periods of "self-renewal" lasting up to 2 years.[41] Presumably, procreation and the care of a baby could be interpreted as a form of self-renewal. The governments of Hungary, Czechoslovakia, and Sweden now offer payments to workers who take time off for child-rearing.

A different kind of approach to part-timing is to divide work into "modules" of various lengths, permitting each worker to put together a package of modules of various kinds. This pattern would make possible the kind of balance among mental, physical, and manual work of which Marx dreamed. Some 10 percent of the work force already does this in a way by moonlighting.[42] But making available large numbers of part-time jobs of a great variety of types and lengths would enormously increase flexibility, to the great benefit of parents. It would also contribute to more flexibility and fluidity in labor markets, as well as providing a remedy for boredom and burnout.

IMPLICATIONS AND COMPLICATIONS

It is important to emphasize that we are talking here not merely about changes in options available to workers but about changes in social norms about the place of work in life. Without a change in norms, the new options will be used primarily by women and by a few marginal male workers and thus will only serve to reinforce the marginality of whoever uses them. Only if the norms about the place of work in life begin to change, so that significant numbers of men want to work less and differently, will women to able to continue to respond to both of their dual pulls and not be at a disadvantage in both worlds.

The Unions' Perspective

A major obstacle to the adoption of all of the alternative work patterns described thus far—from the most timid rearrangement of hours to the most radical rethinking of work time—is the skeptical and in some cases hostile attitude of those institutions which have been the chief advocates of American workers: the unions.[43] The attitude of most unions (with some notable exceptions[44]) has been skepticism about flexitime and downright hostility to efforts to upgrade and expand part-time employment.

The fact that alternative work patterns have usually been initiated by management arouses the suspicions of organized labor. Sometimes the motive of management has been to increase productivity (through flexitime and compact work weeks, for example), sometimes to respond to pressures from people who are not seen by unions as primary workers (women, people about to retire, students). These motives arouse the suspicion in union officials that increases in productivity will not be passed on to the worker and thus that alternative work patterns will become a new form of "speedup."

This suspicion is not entirely baseless. Workers under alternative work patterns do tend to be more productive. Overwhelmingly, firms or agencies that adopt flexitime report increases in productivity ranging from 5 to 15 percent.[45] These increases, however, are rarely caused by pressure on workers but rather by benefits to them, such as the opportunity to adjust their schedules to their biological clocks ("night people" do not have to report to work at 8 A.M. and doze away the first few hours), or to quiet times in the office, or to the length of the projects they work on, or to the times when work flow is heaviest. In these ways, flexitime tends to lead to more self-management and higher morale, which in turn reduces absenteeism, tardiness, and turnover. Not surprisingly, flexitime is overwhelmingly popular among employers.

It is true though that a frequently reported benefit to management from flexitime is reduction in overtime, presumably at least partly because workers voluntarily adjust their schedules to work flow. (Premium pay for overtime work done by flexitime workers who can bank hours is paid only if the extra hours are requested by management.) Reduction in overtime may not be seen as a benefit by workers, especially if they had come to depend on a predictable amount of weekly overtime pay.

Part-time workers often also have higher productivity, even after one takes into account extra administrative and training costs and extra time needed for communication in the case of shared jobs. In one study, people working a 6-hour day were generally producing as much as, or more than, those working an 8-hour day.[46] Part-time work offers some of the same morale and schedule-flexibility benefits as flexitime, and in addition has its own special virtues. People on part-days or even part-weeks suffered less from fatigue and the slackening of attention that often occurs after many consecutive hours or days of work. Probably even more important is Parkinson's Law, which is that work expands to fill the time available. Full-time workers have more time available, so they may simply draw out the work to fill that time, usually unconsciously.

A final factor that applies to part-time professional and some managerial workers is that these people are not really being paid for their time but rather for their expertise, imagination, problem-solving ability, etc. These often cannot be "turned off" when the work day ends, so that the employer may be getting a full-time mind at half-time pay.

An even more fundamental problem with alternative work patterns, arising from the fact that they are not usually initiated by unions, is that they threaten to alter the traditional relationship of workers with management and unions. To begin with, they may increase worker identification with management (though there is no hard evidence of this), mostly by encouraging worker self-management but also because workers on alternative schedules may see themselves as having a special, privileged relationship with management. This may lower their self-protective alertness against management's pressures for higher output or for worker-chosen schedules that are really for the convenience of management—both of which management should be paying for.

Moreover, the kinds of workers who are attracted by alternative work schedules are marginal workers, in the eyes of most unions. Most unions see primary workers as adult males who are heads of families. These are the people seen as most in need of good wages, fringe benefits, and job security and also most likely to be committed to unions who push for such things. For 100 years, unions have put most of their energies into fighting for the "family wage" with which a man could support his wife and children. The assumption behind this fight has been that neither wives nor children will be in the work force themselves except in marginal roles. Unions were major backers of legislation banning child labor and they have cooperated fully with management in the sex segregation of the work force (for example, pushing for protective labor legislation providing different work rules for men and women). They did not make serious efforts to organize into unions the occupations that employ most women (clerical work, teaching, nursing) until about 20 years ago.

The family wage would, of course, be paid to a full-time worker who could reasonably be expected to work all day, every week day, throughout his adult life, except when he is ill, on vacation, or unemployed. The assumption behind the family wage for full-time workers is the traditional patriarchal family—the father at work, the mother at home taking care of the children. In resisting alternative work patterns, unions are still working on this assumption. But with 54 percent of all women in the work force (compared to about 77 percent of men[47]), with the divorce rate at an all-time high, with half or more of the college-age population going to college, most of them wanting to work at the same time, with increasing numbers of vigorous elderly people wanting part-time work, with a new norm for training and employing the disabled—how realistic is that assumption?

At the same time, the structure of the economy is changing so that the traditional blue-collar occupations that have been heavily unionized for many decades are declining relative to the overall economy. Assembly-line workers are now only about 5 percent of the work force. And many of the new occupations—clerical jobs, service jobs, computer-related work—lend themselves much more easily to flexible or part-time schedules. Three-quarters of the workers in Meier's study of job sharing were nonunion.[48]

Unions understandably fear the loss of their central role in setting standards for American working conditions. Such fears are exacerbated by talk of individuals, not unions, bargaining annually with management over work schedules, as in flexiyear, or of people working more than eight hours a day or 40 hours a week, so as to have the "privilege" of banking hours. The tendency to bypass or tamper with collective bargaining agreements or labor laws, for which unions have struggled hard, in order to facilitate alternative work patterns, alarms union leaders. Even when labor laws are not altered, unions often fear that flexible schedules will make them more difficult to enforce.

While objecting to the erosion of the gains they have made for American workers, most unions have been unwilling to take the lead in introducing alternative work patterns in a manner that did not jeopardize what "primary" workers already have. Some unions, usually under pressure from their rank and file, have begun to play this role. The resistance of the other unions can probably be explained in large measure by their attachment to the idea of the family wage as their central goal.

By challenging the family wage, part-time work raises the possibility of a whole new social norm about the relationship between paid work and family life. Part-time work is now used primarily by women as a way of getting them through the difficult years when the children are small and the family budget is tight. As increasing numbers of mothers of small children enter the work force (at last count, 52 percent of mothers of children under 6), the pressure for part-time jobs increases. Women applicants for one job-sharing program outnumbered men by five to one.[49] Over all there are about twice as many women as men in the part-time labor force.[50]

This is very unfortunate because if part-time work continues to be used primarily by women, its main impact will be to reinforce the sex segregation of the work force by enhancing the differences between the way men and women work and thus making it more difficult for each sex to enter the other's occupations. The last thing women need is another wall around the pink-collar job ghetto in which they have less pay, status, influence, autonomy, and room for advancement than men. Only the use of the part-time option by substantial numbers of male workers can make its use by women truly desirable.

This means that the new patterns must be promoted not only as women's rights but as rights for all workers, not only as women's liberation but as workers' liberation. With the slowdown of economic growth, more part-time work for everyone may be the only way of accommodating all the new people who want to enter the work force. Making a virtue of necessity, many workers may come to see the shorter work time as a form of liberation. But it is going to be hard to promote a movement for workers' liberation without the support of the unions, who are the main organized spokesmen for American workers. Though that support has not yet been forthcoming, it must be sought and it can be won.

First, the unions' fears—some of which are quite legitimate—must be addressed. Unions must be reassured, for example, that management will not abuse flexitime. Reassurance might be in the form of laws forbidding pressure on workers to select hours to suit management and providing appropriate penalties (as Public Law 95-390 does), and in the form of studies showing that the exercise of pressure is in fact rare. Unions' fears that part-timers are not good union members can also be assuaged by showing that this is true only insofar as part-timers have been marginal workers. The alternative work patterns movement can play a role both in urging the new breed of part-timers to show more of an interest in unions and in urging unions to show more of an interest in part-timers and their concerns. Unionized part-timers do have better wages and fringe benefits than nonunionized ones.[51]

Probably the most serious concern of unions about job sharing is that rather than being a way of spreading around employment, it is merely a way of spreading around unemployment. This is a very realistic concern. One U.S. Department of Labor survey found that 42 percent of part-time workers had been unable to find full time work.[52] Another study found that between 1970 and 1982 (a recession year) the number of involuntary part-time workers rose far faster than the number of those who preferred part-time work—although there were still twice as many voluntary part-time workers.[53] To deal with this problem, the job-sharing movement should focus initially mostly on full-time jobs reduced voluntarily to part-time and on relatively high-paid jobs which could support individuals and even some families on a part-time basis. In the long run the movement needs to hack away at unions' assumptions about the patriarchal family.

Besides attempting to address the concerns of unions, the alternative work patterns movement should work to see to it that unions are fully included in all moves to introduce or expand flexitime or job sharing in unionized workplaces. Where there is collective bargaining, the reforms should be part of the contract. Where there is a grievance procedure, grievances arising from the new patterns should be covered under it. Where there are genuine and unavoidable hardships to individuals—say, during a period of transition to more part-time jobs—the unions can play a vital role by insisting that management and/or the government cushion those hardships. For example, full-time workers who are reduced involuntarily to part-time status should be made eligible for partial unemployment insurance, as they are in some European countries and in a few places in the United States. This reform could mitigate the hardship of layoffs by encouraging reductions in hours rather than the brutal severing of junior employees—a disproportionate number of whom are, of course, women and minority males.

In general, the movement for alternative work patterns, as it grows, should offer more support to the unions in some of their favorite causes—most notably, a shortening of the work week. That reform is certainly fully compatible with the other discussed here. In fact, the alternative work patterns movement should probably be arguing from the outset that someone who works, say, half-time, should get, say, 60 percent of pay, on the grounds that part-time work is more productive. Thus, part-time work should not be in competition with the shorter work-week; the two causes should be natural allies.

A Feminist Perspective

Union leaders, of course, are not the only ones who assume that the only serious and important workers are male heads of families, who will of course want full-time work. This view is endemic in management as well. So is the related view that the large majority of workers will consider work the central activity of their lives, either because of the intrinsic value of what they do or because of the money they earn, or a combination of the two.

This world view is not seriously challenged by flexitime and the other schedules that merely rearrange the hours worked without reducing them. Perhaps for this reason flexitime is relatively uncontroversial (one manager called it a "motherhood apple pie" issue),[54] and also has little or no significant effect on easing the burden of employees with major child-care responsibilities.

Part-time work could mean much bigger changes if more men were to choose it. But why would substantial numbers of male workers choose to work part-time? Presumably because they had some other rewarding and important way to spend much of their time and they were assured that a wide range of jobs, with full fringe benefits and job security, were available to them.

What other socially useful, rewarding, and important way is there for men to spend their time? The only one that is comparable in the strength of its pull to paid work is raising children. Yet raising children has been so cut off for so long from the "man's world" of paid work that most men have long since ceased to feel a major pull toward it (if they ever did). They serve their children by abandoning them daily when they leave for their jobs. The world of "real" (paid) work and the world of child rearing are connected only by the flimsy bond of cash.

Housewife-mothers attempt to raise their children for the world of work without any participatory sense of what that world is about and with only the barest and most indirect influence in that world. Meanwhile, worker-fathers toil daily in order to earn money for the sustenance of children they barely know, especially if, as is increasingly so, they do not even live in the same household because of divorce.

What is clearly needed is a reintegration of the worlds of home and work, in which both men and women will be drawn to both but will experience this double pull not as tearing their lives apart but as weaving them together, as reuniting two halves. Work and love, Freud's famous pair, can serve each other instead of battling each other from their fortresses in men's and women's worlds.

Men who attempt to do this will find themselves at a competitive disadvantage in the world of paid work, as "Dustin Hoffman Kramer" soon found, and as employed mothers have known all along. In the face of this disadvantage, they are likely to make the change only if they experience a radical change of values, away from ever-expanding material wealth and toward a recreation of meaning and wholeness in their lives.[55] Such a revolution in values would have profound implications for the entire economic system. There were foreshadowings of that revolution in the "counter-culture" movement of the 1960s and there are new harbingers in the alternative work patterns movement of today.

Without a transvaluation of values, alternative work patterns are mere gimmicks. Flexitime is likely to make little difference in easing the strain of women's double lives. Job sharing may bring short-term gains for women workers while making the long-term breakdown of the sex-segregated job market less likely. Only with a profound shift in social values will women—and men—be able to experience the double life not as doubly burdened but as doubly enriched.

Neither the unions nor the alternative work patterns movement is likely to bring about such a shift in values. The only social movement that is

WPP—E

likely to do so is the women's movement. A major part of that movement has always defined its purpose as freeing men and women from the prison of sex roles. Moreover, at the very core of its goal is the empowerment of women in all their roles. Feminists know that women cannot be liberated in the "man's world" without also being liberated at home, nor can they be liberated at home while they are powerless everywhere else. Thus, feminism can give the movement for alternative work patterns a clear sense of purpose.

A political alliance among the unions, the alternative work patterns movement, and the women's movement offers the best hope that alternative work patterns can make a significant difference in the future of Americans.

NOTES AND REFERENCES

1. Good descriptions of the advantages, drawbacks, and detailed functioning of the various types of flexible schedules can be found in Pam Silverstein and Jozetta H. Srb, *Flexitime: Where, When, and How?* (Ithaca, N.Y.: Cornell University, 1979); Virginia Hider Martin, *Hours of Work When Workers Can Choose* (Washington, D.C.: Business and Professional Women's Foundation, 1975); George W. Bohlander, *Flexitime—A New Face on The Work Clock* (Los Angeles: UCLA Institute of Industrial Relations, 1977); Albert S. Glickman and Zenia H. Brown, *Changing Schedules of Work: Patterns and Implications* (Kalamazoo, Mich.: W.E. Upjohn Institute of Employment Research, 1974).

2. Silverstein and Srb, *Flexitime*, p. 2.

3. Glickman, *Changing Schedules of Work*, pp. 24–25, 27, 32.

4. Ibid., pp. 24–25.

5. Silverstein and Srb, *Flexitime*, p. 10; Stanley D. Nollen and Virginia H. Martin, *Alternative Work Schedules, Part 3: Compressed Workweeks* (New York: AMACOM, 1978), p. 39.

6. *Newsweek*, May 13, 1980.

7. Nollen and Martin, *Alternative Work Schedules*, Part 1, p. 6, for the 1977 figure. The 1985 survey figures are on file at New Ways to Work in San Francisco.

8. Ana L. Bishop, " Flexitime in Manufacturing," *American Machinist* (April 1979).

9. Halcyone H. Bohen and Anamaria Viveros-Long, *Balancing Jobs and Family Life: Do Flexible Work Schedules Help?* (Philadelphia: Temple University Press, 1981).

10. Unpublished study by Dr. Richard A. Winett, Institute of Behavioral Research, Silver Spring, Maryland.

11. Personal communication with Lynne McCallister, author of an extensive survey of middle-American mothers.

12. Joseph H. Pleck, Graham L. Staines, and Linda Lang, "Work and Family Life: First Reports on Work-Family Interference and Workers' Formal Child Care Arrangements, From the 1977 Quality of Employment Survey," Working Paper No. 11, Wellesley College Center for Research on Women, 1978, p. 9.

13. Personal communication with Lynne McCallister.

14. Cited in Gretl S. Meier, *Job Sharing: A New Pattern for Quality of Work and*

Life (Kalamazoo, Mich.: W. E. Upjohn Institute for Employment Research, 1979), p. 7.

15. Nollen and Martin, *Alternative Work Schedules*, p. 3.

16. *A Statistical Portrait of Women in the United States, 1978* (U.S. Census Bureau, Current Population Reports, Special Studies, Series P-23, No. 100), pp. 54, 56.

17. Silverstein and Srb, *Flexitime*, p. 1.

18. Joann S. Lublin, "Mutual Aid: Firms and Job Seekers Discover More Benefits to Part-time Positions," *Wall Street Journal*, October 4, 1978, p. 1.

19. Stanley D. Nollen, Brenda B. Eddy, and Virginia H. Martin, *Permanent Part-Time Employment: The Manager's Perspective* (New York: Praeger, 1978), p. 126.

20. Personal communication with Barbara Fiss of the Office of Personnel Management.

21. *National Council for Alternative Work Patterns (NCAWP) Newsletter* (Winter 1979), pp. 4–6; Meier, *Job Sharing*, pp. 15–22.

22. 1985 survey by the Administrative Management Society, on file at New Ways to Work in San Francisco. Figures on shared v. split jobs from Meier, *Job Sharing*, pp. 48, 61.

23. Ibid., p. 61.

24. Ibid., p. 36.

25. Ibid., p. 62.

26. Ibid., p. 83.

27. Nollen and Martin, *Alternative Work Schedules, Part 2*, p. 4.

28. Ibid., p. 5.

29. Research Institute of America, "One Answer to Hard-to-Fill Jobs: Let Two People Share the Work," *Alert* (April 20, 1977); and "Job Sharing as a Way to Hold the Work Force," *Alert* (February 7, 1979), W. F. Thompson et al., "An Answer to the Computer Programmer Shortage," *Adult Leadership* (January 1970), *Jobs for the Hard-to-Employ: New Directions for a Public-Private Partnership* (New York: Committee for Economic Development, 1978).

30. Nollen, Eddy, and Martin, *Permanent Part-Time Employment*, p. 145.

31. Meier, *Job Sharing*, pp. 42, 45.

32. Ibid., pp. 72–74.

33. Ibid., pp. 60, 44.

34. Ibid., p. 84.

35. ibid., p. 80.

36. Ibid., p. 78.

37. William Arkin and Lynne R. Dobrofsky, "Job Sharing," in *Working Couples*, ed. R. and R. Rapoport (New York: Harper & Row, 1978), p. 132.

38. Nollen, Eddy, and Martin, *Permanent Part-Time Employment*, p. 155.

39. Silverstein and Srb, *Flexitime*, p. 42; Willi Haller, *Flexyear: The Ultimate Work Hour Concept* (New York: Interflex, 1977); Bernhard Teriet, "Flexiyear Schedules—Only a Matter of Time?" *Monthly Labor Review* (December 1977) pp. 62–65.

40. Silverstein and Srb, *Flexitime*, p. 43.

41. Glickman, *Changing Schedules of Work*, p. 68.

42. Ibid., p. 72; *NCAWP Newsletter* (Winter 1979), p. 12.

43. See Silverstein and Srb, *Flexitime*, pp. 33–37; Bohlander, *Flextime*, pp. 49–57; Martin, *Hours of Work*, p. 50; Nollen, Eddy and Martin, *Permanent Part-Time Employment*, pp. 128–36, 171.

44. Glickman, *Changing Schedules of Work*, p. 66.

45. *Newsweek*, May 13, 1980.

46. *NCAWP Newsletter* (Summer 1979), p. 4.

47. *Statistical Portrait*, p. 46.

48. Meier, *Job Sharing*, p. 39.

49. "Project JOIN: Final Report Available Shortly," *NCAWP Newsletter* (Spring 1979), p. 3.

50. "Employment in Perspective: Working Women," Report 713, Washington: Bureau of Labor Statistics, Second Quarter 1984.

51. Nollen, *Permanent Part-Time Employment*, pp. 133–4.

52. "What the Boom in Part-Time Work Means for Management," *International Management*, May 1984, p. 39.

53. Saseen, *op. cit.*, p. 12.

54. Carl Selinger, past manager of the Port Authority of New York and New Jersey Staggered Work Hours Project, quoted in *NCAWP Newsletter* (Winter 1979), p. 11.

55. Glickman, *Changing Schedules of Work*, pp. 55, 80–83.

6

Toxic Exposure in the Workplace: Balancing Job Opportunity with Reproductive Health

Louise A. Williams

INTRODUCTION

The protection of reproductive health in the workplace is extremely complex because reproduction is simultaneously intensely private and glaringly public; individuals control when or whether they will reproduce but government agencies are charged to protect their reproductive health. This public–private interface means that personal value systems, the level of scientific knowledge, economic realities, and legal precedents often collide. In order to grasp the nature of the complex issues surrounding the protection of reproductive health in the workplace, it is necessary to examine the disparate knowledge bases and philosophies that surround the issue. Thus, I begin with a review of recent historical events that have led to heightened concern for reproductive health, then consider separately the physiology of reproduction, the population potentially exposed, the number of reproductive toxins and the state of knowledge concerning their toxicity, followed by a discussion of the legal and regulatory statutes that provide for the protection of reproductive health and for compensation when reproductive health has been damaged. I conclude with a consideration of the role of individuals and interest groups in changing and informing government and private sector policies.

Interest in and concern for protecting reproductive health[1] has increased in recent years due to several factors.

1. The rapid rise in the number and percentage of women in the workforce. Prior to World War II nearly 30 percent of women were employed outside the home. This proportion rose to 38 percent during the war, returned to 30 percent immediately thereafter, and has risen steadily

since 1945. In 1960, 38 percent of women over 15 years of age were employed; by April 1984, 54 percent were employed. Some 58 percent of American women are projected to be in the labor force by 1990.[2]

The proportion of married women who are employed has also increased rapidly, from 31 percent in 1960 to 55 percent in 1982. Married women with children accounted for most of this increase. Among married mothers with younger children, the proportion employed more than doubled, from 19 percent in 1960 to 45 percent in 1980.[3]

2. Damage to children whose mothers ingested apparently harmless drugs during pregnancy. The use of the nonprescription drug thalidomide by European women to treat minor headaches and insomnia during pregnancy caused major congenital malformations in their children. This tragedy heightened public awareness that a drug can damage the fetus even when it is not harmful to adults.[4] In addition, the use of a prescription drug, diethylstilbestrol (DES) by pregnant women to reduce the risk of miscarriage caused an increased frequency of a rare form of vaginal and cervical cancer in daughters born to these women.[5]

3. Publicity given to suspected reproductive effects of prolonged exposure to video display terminals (VDTs). Several major studies are now under way; a recently announced study indicates that exposure of less than 20 hours per week is not associated with any increase in spontaneous abortion.[6]

4. Evidence of workplace-induced reproductive damage to men. Workers in a chemical plant in California exposed to the pesticide DBCP (dibromochloropropane) became infertile. Moreover, male Vietnam veterans exposed to Agent Orange have reported increased frequencies of birth defects among their children.[7]

5. Lawsuits charging sex discrimination brought by female workers. Women working at the American Cyanamid Co. plant in West Virginia charged the company with discrimination when they were forced to undergo surgical sterilization in order to keep their jobs.[8]

These events are taking place within a milieu of heightened public awareness of adverse health effects from hazardous waste sites, contamination of our drinking water, and criticism of public officials and agencies charged with the protection of our health and environment. Workers are also becoming fearful that they may not be protected; a company can file Chapter 11 proceedings (for bankruptcy) in order to escape payment of damage claims, as the Johns Manville Company has done to protect itself from claims for adverse health effects resulting from exposure to asbestos.

The protection of reproductive health is an essential component of overall health protection because reproductive health is fundamentally important to individual well-being and safeguards the health of future generations. The major issue in the protection of reproductive health in the workplace is how to balance equal job opportunity for women with protection of the developing embryo/fetus. It is a problem in risk management. Not enough is known about toxic substances so that exposure levels can always be set; moreover, there is a time when a woman may not know she is pregnant. There are also the economic and privacy issues to be considered. Male and female workers may not wish to communicate to their employers that they are planning to have a child out of fear of losing a job or out of a fundamental desire for the right to privacy.

REPRODUCTIVE FUNCTION DEFINED

Normal reproductive function in the narrowest sense is the union of sperm and ovum to form a new organism. However, this union is only one event in a process that begins before birth. Reproduction function actually encompasses:

- The functional and structural integrity of the sperm and ova
- Differentiation and development of the internal and external reproductive organs and endocrine glands
- Activation of the adult reproductive system at puberty
- Senescence of the adult reproductive system
- Behaviors associated with or serving reproduction (libido)
- Maternal and paternal prenatal events
- Embryonic and fetal events (organogenesis)
- Maternal postnatal events (lactation)
- Child health and development.

Although seemingly impossible to measure, reproductive function can be assessed using a detailed patient history, a physical examination that includes blood samples, and a semen or urine sample.[9]

Reproductive function is an integral part of everyday human health and well-being and consists of interactions among multiple physiological systems. It is easy to assume that reproductive function not directly related to fertility is unimportant; however, impotence, menstrual pain, loss of libido, and contaminated breastmilk can have devastating consequences on individual well-being and human relationships.

THE LEVEL OF REPRODUCTIVE DYSFUNCTION[10] IN THE POPULATION

An estimated 2.4 million (8.4 percent) of American couples in which the wife is of childbearing age are unintentionally infertile. In many cases the infertility is transient and corrects itself without medical intervention; in other cases the infertility persists. In roughly one-third of infertile couples both are; in the remaining two-thirds, about half are women and the other half men.[11]

Spontaneous abortion (embyronic or fetal death before the 20th week) is a form of infertility since the inability to bring a pregnancy to term is the medical definition of infertility. The incidence of spontaneous abortion is difficult to determine, largely because most occur during the first few weeks when the woman may not realize she is pregnant. Estimates range from 30 to 75 percent of all pregnancies. One carefully controlled prospective study found that 43 percent of the embryos were lost by the 20th week of pregnancy.[12]

About 7 percent of all live-born infants manifest birth defects.[13] In 1982, 21 percent of all infant deaths were attributed to congenital anomalies, a proportion second only to that claimed by unspecified perinatal conditions.[14]

Elucidating cause is difficult; nevertheless, the etiology of birth defects has been apportioned as follows:

- genetic transmission—20 percent
- chromosomal abnormalities—5 percent
- therapeutic radiation—1 percent
- infection—2 to 3 percent
- maternal metabolic imbalance (e.g., diabetes)—3 to 5 percent
- drugs and environmental chemicals—2 to 3 percent.[15]

The origin of the remaining 63 to 67 percent of birth defects is unknown.

Infertility, birth defects, and spontaneous abortions are but three manifestations of reproductive dysfunction. Because reproductive function encompasses many processes, reproductive dysfunction can cause other health problems because of the interaction of the reproductive system with other systems. Alterations in sex hormone metabolism or production may, for example, increase the risk of heart disease or certain cancers in men and women. Early menopause increases the risk of osteoporosis. The prevalence of these manifestations of reproductive dysfunction in the population is unknown.

WHO IS EXPOSED IN THE WORKING POPULATION

Ascertaining the extent of exposure to hazards in the workplace is crucial. How many workers are at risk? How many workers are of reproductive age and how many of these workers are exposed to reproductive hazards? In what occupations are workers more likely to risk reproductive impairment? Unfortunately, the answers to several of these basic questions are unavailable.

In July 1986, there were 111.5 million employed workers (65.7 percent of the workforce). Men constituted 55.9 percent (62.3 million) and women, 44.1 percent (49.2 million).[16] About three-fourths of employed women were of reproductive age (16–44). Reproductive age limits for men are more difficult to identify because reproductive function is less strongly correlated with chronological age.

At present, there are no reliable estimates of the number of workers potentially exposed to reproductive or other health hazards. The National Institute for Occupational Safety and Health (NIOSH) is tabulating data from a recent survey, but these data will be tabulated only by sex, not by age.[17]

To date, only one study[18] has attempted to estimate the proportion of women who were employed during their pregnancies. In 1980, 63.2 percent of married women over 20 years of age who had delivered a live infant were employed at some time during the 12 months prior to the birth of their children. Of these women, an estimated 17 percent, or 314,000 mothers, worked in industries and occupations in which they faced possible exposure to 10 potential teratogens (agents that interfere with embryonic or fetal development).

Not only are data on the numbers of workers potentially exposed and the agents to which they are exposed generally unavailable, there is also a paucity of information on the reproductive effects of various agents found in the workplace.

THE NUMBER OF REPRODUCTIVE TOXINS IN THE WORKPLACE

The protection of workers and others from the harmful effects of ionizing radiation emitted at nuclear power plants was, until recently, a major focus of concern. As more and more chemicals have been produced, the emphasis has turned to the evaluation of the effects of chemicals that may be toxic. Attention has shifted from protecting the human genome (the total genetic information carried by an individual or a population) from the mutagenic effects of X-rays and radiation to protecting the population from the specific disease effects of specific chemicals produced by individual companies. Thus, the primary issue has moved from one of federally-regulated utilities and medical facilities, to one of government regulation of private companies that manufacture proprietary chemicals, with the result that more emphasis is placed on lawsuits for compensation of specific diseases or injury.

Most of the 5 million chemicals now in existence are probably not harmful at typical exposure levels. The National Academy of Sciences (NAS) estimates that there are about 53,500 chemicals to which individuals in the population potentially could be exposed. This total includes everything from industrial solvents to food additives. Many chemicals are manufactured in small quantities or are used in small amounts in research laboratories. In 1982, NAS estimated that of the more than then 48,000 chemicals (the number now exceeds 63,000) listed in the Toxic Substances Control Act (TSCA) inventory, only about 12,800 are manufactured in quantities of more than 1 million pounds per year; 13,900 are manufactured in quantities of less than 1 million pounds per year; and 21,700 are produced in unknown amounts. It is therefore unlikely that many people will be exposed to more than a few of these chemicals. But, because no publicly available toxicity information exists for more than 70 percent of the chemicals included in the TSCA inventory, it is not possible to evaluate their health effects.[19] In short, we don't know.

WHAT IS KNOWN REGARDING REPRODUCTIVE TOXINS

First, it is important to note that there must be exposure at high enough levels and for a long enough time period(s) to a toxic agent for damage to occur. The relationship between exposure and toxicity is crucial. There is essentially no risk if exposure duration(s) and amounts are insufficient. The issue—establishing safe exposure levels—is not just a scientific issue. It is an economic, social, value-laden, and, ultimately, a political issue.

Risk Assessment

The process whereby safe exposure levels are established is called risk assessment and management. Risk assessment is concerned with amassing and analyzing the scientific data; the management phase begins when economic, social, and legal ramifications are considered.[20] Risk assessment and management activities are carried out in industry but, also, most importantly in federal and state regulatory agencies (see next section for discussion). The two primary sources for scientific information are epidemiology and toxicology studies. Both are necessary to provide sufficient information, but both contain design considerations that make interpretation of results difficult.

Epidemiology Studies

The results of epidemiology studies[21] can be invalid because of the complexity of factors that must be dealt with in the design and execution of these studies. For example, if the investigator has not selected a carefully matched set of individuals for the control group, the results will not be valid. Measurement of reproductive endpoints (the particular biological response) is very difficult. Many endpoints are rare in the population, so large sample sizes are required to show whether the difference observed is a significant difference. For example, in order to detect a twofold increase in the spontaneous abortion rate (measured as the loss of a pregnancy from the time when a pregnancy is recognized to 20 weeks gestation), 161 pregnancies are needed in the exposure and control groups. Using customary assumptions about the birth rate and number of working women, the investigator would have to draw from a population of more than 11,000 workers to find a sufficient number of pregnancies to study. This is one of the difficulties in studying the effects of exposure to VDTs and suspected increases in spontaneous abortion rates. Many reproductive endpoints such as birth defects are very rare in populations so they require even larger samples.

Another problem is confounding factors. Confounding factors are correlated with both exposure and the outcome or effect being studied. For example, Down syndrome is associated with maternal age and with occupational exposure to radiation. Older workers would be likely to have higher cumulative exposure than younger workers. A finding that radiation exposure is associated with Down syndrome might be invalid because the Down syndrome might actually be associated with greater maternal age of the workers. Other confounding factors include smoking or alcohol consumption, and ethnic status. Thus, results from all epidemiological studies must be interpreted carefully.

Toxicology Studies

Toxicology studies[22] have a different set of methodological constraints. It is very difficult to extrapolate the effects observed at a particular dosage level in animals to similar effects that might occur in humans at comparable dosage levels (adjusted for body size, for example). One important goal in many toxicology studies is to establish a no observed effect level (NOEL). Since there is always a background rate of say, congenital malformation in an animal population, finding a NOEL is difficult. In addition, many indices, such as organ size or weight are continuously distributed; thus a decision must be made as to how much of a weight or size change is normal variation and thus a NOEL.

In spite of these and other constraints, toxicology studies are invaluable because they can predict a possible association with agents to which humans are exposed, in contrast to epidemiology studies in which humans will already have been affected by exposure to the hazard.

Risk Management

It is during the risk management phase that scientists and regulators must decide what is an acceptable risk and who will bear the burden of this risk. For example, assume that one case per 1,000 exposed workers is determined an acceptable level of risk. If industry justifiably (sometimes claims are unjustified) claims that installing equipment in order to lower the risk of uterine cancer to that level will be economically infeasible—actually disastrous—then less stringent acceptable levels must be established. Does this mean that only women who have had hysterectomies will be able to work in that environment? Or, will all workers be allowed to work after being informed of the risk? These are the policy decisions that must be made. And the science, itself, is inexact, calling for judgment calls because of gaps in information.

FEDERAL STATUTES ENACTED TO PROTECT WORKERS

Two federal statutes[23] have been enacted to manage the extent of exposure and protect the rights of workers: The Occupational Safety and Health Act (OSH Act), which gives the federal government the authority to protect workers to the extent feasible from substances that could damage their general and reproductive health; and Title VII of the Civil Rights Act, which forbids employment discrimination on the basis of sex or pregnancy.

The OSH Act

The OSH Act of 1970 gave the federal government responsibility for the occupational safety and health of more than 75 million working Americans, or some three-fourths of the work force (certain workplaces are exempt). The Occupational Safety and Health Administration (OSHA), the agency established by the OSH Act, is the primary regulator of hazardous occupational exposures. Some 25 states have federally approved OSHA programs that allow the states to implement and enforce the provisions of the OSH Act.

The OSH Act created two other agencies. One, the Occupational Safety and Health Review Commission (OSHRC), will not be discussed here.[24] The second, the National Institute for Occupational Safety and Health (NIOSH), is the agency that conducts research activities leading to the development of criteria or recommendations for OSHA's use in setting health and safety standards. NIOSH is a part of the Centers of Disease Control (CDC), which is, in turn, a part of the Public Health Service, while OSHA is a part of the Department of Labor. The separation of OSHA and NIOSH is controversial. The original intention was an attempt to keep scientific activities neutral; however, they never are. The result has been inefficiency and duplication. The separation has come under recent criticism because NIOSH recommendations are not binding on OSHA and reductions in technical staff at OSHA have limited OSHA's ability to evaluate the information it receives from NIOSH.[25]

OSHA has promulgated permanent standards for three substances—DBCP, lead, and ethylene oxide (EtO)—which include specific provisions for the protection of reproductive health. The DBCP standard resulted from observation of depressed sperm counts in 14 of 38 workers in a pesticide plant in California. Based on evidence of DBCP's carcinogenicity and gametoxicity, OSHA first issued an Emergency Temporary Standard in September 1977, followed by a permanent standard in March 1978. The DBCP standard requires workers to avoid dermal and eye contact and to wear protective clothing and respirators; requires employers to post signs and labels and provide worker information and training; and calls for preplacement and annual physical examinations that must include several specific tests of reproductive function. Although DBCP has subsequently been banned,[26] the standard is important for its recognition of hazards to male reproductive function.

The lead standard, promulgated in 1978 to prevent other health problems, especially neurological disorders, is significant because it is a precedent-setting gender-neutral standard with provisions designed to minimize reproductive harm. It is gender-neutral in its recognition that harmful effects can be transmitted from either or both parents to the embryo/fetus. In addition, the standard contains statements that specifically prohibit sex discrimination.[27] Promulgated in 1984, the EtO standard[28] is very similar to the lead standard in its provision for physical examinations that include reproductive histories, provisions for training of employees, and for the prominent display of information about potential health effects of EtO.

No substance will ever be regulated solely for its reproductive effects since any substance that causes reproductive impairment would cause other damage as well. The important consequence of these standards is that substances are now being evaluated for reproductive risk as well as carcinogenic or mutagenic risks.

The Civil Rights Act

Title VII of the Civil Rights Act prohibits sex discrimination by an employer of 15 or more persons engaged in an industry affecting commerce. In 1978, Congress amended Title VII to explicitly prohibit discrimination based on pregnancy. An employer cannot violate the act unless he or she can justify a Bona Fide Occupational Qualification or Business Necessity exemption.[29]

Three federal courts[30] have held that exclusion of fertile or pregnant women due to the existence of alleged hazards to the embryo/fetus is permissible if scientifically justified and if less discriminatory alternatives do not exist. Otherwise, such policies constitute illegal sex discrimination. Three general principles that guide exceptions have emerged from these cases:

1.   A fetal protection policy (FPP) that applies only to women is presumptively discriminatory. In the absence of strongly supportive scientific evidence, the employer will be liable under Title VII.
2.   To overcome this presumption, the employer must present scientific evidence supporting legal findings that (a) exposure at the level encountered in that workplace poses a significant risk of harm to the unborn children of women employees; (b) the exposure does not pose a similar risk to the offspring of male employees; and (c) the FPP is effective in significantly reducing the risk.
3.   Even if the employer proves both points 1 and 2, the plaintiff may still prevail by proving that an acceptable alternative policy would promote embryo/fetal health at least as well with a less adverse impact on one sex; or the plaintiff may prevail by showing that the FPP is in fact a pretext for discrimination.

It is sometimes argued that there is an inherent inconsistency between the OSH Act and Title VII—that the two cannot be reconciled in cases where protection of the health of an embryo/fetus is the primary goal. In general, an employer who provides a place of employment that is free of recognized hazards[31] and employs workers in a nondiscriminatory manner violates neither law. The difficulty arises because so little is known about the effects of exposure on either adults or on the developing embryo/fetus that it becomes a formidable task to determine that the workplace is free of recognized hazards or to estimate the risk of suspected hazards.

COMPENSATION WHEN IMPAIRMENT HAS OCCURRED

The OSH Act and Title VII of the Civil Rights Act are preventive measures. Other statutes come into play when reproductive impairment has occurred. Compensation, when it is available, must be obtained from the state workers' compensation system, or failing that, and if eligible, through litigation in the courts (tort liability).

States have jurisdiction over legislation and regulation of workers' compensation systems (Workmen's Compensation). Workers' compensation laws are relevant for reproductive disease or injury claims for the following reasons:

- most systems do not compensate for reproductive injury or impairment, and
- in most states, uncompensated workers are barred from suing their employers due to the exclusivity of remedy provision contained in workers' compensation statutes.

The latter condition means that in most states, even if *not* compensated for the workplace-induced injury or illness, the worker is barred from seeking tort redress. In addition to this constraint, qualifying for compensation is difficult. Workers are compensated only if the disease or injury is "personal," if it results in job disability, *and* if it is caused by workplace accident or exposure.[32]

Aside from values for accidental loss of a body part such as a testicle or breast, compensation schedules do not contain valuations for workplace-induced reproductive impairment. In addition, most reproductive impairment is treated through a worker's health insurance plan; that is, a worker who has a miscarriage or is suffering from impotency will go to a physician.

A central issue in compensation for reproductive impairment, which is also true for other occupational diseases such as cancer, is determining cause. Often there are several contributing factors, some of which may be due to the lifestyle of the individual or to exposure to toxins outside of the workplace. Furthermore, the evidence linking reproductive impairment to specific toxins is tenuous or unknown for many substances.

The personal injury requirement has another serious repercussion, which is a problem for parents and employers. In theory, though not usually in practice, both male and female workers are compensated for workplace-induced accidents or disease. But the embryo/fetus is not covered by this system. If a child is born with defects that have been caused by workplace exposure of either or both parents, the company could be liable for the damage caused to that child, if litigation is pursued. Hence many companies and hospitals rush to formulate fetal protection policies in order to protect themselves from this liability.

What are the consequences of these policies? First, there is the personal suffering and loss to the parents and the damaged child. Second, the tort system is capricious and uncertain. Often the plaintiffs lose, and do so after a great deal of money is spent. The workers' compensation system was implemented to avoid the inadequacy of the tort system. Third, there are further repercussions for the employers: an employer can be sued for care and maintenance and for punitive damages if the plaintiffs can prove that a damaged child sustained that injury because of toxins to which either or both parents were exposed in the workplace. To avoid potential liability, a company formulates a policy that excludes women of childbearing age and is not based on solid scientific evidence; the employer is then potentially liable for sex discrimination. Nevertheless, scientific information is scanty and the interpretations of scientists differ. For some employers, taking the less risky course bcomes the option acted upon: it is less risky to be sued for sex discrimination than for tort liability for a damaged child. Thus employers implement FPPs that exclude women of childbearing age. The fallacy of this extends beyond discrimination of women, however. Males exposed to toxins may transmit effects, especially genetic damage, to their offspring.

Even for employers desiring to comply, the legal risk must be reconciled with competing interests. The employer is justifiably concerned with profitability. Small businesses may not be able to afford medical removal programs that include placement of workers in other positions with maintenance benefits, salary, and seniority. If workers are harmed, there may be an increase in absenteeism due to health problems—some due to reproductive system impairment itself, others to the physical and emotional consequences of such impairment. In addition, workers may consider being required to inform their employer of intentions to procreate an invasion of privacy.

CONCLUSION

The management of exposure to reproductive toxins in the workplace is exceedingly complex and difficult. Risk assessment rests on an inadequate scientific base. Not only is there not enough known but methodologies are flawed. New substances are entering the workplace each month and research cannot keep up with evaluation of even the substances in existence.

Women are entering the workforce in unprecedented numbers. This is a result of the women's movement and is a part of a social and economic transformation of our country. Paternalistic attitudes and protectionist policies have been enacted in years after women have entered the labor force in relatively larger numbers.[33]

Many legal experts and labor leaders believe that it is difficult, if not impossible, to reconcile the provisions of Title VII with the OSH Act. Although there is always uncertainty regarding risk, large companies can institute medical removal policies (MRPs) that will protect the seniority and wage levels of men and women who wish to procreate. For small businesses, however, who employ the larger proportion of workers in this country, MRPs may be economically infeasible.

Ultimately, however, a damaged child can sue its parents' employer(s) no matter what kind of MRPs are in force. This is the dilemma for employer, employee, and legislator. For politicians, resolution of the issue rests on competing value systems. Should laws be enacted to protect the hypersusceptible (translate: pregnant) worker, or should laws be enacted to protect the majority of workers? Those arguing for protection of all workers maintain that if we do not legislate to protect even the hyper-susceptible worker, industry will not clean up the workplace, but will, instead, state that certain workers are hypersusceptible and therefore barred access to particular workplaces (which is sex discrimination). Industry argues that cleaning the workplace to the degree necessary to protect the hypersusceptible worker is economically and scientifically infeasible and that there is no such thing as zero risk.

Obviously everyone wants to have his or her health and opportunity to obtain a job protected. Many individuals do not wish to inform their employers when they wish to procreate because they fear discrimination. At the same time, reproductive health may not be even as well protected as it has been. With recent budget cuts at OSHA, the number of workplace inspections has decreased. In addition, recent shifts in the Supreme Court may mean changes in the interpretation of Title VII and the OSH Act.

What means are open to workers who wish to protect their reproductive health? First, become informed. There are agencies, both state and federal, as well as newsletters and publications, with specific information on toxic substances and their effects.[34] Second, workers must talk with their employers to find out what substances they are being exposed to and whether the employer has information on those substances and the levels of exposure to those substances. Find out if the employer has a medical removal policy (MRP) for men and women who wish to procreate and/or a fetal protection policy (FPP) for pregnant women.

What are the essential features of a MRP or FPP? First, the company should have a stated, preferably written, policy or set of procedures. Second, the management should be informed regarding the substances in the workplace and have taken measures to eliminate or significantly reduce exposure to hazards wherever feasible. Ambient air levels should be monitored. There should be an active campaign to educate and inform workers. (Under the Hazard Communication Standard, or Right to Know, employers are required to inform workers about the substances to which they are exposed.) If reproductive hazards are present at levels that pose a risk, an MRP should be in force. Note that an MRP that excludes only pregnant workers ignores possible effects of agents to which the father or mother may have been exposed prior to conception. An MRP should assure the worker equal pay and benefits and retention of seniority. The employer should recommend or require notification of pregnancy or planning for procreation, and should provide for employee counseling from an occupational health physician or the employee's private physician. Most importantly, the individual worker must become informed, then set up a dialogue with employers, unions, and organizations interested in protecting worker health and safety.

Finally, the center of concern for reproductive health hazards must change. All parties must become aware that reproductive health is not just a women's issue. Men suffer reproductive impairment and can pass genetic changes to their offspring. When the protection of reproductive health is viewed as a part of total health protection and well-being for all individuals as well as the developing embyro/fetus, FPPs that discriminate against women workers are less likely to be implemented.

NOTES AND REFERENCES

1. The author served as project director for the OTA assessment, *Reproductive Health Hazards in the Workplace*, U.S. Congress, OTA, Dec. 1985, U.S. Government Printing Office, OTA-BA-266. Further discussion of the issues raised in this chapter can be found there as well as in the references listed below.

2. U.S. Department of Labor, Bureau of Labor Statistics, *Handbook of Labor Statistics*, Bulletin 2175, December 1983.

3. D. Makuc and N. Lalich, "Employment Characteristics of Mothers During Pregnancy," *Health, United States, and Prevention Profile, 1983*, National Center for Health Statistics, DHHS Publication No. (PHS) 84-1232 (Washington, DC: U.S. Government Printing Office, December 1983), pp. 25–32.

4. The thalidomide tragedy focused research on teratogenic effects, when, in fact most toxins are harmful to the mother as well as to the developing embyro fetus. In fact, thalidomide is an atypical teratogen.

5. For effects in daughters and sons see W. Gill, "Transplacental Effects of Diethylstilbestrol on the Human Male Fetus: Abnormal Semen and Anatomical Lesions of the Male Genital Tract," *Proceedings of a Conference on Women and the Workplace*, Society for Occupational and Environmental Health, June 17–19, 1976; 1977, p. 39–46; S. J. Robboy, K. L. Noller, P. O'Brien, R. H. Kaufman, et al., "Increased Incidence of Cervical and Vaginal Dysplasia in 3,980 Diethylstilbestrol-Exposed Young Women," *J.A.M.A.* 252 (Dec. 7, 1984): 2979–2983; and W. R. Welch, "Transplacental Carcinogenesis: Prenatal Diethylstilbestrol (DES) Exposure, Clear Cell Carcinoma and Related Anomalies of the Genital Tract in Young Females," *Proceedings of a Conference on Women and the Workplace*, pp. 47–50. A recent study disputes findings in male offspring: F. J. Leary, L. J. Resseguie, L. T. Kurland, P. C. O'Brien, et al., "Males Exposed In Utero to Diethylstilbestrol," *J.A.M.A.* 252 (Dec. 7, 1984): 2984–2989.

6. NIOSH is currently conducting a 3-year study that involves a cohort of 2,000 VDT-exposed women and 2,000 nonexposed controls. All women are employed in nonmanagement positions in one geographic area. Reproductive, health, and work histories will be obtained by self-administered questionnaires completed at three 9-month intervals. Personal habits such as alcohol, tobacco, and caffeine use will also be measured. NIOSH is not planning any similar studies of men. Another prospective study of 10,000 office workers has been initiated by Mount Sinai School of Medicine in cooperation with the Service Employees International Union and

the 9 to 5 Association of Working Women. Both male and female workers exposed to VDTs will be compared with a group of nonexposed workers. Participants will complete extensive health questionnaires on a regular basis. Follow-up studies are planned to determine whether children of VDT workers suffer increased incidence of cancer. Recent study results announced at the 1986 annual meetings of the American Public Health Association indicated that exposure to less than 20 hours per week is not associated with adverse pregnancy outcomes.

7. The DBCP case was the first to highlight the importance of hazards that affect male reproductive function. Prior to this, most studies of reproductive hazards had been carried out on wives of workers and their offspring or women and their offspring. Informal discussion among male workers in a California pesticide factory manufacturing DBCP disclosed the fact that their wives had been having trouble conceiving since the husbands began working at the plant. After considerable urging, one worker convinced five others to submit semen samples for analysis; all samples were determined to be grossly abnormal. A subsequent study indicated that, except in cases of exposure greater than 100 hours, the effects of DBCP on male fertility appear to reversible. However, there is some evidence of an altered sex ratio in subsequent births to wives of the exposed workers (far more females than males). The policy ramifications are significant. When male reproductive capacity was endangered, men of reproductive age were not removed from their jobs. Instead, the hazardous agent was banned. The treatment of women workers in similar circumstances has sometimes been reversed; when developmental hazards to the embryo/fetus have been identified, the women, rather than the hazards, have been removed. In at least two instances female X-ray technicians were removed from their jobs because of suspected risks, and in another case women had themselves sterilized because they believed it was the only way they could retain their jobs (for discussion of these cases, see chapter 8, U.S. Congress, OTA, December 1985). For information on Agent Orange, see: M. Gough, *Dioxin, Agent Orange, The Facts* (New York: Plenum Press); P. H. Schuck, *Agent Orange on Trial, Mass Toxic Disasters in the Courts* (Cambridge, MA: Harvard University Press, 1986).

8. For further discussion of this case, see U.S. Congress, OTA, Dec. 1985, Chapter 8.

9. For discussion of reproductive function tests, see J. H. Belina and J. Wilson, *You Can Have A Baby*, (New York: Crown Publishers, 1985).

10. Reproductive dysfunction is naturally occurring levels of reproductive or infertility problems; reproductive impairment connotes reproductive dysfunction that is caused by an agent, such as exposure to a toxic substance in the workplace.

11. W. D. Mosher, "Fecundity and Infertility in the United States, 1965–1982," National Center for Health Statistics, paper presented at the Annual Meeting of the Population Association of America, Minneapolis, MN, May 3–5, 1984.

12. F. D. Abramson, "Spontaneous Fetal Death in Man," *Social Biology* 20 (1973): 375–403; J. F. Miller, E. Williamson, J. Glue, Y. B. Gordon, J. G. Grudzinska, and A. Sykes, "Fetal Loss After Implantation: A Prospective Study," *Lancet*, Sept. 13, 1980, pp. 554–556.

13. A birth defect is any structural, functional, or biochemical abnormality, whether genetically determined or induced during gestation.

14. March of Dimes, *Facts/1984*, White Plains, NY, March of Dimes Birth Defects Foundation, 1984; U.S. Department of Health and Human Services, National Center for Health Statistics, "Advance Report of Final Natality Statistics, 1981" *Monthly Vital Statistics Report*, Vol. 32, No. 9, Supplement, Dec. 29, 1983.

15. J. G. Wilson, "Environmental Effects on Development—Teratology," in *Pathophysiology of Gestation*, Vol. 2, N. S. Assali (ed.) (New York: Academic Press, 1972), pp. 269–320.

16. Department of Labor, Bureau of Labor Statistics, *Employment and Earnings,* August 1986.

17. Contact NIOSH information office, Cincinnati, Ohio for tabulations.

18. The results of this survey are limited because only married women who delivered a term live birth were included, only three physical agents and seven chemicals were labeled potentially teratogenic, and the exposure of the women in the sample was not measured. Potential exposure was linked to the occupations that women reported. Nevertheless, the study is a beginning. See D. Makuc and N. Lalich, "Employment Characteristics of Mothers," 1983.

19. National Academy of Sciences, Steering Committee on Identification of Toxic and Potentially Toxic Chemicals for Consideration by the National Toxicology Program, Board on Toxicology and Environmental Health Hazards, Commission on Life Sciences, National Research Council, *Toxicity Testing: Strategies to Determine Needs and Priorities* (Washington DC: 1984).

20. For further discussion of risk assessment and management, see C. Coodley, "Risk in the 1980's: New Perspectives on Managing Chemical Hazards," *San Diego Law Rev. 21* (5): 1015–1044, Sept.-Oct., 1984; National Academy of Sciences, *Risk Assessment in the Federal Government: Managing the Process* (Washington, DC: National Academy Press, 1983); J. V. Rodricks, and R. C. Tardiff, "Risk Assessment: How It's Done, and How It Might Be," *Chemtech.* 14: 394–397, July, 1984.

21. Epidemiology is the study of relationships between the frequency and distribution, and the factors that may influence frequency and distribution of diseases and injuries in human populations. For discussion of difficulties in epidemiology research on reproductive hazards, see A. D. Bloom (ed.), *Guidelines for Studies of Human Populations Exposed to Mutagenic and Reproductive Hazards*, Proceedings of a Conference held Jan. 26–27, 1981, Washington, DC, March of Dimes Birth Defects Foundation, White Plains, NY, 1981; J. Kline, Z. Stein, B. Strobino, M. Susser, and D. Warburton, "Surveillance of Spontaneous Abortions: Power in Environmental Monitoring," *Prev. Med.* 9: 267–274, 1977; I. C. T. Nisbet and N. J. Karch, *Chemical Hazards to Human Reproduction*, Park Ridge, NJ: Noyes Data Corp., 1983; E. Sever and N. A. Hessol, "Overall Design Considerations in Male and Female Occupational Reproductive Studies," *Reproduction: The New Frontier in Occupational and Environmental Health Research*, New York: Alan R. Liss, Inc., 1984, pp. 15–47; Z. Stein, M. Hatch, J. Kline and D. Warburton, "Epidemiologic Considerations in Assessing Health Effects at Chemical Waste Sites," *Assessment of Health Effects at Chemical Disposal Sites*, Proceedings of a Symposium held June 1–2, 1981, New York, W. W. Lowrance (ed.), New York: The Rockefeller University Press, 1981, pp. 126–145; D. Warburton, "Selection of Human Reproductive Effects for Study," in W. W. Lowrance, 1981, pp. 106–124; M. J. Rosenberg and L. H. Kuller, "Reproductive Epidemiology: What are the Problems in Methodology?" *Reproductive Health Policies in the Workplace*, 1983, pp. 201–226.

22. Toxicology studies are in vitro and whole animal tests of suspected hazards. For discussion of animal testing, see S. M. Barlow and F. M. Sullivan, *Reproductive Hazards of Industrial Chemicals* (New York: Academic Press, 1982); C. A. Kimmel, *Reliability of Experimental Studies for Predicting Hazards to Human Development*, National Center for Toxicological Research, Technical Report for

Experiment No. 6015, Jefferson, AR, Jan. 1984; I. C. T. Nisbet and N. J. Karch, 1983.

23. Three additional major statutes that apply to occupational reproductive risk are the Toxic Substances Control Act (TSCA); the Federal Insecticide, Fungicide, and Rodenticide Act (FIFRA); and the Atomic Energy Act (AEA). Standards under these acts are all set in the Environmental Protection Agency (EPA). Under these mandates, EPA is required to protect farmworkers although these mandates are not specifically written to protect occupational health. This lack of clear authority has been one of the reasons why protection of farmworkers has often "fallen through the cracks."

24. OSHRC is an independent, quasi-judicial review board whose duties are limited to reviewing OSHA citations issued to employers charged with violating OSHA standards. OSHRC is composed of three members, appointed by the president with the advice and consent of the Senate, for staggered terms of 6 years.

25. For discussion of OSHA and NIOSH, see U.S. Congress, OTA, December 1985; U.S. Congress, OTA, *Preventing Illness and Injury in the Workplace*, April 1985, U.S. GPO OTA-H-256; M. A. Rothstein, "Substantive and Procedural Obstacles to OSHA Rulemaking: Reproductive Hazards as an Example," *Boston College Environmental Affairs Law Review 12* (Summer 1985): 627–700.

26. DBCP was banned by EPA in 1979, except for use in Hawaiian pineapple fields. In January 1985, EPA canceled registration even for Hawaiian pineapple fields after finding DBCP contamination of groundwater. Unfortunately, the ban did not go into effect until 1987; also see not #7.

27. The lead standard contains the following gender-neutral provisions for protecting reproductive health: Male or female workers who plan to procreate can request pregnancy testing or laboratory evaluation of male infertility. The standard sets a technologically feasible permissible exposure level (50 $\mu g/m^3$ which yields average blood levels of 35 to 40 $\mu g/100g$) and minimizes adverse reproductive effects by: (a) establishing a 30 $\mu g/100g$ action level above which biological and air monitoring are initiated; (b) utilizing the provisions of medical surveillance, including infertility testing, physician reviews, and medical removal to identify and perhaps remove workers who may wish to plan a pregnancy or who are pregnant; and (c) ensuring, through the education and training provisions of the standard, that workers are fully informed of the potential reproductive as well as other health hazards from exposure to lead. The preamble to the lead standard in 43 Fed. Reg. 220:52966 (1978) details the arguments for different action levels put forward by industry and scientists.

28. EtO is a clear, colorless gas that is used as a chemical intermediate in the production of pesticides and as a sterilant and fumigant for hospital equipment. Because of its use in farm and nonfarm environments, regulation could fall under FIFRA by EPA or the OSH Act by OSHA. OSHA finally set the standard.

29. A BFOQ exception is an exception to Title VII's prohibition against employment policies that intentially discriminate against one sex. Intentional discrimination is permitted if sex is a bona fide occupational qualification (e.g., a male actor to portray a male character). The Business Necessity Exception is an exception to Title VII's prohibition against sex-neutral employment policies that have a disparate impact on one sex. A policy with a disparate impact on one sex is permissible if the policy is necessary to achieve a business purpose.

30. Three cases have led to the development of these principles, *Hayes v. Shelby Memorial Hospital*; *Zuniga v. Kleberg County Hospital*; and *Wright v. Olin Corp.* In the *Hayes* case, an Alabama hospital hired a female X-ray technician. Two

months later, the technician was fired after she informed her supervisor that she was pregnant. The technician filed a sex discrimination suit against the hospital in Federal court. The hospital defended on the grounds of a BFOQ and business necessity. The trial court concluded that the hospital violated Title VII and awarded the technician damages. The hospital appealed and the appellate court upheld the lower court's decision. The *Zuniga* case was another one of the hospital firing a pregnant X-ray technician, but the case occurred prior to the effective date of the Pregnancy Act of Title VII. Nevertheless, the court held the policy to be discriminatory because of its impact on women. The *Wright v. Olin* case, better known as the Cyanamid case (Olin is a subsidiary), resulted from a FPP that required fertile women to be excluded from certain work environments. As a result of this policy two women workers were transferred to janitorial jobs, while several other women underwent surgical sterilization because they feared they would lose their jobs. A settlement for $200,000 plus costs and attorney's fees was agreed to. Thus the company never admitted liability under Title VII. For discussion of these and other cases see OTA, Dec 1985, ch. 8 and M. A. Rothstein, "Reproductive Hazards and Sex Discrimination in the Workplace: New Legal Concerns in Industry and on Campus," *The J. of Coll. and Univ. Law, 10* (Spring 1983–84): 495–514.

31. A recognized hazard under OSHA is (a) common knowledge in the employer's industry, and (b) employer's actual or constructive knowledge of the hazardous condition.

32. A personal injury or disease precludes compensation for injuries or diseases suffered by others, such as the worker's spouse, fetus, child, or descendant. Although states differ, the laws generally provide for several classes of benefits for different classes of liability such as loss of earnings, medical costs, death, etc. The injury or illness must have been caused by exposure to a hazard in the workplace. This also makes claims for reproductive damage difficult since many reproductive injuries are caused by other factors in addition to workplace exposure.

33. J. M. Stellman, *Women's Work, Women's Health* (New York: Pantheon Books, 1977).

34. Sources for help: Committees on Occupational Safety and health (COSH) groups were formed during the Carter administration. Forty still exist although most are underfunded; the Public Citizen Health Research Group in Washington, DC is a part of the Ralph Nader network of organizations; the Women's Occupational Health Resource Center at Columbia University in New York publishes a bimonthly newsletter and publishes "factpacks" on various occupational hazards; the National Campaign Against Toxic Hazards, Washington, DC assists in organizing and lobbying; the Occupational Health Legal Rights Foundation, Washington, DC assists union members and their families; the Workplace Health Fund, Washington, DC provides research and education; and the Health Hazard Evaluation Program, a part of NIOSH in Cincinnati, Ohio, conducts hazard evaluations of workplace environments.

7

The Womb Factor: Policy on Pregnancy and the Employment of Women

Patricia Huckle

Men and women are biologically different; that is not a political statement, but a fact. What does having a womb mean in terms of employment? What are some of the consequences assumed to follow from women's capacity to reproduce, as reflected in public law and policy?

Since the mid-1960s, feminists have acknowledged the importance of public policies and programs in generating opportunities for women, and have geared much of their political efforts toward changing existing laws and developing strategies that will result in greater social, political and economic independence for women.[1] This chapter examines legislative and judicial decisions with respect to treatment of pregnancy as a public policy issue. Its context is the interaction of judges, career bureaucrats, lobbyists, and legislative committees as they set the terms by which employers treat women workers.

By reviewing restrictions on women's employment it is possible to see more clearly the relationship between social structure and individual options. It is also possible to examine the development of a feminist political strategy that is both pragmatic (acknowledging the incremental nature of social change) and drastic in its long-range implications for defining work and women's relationship to both production and reproduction.

The issue of employment policies and pregnancy becomes increasingly significant as women who might and do bear children join the labor force. Most women in the United States will be employed at some time in their lives. Pregnant women and mothers are employed in dramatically larger numbers today than in the past, with 64 percent of women in childbearing years employed in 1984.[2] As Sheila B. Kamerman testified, "More than 80 percent of employed women are in the child bearing years and 93 percent of these are likely to become pregnant during their working lives."[3]

How do employers, lawmakers and judges deal with the fact that women have the capacity to become pregnant? Implicitly the question comes down to whether women are just like men, and therefore should be treated the same for employment purposes, or whether women are not only different, but deserve special treatment. This chapter briefly traces the historical treatment of pregnant or potentially pregnant women, and describes the process of amending the Civil Rights Act of 1964 to include pregnancy discrimination as sex discrimination. The changing patterns of public policy are weighed against prevailing expectations.

SEVENTY YEARS' WORTH OF ASSUMPTIONS

A review of U.S. Supreme Court decisions and employer policies illustrates the attitudes toward women that affect current policy-making. From *Muller v. Oregon*[4] to *Gilbert v. General Electric*,[5] the womb factor has affected women's employment opportunities. Quite often, restrictive policies developed out of an interest in "protecting women." Often these "protected" women from not only long hours but also overtime pay and advancement.[6] The Muller case was one step in the long labor movement struggle to achieve better working conditions for all workers. It was also a case with dramatic long-term consequences for women. The rationale in *Muller v. Oregon* assumed the physical frailty of women because of their capacity to reproduce, and took for granted women's dependency on men (reinforced by marriage and property laws):

> That woman's physical structure and the performance of maternal functions place her at a disadvantage in the struggle for subsistence is obvious. This is especially true when the burdens of motherhood are upon her. Even when they are not . . . continuance for a long time on her feet at work . . . tends to injurious effects upon the body, and as healthy mothers are essential to vigorous offspring, the physical well-being of a woman becomes an object of public interest and care in order to preserve the strength and vigor of the race . . . she is properly placed in a class by herself. . . . "[7]

The protective rationale and classification by sex have continued to define the boundaries within which women provide economic support for themselves and their families. As a result of these assumptions, the law, employer policies, and judicial interpretations might be summarized as follows: if she is pregnant, woman needs protection; if she is not pregnant, she might some day be, and therefore it is rational to protect (or exclude) her in advance.[8]

Because of their assumed frailty and dependence, women have been excluded from many jobs. Only when "manpower" has been diverted for other purposes such as war have employers encouraged women to accept a wider range of tasks. During the 1920s and 1930s, when jobs were scarce, women were assumed to be disposable workers. In congressional testimony, Kathleen Williams reported that women were told home and child rearing should be their primary goals: "A National Education Association study in 1930–31 revealed that 77 percent of all school systems surveyed refused to hire wives; sixty-three percent dismissed women teachers if they subsequently married."[9] During the Depression, cities campaigned against hiring married women and many state legislatures considered restrictive laws.[10] If women were employed and retained after marriage, they were frequently fired as soon as pregnancy became known.[11] In a 1942 study the Children's Bureau observed that protection of the woman and fetus was the formal justification, but there was also some indication that "aesthetic and moral" qualms about the presence of pregnant women in the classroom influenced such dismissals. In these cases, women lost jobs because their "natural" and primary role offended others.[12] Nancy Erickson notes resistance by women workers in the 1952 effort by the New York Women's Trade Union League to amend the state disability benefits law "to cover disabilities caused by pregnancy and childbirth."[13]

Although there have been some legal modifications since World War II, a heritage lingers. Despite antidiscrimination laws, some employers ask women if they are married or plan to be, if they intend to have children, and what form of birth control they use. In the event that they exercise a right to bear children, women have been fired or forced to take extended leaves of absence whether capable of working or not. They have been denied unemployment benefits. Women on pregnancy leave have lost seniority and returned to work as new employees at lower levels.[14]

Several Supreme Court decisions in the 1970s dealt with the issues of marriage and reproduction as they affect employment. A regulation forbidding employment of married women was ruled illegal under Title VII of the Civil Rights Act of 1964,[15] in *Sprogis v. United Air Lines, Inc.*[16] Also declared illegal in *Phillips v. Martin-Marietta Corp*[17] was the refusal to hire women with pre-school age children. In *Cleveland Board of Eduction v. LaFleur*,[18] the Supreme Court declared aribtrary, mandatory maternity leave requirements unconstitutional, and indicated that maternity leaves should be determined on an individual basis. In *Turner v. Dept. of Employment Security*,[19] the Court decided that a state may not exclude pregnant women from eligibility for unemployment benefits solely because they are pregnant. In *Nashville Gas Co. v. Satty*,[20] the Court decided that a policy of not awarding sick leave pay to pregnant employees was not *prima facie* evidence of sex discrimination, but did rule that a policy that employees on pregnancy leave lose all job-bidding seniority resulted in discrimination against women.

Partly in response to the Supreme Court decisions interpreting the scope of Title VII's sex discrimination provisions, partly due to the development of guidelines from the Equal Employment Opportunity Commission (EEOC),[21] and partly due to the sharpened awareness of employers and employees, policies have changed. In one Prentice-Hall survey of employers, conducted in 1965, 40 percent of offices and 75 percent of plants had pregnancy leave policies. Most employers who had policies required early leave, and fewer than 10 percent permitted the employee to decide at what point the leave would begin.[22]

By 1972, the EEOC had issued new guidelines for treatment of pregnant employees. It was clear that EEOC considered refusal to hire pregnant applicants sex discriminatory. The guidelines also addressed treatment of pregnant employees:

> Disabilities caused or contributed to by pregnancy, miscarriage, abortion, childbirth, and recovery therefrom, are, for all job-related purposes, temporary disabilities and should be treated as such under any health or temporary disability insurance or sick leave plan available in connection with employment.[23]

By 1972 three-quarters of employers surveyed by Prentice-Hall had maternity leave policies, and 60 percent allowed the employee and her physician to determine length of employment.[24] In their 1973 survey, Prentice-Hall was able to report that 90 percent of the employers surveyed had formal maternity leave provisions. They noted:

> The most frequent policy change reported is the switch to paid maternity leaves. Many firms told us their former policies included paid sick leave, but no pay for maternity leave; most of these companies said they now pay accrued sick pay to employees on maternity leave.[25]

These surveys suggest the extent to which employers, by the early 1970s, were beginning to respond to pressures from women employees, and from the courts and administrative agencies to make some provisions which treat pregnancy as a work disability. Most of these changes were occurring in places of employment, not in government subsidy to women.[26]

In a 1976 telephone survey of California cities, 70 percent of the respondents allowed women to use accrued sick leave for absences due to childbirth, although most of these cities also said they had no formal policy, and women were able to take leave without pay. In some California cities there were no women employees, or so few that the question had never been raised. The small city of Mill Valley stated that they didn't have a maternity leave policy because, "We don't get pregnant."[27]

Two Supreme Court decisions in the 1970s highlighted both resistance to change and the continuing legacy of the *Muller v. Oregon* assumptions. At about the same time that mandatory maternity leaves were held unconstitutional, the Supreme Court held in *Geduldig v. Aiello* that exclusion of pregnancy from a state disability plan was constitutional, since the issue was "not one of gender discrimination" prohibited by the 14th Amendment.

In explaining its decision that exclusion of pregnancy from income protection insurance was not sex discrimination, the Court said:

> The California insurance program does not exclude any one from benefit eligibility because of gender but merely removes one physical condition—pregnancy—from the list of compensable disabilities. . . . Normal pregnancy is an objectively identifiable physical condition with unique characteristics. . . . The lack of identity between the excluded disability and gender becomes clear . . . the program divides potential recipients into two groups—pregnant women and nonpregnant persons. While the first group is exclusively female, the second includes members of both sexes. . . . There is no risk from which men are protected and women are not. Likewise, there is no risk from which women are protected and men are not.[28]

The state could exclude pregnancy from conditions covered by its disability plan without infringing on constitutional rights. Feminists expected that the broader scope of Title VII would yield a different result, but this was a false hope since the Court's interpretation in *Gilbert v. General Electric*, as in the *Geduldig* case based on state law, was the same. Writing for the majority, Justice Rehnquist stated:

> There is no more showing of discrimination here than in *Geduldig* that the exclusion of pregnancy benefits is a "mere pretext" designed to effect an invidious discrimination. . . . Respondents have not made the requisite showing of gender-based effects. . . . There is no proof that the package is in fact worth more to men than women.[29]

Although six federal courts of appeals and 18 federal districts had by this time accepted the EEOC's pregnancy guidelines, the *Gilbert* decision disagreed. In his dissenting argument, Justice Brennan wrote that: "A violation is triggered because omission of pregnancy from the program has the intent and effect of providing that only women are subjected to a substantial risk of total loss of income because of temporary medical disability." He further argued that the General Electric plan should have been examined in light of their employment history with respect to women, and the broad social objectives of Title VII. He went on, "Surely it offends common sense to suggest . . . that a classification revolving around pregnancy is not, at a minimum, strongly sex-related." He commented that pregnancy is not always voluntary, and that the plan covered other voluntary disabilities, some of them specific to men, including sports injuries, attempted suicides, cosmetic surgery, prostatectomies, vasectomies and circumcisions. Justice Stevens also dissented, commenting: "The rule at issue places the risk of absence caused by pregnancy in a class by itself. By definition, such a rule discriminates on account of sex; for it is the capacity to become pregnant which primarily differentiates the female from the male."

THE RESPONSE: THE ONGOING POLITICAL STRUGGLE

The *Gilbert* decision triggered media and organizational response. Surprise and rage characterized the women's movement's statements. Karen DeCrow, speaking for the National Organization for Women (NOW), stated that NOW had been so sure of an opposite conclusion that they had prepared a 2-year implementation strategy. Susan Ross, of the ACLU Women's Rights Project, said, "The Supreme Court today legalized sex discrimination."[30]

Womanpower published a selection of comments from newspaper editorials criticizing the *Gilbert* decision[31]:

> . . . flies in the face of reality, makes little economic sense, and is bad social policy. . . . Asked to carry on the race by bearing children [women] are penalized economically for doing so. (Boston, *Evening Globe*)

> The French exclaim: Vive la difference! when talking about women. The U.S. Supreme Court states on the same subject: Too bad about that difference! (*Hartford Courant*)

> There is, of course, an ultimate remedy. If more of the people who run the corporations, make the country's laws, and sit on the Supreme Court were capable of becoming pregnant, we have no doubt that pregnancy benefits would be the norm. (Hackensack, *Sunday Record*)

At the time of the decision, 22 states required employers to pay disability benefits to pregnant workers.[32] The California law upheld in *Geduldig v. Aiello* had been changed, and several other states notified employers that failure to follow EEOC guidelines would be discriminatory.[33] Within weeks of the *Gilbert* decision, a coalition of civil rights and women's groups, the Campaign to End Discrimination Against Pregnant Workers, had formed " . . . to secure legislation assuring that prohibitions against sex discrimination in employment also prohibit discrimination because of pregnancy."[34] Two months later it was reported that a group of businessmen had begun to organize to lobby for elimination of the pregnancy disability coverage required by Connecticut law.[35]

By spring 1977, hearings were being conducted on new legislation to amend the Civil Rights Act. The Senate committee opened its hearings as follows:

> By concluding that pregnancy discrimination is not sex discriminatory . . . the Supreme Court disregarded the intent of Congress in enacting

Title VII. That intent was to protect all individuals from unjust employment discrimination, including pregnant women.[36]

Analysis of both hearings points out some basic threads that go beyond the specific concern for income protection of pregnant women. The larger questions for both sides include: (a) What is the role of women as workers in the United States? (b) Who bears the responsibility for child bearing in this society? (c) Who must bear the costs for social change or maintaining the status quo? (d) What is the appropriate role of government in regulating employment?

Among those who spoke in favor of the bill were many who had also participated in the *Gilbert* case, many of them also members of the Campaign to End Discrimination. The coalition of interests included in part: Ruth Weyand, attorney, International Union of Electrical, Radio and Machine Workers, and counsel in *Gilbert*; Susan D. Ross, ACLU; and representatives from NAACP, AFL-CIO, American Nurses' Assoc., Joseph & Rose Kennedy Institute, United Automobile, Aerospace and Agricultural Implement Workers of America, United Steelworkers of America, Communications Workers of America, American Citizens Concerned for Life, Inc., and the National Conference of Catholic Bishops. Some of the opponents were also familiar from the *Gilbert* days, including National Association of Manufacturers, Metropolitan Life Insurance Association of America, American Retail Federation, and the U.S. Chamber of Commerce. Patterns in the testimony of these groups and individuals as they speak to the larger societal issues are outlined above.

Women as Workers

Advocates for the bill emphasized that women are an integral, not temporary, part of the work force. Most women, in this view, are employed because of economic need; all need job protection just as men do. The social goal is to generate employment opportunities so that the most productive use of human resources can be made. Employment and career patterns should be determined by individual capabilities and not sex role expectations. Opponents testified primarily about the negative consequences of providing pregnancy disability benefits to pregnant women. Pregnant women would malinger, inclined to stay away from work longer, and insist on the maximum period of benefits. They might convince physicians that their condition required extended leave; employers would then be paying much greater benefits than for other employees. Beyond this, they argue that pregnant women would quit after maternity leave, and receive severance pay not available to others.

In response, advocates argued that while data on terminations following pregnancy are incomplete, preliminary evidence from employers currently providing income protection for pregnant workers indicates no serious changes, and there may even be some incentives to return to work following pregnancy. Further, they questioned the assumption that women are more likely than men to malinger, especially given employer requirements for medical certification of leaves. This assumption supports the traditional view of women as temporary workers and perpetuates the stereotype of the devious female.

There is tension here between the traditional perspective and the vision of advocates for change. Advocates for change see women as full members of the labor force, not exactly as men are, but as women who are workers and who also bear children. The traditional perspective is that if women are to be employed, they must not expect more than equal treatment—meaning the same as what men receive.

Childbearing

Those who opposed this legislation followed the line of argument used in the *Gilbert* case. Pregnancy is by and large a voluntary condition in these times: " . . . commonly desired and generally planned. The resulting expenses are usually predictable and can generally be planned for."[37] Pregnancy, in this view, is not a disability but rather an unique physical condition. Women who choose to have children are responsible for that decision, and should take it into account in their plans. Since society protects the right to have children, individuals (women) must be responsible for the consequences.

Advocates questioned the extent to which pregnancy is voluntary. They argued that pregnancy is no more (or less) disabling than many other conditions. A man who has elective surgery can hardly be said to have an involuntary condition but his surgery would be covered by a disability insurance program. In this view, pregnancy may be voluntary or involuntary for the individual woman, but the important point is that it is a disability like other temporary disabilities. Beyond this is raised the issue of society's collective responsibility for children as resources. It is pointed out that children are the workers and citizens of tomorrow, and that the issue of their future contributions to society goes beyond the individual mother or family. Opponents responded that employers and taxpayers do not own children, but parents do. And, they argued, that in U.S. society it is inappropriate to usurp the rights and responsibilities of individuals, or to require employers to bear the consequences of individual reproductive decisions.

Costs

As is often the case, political issues sooner or later evolve into discussions of money. Supporters of the antidiscrimination amendment to Title VII stated that equity not cost was the basic issue. They contended that women have borne both children and secondary status in the work force, and that social justice requires equalization. Advocates argued that there are hidden costs, psychic and actual, in depriving women of a chance to maintain income during pregnancy.

Cost estimates of the potential impact of legislation vary widely. Table 7.1 shows a range of projected additional costs if employers are required to include pregnancy in disability programs. It should be noted that these are not entirely direct costs to employers, since plans often require contributions from workers. As the table shows, the range of predicted additional cost per year is from $120.5 million to $1.7 billion. The totals differ because of differences in projections of fertility rates, average duration of coverage and average payment level.

The Chamber of Commerce estimated the cost would be $1.7 billion each year. Ruth Weyand suggests those figures reflect high fertility rates and inclusion of women already covered by pregnancy disability programs, rather than additional coverage.[38] Metropolitan Life Insurance Association used the highest estimates for duration of leave (11.3 weeks), for wages (94 percent of the industry average wage, not women's average way), and an estimated 435,000 additional births expected, for a total additional cost projection of $611 million per year. Murray Latimer, an industrial relations consultant, projected costs for the year 1978, using an 8-week duration of leave, $80.45 average wage (55 percent of $146.28) and 364,000 additional births, for a total cost for 1978 of $234 million, or an additional cost of $198 million. The latter figure, he estimated, would be about 3.75 percent of total disability payments made (5.3 billion). The lowest estimates were provided by the AFL-CIO, with a total additional cost of $130 million, which they say would be about $1.50 per worker. Alexis Herman, discussing Department of Labor estimates, stated that disability payments for pregnancy represent "only about one-third of one percent of the total lifetime earnings of the average female worker."[39]

These estimates are an interesting example of the manipulation of data to match predetermined expectations or viewpoints. It is probably true that change is costly, both psychically and economically. It is equally true that failure to change may restrict opportunities. Who bears the cost for change is a constant political question, as is who bears the cost for not changing. The issue of responsibility raises the traditional question of the proper role of the federal government.

Table 7.1 Costs Predicted on the Basis of Required Coverage of Pregnancy Disability Programs

Source	Duration of Disability	Average Payment Per Week	Additional Women Covered	Total Additional Cost
Chamber of Commerce (Sen. pp. 480–98)	6 weeks	$100	5% of 25 million female workers?	$1.7 billion
Metropolitan Life Insurance Association (Sen. pp. 420–31)	11.3 weeks	$149 (94 percent of average gross weekly earnings, weighted)	435,000	$611 million
Murray Latimer, Industrial Relations Consultant (Sen. p. 499)*	8 weeks	$80.45 (55 percent of 146.28)	364,000	$198 million
AFL-CIO (Sen. pp. 218–19)	6 weeks	$78	276, 273	$130 million†
U.S. Dollars (Sen. pp. 554–74)	6 weeks	$80 (60 percent of $314)	208,000	$120.5 million
	7.5 weeks	"	"	$191.5 million
	9 weeks	"	"	$262.5 million

*Latimer is projecting for 1978, and estimates a total for all disability payments of $5.3 billion, so that the increase of $198 million represents an increase of 3.7 percent.

†AFL-CIO estimates this cost to be about $1.50 per worker and represents plus .004 to 0.01 cents per hour increase in wage rate.

Source: Derived from U.S. Senate Hearings on SB 995, Discrimination on the Basis of Pregnancy, Subcommittee on Labor of the Committee on Human Resources, 95 Congress, April 1977.

Private Versus Public Roles: The Government Role

The Civil Rights Act is an acknowledgement of government responsibility to provide employment opportunities and restrict discrimination on the basis of sex. Business has historically argued for limited (if any)regulation. Opponents argued that Congress and the EEOC would become arbiters in essentially private matters of labor/management negotiation. Further, they argued, businesses would be required to provide maximum benefits for pregnancy regardless of previous labor contracts. Those employers who do now have disability programs (about 40 percent) would be discouraged by this legislation from adding them, thus denying all workers additional protection.

Advocates argued that a uniform national policy was required. Some states required coverage of pregnancy under disability programs, and others did not. The result was not only confusion but an unfair situation for employers and employees in different states. In addition, they argued, federal regulation was required to provide guidelines for businesses that had not already taken the initiative to eliminate sex discrimination.

THE PREGNANCY DISCRIMINATION ACT OF 1978

Following debate in both the U.S. House and Senate, and committee resolution of final wording, the bill was passed.[40] Sex discrimination on the basis of pregnancy is now prohibited in employment. However, an abortion rider to the bill was proposed. Some supporters of the bill assumed that since there would be job protection, then abortions could be avoided. Opponents argued that by requiring coverage pregnancy and pregnancy-related conditions, the bill would require employers to pay for abortion. The compromise states:

> This subsection shall not require an employer to pay for health insurance benefits for abortion, except where the life of the mother would be endangered . . . or except where medical complications have arisen from an abortion: provided, that nothing herein shall preclude an employer from providing abortion benefits or otherwise affect bargaining agreements in regard to abortion.[41]

The result reflects the ongoing public debate about the role of government in regulating reproduction, and the complicated patterns of interaction among competing groups.

CONCLUSIONS

The passage of the Pregnancy Discrimination Act demonstrates the developing ability of women's groups to organize and present political arguments effectively in the male political arena. The testimony at the hearings shows an understanding of the complexity of sex discrimination issues and the interconnectedness of women's reproductive choices and structural obstacles in employment. The coalition brought together those who believe women should be protected as well as those who believe that women need no protection. It was recognized that women's life circumstances are not the same as men's. The process has been a long and slow one. The resistance to implementation of anti-discrimination laws has been substantial, and has certainly not ended with this incremental change. One strategy for increasing women's economic, political, and social opportunities has been to use the legal/political structure as a catalyst for social change. It is not the only approach, but has led since the 1960s to increase political sophistication.

Resistance to increased options for women is also clear. It would be a mistake for feminists to underestimate the strength of traditional views and male control. Employers understand the implications of changing the rules so that women are paid equally and can compete for a wider range of jobs. Those who wish to control (or eliminate) access to abortion are a considerable political force as well. The addition of the modified abortion rider is a sign of the vigilance and political strength of anti-abortion groups. The Campaign to End Discrimination Against Pregnant Workers interprets the language and legislative history of the new law as making it "clear that women who have abortions are protected by federal law from all discrimination in employment except for the hospital and medical expenses for the performance of the abortion."[42]

This incremental change is only one step in the ongoing effort to deal with the increased entrance of mothers into the work force, and their responsibilities in childbearing and childcare. There are still conflicting views on how society ought to treat sex differences. While there is some acceptance that women should have employment opportunities, it is not clear what that means. It has often seemed to mean entitlement as long as women are similar to the "standard, fully developed person who is male as well as white."[43]

In the period since the passage of the Pregnancy Discrimination Act pressures for maternity leave policy have continued to mount. Most employers now have some form of unpaid maternity leave, though guarantees of career continuity or return to the same job are scarce.[44] Small scale employers have been particularly reluctant to hold jobs for any extended period of time, arguing prohibitive costs. Their concerns are part of the debate over the proposed federal parental leave bill. The Supreme Court has, however, recently affirmed the right of states to require employers to provide both leave and reinstatement to pregnant employees, even where it does not require similar treatment for other temporary disabilities (*Calif. Federal Savings and Loan Assn. v. Guerra, Dir., Dept. of Fair Employment and Housing*, No. 85–494, decided Jan. 13, 1987). Also, some employers are now permitting both parents to use vacation time and/or sick leave for care of children. Finally, there has been some increase by top corporations in providing job sharing and flexible hours as supports for parents. As has always been the case in the United States, however, there is only very limited income replacement for maternal or parental leave. For most women workers no income means no leave. As Sheila Kamerman testified: "Most working women have no right to a paid maternity disability at all (beyond a few days) and none have a right to a paid leave that goes beyond a brief period of 'disability'. No firm and no state provides for a paid maternity-related leave that lasts more than an absolute maximum of 12 weeks and most provide far less or none at all."[45]

Her research contrasts the non-existent U.S. parental leave policy with those of several European countries, which not only provide longer leaves (up to a year in Sweden) but much better benefit levels (90 percent of wage for 9 months, and a flat rate beyond that).[46]

The Pregnancy Discrimination Act attempts to protect against employment discrimination based on a woman's capacity to reproduce. Its passage reflected both the growing political sophistication of feminists and the general social climate recognizing permanent inclusion of women in the work force. But the general issues raised in the process are still controversial. The current struggle has been restructured to address not only women's roles, but also the intersection of work and family. The question goes beyond whether women are to be punished for bearing the next generation to how the work force can be modified to protect families. Employers are beginning to see that they need to provide support for child care and some form of parental leave (albeit unpaid for the most part) as incentives for employees.[47] The question of whether women should work is discussed less frequently, but the debate over the role of government and responsibility for social/economic costs for child bearing and rearing continues. Thus, the womb factor has been modified but not eliminated.

NOTES AND REFERENCES

1. For the purposes of this discussion, I am borrowing Linda Gordon's definition of feminism: "An analysis of women's subordination for the purpose of figuring out how to change it." *Woman's Body, Woman's Right* (New York: Viking, 1976).

2. Economic Policy Council of UNA-USA, "Work and Family in the United States: A Policy Initiative," (New York: United Nations Association of the U.S.A., Inc., 1985), p. 10.

3. U.S. House of Representatives, "Parental and Disability Leave," Hearing before the Committee on Post Office and Civil Service and the Committee on Education and Labor, 99th Congress, 1st Session (October 17, 1985), p. 27.

4. 208 U.S. 412 (1908).

5. 429 U.S. 129 (1976).

6. Barbara Allen Babcock, Ann E. Freedman, Eleanor Holmes Norton and Susan C. Ross, *Sex Discrimination and the Law* (Boston: Little, Brown, 1975), chapter 1.

7. *Muller v. Oregon*, 208 U.S. 412 (at 422).

8. For discussion of these issues, see Jane Roberts Chapman and Margaret Gates, *Women Into Wives*, (Beverly Hills: Sage, 1977); Ruth Bader Ginsburg, "Sex Equality and the Constitution: The State of the Art," *Women's Rights Law Reporter* 4, 3 (Spring 1978): 143–47; Kathleen Peratis and Elisabeth Rindskopf, "Pregnancy Discrimination as a Sex Discrimination Issue" (California Commission on the Status of Women, Equal Rights Project, 1975); Adrienne Rich, *Of Woman Born* (New York: Bantam, 1977); Ruth Weyand, "Discrimination Because of Pregnancy," *Equal Opportunity Forum* (February 1977), pp. 4–23; Linda H. Kistler and Carol C. McDonough, "Paid Maternity Leave—Benefits May Justify the Cost," *Labor Law Journal* (December 1975): 782–94; and Shiela B. Kamerman, Alfred J. Kahn, and Paul W. Kingston, *Maternity Policies and Working Women* (New York: Columbia University Press, 1983.

9. U.S. Senate, "Discrimination on the Basis of Pregnancy, 1977," Hearings before the Subcommittee on Labor of the Committee on Human Resources, 95th Congress, 1st Sess., on SB 995 (April 1977), p. 124.

10. U.S. House of Representatives, "Legislation to Prohibit Sex Discrimination on the Basis of Pregnancy," Hearing before the Subcommittee on Employment Opportunities of the Committee on Education and Labor, 95th Congress, 1st Sess., on HR 5055 and HR 6075 (April 6, 1977), p. 7.

11. In this same time period there was some development of national maternity programs to provide medical aid, counseling centers, and visiting nurses. The Maternity and Infant Protection Act of 1921 provided national funds to local units. The program of family support services is now administered under Title XX of the Social Security Act. See Carolyn Teich Adams and Kathryn Teich Winston, *Mothers at Work* (New York: Longman, 1980), pp. 34–36.

12. U.S. House of Representatives, p. 7.

13. Nancy S. Erickson, "Pregnancy Discrimination: An Analytical Approach," *Women's Rights Law Reporter* 5, 2–3 (Winter-Spring 1979): 83.

14. U.S. House of Representatives, p. 31.

15. 42 U.S.C. Sec. 2000e, forbids all discriminatory employment practices based on sex. Hereafter referred to as Title VII.

16. 404 U.S. 999 (1971).

17. 400 U.S. 542 (1971).

18. 414 U.S. 632 (1974).

19. 96 S. Ct. 249 (1975).

20. 434 U.S. 136 (1977); see Erickson, "Pregnancy Discrimination," pp. 92–93.

21. Hereafter referred to as EEOC. The commission was established by the Civil Rights Act of 1964, and its guidelines and procedures have often been deferred to by the courts.

22. U.S. House of Representatives, p. 457.

23. 29 C.F.R.§ 1604.10(b).

24. U.S. Senate, p. 244.

25. Ibid., p. 245.

26. Adams and Winston, *Mothers at Work*, p. 33.

27. California League of Cities, "Spot Checks on Maternity Leave Survey,"

December 1, 1976, p. 1.

28. 417 U.S. 484 (1974).

29. 429 U.S. 129 (1976).

30. "Reaction to the Supreme Court Decision Against Disability Pay for Pregnancy," *Womanpower* (February 1977), pp. 1–5.

31. Ibid., p. 2.

32. "Civil Rights for Pregnant Workers," *Congressional Clearinghouse on Women's Rights* 4, 5 (April 10, 1978).

33. California Commission on the Status of Women, "California Women: A Bulletin," (November/December 1976).

34. Campaign to End Discrimination Against Pregnant Workers, "Fact Sheet" (December 1976).

35. "Reaction to the Supreme Court Decision . . . " *Womanpower*, p. 3

36. U.S. Senate, p. 1.

37. Ibid., p. 399.

38. U.S. House of Representatives, 1978, p. 202.

39. Ibid., p. 181.

40. Public Law 95-555, 92 Stat. 2076.

41. U.S. House of Representatives, 95th Congress 2d Session, Conference Report No. 95-1786, "Pregnancy Discrimination" (October 1978).

42. *Spokeswoman*, December 15, 1978, p. 47.

43. Richard A. Wasserstrom, "Racism and Sexism," in *Philosophy and Women*, Sharon Bishop and Marjorie Weinzweig, eds., (San Francisco: Wadsworth, 1979), p. 8.

44. Catalyst, "Report on a National Study of Parental Leaves," (New York, 1986).

45. Ibid., p. 13.

46. U.S. House of Representatives, 1985, p. 29.

47. Economic Policy Council, op. cit., p. 121–122, and *Business Week*, October 6, 1986, p. 53.

PART III

PUBLIC POLICY ON WOMEN AND REPRODUCTION

Introduction

The last chapter in the previous section dealt with public policy changes affecting the work life and finances of pregnant women. But far more heady and potentially revolutionary changes are taking place in the area of pregnancy. Chapters in this part will explore the impact of public policy on women as they struggle to raise children after they are born. However, the social role of motherhood seems to follow, not logically but nevertheless inexorably, from women's biological role in reproduction, so it is with biology that this section will begin.

Irene Diamond's chapter examines one part of a fascinating area: changes in reproductive biology brought about by technological advances. In this century, women's lives have been transformed by the invention and popularization of relatively safe and effective methods of contraception, which began in the 1920s and made a great leap with the introduction of the birth control pill in 1960. Motherhood as an institution took on a new meaning when it became far more (though still not perfectly) voluntary. It has become easier for women to plan the number and spacing of their children so as to fit them into a life that includes other major commitments. And in the past 15 years, increasing numbers of women have realized that birth control makes it possible to choose not to be a mother at all and still enjoy a heterosexual sex life.

These choices have been further enhanced by advances in surgical techniques that have made both sterilization and abortion virtually free of medical risk. The crumbling of the old myth that the only legitimate purpose of abortion was to protect the mother's health helped pave the way for the legalization of abortion in the United States in 1973, which in turn increased the number of abortions to the present 1.7 million each year.

For some women faced with an unwanted pregnancy, the existence of safe and legal abortion has presented a moral/theological dilemma. At the level of public policy, this conflict that began in the hearts of individual women has become probably the ugliest political battle of recent years, escalating in the middle 1980s to the widespread bombing of abortion clinics. The Justice Department under President Reagan has refused to involve itself, leaving the protection of abortion clinics to the discretion of local police forces. This may be a significant factor contributing to the paucity of abortion clinics in rural areas in the United States.

Other moral dilemmas in the area of reproduction arise because advances in medical technology make it possible to preserve the lives of extremely premature babies and babies born with severe, often permanent medical defects. Some conservatives have insisted that the state should have the power to appoint committees that can veto the parents' decision about whether or when to withhold medical care. (The same issue has arisen with adult family members, such as in the case of Karen Quinlan in New Jersey several years ago.) In most of these cases, the decision made by a committee will most profoundly affect the mother, who will have to devote a great deal of her life to the case of a severely handicapped person.

Interestingly, in the areas of abortion and medical decisions, conservatives tend to favor more state power, though they decry such power in the area of child care. Perhaps the real issue here is not government power but the proper role for women in reproduction.

In chapter 8, Irene Diamond goes straight to the heart of this question by looking at technologies that are even closer to the cutting edge than the ones we have so far discussed here: the issues of pre-natal screening for abnormalities and the various forms of fertilization, including gestation outside the uterus. She raises vital questions about the meaning of these new technologies for women's experience of procreation.

The remainder of the chapters in this section concern the mothering of children after they are born. Motherhood is at the heart of the social differences between men and women. It is the role that most strongly ties women to the most traditional of American institutions—the family; that most clearly defines the stereotypically feminine personality—as nurturing; and that most effectively limits some women to the traditional sphere of influence—the home. Sexist ideology uses motherhood, even the capacity to be a mother, to establish woman's place and to restrict her ability to succeed in nontraditional roles. Thus, it is not surprising that policymakers have resisted measures that would allow women to combine motherhood with other economic social and political roles; to do otherwise would be to legitimate the process of role change.

Despite the failure of the political process to assist women in developing a range of life options, women are doing so at a rapid pace. More women than ever before are choosing to combine roles as mothers with roles as workers outside the home. While such choices are usually motivated by economic necessity, most working mothers feel that they combine these roles relatively successfully. In the 1980 Virginia Slims American Women's Opinion poll, 47 percent of employed mothers believe they are as good mothers as they would be if they were not employed, as compared to 16 percent who do not.[1] The 1985 Gallup poll found that only 34 percent of

Americans see being married with children and with no full-time job as the ideal life-style for American women. And in response to the question "What kind of work would you recommend to a young woman just starting out?" only 5 percent of the Gallup respondents said "housewife."[2]

Perhaps in part because of these new social attitudes, the Virginia Slims poll also showed that Americans have increasingly favorable attitudes toward child care. Seventy-five per cent of the women and 66 percent of the men in 1980 favored an increase in day-care facilities, as compared to 63 and 47 percent, respectively, in 1970. Almost half the women under 30 who were not working indicated that they would probably look for jobs if day-care facilities were available.[3]

In chapter 9, "In Search of a National Child-Care Policy," Jill Norgren leads a journey from a not very distant past when day care was associated with poverty and pathology, through the 1970s and 1980s, when the American myths of mother-at-home and family independence came in conflict with the reality of the ever-growing percentage of mothers in the work force (in 1984, 68 percent of mothers of children ages 6–17 and 52 percent of mothers of children under age 6[4]). Norgren's chapter explores the debates about how children of employed mothers should be cared for and whether government should assist them.

One of the primary motives for maternal employment is to earn money to contribute to the support of their children. For many working mothers, this goal is accomplished. But many others find themselves and their children living in poverty in spite of their earnings. This "feminization of poverty" happens particularly when there is no husband present. Female-headed households represent the largest and only increasing category of families below the poverty line. Such households make up only 17 percent of families but nearly half (48 percent) of all poor families and 73 percent of poor black families.[5]

A woman without a husband often finds great difficulty in finding affordable rental housing that accepts children. The escalation of real estate values and rental costs within the last 10 years is compounded by housing discrimination against families with children. Much of the nation's housing was constructed to serve mom-dad-and-the-kids suburban families, who are a surprisingly small and declining percentage of the nation's households. New, conveniently located housing is often designed to serve the affluent and childless. In 1978, only 48 percent of families headed by women with no husband present resided in nonrental housing, compared with 76 percent of married couples. Whether owning or renting, women without husbands pay a larger proportion of their incomes (57 percent) for shelter than do single men (30 percent) or married couples (22 percent).[6]

Housing problems are a direct result of the feminization of poverty. The first cause of this phenomenon is that the earnings gap between women and men is not decreasing. Since the 1950s, women full-time workers have been earning about 60 percent of what men full-time workers earn, give or take about 4 percentage points.

The mother, who is thus almost always the parent with the lower earning power, is also the parent of last resort. Fathers often leave their children; mothers almost never leave their children, no matter how much hardship they face. Sometimes their plight forces them to go on welfare.

Emily Stoper in "Raising the Next Generation: Who Shall Pay?" (chapter 10) sorts out myth and reality, perception and true problem with respect to the perpetually controversial U.S. program known as Aid to Families with Dependent Children (AFDC). About half the mothers on AFDC seem to be permanently trapped in the lower class, able to find only the lowest paying jobs and to work intermittently, able to meet only men who have the same job problem. Many other mothers are forced to use AFDC for a year or two after the loss of a better job or after separation or divorce. The chapter explores policy changes that might assist both groups of AFDC mothers.

The second reason for the feminization of poverty (besides the persistent wage gap) is the rising divorce rate resulting from the greater social acceptance of divorce and the liberalization of the divorce laws. Between 1970 and 1984 the percentage of divorced American women over age 18 rose from 3.9 to 8.3.[8]

Even middle class mothers often suffer economic hardship after divorce. In chapter 11, Emily Stoper and Ellen Boneparth examine how public policies about child custody and child support make the lives of divorced mothers difficult in the United States. Although the financial impact may be eased by social policies, as in Israel, there are significant social difficulties associated with being a divorced mother.

The disastrous financial effects of divorce in the United States have caused some Americans to question the wisdom of the policy of "no-fault divorce," which began in California in 1970 and had become the policy of every state by the mid-1980s. Under the old divorce laws women were allowed to sue their husbands for divorce on specific, and rather limited, legal grounds. The husbands were then legally assigned fault; consequently, the wives usually received more than half of the couple's property. This generally meant that they received the home (if there was one, of course) where they could raise the children, and usually the custody of the children. Today, when no fault is assigned, in states where there is community property, the marital property is usually divided equally and the woman is often left without a home—and sometimes without the children, in some cases because a judge deems the father better able financially to provide them with a middle-class lifestyle.[9] In spite of the financial plight of divorced mothers, the divorce rate remains very high.

Presumably, many divorces are chosen by the wives. In the 1970s the public became increasingly aware of the role played by the battering of wives in driving women out of their homes and of the possibilities for state programs to assist such women.[10]

In the 1980s two new issues surfaced that might help explain the high divorce rate: marital rape and child sexual abuse. Ten years ago, there were no laws against marital rape and the very idea seemed strange to most people, so accustomed were they to the patriarchal notion that a man had a right to demand sex from his wife. By 1986, opinion on this question had changed so much that 24 states had passed laws against marital rape.

Even more horrifying than the rape of wives was the growing revelation of the number of fathers and stepfathers who were committing incest with their minor daughters. In such a situation, some mothers face accusations of complicity from their daughters, especially in the new climate of awareness, if they failed to divorce a father who would not stop such behavior. Public policy is beginning to respond with both education of daughters and legal penalties against the fathers. Child sexual abuse in child-care centers has also become a hot issue, raising new needs for the public regulation of child care.

Taken together, the problems discussed in this section reveal that the institution of motherhood is undergoing some painful changes. The increase in maternal employment, rising divorce rates, and the feminization of poverty all demonstrate the need for some major rethinking of public policies that touch on motherhood. Mothers themselves must play a major role in this process. To become a mother is no longer the signal for a retreat into private life; in late twentieth-century America, the institution of motherhood can no longer function well without the voices of mothers in the public sphere.

NOTES AND REFERENCES

1. Roper Organization, *The 1980 Virginia Slims American Women's Opinion Poll*, p. 12.

2. *The Gallup Poll* (Wilmington, DE: Scholarly Resources, Inc., 1985), p. 105.

3. Roper, *Virginia Slims Poll*, p. 12.

4. *Working Women and Public Policy* (Washington, DC: Bureau of Labor Statistics, Report 710, August 1984), p. 5.

5. *Facts on Women Workers*, (Washington, DC: Women's Bureau, 1986), p. 3.

6. *A Statistical Portrait of Women in the U.S.: 1978* (Washington, DC: Bureau of the Census, February 1980), p. 22.

7. *Working Women and Public Policy*, p. 5.

8. *Statistical Abstract of the United States* (Washington, DC: Bureau of the Census, 1986), p. 35.

9. Lenore Weitzman, *The Divorce Revolution: The Unexpected Social and Economic Consequences for Women and Children in America* (Glencoe: Free Press, 1985).

10. Del Martin, *Battered Wives* (San Francisco: Glide Publications, 1976).

8

Medical Science and the Transformation of Motherhood: The Promise of Reproductive Technologies

Irene Diamond

With the birth of Louise Brown, the world's first "test-tube" baby, in July 1978, the debate about alternative forms of conception moved from the pages of medical and professional journals to the center of the nation's media attention. In our litigious society, when the accidents of life throw kinks into the contracts and laboratories of lawyers and scientists—when a "surrogate mother" decides she does not want to turn over the child she has contracted to "produce" or when she produces an imperfect product, or when the parents of a frozen embryo die in a plane crash—legal conflicts typically emerge. Such conflicts provide lively material for television talk shows while also creating pressure for new legislation that will help us come to grips with the realities of scientific advances. Are these new "problems" susceptible to policy resolution? Can we identify a feminist perspective that can help us sort through these issues? American feminism is so divided about these technologies that a coherent feminist policy position is unlikely to develop.

The medical advances that permit alternatives to traditional male/female sexual conception grip our imaginations and magnify our fears because they portend radically different scripts for the drama of human procreation. For women who are infertile or for those who through choice or circumstance do not engage in male/female sexual encounters, the scripts have already changed. If they want to have babies, the presence of the new reproductive technologies has radically altered the terrain of their choices. As of late 1986 the number of women who have chosen some of these new alternatives is still relatively small, though growing. However, the routinization of reproductive technologies that permit the prenatal detection of fetal abnormalities has already transformed the experience of pregnancy for all mothers.[1] The overload of information these technologies provide creates moral dilemmas that lack the human intrigue the media finds in the battles over baby contracts and the disposition of frozen embryos. Nonetheless, technologies that screen for birth defects raise equally troubling questions regarding the choices created through medical advances. This chapter examines both technologies that facilitate alternative conceptions and those that facilitate control of the "quality" of conceptions.

Before discussing the theoretical and policy questions raised by contemporary reproductive technologies I want to offer some clarification of terminology. This is an almost impossible task because the speed with which science fiction fantasies have become reality has created a world in which the state of the art has no stability. As a baby boomer who had a child in 1971, I am continually struck by how my own experiences of pregnancy are so radically different from those of my contemporaries who are having babies in the closing phase of their reproductive years. Today, ultrasound provides a sonogram picture that permits a mother to see her baby on a screen before its birth; alpha-fetoprotein screening, a relatively simple blood test, gives a mother some information about the probability that she is carrying a fetus with a neural tube defect; amniocentesis, a procedure performed no earlier than the sixteenth week of pregnancy in which a needle is inserted into a mother's abdomen, provides information about the fetus's chromosomes as well as revealing its sex; chorionic villus sampling, a still experimental procedure performed during the first trimester of pregnancy before a woman has begun to feel her baby, also provides information on chromosomes and sex. If one of these procedures comes up with something that falls within the medically established abnormal range, there may be more tests and more probabilities, and with them the choice of terminating a wanted baby, or the choice of entering the uncharted world of fetal medicine and fetal surgery. If the pregnant mother makes it to a delivery room, she will have the option of having an electronic fetal monitor that will provide information on the condition of the fetus. These printouts may then be used to determine whether a caesarean section is advisable. In the context of technologies that focus on ever small pieces of the life process, the mother and her baby will come to be viewed as two separate and distinct patients.

These are some of the technologies currently shaping the hopes, anxieties, and fears of women who have achieved pregnancy. But for those who have been unable to conceive, another range of medical technologies is reshaping expectations about the possibilities. The simplest of these, artificial insemination, in which sperm is deposited in a woman's vagina, is neither particularly "high-tech" nor particularly new, but as state regulations have attempted to contain this procedure within the purview of physicians, and as the use of anonymous donor sperm has become institutionalized, it has come to be classified as a new reproductive technology. In vitro fertilization, the procedure that produced Louise Brown, refers to a surgical procedure in which an egg is removed from a woman's ovary and fertilized in a laboratory dish, after which the fertilized egg or embryo is implanted into the uterus of a woman (referred to as embryo transfer). Ovum transfer or uterine lavage refers to a procedure in which a fertile donor is inseminated with sperm, after which the woman's uterus is washed or "lavaged" and the embryo is transferred to the uterus of an infertile recipient. Cyropreservation or embryo freezing is a process by which an embryo is stored for implantation at some future date. Surrogate motherhood typically refers to a contractual arrangement in which a woman agrees to gestate a baby for a contracting couple; she is artificially inseminated with the sperm of the male of the contracting couple. (There have been two reported instances in which the surrogate did not supply her own egg and was instead implanted with an embryo. Predictions abound that this form of surrogacy in which the gestational mother has no genetic link to the baby she carries will soon become the preferred method of surrogacy.)

These are some of the technologies that are currently being used to promote the production of wanted babies. At this point, these procedures have not been combined with gene therapy techniques. However, the fact that such experiments have been performed with non-human animals has led to the fear that in the not too distant future, quality control mechanisms will have advanced to the point where the production of human beings to specification will be the norm. We already know that in areas of the developing world where the birth of a female baby may be viewed as highly undesirable, amniocentesis is being used in a manner that some have termed femicide or gynicide.[2]

Why is this all happening? Is this a gigantic male plot to subvert women's power as mothers? The British sociologist Jalna Hamner has suggested that the tightening control over female reproductive processes and motherhood is a male counterattack against women's attack on the institutions of patriarchy.[3] Alternatively, we might ask if technology would be developing differently if women scientists were running the laboratories. Shulamith Firestone's cybernetic vision in *The Dialectics of Sex* seemed to offer that hope.[4]

Clearly, the practice of these technologies raises many complicated theoretical and historical questions that cannot be dealt with in an essay that is focused on contemporary policy dilemmas. While I cannot untangle these larger questions here, I am also acutely conscious that these technologies are necessarily products of the historical context in which they emerged. My own interpretation is that this industrialization or techno/ medico-rationalization of human procreation and birth cannot be understood solely through the lens of male/female conflict. The advances of the past few years have occurred in the midst of grass-roots feminist efforts to de-medicalize and de-pathologize human birth.[5] However, we also need to acknowledge feminism's intimate entwinement with the long-term historical forces that propelled the development of these technologies, namely, the modern world view that the phenomena of society and the natural world are proper objects for the exercise of human will and control.

The paradoxes of feminism's indebtedness to this world view are vividly illustrated by the fact that in the early 1970s when Louise Brown was still a distant fantasy, and the debate about laboratory attempts to manipulate the creation of life was relatively closed, a crucial text for radical feminists was Firestone's call for artificial reproduction.[6] For Firestone, modern science and technology held the promise of transcending the limits of biology and the fundamental inequality that had been produced by nature.

In the mid-1980s, pregnancy is no longer viewed as a debased state of being. Indeed, in the midst of the feminist revaluation of motherhood and the wisdom of the natural world, the desire to transcend biology and manipulate the cycles of nature is often viewed as characteristically male. Many radical feminists are moved to calls for prohibition on reproductive technologies and genetic engineering by the frightening scenarios of gynicide, industrialized breeding brothels, and the marketing of women's reproductive parts depicted by Gena Corea's *The Mother Machine*. For Corea, "Reproductive technology is a product of the male reality. The values expressed in the technology—objectification, domination—are typical of the male culture."[7]

The more positive stance on motherhood has not, however, led to a total feminist reversal on the liberating aspects of alternative conception technologies. For many, the interest in motherhood has been accompanied by an insistence that access to available technologies is necessary if women are to mother in arrangements of their own choosing. Access to alternative conception technologies has increasingly become an issue for lesbians and single women. In 1981, in the *Harvard Women's Law Journal*, Barbara Kritchevsky argued, "A lesbian is a woman who possesses a fundamental right to bear and rear a child."[8] It is now estimated that 1,500 single women are artificially inseminated each year.[9]

Many feminists who have been most vociferous in their critiques of the harm and danger of new reproductive technologies have at the same time argued for access to artificial insemination. The distinction typically made is that as a technical procedure, artificial insemination does not necessitate dependence or reliance on the high-tech medical establishment. While those who are most critical of the medicalization of women's lives draw the line at artificial insemination, for others who are primarily interested in establishing the rights of procreation and childrearing for individuals who do not fit within traditional definitions of the family, the issue is access to technological advances. In the latter view, "If reproductive technology makes it possible for an unmarried person to have her or his own child, it is discriminatory and socially unwise to deny that person the right to procreate simply because she or he may be unable to find a suitable spouse, be unwilling to marry, or object to heterosexual intercourse."[10]

This question of access often arises in debates about reproductive technologies. And, as we might expect, consideration of access often brings the complexities of race and class to the fore. Minority women and low-income women typically do not have the same access to these technologies as do white and middle-income women; thus low-income advocacy groups often stress the hardship that arises from inequities in the availability of services. There are paradoxes and contradictions to a focus on the issue of access. Indeed, in this area that touches so directly on matters of ultimate meaning and purpose, the very framing of issues in these terms tends to obscure basic questions regarding state power and the dynamics of contemporary society. I will first treat some of the policy issues that have been raised in the area of prenatal diagnosis and then turn to a consideration of alternative conception technologies.

Technologies that permit prenatal detection of fetal problems have not captured the public imagination in quite the same way as have technologies that provide alternatives to traditional male/female mating. The latter appear to directly challenge societal conceptions of what is natural and traditional family life, whereas efforts to ensure the birth of healthy babies are more typically seen as appropriate and supportive of family life. To question whether access to more knowledge facilitates individual well-being or whether efforts to control and limit the accidents and risks of life contribute to societal well-being is to question the foundations of modern life. Yet, it is precisely these sorts of questions that are beginning to be raised by feminist scholars as well as advocates for the disabled who are troubled by the social impact of prenatal diagnosis procedures. The biologist Ruth Hubbard, who has been especially eloquent in explicating the trade-offs of scientific progress, warns, "The danger is that with the availability of an increasing number of tests, more and more women will feel that they must be at risk of something."[11] Feminist advocates for the disabled question the medical view of disability as a tragedy and argue that, in many cases, the problem is not the disability but how people are treated because of it. They ask what the ability to choose not to give birth to *particular* fetuses means for the value of the lives of disabled people.[12]

To date, the routinization of amniocentesis and other prenatal diagnostic procedures has evolved from a complex set of informal voluntary practices.

In a cultural and legal context that presumes modern technological medicine can guarantee the birth of "perfect" babies, pregnant women and physicians both seek to reduce risks and uncertainties. On one side, mothers seek to reduce their anxieties and fears, and on the other, physicians seek to allay those fears and to protect themselves against malpractice suits. Shifting standards of sound medical practice, rather than formal state guidelines, have been the primary shaping force in the routinization of quality control mechanisms and the transformation of pregnancy into what the sociologist Barbara Rothman has termed "the tentative pregnancy."[13] It is this context that makes recent genetic screening legislation in California, often a leader in policy innovation, particularly noteworthy.

Why California chose to launch a statewide alpha-feto-protein screening program when the president's Commission for the Study of Ethical Problems recommended against the routine screening of all pregnant women cannot be dealt with here.[14] Moreover, it is too early to assess the actual impact of this effort to directly wed state policy to the advances of seemingly benevolent prenatal technologies. Nonetheless, this effort to facilitate mass access highlights some of the complicated questions regarding social coercion, state responsibility, and attitudes toward disability that are raised by the practice of prenatal screening technologies more generally.

One of the particularly interesting features of the California screening program is the way in which it builds on the "voluntariness" that characterizes the existing genetic counseling system to induce mass participation. Prenatal care providers in California are required to provide *all* their patients with a state-prepared brochure that discusses the screening program for anencephaly and spina bifida. The brochure explains that anencephaly, in which a large part of the skull is missing, is untreatable, while spina bifida, in which there is an opening in the bone of the spine, is treatable depending upon its seriousness. The blood test for these defects is explained and the fact that a positive test does not prove the fetus has a neural tube defect is emphasized in bold type. The brochure explains that in the event of a positive test (5 out of every 100 women will test positive), another blood test, ultrasound, or amniocentesis will be needed. Voluntary participation in the program is also emphasized by bold type; if a woman does not want to have the test, she is asked to sign an informed refusal statement, which reads "I REFUSE to have the AFP blood screening test done. I understand and accept the consequences of this decision." Thus, in addition to mandating informed consent, a fairly routine practice in genetic counseling systems, the program also provides for a version of what might be termed informed refusal.

Because the program is so new, how the courts and insurance companies will treat persons who are born with neural tube defects in instances where their mothers have refused the test remains to be seen. Will insurance companies, for example, argue that they are not liable for the expenses of treatment? It is worth noting the arguments of the State Commissioner of Genetic Services regarding the cost-saving features of the program, who commented that "if 90 percent of women found to be carrying severely malformed babies choose abortions, $13.3 million will be saved statewide in lifetime medical costs for every 100,000 women screened and $3.7 million will be saved for Medi-Cal."[15] Will such reasoning lead to the erosion of support services for persons with special needs? (Some feminist scholars have observed that the right to bear healthy children too easily translates into a woman's obligation not to burden society with unhealthy ones.) Will courts permit children to sue their mothers for wrongful life, to sue for having been born? The availability of written evidence regarding the mother's refusal to take advantage of available medical procedures certainly raises the spectre of mothers being sued for "negligence."[16] Here we have an example of an apparently beneficent technology for which democratic access has been made available and where the result may be ambiguous at best.

At this point we do not know what kinds of women will actually have the courage to refuse the test. Most women will probably enter the system. As Ruth Hubbard insightfully comments, "as long as childbearing is privatized as women's individual responsibility and as long as bearing a disabled child is viewed as a personal failure for which parents (and especially mothers) feel shame and guilt, pregnant women are virtually forced to hail medical 'advances' that promise to lessen the social and financial burdens of bearing a disabled child." [17] For many of the 95 out of 100 women whose tests are negative, their participation in the system may prove to have little impact on their experience of pregnancy. But let us consider that out of 200,000 births a year (if all pregnant women are tested), 10,000 will have a positive test, 9,800 of them false positives. Hubbard observes, "Those 10,000 women will now have to undergo the stress of worrying and further tests, including for some, amniocentesis . . . in order to determine who among them is in fact carrying a fetus with NTD. And *no test will tell* the 200 who are carrying one *how severe the defect* will be"[18] (emphasis added).

The California program will pay for genetic counseling and the additional diagnostic tests for the 10,000 women who test positive, which is part of the argument of its proponents that its careful planning will not lead to unnecessary abortions and parental anxiety. What is neglected in this complex screening plan is the fact that ordinary low-tech prenatal care and nutrition care, typically the best preventatives for birth defects, are not covered, nor are they particularly well covered by other state pregnancy programs. The expenditure of resources for a complicated screening program may actually divert resources from an already strained system for meeting the prenatal needs of low-income women.

It is these larger contexts that point to the paradoxes and moral quagmires of approaches to pregnancy and birth that seek to maximize access to high-tech technologies that focus on inherited diseases. Helping individual women to avoid bearing children with disabilities can weaken a society's commitments and responsibilities to the needs of people who because of poverty or disabilities (whether acquired through inheritance or the accidents of living) require special support. While proponents argue that access to advanced technology is necessary to ensure basic rights to bear healthy children, critics argue that routine prenatal screening medicalizes every pregnancy and nourishes eugenic ideologies.

The public debate about alternative conception technologies is particularly intense and complicated. On the one hand, these technologies are viewed as threats to traditional family life. On the other, they are promoted as solutions to the problems of infertility. In this latter view, barriers to their use are said to undermine people's abilities to maintain and produce stable family lives. Indeed, it is the promise of alleviating infertility, currently estimated to affect 15 percent of American married couples, that has propelled the rapid development of these technologies during the past decade and created the impetus for policy proposals to remove barriers to their use. Different barriers such as federal and state laws restricting fetal and embryo research, insurance companies' refusal to cover services or state laws that prohibit mothers from accepting payment in connection with releasing a child for adoption, are problem areas. From this client or consumer perspective (which is also often held by feminists), policies that thwart the infertile from taking advantage of the advances of medical science are inhumane and attempts to hold back the clock.[19] Others, however, who focus on the potential damages to society or the exploitation of women (feminists are here as well) have called for policies that would curtail the modification of reproduction.

One of those reproductive technologies currently being debated as a public policy question is surrogate motherhood. Ironically, surrogate motherhood, when the birth mother (the woman who has mistakenly been labeled the surrogate) is artificially inseminated with the sperm of a man who has contracted for a baby, does not entail any of the new complicated medical technologies. As George J. Annas has noted: "The only 'new' development in surrogacy is the introduction of physicians and lawyers as baby brokers who, for a fee, locate women willing to bear children by AID and hand them over to the payor-sperm donor after birth."[20] While the media has tended to focus on the moral and psychological character of women who are willing to "rent" their wombs, this lens tends to obscure other salient moral questions: (a) the profiteering of brokers; (b) the desperateness of men who want "perfect" children that are biologically theirs; (c) the market system that permits professional women who have chosen not to assume the risks and inconvenience of pregnancy to purchase birthing services from women who are in a disadvantaged position in the labor market;[21] and (d) the social control mechanisms enacted to ensure that buyers receive what they have contracted for.

No state has specific laws that govern surrogacy. Thus the first round of policy proposals were introduced by the lawyer-brokers who proposed legislation that would both give official state sanction to the contracts by which the industry operates and clearly establish the seed rights of male clients. For example, in California, a center for the surrogate industry, proposed legislation would clarify that the financial transactions that undergird the institution do not constitute a violation of the state ban on baby selling.[22] (Payments to the surrogate for her services are usually $10,000. The brokers who arrange for the transactions typically charge clients between $35,000 and $40,000 for their legal, psychological, and medical services.) The legislation would also establish that the payor-sperm donor is the father, rather than the husband of the biological mother. Legal commentators have stressed the need for surrogacy policy to clarify legal paternity since California (as with a number of states that regulate artificial insemination) provides that if a man donates sperm to a woman who is not his wife, he is *not* the legal father.[23]

New legal doctrine is necessary in order to protect the rights of sperm donors who want to maintain relations with the child born as a result of a surrogate arrangement. Yet what is particularly noteworthy about the surrogacy regulatory policy of the sort proposed in California is the extensive provisions to ensure that the payor-sperm donor is in fact the biological father, that the child is born free of genetic defects, and that all the relevant participants are "certified" by licensed mental health professionals. Indeed, it would appear that a subsidiary goal of broker-initiated surrogacy legislation is to regulate and legalize the industry so that less professional entrepreneurs who do not abide by developing therapeutic standards cannot continue in the field.

Lawyer-brokers are interested in therapeutic regulation because they want to ensure that surrogates do not change their minds; thus, one of the most professionally minded firms in the industry has crafted ingenious procedures such as *required* attendance at surrogate support groups.[24] Not surprisingly, surrogates must also agree to abide by prevailing medical instructions concerning prenatal care. But quality control mechanisms, such as amniocentesis, take on a slightly different cast in the contractual context of the surrogate industry. Thus, for example, in this professionalized firm, if amniocentesis is medically indicated and if a "problem" is detected, the payor can ask that the pregnancy be terminated. If the surrogate refuses she is considered in breach of the contract and forfeits her fee.[25]

Clearly, the institution of surrogacy raises complicated moral problems that have no easy policy solution. In England, the Warnock Committee recommended that the recruitment of women for surrogacy be criminalized. The worldwide publicity generated by the *Baby M* case in New Jersey in which Mary Beth Whitehead and William Stern fought for custody over the baby Mrs. Whitehead bore for William and Elizabeth Stern intensified the calls for legislative answers. Some of the proposed legislative solutions have moved in the direction of curbing surrogacy, either through the prohibition of payments to surrogates or requirements modeled on adoption law that would grant the surrogate a specific time period after the birth to change her mind about giving up the baby. The other response has been the argument that future *Baby M* battles can be avoided if state-monitored surrogate contracts mandate professional counseling. In this informed-consent model, appropriate psychological counseling would screen surrogates who are psychologically or emotionally not prepared to surrender the baby to the contracting parents.

It is impossible to predict how legislatures are likely to respond to the call for policy clarification. My own hunch is that few restrictive laws, particularly restrictions on the commercial aspects of surrogacy, are likely to be enacted in the United States in the next few years. The constitutional right to privacy, especially in matters of procreation, is deeply embedded in the American consciousness.[26] Moreover, the American interest in fixing things is not likely to overlook the potential of "fixing" the most "natural" and human thing there is: procreation. Legislative efforts to block such fixing would therefore be much resented.

However, as this chapter has argued, the act of fixing is neither an unambiguous good nor in certain contexts even good at all. The very lack of coherent current policy might thus be seen as perhaps a desirable state of affairs. In the impending political debate concerning reproductive technologies feminists might have the welcome opportunity to raise deeper questions concerning the value of modernity, especially in its guise of technical rationalism and the omnipotent central state.

A final note on infertility: the medicalization of this emotionally painful affliction has caused some commentators to focus too narrowly on the individual trauma. Others point to aggregate statistics concerning the increasing incidence of the "disease." Few, however, choose to focus on the meaning of infertility as a signal ecological metaphor. While such an ecological focus depersonalizes the experience because it takes a holistic look at what the general phenomenon of infertility says, there is the benefit of bringing questions of birth technologies out of a rather narrow policy debate and into the much larger arena of planetary survival. Among certain Green or ecofeminist activists, infertility is nothing less than nature's agonized plea for people in the advanced industrialized societies to reevaluate the price of industrialism and the hubris of technological progress.[27]

NOTES AND REFERENCES

1. When amniocentesis was first introduced it was recommended for women over the age of 40. Within ten years the recommended age had dropped to 35 and in some areas of the country it is already inching its way down to 33. Sonograms which are used in conjunction with every amniocentesis, are also often used to simply monitor the pregnancy whatever the mother's age. My general point here is that the pervasiveness of prenatal screening, even when it may not be used in a particular instance, has transformed the experience of pregnancy because of the anxieties about normalcy it creates.

2. Madhu Kishwar reports that in India the sex ratio balance is changing as a consequence of amniocentesis followed by abortion of female fetuses. Madhu Kishwar, "The Continuing Deficit of Women in India and the Impact of Amniocentesis" in Gena Corea et al., ed., *Man-made Women: How the New Reproductive Technologies Affect Women* (London: Hutchinson and Co., 1985): 30–37.

3. Jalna Hamner, "Transforming Consciousness," in Corea et al., *Man-Made Woman*.

4. Shulamith Firestone, *The Dialectic of Sex* (New York: Morrow, 1970).

5. Pamela S. Summey and Marsha Hurst, "Ob/Gyn on the Rise: The Evolution of Professional Ideology in the Twentieth Century" *Women and Health, 11* (Summer 1986): 103–122.

6. It is interesting to note here that in 1972 when radical feminists were considerably more enthusiastic about the possibilities of birth outside the female body than they are today, the *Journal of the American Medical Association* editorially called for a moratorium on human in vitro. "Genetic Engineering in Man: Ethical Considerations" *Journal of the American Medical Association, 220* (1972): 72.

7. Gena Corea, *The Mother Machine* (New York: Harper and Row, 1985) p. 4.

8. Barbara Kritchevsky, "The Unmarried Woman's Right to Artificial Insemination: A Call for An Expanded Definition of the Family," *Harvard Woman's Law Journal,* 1981: 3.

9. Cited in Note, "Reproductive Technology and the Procreative Rights of the Unmarried," *Harvard Law Review, 98* (January 1985): 671.

10. Ibid., 685.

11. Ruth Hubbard, "Some Legal and Policy Implications of Recent Advances in Prenatal Diagnosis and Fetal Therapy," *Women's Rights Law Reporter* (Symposium of Reproductive Rights) (Spring 1982): 206.

12. Anne Finger, "Claiming All of Our Bodies: Reproductive Rights and Disabilities" and Marsha Saxton, "Born and Unborn: The Implications of Reproductive Technologies for People with Disabilities" in Rita Arditti, Renata Duelli Klein and Shelly Minden (eds.), *Test Tube Women: What Future for Motherhood* (London: Pandora Press, 1984) and Adrienne Asch and Michelle Find, "Shared

Dreams: A Left Perspective on Disability Rights and Reproductive Rights," in *Radical America, 18* (1984): 51–58.

13. Barbara Rothman, *The Tentative Pregnancy* (New York: Viking, 1986).

14. See George J. Annas "Is a Genetic Screening Test Ready When the Lawyers Say it Is?" *Hastings Center Report* (December 1985): 16–18; and Robert Steinbrook, "In California, Voluntary Mass Prenatal Screening," *Hastings Center Report* (October 1986): 4–7. On contextual explanation not discussed in these articles but noted by other observers is the large number of genetics centers in California which prosper as the client base grows.

15. Steinbrook, "In California," p. 6.

16. For a discussion of wrongful life suits more generally and the prospect of mothers being sued see Mary Sue Henifin, "Wrongful Life Cases and the Courts," *Women and Health, 11* (Summer 1986):

17. Ruth Hubbard, "Personal Courage is Not Enough" in Rita Arditti, Renata Duelli Klein and Shelly Minden (eds.), *Test-Tube Women*, p. 350.

18. Ruth Hubbard, "Prenatal Diagnosis and Eugenic Ideology," *Women's Studies International Forum, 8* (1985): 574.

19. See for example the work of Lori B. Andrews, *New Conceptions: A Consumer's Guide to the Newest Infertility Treatments* (New York: St. Martin's Press, 1984); testimony in *Hearings on Human Embryo Transfer before the Subcommittee on Investigations and Oversight of the Committee on Science and Technology*, House of Representatives, 98th Congress, August 8, 1984; and "Reproductive Technology in the 1990's," a forthcoming paper in the Rutgers University Reproductive Laws for the 1990's project.

20. George J. Annas, "The Baby Broker Boom," *Hastings Center Report* (June 1986), p. 30. Surrogacy with embryo transfer does involve the new technologies and this combination creates the situation where the gestational mother is not the genetic mother.

21. Available evidence suggests that most women in couples who seek surrogate services are genuinely infertile, but the fear that an unregulated market will also serve women who want to avoid pregnancy is part of the argument for state regulation. In the celebrated *Baby M* case the question of whether Dr. Elizabeth Stern's mild multiple sclerosis represented a grave risk to her life if she were to become pregnant was a subject of contention.

22. The Michigan Court of Appeals in 1981 held that this ban on payment applies to the surrogate situation as well, whereas in 1986, the Kentucky Supreme Court, not wanting to interfere with the "solutions offered by science," sided with Surrogate Parenting Associates, Inc. The court emphasized the constitutional protection of autonomy in child-bearing decisions and contended that the baby-selling ban did not apply if the price was agreed to *before* conception.

23. Interestingly, these laws were passed to absolve sperm donors from child support.

24. In William Handel's surrogate firm in Los Angeles the surrogate contract stipulates that the surrogate will participate in monthly support groups throughout the pregnancy and for several months after delivery. The group would consist of a counselor, surrogates who are pregnant, and surrogates who have already given up their babies.

25. Based on conversations with Handel's psychological staff.

26. The long-term legal significance of Judge Harvey Sorkow's decision to award full custody of Baby M to William Stern is yet to be determined. Nonetheless, it is worth noting that Sorkow accepted the argument that "the refusal to enforce these

contracts and prohibition of money payments would constitute an unconstitutional interference with procreative liberty since it would prevent childless couples from obtaining the means with which to have families."

27. For a general discussion of the worldview of Green activists see Charlene Spretnak and Fritjof Capra, *Green Politics*, rev. ed. (Santa Fe, New Mexico: Bear and Co., 1986) and Charlene Spretnak, *The Spiritual Dimension of Green Politics* (Santa Fe, New Mexico: Bear and Co., 1986). For a general introduction to ecofeminist writings see Leonie Caldecott and Stephanie Lelands, (eds.), *Reclaim the Earth: Women Speak Out for Life on Earth* (London: Women's Press, 1983). The specific subject of reproductive technology was taken up in April 1985 at a conference in Bonn, "Women Against Genetic Engineering and Reproductive Technologies," organized by the West German Green Party's Parliamentary Working Group and the Institute on Women's Social Science Research. That conference passed a resolution that declared, "For us women, for nature, and for the people of developing nations, this technology is a declaration of war. . . . The human and nature despising character of this technology reveals itself in the reduction of human and nonhuman living organisms to a few exploitable properties and functions. Once we fall into the double trap of the technology's power and our mere ability to make it happen, living organisms are going to be arbitrarily constructed, changed, and improved, without any regard for the far-reaching consequences of such activity for life on earth. Spontaneity, vivacity, nonconformity—in short, the multi-faceted character of all life, including human life—will thus become factors which disrupt the production process."

My specific argument regarding the need for an ecological perspective on infertility is informed by the evidence that much infertility derives from toxic contamination of the environment and the side-effects of high-tech birth control devices such as the I.U.D. The infertility that is often attributed to the "delayed childbearing" that is a consequence of women's entrance into the labor market can also be interpreted as an example of forcing natural time to march to the clock of industrial time.

9

In Search of a National Child-Care Policy

Jill Norgren

Americans express ambivalence about the desirable role of the state in the upbringing of their children. The imposition of compulsory school attendance achieved between 1852 and 1918 occurred in an atmosphere rife with dissension. Compulsory attendance laws brought unresolved issues of the republic into sharp relief by imposing explicit values, and their resulting costs, on the lives of citizens and their offspring. These education laws not only authorized the state to demand the presence of a child in school but also, once there, to inculcate uniform and increasingly national values and attitudes. At one level, debate centered upon the question of state versus parental custody of the child, but the broader issue was the spectre of standardized behavior and thought, which threatened the American tradition of "being one's own man"—the liberal value of individualism.[1]

Today Americans have arrived at a consensus concerning the need for compulsory schooling and the acceptability of the government's role in this function. The same cannot be said for child-care programs. Despite periodic momentum over the past two decades and a monotonically increasing rate of employment among women with small children, a clearly defined national policy in the area of child care has yet to be enacted. Nevertheless, the issue fundamental to the debate concerning child care—one the child-care lobby must continue to address—is the same as that presented by the compulsory school attendance controversy: in what ways do changing social and economic conditions require new relationships between the family and the state? While Americans accept schooling as necessary preparation for an increasingly technological, homogeneous society, rejection of a comprehensive, national child-care policy continues despite conditions that advocates cite as justification for government involvement.[2] Between 1971 and 1979 three major congressional initiatives toward the development of comprehensive child-care policy were defeated, including one by presidential veto. A comprehensive measure pending in the 1986–87 congressional session is given little chance of passing in its entirety.[3]

This chapter reviews the history of day care in the United States and examines the political events and ideological background that contributed to the defeat of committed congressional sponsors and a broad coalition of lobby groups over this 15-year period. The specifics of cach legislative episode vary, but similar factors undermined all the efforts. Political factors including the cost of potential programs, a diffuse and contentious coalition of lobby groups, and substantive programmatic differences precipitated defeat. Fundamental myths about American life exacerbated by the bleak popular image evoked by day-care centers fed a political atmosphere that permitted these repeated defeats to take place. Political conservatives continue to manipulate these myths as part of their effort to defeat the concept of a national family policy. But the undeniable feminization of the workplace, and the growth of female-headed families may alter this pattern in coming years.

THE DEVELOPMENT OF PUBLICLY FUNDED DAY CARE: THE POWER OF IMAGES AND IDEOLOGY

Early Years

In 1971 President Nixon vetoed the first comprehensive child-care legislation passed by Congress.[4] In the message accompanying his veto Nixon referred to the legislation as having "family-weakening implications," suggested that it would "commit the vast moral authority of the National Government to the side of communal approaches to child care rearing over against the family-centered approach," and claimed that the legislation before him would be "truly a long leap into the dark for the United States Government and the American people."[5] The severe, even caustic language reflected significant differences between the White House and Congress over technical content: the nature of the means test, the prime sponsor provision, and the level of funding for a comprehensive program. More than this, however, the Nixon veto underscored the negative social and political image long attached to day care in the United States.

Americans traditionally have viewed day-care centers as bleak, understaffed institutions in which children from poor or troubled families could be cared for under the aegis of a charitable organization or the state. More recently, the use of day-care centers in socialist and communist nations has touched the already negative physical image with political tones suggestive of state-controlled, and therefore critics say family-weakening child rear-

ing. The images of grim physical surroundings and the incipient commun-
ism referred to in the Nixon veto stand in sharp contrast to the generally
positive regard for nursery school, kindergarten and, more recently, Head
Start—all programs designed for preschool children but perceived as
educational rather than custodial.

Day care began as a charitable service for the children of poor, working
mothers, perhaps as early as the 1820s or 1830s.[6] Following the Civil War,
the number of centers expanded as veterans' widows and an increasing
number of immigrant women found it necessary to work. Virtually all
day-care histories describe the surroundings as dreary, with time devoted
to the teaching of moral principles, cleanliness, and useful skills. While this
may not present a particularly attractive picture to the twentieth-century
mind, the nineteenth-century schoolhouse was similar both in physical
appearance and pedagogical goals.

Reforms of various kinds were introduced at the turn of the century,
with the earliest centering on health and safety conditions and some
municipalities initiating procedures for the supervision and inspection of
centers. At the same time, the effects of the kindergarten movement began
to filter down. Trained staff were hired; in more progressive centers this
included teachers with training in the methods of Froebel and Montessori.
Prior to the 1920s the clientele appears best described as working class with
some children from poor or troubled families.

In retrospect, we might expect that day care would have evolved into an
institution similar to an all-day nursery school with a relatively positive
image. This did not prove to be the case owing in large measure to the
influence of newly professionalized social workers, hired by the centers in
the 1920s. Their emphasis on the existence of social pathologies among
day-care families and their insistence on the use of intake procedures and
formal casework eventually imparted the aura of a social welfare service to
the programs.[7] As a result, fewer families resorted to day care and, in
many instances, those that did were in some way or another "troubled
families." Reputation and reality chased each other. In the period between
World War I and the Depression, the public began to build a negative
image of day care based on this social welfare orientation, and has
sustained this image into the present.

Early Government-Sponsored Programs

Until the 1930s group day care evolved in each community according to
need and the response of local philanthropic and social welfare organizations. The Depression strained or bankrupted the resources of these
private agencies and forced the closing of most centers. In 1933, however,
the federal government inaugurated a day-care program administered by

the Federal Emergency Relief Administration (later the Works Progress Administration). By 1937 nearly 2,000 centers were established with federal funds by state departments of education. Although the needs of children were discussed, the primary purpose of the program was the creation of jobs for unemployed teachers, nurses, and other school personnel. This was the first of repeated uses of day care as an employment program rather than as a child-focused service. (As we will see, the "workfare" lobby in the 1960s supported day care as an adjunct to welfare reform. More recently, the AFL-CIO has recognized that expanded day care could provide career opportunities for the unemployed elementary and secondary school teachers and has become an active, identifiable participant in the child-care lobby.) The employment bias of the federal commitment became more apparent when the economy improved enough to permit the rehiring of center personnel at their original jobs. Rather than move toward a child-focused day-care policy, federal funding was decreased and officials prepared to terminate the program.

The entry of the United States into World War II, however, revived interest in day care and triggered a second, brief era of nationally subsidized centers. Congress authorized funds for the care of children of working mothers, but official reluctance to encourage working mothers except where required by the war effort resulted in allocations only to defense areas with war-related employment.[8] Some major population centers, including New York City, did not qualify.[9] As with the earlier New Deal legislation, this wartime legislation was not the beginning of an ongoing program of nationally subsidized day care. Both programs represented no more than specific responses to adult problems of the times. Neither involved long-term policy commitments to children.

THE POSTWAR YEARS: TRADITIONAL ATTITUDES AND NEW SOCIAL FORCES

Although women with children entered the labor market in ever-increasing numbers after an initial postwar lull, the federal government made no effort to respond to the needs of children of working parents. Many officials felt that a mother's place was at home and discouraged policy discussion. Moreover, nothing on record suggests lobbying by parents of young children to counter this government position.

Despite the wartime experience and contemporary evidence to the contrary, day care was characterized as a social welfare service for problem families. Well into the 1960s articles by psychologists and social workers focused on day care in terms of social or individual pathology. At the 1965

National Conference on Day Care, the Children's Bureau distributed a pamphlet which asked,

> Who needs day care?
> Giorgi does. When his father deserted the family . . .
>
> Alice does. Her father . . . was seriously disabled in an automobile accident . . .
>
> Esther does. She is 4 and mentally retarded. Her parents want her to live at home but are finding this . . . difficult . . .
>
> Paul does . . . and so do his (8) brothers and sisters . . .
> Their father is unemployed, their mother hospitalized. The family lives in two rooms in a slum tenement. . . .[10]

The orientation of the Children's Bureau and many of other institutions and professionals caught up in this debate mirrored deeper attitudes concerning the American family and maternal roles. Alice Rossi has written of the postwar period:

> For the first time in the history of any known society motherhood has become a full-time occupation for adult women. Why? American woman has been encouraged by the experts to whom she had turned for guidance in childrearing, to believe her children need her continuous presence, supervision, and care and that she should find complete fulfillment in the role.[11]

The dramatic growth in female employment over the past 40 years, however, strongly indicates other social and economic forces at work[12]: the rapidity of change from a rural to an urban-orientated economy, requiring cash income; an expanding economy, in particular service industries offering employment opportunities to women; higher levels of female education; a dramatic increase in the number of divorced parents and single mothers; the monetary demands of a materialistic society exacerbated by inflation and the disappearance of the so-called "family wage"; and finally, the influences of the feminist movement.

While the social and economic landscape of America was undergoing change, the small but persistent National Committee for Day Care successfully lobbied Congress for the resumption of federal day-care funding. In 1962, 16 years after the federal government had terminated its funding of day care, Congress tentatively recommitted funds to the program as part of the Public Welfare Amendments to the Social Security Act.[13] This legislation reflected the efforts of traditional day-care advocates with a social-welfare, child-focused viewpoint and a new congressional "workfare" caucus that considered day care a necessary adjuvant to welfare reform and job training programs. The disparate goals of this legislative coalition were mirrored by the bill it produced, which failed to delineate whether the government's commitment was to the needs of children or the reduction of welfare dependency.

In 1967, amendments to the Social Security Act were passed, establishing an open-ended day-care funding authorization (up to 75 percent of costs) for any parent participating in the government's Work Incentive Program (WIN), and individuals identified by state welfare departments as "past, present or future recipients of Aid for Dependent Children" (AFDC). Whatever the ambiguity of objectives in the 1962 legislation, the intent of the 1967 amendments appeared clear: the equation of expanded day care with a reduction in welfare dependence. As social policy, the 1967 legislation marked the first time since the federal government initiated social welfare programs that "it became acceptable to think of mothers with dependent, small children as proper objects of the effort to get the very poor off the relief rolls and onto the tax tolls."[14]

Ironically, the impact of the 1967 legislation was not on welfare rolls. The funding authorization and liberal eligibility guidelines did encourage substantial growth in the number of day-care centers. Enrollment in New York City's group day-care program, for example, rose dramatically from 8,000 children in 1970 to 15,000 in 1971.[15] The children enrolled, however, were primarily the offspring of already employed mothers of working and occasionally middle-class, professional background. This 1967 legislation initiated an era of rapidly expanding day care and provided a policy base from which a radically reconstituted day-care coalition would work in its struggle to refashion federally subsidized day care into a comprehensive child-care policy.[16]

COMPREHENSIVE CHILD-CARE POLICY: CREEP OR CRESCENDO

Charles Lindblom has described our political process as one that permits only incremental policy change.[17] The politics of child care from 1969 to the present support Lindblom's contention, suggesting that even in a near-ideal policy environment, incrementalism will prevail. The 1971 Comprehensive Child Care Act, which proponents hoped to use as a vehicle for instituting the new era of child care, was considered in such an environment. The country's new preschool program, Head Start, was held in high regard. The 1970 White House Conference on Children had also endorsed the concept of child development. The Nixon administration, which might have been expected to oppose the intervention of the state in family life, had committed itself to aid children in the first 5 years of life and specifically supported day care as a program necessary to welfare reform. Several congressmen stood ready not just to sponsor child-care legislation, but to work actively for it. Public awareness and interest in the use of community programs for community change was growing, as was the impact of the feminist movement. In addition, there was no lobby organized to oppose day care during this period. With all these positive factors operating on their behalf, day-care advocates had only to find a common ground to command support in Congress and the White House.

With little congressional debate and even less public dialogue, several measures were considered in committee over this 2-year period.[18] The bill ultimately receiving serious attention was the Comprehensive Child Development Act, Title V of the Economic Opportunity Amendments of 1971 (S. 2007). This legislation was backed by a coalition of two dozen interest groups including day-care and early childhood education professionals, labor, community control advocates, and feminists, coordinated by Marion Wright Edelman of the Children's Defense Fund. These potentially fractious partisans, with limited funds and lobbying experience, and disparate objectives, nonetheless propelled a major social policy measure through Congress in amazingly little time.[19] Their final bill, S. 2007, outlined an extensive network of federally funded day-care centers with comprehensive medical, educational, nutrititional, and social services for preschool and school-age children. The appropriation request for fiscal year 1972–73 was $2 billion. Congressional sponsors originally had proposed free day care to families with incomes below $6,900, with sliding scale fees for families above this figure, which was an attempt to broaden the potential clientele. Eventually the figure for totally subsidized services was dropped to $4,320, a move meant to appease the Nixon administration whose representative, Health, Education and Welfare Department Secretary Richardson, was caught off guard by the efforts of the bill's sponsors—Mondale and Brademas—and had failed to structure meaningful countermeasures in Congress. The final bill mandated extensive community and parental involvement, including a highly controversial provision for prime sponsorship by communities with populations as few as 5,000. The emphasis in the day-care centers, drawing upon the Head Start model, would be on cognitive as well as social development with all the necessary support services. Short of the universal, free day care somewhat glibly demanded by radical feminists, who did virtually no lobbying, most lobbyists felt S. 2007 represented a fairly satisfactory initiative which would catapult the United States into an era of child development-oriented day care.

S. 2007, adopted by both houses of Congress, became an unfulfilled dream rather than public law when President Nixon vetoed the bill late in 1971. Explanations for the president's veto abound. First, the nation's governors were virtually unanimous in their opposition to the community control–prime sponsor provisions of the legislation and had communicated this opposition to the White House. Second, the administration was concerned that approval of the bill might further antagonize the conservative wing of the Republican party, already angered by Nixon's new China policy. The veto was intraparty fence mending and a sign that Nixon had not abandoned all conservative standards. Finally, the veto was consistent with the social and fiscal philosophies of the Nixon administration.

POST-1971 POLITICS

Gilbert Steiner has observed that comprehensive child care "had a quick fling" on the congressional agenda and was gone. In his study, *The Children's Cause*, published 5 years after the Nixon veto, Steiner implied that child-care proponents had ceased to work for child care after the 1971 defeat; they had failed to consider that success might "ultimately take a decade and that interim failures were not final." In Lindblom's terms, they failed to learn the lesson of incrementalism.[20] Congressional sponsors and child-care lobbyists used a confluence of positive attitudes and events to work swiftly on comprehensive policy proposals between 1969 and 1971. This legislative blossoming, however, was the culmination of a decade of social debate and political action concerning child care, child development, and preschool education. Congress passed two day-care bills during the 1960s, reestablishing federal funding for child care for the first time since World War II. Head Start was born mid-decade. The 1969–71 comprehensive child-care legislation married the older tradition of custodial day care with newer concepts of comprehensive, educationally focused programming. These policy increments suggest not a brief fling but sustained political wooing.

While the 1971 legislation is the benchmark of national comprehensive child-care politics, the Nixon veto did not signal the end of lobbying or congressional action: hearings were held in three separate years—1964, 1977, and 1978—and bills were considered or sent to committee in 1972, 1975, 1979, and 1984.[21] But the political climate did change significantly after the veto. Steiner correctly observes that proponents could not expect the same highly favorable environment. The defeat also strained the solidarity that existed among groups like the Child Welfare League of America, the National Association for the Education of Young Children, the Day Care and Child Development Council of America, the UAW, the National Welfare Rights Organization, religious organizations, women's groups, and the many local community control-oriented organizations.[22] Differences in approach to policy that were adroitly compromised when success appeared imminent reemerged after the propitious moment passed.

The immediate realization of a national child-care policy may now prove beyond reach. First, as one Senate aide recently remarked, "neither Congress nor the White House is in the mood for a new program . . . only cutbacks and fiscal austerity." Second, the strong and longstanding social and political biases militating against a national child-care policy, which were almost neutralized for a few years, have been reasserted, perhaps more vigorously than ever. On the positive side, opposition from conservatives may have pressed those committed to child-care policies to work harder and to be supported by a larger constituency. And while Washington may not be in the mood for new social programs, public opinion data indicate that the public has increased its support for social spending during the Reagan presidency.[23]

In short, the steadily increasing number of working mothers, the long-term nature of female employment, and growing concern in many quarters over the perceived breakdown of the American family may be changing the nature of child-care politics.[24] Elected officials sense an ever-growing electorate with child care on its mind—women and men who variously support a right to maternal or parent leave, flexible work schedules, as well as the availability of day-care centers. There is more bipartisan support for child-care policies, which increasingly are accepted as supportive of family life rather than "family-weakening." Officials are concerned about homeless families, poverty, divorce, financial stress in working and middle class families, and a birth rate that stood at 1.8 percent (below replacement level) in 1985.

Reflecting these changes, more than 60 bills having to do with child care were pending in Congress in the summer of 1986. Analysis of congressional politics, however, does not reveal sympathy for broad change. Congressional aides predict incremental change rather than passage of the comprehensive bill offered by Representative George Miller. Sponsors of most bills have planned for this by writing legislation that is easily divided into component pieces. New child-care legislation will come as reasonably invisible, relatively inexpensive programs.

The next section compares current child-care policies in the United States with those in other western industrial societies. It considers further whether, as happened earlier with compulsory school attendance, the imperatives of new social values and economic forces will eventually lead to major changes in federal child-care policies even if immediate prospects are not bright.

CHILD-CARE POLICY TODAY

President Nixon's veto of the 1971 Comprehensive Child Care Act portrayed child-care programs as "family weakening" and likely to "commit the vast moral authority of the National Government to the side of communal approaches of child rearing." "All other factors being equal," Nixon stated, "good public policy requires that we enhance rather than diminish both parental authority and parental involvement with children –

particularly in those decisive years when social attitudes and a conscience are formed and religious and moral principles are first inculcated."[25] Conservative rhetoric? It is easy to dismiss it as such, but to do so precludes any understanding of the failure of the United States to develop a national child-care policy, or more broadly, family policy similar to that found in many of the industrialized nations of Europe.[26] Although couched in particularly forceful language, in fact, President Nixon's sentiments may be shared by a great number of Americans.[27]

Opposition to a national child-care policy has found expression in a variety of arguments, ranging from the issue of expense to statements of insufficient evidence of demand, or unwillingness to accept the particular technical language of the bill. The "issues of the moment," it would seem, are vehicles through which underlying biases are expressed concerning the relationship of the individual and the family to the state, and the proper role for mothers. Those who favor a national child-care policy are aware of these biases, but have failed to counteract their influence; as a result, child-care policy currently exists only as a stepchild to welfare policy for the poor and tax policy for the middle class.

The federal government subsidizes child care either directly through social service programs aimed at welfare recipients and families living below the poverty line, or indirectly through the child-care tax credit under the Internal Revenue Code. The government contributes direct payments primarily through Title XX of the Social Security Act. Other direct subsidy child-care programs also aimed at welfare or below-poverty-income families include Head Start and those administered by the Departments of Agriculture, Interior, Housing and Urban Development, and the Community Services Administration.[28] In contrast, the government's indirect subsidy via the child-care tax credit suggests broader eligibility. In reality, however, because of "the nature of the tax credit and the structure of our tax system—the credit is not refundable and, on the average, four-person families with incomes below $7,500 do not pay any federal income taxes—the credit is largely of use to middle and upper-income families."[29] Congressional Budget Office figures indicate that two-thirds of the tax expenditure funds went to middle- and upper middle-class families.[30] Thus, despite the estimated $2.3 billion currently spent on direct and indirect subsidy of child care by the federal government, our child-care policy fails to provide any assistance for a large portion of the population, lacks flexibility for many of those families using direct subsidy programs, and provides no service per se for families using the indirect subsidy tax credit.

What most critically mars the current collection of child-care programs in the United States is the dearth of assistance for low-income, working parents. Parents in this population find that their incomes are too high to benefit from Title XX assistance (or that of other programs), while their incomes are too low to benefit from the tax credit. The 1979 Cranston bill took particular note of this group and was intent upon providing a remedy.

In contrast, welfare and low-income families qualify for a variety of family or day-care center programs. Critics of these programs, however, argue that they fail to provide for parental discretion and urge a policy of vouchers—permitting the choice of center and encouraging institutional accountability—or a negative income tax option.[31] Waiting lists or total lack of facilities, of course, preclude an unknown number of low-income children from receiving any kind of government subsidized care. Middle- and upper middle-income families face yet another set of child-care problems. Like most working-class families, their children are ineligible for government-subsidized family or group day care; they must reach into the private marketplace for suitable arrangements. Limited financial relief from child-care costs is available for middle- and upper middle-income families as a result of the child-care tax credit.[32] Thus, the net effect of current federal programs may be described as directly providing child-care services only for children of the poor.[33]

The record of the United States stands in marked contrast to the child-care policies of other major industrialized nations. France, Czecho-slovakia, the two Germanys, Hungary, Israel, Norway, and Sweden, among others, have evolved various child-care, or more accurately, family policies that provide benefits and/or services as a matter of social right. These include family allowances and housing allowances or priorities; maternity and paternity leave with job protection, full salary, and leave to care for sick children; child-care grants for mothers who stay home with prekindergarten children; universal neonatal and child health care; and various kinds of child-care centers.[34] Universal eligibility governs some of the programs; fees and benefits are scaled according to income in most of the countries.

Child-care policy does not follow any set pattern in these countries. Each combines some form of income maintenance with day-care centers and family day-care programs. The basic and often bitterly debated policy question in almost all of these countries concerns the balance of income maintenance and day care. Many societies accept the principle of general child support through paid maternity leave and child allowances, preferr-ing this approach to day care because children will be cared for at home by mothers. Pressure from women's movements, the financial inadequacy of some income maintenance programs, and the inescapable statistics of increased maternal employment have led recently to almost universal expansion of child-care facilities even where there is also a policy of paid leave.

Sweden's approach combines the use of child-care centers with a developmental emphasis, family day care, "child-minding" homes-after-school centers, and paid maternity or paternity leave (parenthood insurance). Sweden's more conservative, less industrialized neighbor, Norway, had pursued an income policy that discouraged maternal employment through the inclusion of "family support" in the salaries of men. This changed in the 1970s. In 1975 the Norwegian government laid plans to increase the number of places in day-care institutions from 40,000 (1975) to 100,000 (1981–82). These centers are planned and operated by municipalities with financing from the state. Employed women in Norway may use up to 18 weeks of paid maternity leave (if married—part of which may be shared with the father) and take further leave up to a year with full job protection but no pay. Norwegian parents are also entitled to 10 days' leave for sick children under the age of 10.

Neither France nor West Germany has yet to provide sufficient facilities for the care of very young children, although programs for children over the age of 3 are more extensive. Both countries have maternity leave or allowance policies. German women, for example, may take 14 weeks' paid maternity leave and have 5 days' leave available each year for the care of sick children. The development of day-care centers appears less urgent in the Federal Republic of Germany, where grandparents care for almost half of all children under 3 with working mothers. Observers in France believe that the expansion of day care will turn on the strength of natalist arguments and those of income-maintenance versus out-of-home care proponents.

Child-care and income-maintenance policies in Eastern Europe are similar. Programs in Hungary and Czechoslovakia appear somewhat more supportive of the working mother than those in Poland. All three countries provide immediate postnatal maternity leave at different reimbursement levels and for varying numbers of weeks, but Poland fails to grant paid child-care leave for mothers of 1 to 4-year-olds. Hungary permits a grant until the child is 3 at one-third to one-half of the average salary of the young mother cohort and counts this toward pensionable years; Czechoslovakia gives all "economically active" women birth grants and a maternity allowance after maternity leave for second, third (and later) children. Parents, in some cases only mothers, may take many more leave days (up to 60 in Hungary and Poland) to care for sick children than in Western European countries. Approximately 10 percent of children under 3 in these Eastern European countries attend a day nursery, and 66 to 90 percent of 3- to 6-year-olds are enrolled in kindergartens.[35]

Proponents of comprehensive child-care or family policy in the United States tend to emphasize the client orientation of European programs. They portray these governments as altruistically redistributing resources in order to promote employment, equality, adequate housing, child care, and social security. Family policy may also be a tool for social control. Nations with comprehensive family policies use the family to structure population and employment policies. Governments similarly recognize the importance of the family in the dissemination of social and political values. The sum of these European programs and benefits reflects public concern for, and commitment to, the family as a national resource. In the United States, concern for the family seems as high, but the commitment of government remains incoherent.

The American position, or more accurately, lack of position derives from the persistence of several myths about American life that support a deep current of opposition to any national child-care policy. The older of the two myths concerns the individual unfettered by government, and harkens back to classical liberal thought and the experience of the American frontier. The reality of the American experience, particularly in the twentieth century, impinges and reduces this to rhetoric and enco-miums for the Algers, Ingallses, and Lincolns of another era. We adhere to a philosophy that demands freedom for the individual and the family from government interference and extols the virtues of self-sufficiency. Yet the state has intervened in matters of property and the family from the earliest colonial times.

A 1642 Massachusetts General Court educational ordinance, for example, empowered the selectmen of each town to "[T]ake account from time to time of all parents and masters, and of their children, concerning their calling and employment of their children, especially of their ability to read and understand the principles of religion and the capital laws of this country" and specifically authorized them, with the consent of any magistrate or court, to "put forth apprentices the children of such as they shall 'find' not to be able and fit to employ and bring them up."[36] Two hundred years later the stability, predictability, and national social codes sought as a result of industrialization and the Civil War extended such public guardianship to its logical conclusion in the compulsory school attendance laws. C. J. Greer, county superintendent of the Washington Territory, summed up the extreme position stating, "the children belong to the State and the State should see that they are educated."[37] Certainly in the twentieth century the liberal tradition does not manifest itself in the child–state relationship. Compulsory education is only the most visible in a long list of encroachments that include, or have included, registration of births, mandatory immunization, chemical treatment of children's clothing against fire, residential housing, health and safety regulations, prayer and religious holiday celebrations in schools, control of information about and access to birth control and abortions, fluoridation of public water supplies, and child labor laws. While most parents view these laws and regulations as benign and protective, they are nonetheless counter to the liberal tradition of individualism.

Opponents of child care, however, often ignore the degree to which the relationship between the individual and the state has changed, and portray child-care programs as antithetical to established values. For this group, day-care centers, with their capacity to socialize the very youngest members of society, represent the shadow of Big Brother. "Day care is powerful. A program that ministers to a child from six months to six years has over 8,000 hours to teach beliefs and behavior. The family should be teaching values, not the Government or anyone in day care."[38] The 1979 Cranston bill openly acknowledged this position in Section 3, Protection of Parental Rights, which states: "Nothing in this Act shall be construed to authorize any public agency or private organization or any individual associated therewith to interfere with, or to intervene in, any child-rearing decision of parents."[39] A national child-care benefits and services policy is further opposed on the grounds that such policy is both an admission of, and an encouragement to, a lack of self-sufficiency in the public. Government intrusion, they argue, engenders dependency.

A second, more recent myth, the importance of the mother-at-home, acts in concert with the liberal tradition in retarding the enactment of a national child-care policy. In the mid-nineteenth century, the social and economic revolution altered the lives of middle- and later working-class women. Industrialization and new wealth permitted some women to withdraw from the labor force and remain at home. The nonworking, "pampered" wife became a Victorian male status symbol. After the turn of the century, and particularly after World War I, this liberation from the work force actually resulted in more women becoming educated and entering professions, but the vast majority in this expanded middle stratum of society made homemaking a profession. The Depression militated against this trend, but following the temporary acceptance of female employment during World War II, it was clearly expected that women would return to their homes and families, leaving men to be the breadwinners. Most women, particularly mothers, complied. Three years after the conclusion of the war, only 18 percent of mothers in the United States worked outside their home. For a decade little change occurred, owing in part to minimal inflation, the growth and demands of suburban family life, and increased mechanization of industry.

Various schools of professionals and intellectuals pressed this norm upon women by arguing the imperative of staying at home with one's child. Among the most influential was British psychologist John Bowlby, whose theory of maternal deprivation had an enormous impact on the type of mother–child relationship supported by professionals and adopted by many families.[40] Ironically, as the influence of conservative theorists like Bowlby grew, mothers began returning to work in increasing numbers. Forty-three percent of women with children under 18 were working in 1971 in contrast to 30 percent in 1960; by 1977 a majority of women in this category had entered the labor force. Figures for 1985 indicated that 52 percent of mothers with children under the age 6 were employed.[41] Inflation, divorce, migration, and the women's movement negated the desirability or opportunity of staying at home. The expansion of service industries, the Vietnam War, the women's movement, and affirmative action created the possibilities. Nevertheless, the myth of the mother-at-home retains enormous power, and influences the development of family and child-care policy in the United States.

Both these biases are currently best expressed in the statements of the "new right," which has been characterized as consisting of individuals working for the defeat of ERA, and opposed to abortion, sex education in schools, feminism, and government-sponsored day care. Well organized and aggressive in the assertion of their position, this relatively new political faction has indicated, most recently in connection with the While House Conference on the Family and the Family Protection Act, that it intends to be influential in any dialogue on the role of the state in family life.[42]

CONCLUSION: PROSPECTS FOR A NATIONAL CHILD-CARE POLICY IN THE NEXT DECADE

The history of day care in the United States reflects a society that has moved slowly and reluctantly in the direction of a broad national child-care policy. The constellation of values described here as the myths of individualism and mother-at-home have resulted in social and political resistance, which the fragmented and poorly funded child-care supporters to date have failed to overcome.

In their analysis of women's policy issues, Gelb and Palley hypothesize that several factors are crucial to a successful lobby effort: an issue with the image of broad-based support; an issue narrow enough not to challenge basic values or divide supporters; a policy network capable of securing access to decision makers and providing them with information; an ability to compromise with constituents and during the political process; the additional ability to define success in terms of increments of change; and, in the case of policy affecting social relations, an issue that focuses upon role equity not role change.[43] The issues and politics of child care fulfill only a limited number of these conditions. It is not clear that a broad base of support for comprehensive child care exists. Within the coalition of groups currently declared for a national child-care policy, there is no consensus on policy approach. Finally, as outlined above, day care challenges basic values and is perceived to imply role change, some argue on the part of the children as well as the mothers. Given this diagnosis, will a comprehensive child-care policy be forthcoming?

Until groups lobbying for a national child-care policy can diminish the influence of the myths of individualism and mother-at-home, comprehensive programs and benefits are not likely. Lobbyists have two tasks before them. The first involves convincing a far broader audience of the realities of contemporary American life. Proponents must use the media to show that a domestic revolution has already occurred, that family structure had changed and child-rearing practices have been altered in the wake. Marion Wright Edelman of the Children's Defense Fund has testified that "public policy . . . should proceed from reality. There are mothers who are already working. There are children who are already handicapped. There are children who need to be cared for."[44] Psychologist Urie Bronfenbrenner has written that the family as the "institution bearing primary responsibility for the care and development of the nation's children has suffered progressive fragmentation and isolation in this child rearing role."[45] Both these observers, and many others as well, emphasize that the family should remain primary in child-rearing decisions, but feel that this new structure requires altering the relationship between the state and the family in order to ensure family stability. The second task for the child-care lobby is to convince the public that child-care programs are an adjunct to parental primacy and family stability, not their antithesis. In terms of child-care policy, the myths of individualism and mother-at-home translate into a belief that the substance of child rearing is both the duty and the right of parents. Placement of one's children with nonfamily members for any portion of the day introduces children to new and different norms, particularly if parents have limited control and input with respect to the individual care giver or day-care center. Progress in the development of national child-care programs has been significantly hindered by limited understanding of the proposed programs. Many people fail to realize that participation in the programs outlined in the 1971, 1975, 1979 and mid-1980s legislation was voluntary. Even fewer comprehend the breadth of the programs and benefits that come under the child-care rubric—family allowances, tax credits, insurance benefits for parents of sick children, maternity leave as well as family day care and day-care centers. In short, despite existing government intervention in their lives, or perhaps because of it, the child-care lobby cannot underestimate the force of parental and societal fears about who controls the lives of young children. The family may be perceived to be the last frontier of individualism, of individual authority. If so, those lobbying for child-care policy will have to portray more effectively their commitment to the family by emphasizing how child-care possibilities increase, rather than decrease, the cohesion of family units when the adults either need or want to work.

The process of neutralizing these myths will be affected by the political environment of coming years. The 1980 and 1984 elections reflected and further encouraged the growth of political conservatism, with its stated desire to limit publicly funded social programs and government regulatory activities. At the same time, social and economic factors that have encouraged maternal employment and female-headed households show no sign of abating. Assuming that these trends continue, the confrontation between conservative political values and the needs of working mothers is likely to be strident. Politicians may find themselves asked why the substantially increased tax revenue derived from this enlarged maternal work force should not be used to support child-care needs. It would be no less an argument than that made by the trucking and automobile industries for government highway building and maintenance programs, or that of the oil companies for the oil depletion allowance. In American politics, interest groups have always expected some taxes to be returned to their members in the form of benefits and services. Acceptance of a national child-care policy, or even more broadly, a national policy on families, poses the following question: do taxpayers, particularly parents, want their tax revenues used to support family services at the price of expanded government and, if so, what are the acceptable conditions of intervention?

NOTES AND REFERENCES

1. Such sentiments were formally expressed by various men in public life. The governor of Pennsylvania, for example, vetoed a compulsory attendance bill in 1893 on the grounds that it was un-American. Jack Culbertson, "Attendance," *Encyclopedia of Educational Research*, 3rd ed. (New York: Macmillan, 1960) p. 94, cited in Charles Burgess, "The Goddess," *Harvard Educational Review, 46* (May 1976): 213.

2. Foremost among reasons given is the increase in the number of working mothers in the United States in the past 40 years, a trend forecasters believe will continue. The Bureau of Labor Statistics recently estimated that labor force participation among women aged 25 to 44 is expected to exceed 80 percent in 1995, up from 70 percent in 1984 and 50 percent in 1970. Prime working age women are expected to account for more than one-third of the labor force in 1995. The proportion of the labor force that is female was 44 percent in 1984 and is projected to reach 46 by 1995. Howard N. Fullerton, J., "The 1995 labor force: BLS' latest projections," 108 *Monthly Labor Review* (November 1985), pp. 17, 19, and 23. The Urban Institute earlier estimated an increase of 3.1 million working women with very young children by 1990—a 56 percent increase over the 1978 level. A large increase in the number of working mothers with children ages 6–17 has also occurred. Ralph E. Smith, *The Subtle Revolution* (Washington, DC: The Urban Institute, 1979) pp. 14, 19 and 133. The growth in numbers of one-parent families and the decrease in extended family child care are also cited by proponents of day care. Studies such as Mary Keyserling's *Windows on Day Care* (New York: National Council of Jewish Women, 1972), for example, indicate the need for child

care by demonstrating the number of latchkey children in the United States. A totally different argument for day care is offered by those concerned with the increasing number of Americans on public assistance who see child-care programs as a means of decreasing welfare dependency. Another justification for day-care centers and supervised family care rests upon arguments made on behalf of compensatory, development education, that is, all-day nursery school or a Head Start-type program. Feminists argue for child-care programs on the grounds that mothers ought to be provided time to develop themselves. Community-focused activists portray day-care centers as institutions capable of enhancing communications and solidarity in neighborhoods, and as agents of social and economic change.

3. In 1971 President Nixon vetoed the Economic Opportunity bill because of his opposition to Title V, "Child Development Programs." Both the 1975 Child and Family Services Act, sponsored by Senator Walter Mondale and Representative John Brademas, and the 1979 Child Care Act, sponsored by Senator Alan Cranston, failed to emerge from committee. Perceiving a dim future, Cranston even withdrew his bill before the completion of hearings. After attempting to build support by holding child care hearings around the country in 1984, Rep. George Miller (Chairman, Youth and Families) introduced HR 2867. A bill approaching child care needs in a variety of ways, this legislation would provide grants to states and to the private sector. A package of similar bills (S803–S810) was introduced in the Senate. Approaching the child-care issue in another way, Representatives Patricia Schroeder and William Clay co-authored HR 4300, The Family and Medical Leave Act of 1986. This legislation would require for the first time in the United States that male or female employees in firms with 15 or more workers be given (unpaid) job protected leave to care for newborn or newly adopted children. It may well be that parent leave legislation will succeed before any comprehensive action by the government to provide more day care and family services.

4. Title V, "Child Development Programs," Economic Opportunity Amendments of 1971 (S. 2007). For the veto message, see Richard Nixon, "Veto of Economic Opportunity Amendments of 1971," *Weekly Compilation of Presidential Documents*, December 13, 1971, pp. 1635–36.

5. Ibid., p. 1636. The message may have taken its language from the September 9, 1971 comments of New York's Conservative Senator James Buckley, who described the child development bill as one that "threatens to destroy parental authority and the institution of the family." *Congressional Record* (daily ed.), September 9, 1971, p. S. 14010, cited in Gilbert Steiner, *The Children's Cause* (Washington DC: Brookings Institution, 1976), pp. 108 and 113–15.

6. For more comprehensive histories of day care as it developed in the United States, see Rosalyn F. Baxendall, "Who shall Care For Our Children? The History and Development of Day Care in the United States," in *Women: A Feminist Perspective*, Jo Freeman (ed.) (Palo Alto, CA: Mayfield, 1979), pp. 134–49; James D. Marver and Meredith A. Larson, "Public Policy toward Child Care in America: A Historical Perspective," in *Child Care and Public Policy*, Philip K. Robins and Samuel Weiner (eds.) (Lexington, MA: Lexington, 1978), pp. 17–42; National Association of Day Nurseries, "Origins of Day Care Nursery Work" (1970), processed paper on file at the Child Welfare League of American Library, New York City; Jill Russack Norgren, "Political Mobilization and Policy Input in Urban Day Care" (Ph.D dissertation: University of Michigan, 1974), in particular chapters 2 and 3; Pamela Roby, *Child Care—Who Cares?* (New York: Basic Books, 1973); Sheila M. Rothman, "Other People's Children: The Day Care Experience in America," *The Public Interest, 30* (Winter 1973): 11–27; and Margaret O'Brien

Steinfels, *Who's Minding the Children?* (New York: Simon and Schuster, 1973).

7. The fact that day care did not always convey such an image—at least to working-class families—prior to the increased use of social work techniques is suggested by the comments of a day-care center social worker: "In most of the families [she complained], the parents' attitude is that the nursery is a community resource, such as the public school, and it is, therefore, for them to use as they wish. Families find it difficult to see the need of discussing financial, social and personal factors." *Case Work Programs in Day Nurseries: A Symposium*, Five Papers presented at the Twentieth Biennial Conference of the National Federation of Day Nurseries, New York, April 1937, p. 7, cited in Steinfels, *Who's Minding the Children?* p. 63.

8. In the Community Facilities Act of 1941 (also known as the Lanham Act), Congress instructed the Children's Bureau to make funds available to states on a 50-50 matching basis for nursery schools and day-care centers.

9. The program continued in New York City when that municipality agreed to contribute funds to privately sponsored centers.

10. U.S. Department of Health, Education and Welfare, Children's Bureau, Welfare Administration, *What is Good Day Care?* (Washington, DC: n.p., 1974).

11. Alice S. Rossi, "Equality Between the Sexes: An Immodest Proposal," *Daedalus, 93* (Spring 1964): 616.

12. Women constituted 36 percent of the labor force in 1944. This figure dropped to 29.8 in 1947, rose to 34.8 in 1960, and increased most dramatically by 1970 (42.6 percent) and in subsequent years. The percentage of women with children under the age of 6 in the labor force registered an even greater increase: 14 percent in 1950, 20 percent in 1960, 32 percent in 1970, and 41 percent in 1977. U.S. Department of Commerce, Bureau of the Census, *Statistical Abstract of the United States* (Washington, DC, 1971), pp. 212–13, and U.S. Senate, Subcommittee on Child and Human Development of the Committee on Human Resources, *Hearings on the Child Care and Child Development Programs*, 1977–78 (Washington, DC: 1978), p. 682. See also, *supra*, note 2.

13. Congress authorized a modest $5 million for fiscal 1963 and $10 million the following year. Although the authorization called for $25 million to be spent in the first 3 years, Congress appropriated only $8.8 million from 1962 through 1965. The modesty of these yearly appropriations is illustrated by a comparison with the day-care budget for just the city of New York in 1963: $7,407,203.

14. Gilbert Y. Steiner, "Day Care Centers: Hype or Hope?" *Transaction, 8* (July–August 1971): 51.

15. Herb Rosenweig, *Agency for Child Development Fiscal Year 1972–73 Request* (Human Resources Administration, Agency for Child Development: Office of Public Affairs, n.d.), p. E-1. Staff at the Agency for Child Development described a ripple-like awareness process with municipalities like New York first discovering the potential of the 1967 legislation particularly as they were pressed by community control and women's rights groups to expand local child-care programs.

16. "Comprehensive," in this context, implies day care that provides for a child's social and intellectual needs as well as his or her physical and mental health—comprehensive rather than custodial care.

17. Charles E. Lindblom, "The Science of Muddling Through," *Public Administration Review, 19* (Spring 1959): 79–88.

18. For a summary and comparison of the various bills, see Day Care and Child Development Council of America, *The Council's 1971 Legislative Analysis* (September 1971, processed).

19. For a detailed discussion of the politics of the 1969–71 bills, see Steiner, *The Children's Cause*, chapters 5 and 7.

20. Ibid., p. 91.

21. Senator Alan Cranston's Child Care Act of 1979, emphasized "the availability and diversity of quality child care services for all children and families who need such services." It did not provide for universal entitlement but rather priorities based upon family need. These priorities were not spelled out, although two-parent working families and single-parent families are repeatedly discussed. The Cranston bill also provided for a variety of auspices, flexible funding arrangements including vouchers, sliding fee payments, and a strong regulatory mechanism. This child-care program was to be administered by the individual states after the approval of a comprehensive state child-care plan. *Congressional Record*, January 15, 1979. See also, *supra*, note 3.

22. The list of organizations and interest groups that speak to the issue of child care is lengthy. A review of the published hearings for the 1975 Child and Family Services Act or, more recently, Senator Cranston's Child Care Act (S.4) indicate additional names, background, and points of view.

23. W. Schneider, "The Voters' Mood 1986: The Six-Year Itch," *The National Journal* (December 7, 1985): 2757–2759.

24. Howard N. Fullerton, Jr. argues that labor force participation among white women ages 30 to 45 will increase rapidly during the next decade. "These women, and their spouses, will have reached a point in their working lives when earnings no longer increase rapidly. Thus, to maintain their living standard, they will have to increase their time in the labor force." "The 1995 labor force: BLS' latest projections." 108 *Monthly Labor Review* (November 1985), p. 21. Representative Nancy Johnson puts it more simply: " . . . Americans need to work to pay the mortgage." Steven V. Roberts, "G.O.P. Congresswoman Pushes Aid for Day Care," *New York Times*, June 15, 1986. And economist Sylvia Ann Hewlett reminds us that many Americans are working just to survive: "75 percent of working women are either single mothers or are married to men earning less than $15,000 a year." "Feminism's Next Challenge: Support for Motherhood," *New York Times*, June 17, 1986, p. A27.

25. Nixon, "Veto of Economic Opportunity Amendments of 1971," p. 1636.

26. For a discussion of the various uses of "family" policy, see Sheila B. Kamerman and Alfred J. Kahn, *Family Policy: Government and Families in Fourteen Countries* (New York: Columbia University Press, 1978), pp. 3–8.

27. Speculation must satisfy us for the moment owing to the lack of national citizen opinion data concerning issues of child-care policy.

28. The Department of Health, Education and Welfare estimates that in fiscal year 1977, $800 million of the $2.7 billion appropriation for Title XX was expended for child care. The Congressional Budget Office has estimated that the federal government provides about $1.8 billion in direct spending for child-care or child-care-related services through these various agencies. *Congressional Record*, January 15, 1979, p. S77.

29. Ibid., p. S77.

30. In the introductory comments to S.4 Senator Cranston estimates that the federal government contributes approximately $500 million a year to the cost of child care through the child-care tax credit., p. S77.

31. For a brief discussion of the application of the voucher system to child care, see U.S. Senate, Subcommittee on Child and Human Development, *Hearings*, pp. 6–14, 20–32, and 170–75. For an argument in favor of the negative income tax

rather than day care, see William V. Shannon, *New York Times Magazine*, April 30, 1972, pp. 13–85.

32. The Tax Reform Act of 1976 provided for a credit of up to $800 a year for child care for families who qualify. The basic formual allowed a credit of 20 percent of child-care costs up to $2,000 per year for one child or $4,000 for two or more. One thousand dollars in child care for one child, for example, would qualify the taxpayer for a $200 tax credit. In 1982 Congress raised the child care tax credit to a maximum of $960 for those families earning over $28,000, rising to $1,440 for those with two or more children in child care and adjusted gross incomes of $10,000 or less. In the private sector, there has been some growth in day care services and benefits as a result both of social change and government encouragement. The 1981 Economy Recovery Act (ERTA) made child care a nontaxable benefit and, thus, a more convenient option to include in corporate benefit plans and salary reduction programs. The legislation made these tax-deductible contributions for the employer. Dana Friedman, *Corporate Financial Assistance for Child Care* (New York: The Conference Board Research Bulletin No. 177, 1985), pp. 3, 6.

33. The federal government also provides limited funds for child care as a preventive tool where a mother's incapacitation might otherwise require foster care, or where other social pathologies are diagnosed.

34. See the report of the Coalition of Labor Union Women Child Care Seminar, "A Commitment to Children" in U.S. Senate, Subcommittee on Child and Human Development, *Hearings*, pp. 775–809; Kamerman and Kahn, *Family Policy*; Kamerman and Kahn, "The Day-care Debate: A Wiser View," *The Public Interest, 54* (Winter 1979): 76–93; and Sheila Kamerman and Alfred Kahn's six-country study, *Child Care, Family Benefits and Working Parents* (New York: Columbia University Press, 1981).

35. The above discussion draws upon materials in Kamerman and Kahn, *Family Policy*: Rita Liljestrom, "Sweden," pp. 41–48; Hildur Ve Henriksen and Harriet Holter, "Norway," pp. 54–64; Nicole Questiaux and Jacques Fournier, "France," pp. 145–82; Friedhelm Neidhardt, "The Federal Republic of Germany," pp. 232–38; Walter Vergeiner, "Czechoslovakia," pp. 102–3, 113–14; Zsuzsa Ferge, "Hungary," pp. 73–77, and Magdalena Sokolowska, "Poland," pp. 252–58. See also Zsuzsa Ferge, *A Society in the Making: Hungarian Social and Societal Policy* (Middlesex, England: Penguin Books, 1979).

36. Lawrence A. Cremin, "Family-Community Linkages in American Education: Some Comments on the Recent Historiography," *Teachers College Record, 79* (May 1978): 687–88.

37. Burgess, "The Goddess," p. 215.

38. Statement by a member of Oklahomans for Life, the Eagle Forum (Phyllis Schlafly's organization), the Pro-Family Forum and Stop E.R.A.—the "new right." Nadine Brozan, "White House Conference on the Family: A Schism Develops," *New York Times*, January 7, 1980, p. D8.

39. *Congressional Record*, January 15, 1979, p. S80.

40. John Bowlby, *Maternal Care and Mental Health* (Geneva: World Health Organization, 1942). Also, R. A. Spitz, "Hospitalization: An Inquiry into the Genesis of Psychiatric Conditions in Early Childhood," *Psychoanalytic Studies of the Child, 2* (1945): 53–74. For a critique of Bowlby, see Milton Willner, "Day Care: A Reassessment, *Child Welfare, 44* (March 1965). For a broad review of the literature, see a two-part article by Mary C. Howell, "Employed Mothers and Their Families (I)" *Pediatrics, 52* (August 1973): 327–42. See also, more recently, Ruth

Zambrana, Marsha Hunt, and Rodney Hite, "The Working Mother in Contemporary Perspective: A Review of the Literature," *Pediatrics, 64* (1979): 862–70. Selma Fraiberg in *Every Child's Birthright: In Defense of Mothering* (New York: Basic Books, 1977), offers a contemporary statement of maternal deprivation theory.

41. These figures translate into more than 6.4 million children under the age of 6 whose mothers work and 22.4 million children ages 6 to 17 whose mothers are in the labor force. U.S. Senate, Subcommittee on Child and Human Development, *Hearings*, p. 682, Bureau of Labor Statistics, and Smith, *The Subtle Revolution*, chaps. 1 and 5. Overall, about 2.5 million children—over half of them with married parents—are in the care of babysitters or day-care centers while mothers work. Kenneth B. Noble, "More U.S. Mothers Are Holding Jobs," *New York Times*, March 16, 1986, p. A33.

42. Brozan, "White House Conference on the Family."

43. Joyce Gelb and Marion Leif Palley, "Women and Interest Group Politics: A Comparative Analysis of Federal Decision-Making," *Journal of Politics, 41* (May 1979): 362–92.

44. U.S. Senate, Subcommittee on Child and Human Development, *Hearings*, p. 874.

45. Urie Bronfenbrenner, "The Challenge of Social Change to Public Policy and Development Research," Paper presented at the President's Symposium, "Child Development and Public Policy," at the annual meeting of the Society for Research in Child Development, Denver, April 12, 1975, p. i.

10
Raising the Next Generation: Who Shall Pay?

Emily Stoper

What is the responsibility of the community or the government in assisting parents to support the next generation financially? In pre-industrial societies the question rarely arises because children become an economic asset at an early age. But the United States is not a pre-industrial society and children often remain an economic liability for their families until they are in their twenties. The resulting vulnerability of children and their parents to economic hardship is intensified by two other factors: the smallness and impermanence of the nuclear family, and the unequal distribution of family incomes.

In modern industrial societies such as ours, children are extremely dependent on their parents; one of those parents, usually the father, often leaves the household before the children are economically independent. In 1983, some 19.4 percent of children under 18 lived in households with a female householder.[1] This leaves the mother, who is at a great disadvantage in the labor market (in large part, directly or indirectly, because of the children) with the task of supporting them. (Chapter 15 discusses the inadequacy of the child support system.) If she happens to be a member of the poorer classes, her position is almost impossible without help from the larger community.

AFDC: REFORM AND RESENTMENT

In the United States, the larger community does give financial assistance to single parents who are poor (and to a few two-parent families) in the form of Aid to Families with Dependent Children (AFDC), popularly known as "welfare."

AFDC's benefits go to some 10.8 million very poor people, whose cash income is brought up to a level still well below the poverty line. AFDC payments averaged $320 a month per family in 1983.[2]

Major reforms have occurred in the welfare system over the last 20 years, and yet a pall of anger and futility still hangs over welfare, affecting policymakers, recipients, and taxpayers. This frustration with welfare is somewhat puzzling. Although no administration has achieved all it set out to do, substantial progress has been made toward each of the major goals of welfare reform: combating poverty, encouraging employment, and reducing costs. President Lyndon Johnson set as his goal no less than the elimination of poverty. Some say this goal has actually been achieved[3]; many others would disagree.[4] However, without question, the amount of government money spent in aid of the poor enormously increased in the 1960s and 1970s. It almost doubled between 1966 and 1977.[5]

Presidents Richard Nixon and Jimmy Carter placed high on their list of goals the employment of all employable welfare recipients. Although neither Nixon's Family Assistance Plan nor Carter's Program for Better Jobs and Income passed Congress, many work incentives did become law. Why? Because policy-makers realized during the 1960s that if the government deducted from welfare benefits the full amount of earnings by welfare recipients, this amounted to a "marginal tax rate" of 100 percent—surely a powerful disincentive to employment. Accordingly, beginning in 1962, the law began to permit welfare recipients to keep some of their earnings. During the 1970s, all AFDC recipients were permitted to keep all of their earnings necessary to cover work expenses, plus $30, plus one-third of their additional earnings up to the poverty line. The Reagan administration has eliminated most work incentives in order to reduce welfare costs.

These carrots are increasingly being supplanted by the stick of work requirements. Currently, all AFDC parents must register for work unless they can meet one of the following conditions: ill health; at least one child under 7 to care for and/or inability to work because of incapacity; old age; student status; or lack of access to day care, transportation, or a job.[6] Even the inability to find a job at the minimum wage is now less frequently accepted as a reason for not working. Since 1977, the federal government has permitted states to require welfare recipients to work off their benefits at public jobs below the minimum wage, and increasing numbers of states and county governments are requiring this "workfare."[7]

In an effort to assist AFDC recipients and other poor people in obtaining jobs, the federal government has also sponsored numerous job training programs and even a large job creation program called the Comprehensive Employment and Training Act of 1973 (CETA). This was replaced during the Reagan administration mainly by the Job Training Partnership Act, which assigns primary responsibility for job creation to local communities. Although none of these programs has been very successful in finding long-term jobs for welfare recipients,[8] there are many employed welfare recipients and the tendency for them to work is increasing slightly.[9] Some 18 percent of welfare mothers are now employed at any given time, and over a period of years many more hold jobs, going on and off the welfare rolls. In fact, about 60 percent of welfare families are off the rolls in 3 years or less, though some of these go back on again.[10] Only 7.9 percent of welfare families remain on the rolls for over 10 years.[11]

The third major goal of welfare reform has been to reduce the costs of the welfare system and to shift those costs to the federal government in order to assure equitable treatment of welfare recipients in poor areas. The latter goal has gradually been met; the federal government now pays slightly over 50 percent of the public assistance bill—consisting largely of AFDC.[12] The size of the AFDC rolls, which more than doubled in the late 1960s, is no longer increasing. The number of welfare recipients peaked in 1975; in 1983, it was almost exactly the same as in 1970, or about 7 million children.[13]

In spite of this stabilizing of the number of recipients, the amount of money spent on poor families increased a great deal in the 1970s, largely because of the rapid expansion of the food stamps program and Medicaid, both of which are available to everyone on AFDC as well as to some of the non-AFDC poor. It is this last category of people who were the target of President Reagan's cuts in food stamps. The costs of Medicaid have increased even more rapidly than those of food stamps, but this is largely a function of the general problem of runaway health care costs, a problem that cannot be solved by welfare reform. Interestingly, the costs of food stamps and Medicaid have seemed more acceptable to the American people than the direct cash payments under AFDC (which have not risen in the 1970s), perhaps because the public does not trust welfare recipients to spend cash wisely.[14]

In sum, a great deal of progress has been made toward all three major articulated goals of the welfare system: combating poverty through income transfers, encouraging employment, and controlling costs. The system is not in crisis with respect to any of these three areas. Yet the view persists among the public, the politicians, and many recipients that welfare is a hopeless mess.

A principal reason for the view of welfare as a mess, and for the sense that it is perennially in crisis and in need of major overhaul, is the failure to address the real question about AFDC: How well is it assisting poor mothers in raising their children? If the public thought that welfare mothers were doing an acceptable job of producing a new generation, then there would be little reason not to see welfare as a legitimate subsidy for mothering, a task for which women have traditionally been wholly or partially excused from market labor. But because the public does not see welfare mothers as doing an acceptable job, it tends to regard AFDC as an evil system that perpetuates dependency and crime from generation to generation.[15]

Welfare mothers themselves do not perceive the task of child rearing very differently from the general public. Studies show that "the child-rearing concerns of the lower class closely approximate those ascribed to middle- and upper-class groups," though actual child-rearing practices differ. Like other parents, lower-class parents want their children to "do better" than they have done.[16] One of the main findings of Elliot Liebow's participant–observer study of poor urban Blacks was that they accept the same norms as everyone else, but find them impossible to attain.[17]

What choice of policies would best serve both the public and the welfare mothers themselves in making the attainment of these shared norms possible? Clearly, policies are needed that would enable the mother to communicate to her children the kind of personal strength needed to overcome the multiple obstacles in their path. She must be able to give them a sense that it is not inevitable that they too follow the path of truncated education and early parenthood that often leads to welfare or to a life of low-paid casual labor, crime, and frequent incarceration. She must be able to convey to them a sense of being in charge of their own lives. Research indicates that the main psychological difference between middle-class and non-middle-class children is that the former see themselves as shaping their own lives, whereas the latter see themselves as victims, buffeted by events and circumstances.[18]

This psychology of victimization is passed on from one generation to the next.[19] The perpetuation of the psychology of victimization cannot be said to be caused by welfare mothers, however. The tendency of the poor to see themselves as hopeless victims is constantly fed by the tendency of the non-poor to "blame the victims" for having caused their plight by their own inherent laziness, immorality, stupidity, "present-orientedness"[20] and the like.

The poor react to this sort of blaming in two ways: they either accept these characterizations of themselves and therefore sink into hopelessness, or they turn the charges around and angrily blame their accusers for blaming them and for failing to change their own behavior, which has contributed to the plight of the poor. In this way, both poor and non-poor become locked into a pattern of mutual blame. This pattern is the real cause of the perpetuation of poverty because it prevents either of them from doing what needs to be done.

During the late 1960s and early 1970s, a political group called the National Welfare Rights Organization (NWRO) used turning the blame back on the accusers as its major strategy.[21] It accepted the view of a number of radical writers that those on welfare were victims of a capitalist system that was so structured that it needed to maintain a class of perpetually poor people who were marginal to the labor force.[22] The logical conclusion was that the only recourse of the welfare poor was to demand that they be supported permanently at a reasonable comfortable level. The work ethic was rejected as unrealistic for the very poor. "Welfare is not a problem," declared the NWRO, "welfare is the solution to the problem of poverty."[23]

When maximally successful, this approach did achieve some real victories, for example, in getting the Supreme Court to acknowledge that welfare was a legal right that could not be removed without due process or for illegitimate reasons.[24] The trouble with this approach, though, was that it doomed the poor to a marginal and limited existence, perpetually resented by the taxpaying public. By reinforcing the psychology of victimization it helped back some of the poor into a corner.

The truth is that the tax burden of AFDC (some $816 billion in 1985) certainly outweighs whatever benefits the existence of a welfare class gives to the capitalist economy, though this may not always have been so. Because of the minimum wage, the welfare class no longer functions effectively to hold down the wages of the working class. In the past, the welfare system served in some places as a way of supporting seasonal unskilled agricultural workers during the off season and forcing them to work when needed by throwing them off the rolls every spring.[25] With the increasing mechanization of agriculture and of unskilled labor in general, however, even this function is largely obsolete. There is probably no systemic reason that many of the mothers now on welfare could not be absorbed into the work force, and it would be better for most of them if they were.

In recent years, however, the U.S. economic system has had difficulty expanding the number of jobs offered to keep pace with the number of potential new entrants into the work force, thus causing an increase in the amount of unemployment even at the peak of prosperity. This situation may ease somewhat now that most of the baby-boom generation have been absorbed into the work force, but it nevertheless presents a serious obstacle for welfare recipients seeking employment. A disturbing trend of the 1980s has been the disappearance of many high-paid manufacturing jobs and their replacement with minimum-wage sales and service jobs, which do not bring in enough income to pull a family out of poverty.

A major difficulty with any strategy (like that of NWRO) that pushes for higher benefits is that such benefits must be balanced against work incentives. Obviously, the higher welfare benefits are, the more people there will be for whom it is not financially worthwhile to be employed.

When there is a combination of high benefits and generous work incentives, people can continue to receive welfare benefits until they have quite a high income. It has been calculated that the NWRO's demand in the early 1970s of a guaranteed income of $5,500 with the right to keep one-third of one's earnings (not a particularly large work incentive) would have cost $7 billion and covered half the U.S. population.[26] These kinds of cost concerns are what motivated the Reagan administration to discontinue even the far more limited work incentives that existed in 1981.

Americans have resisted the idea of a guaranteed income because they fear it involves an acceptance of the legitimacy of welfare status for some people and that in view of the attitudes expressed by welfare rights groups (which in their heyday in the late 1960s and early 1970s received a great deal of media coverage), this acceptance could result in enormous and uncontrollable costs.[27] This fear is understandable but it is a barrier to the achievement of the key requisite to a better welfare system: the replacement of the psychology of victimization by the psychology of responsibility.

WELFARE AND THE PSYCHOLOGY OF RESPONSIBILITY

Paradoxically, in order for welfare recipients to be able to do what they need to do to get *off* the rolls, both they and the public must accept the legitimacy of their being *on* the rolls. Only if both welfare and employment are acceptable can they have the experience of choosing freely between the two. That experience of choice is the key element of the psychology of responsibility.

There are several persuasive reasons for accepting the legitimacy of some people being on welfare. The most obvious is the scarcity of jobs that pay more than welfare and that can be obtained by the kind of adults who are usually on welfare. These are:

- women—only one AFDC home in ten has a father present and over a third of these fathers are incapacitated;[28]
- the poorly educated—55 percent have not completed high school; 13 percent have not gone beyond the seventh grade;[29]
- the chronically ill;
- members of minority groups—some 44 percent are Black[30] and about 15 percent are Hispanic;[31]
- those with little or no job experience—a quarter of the women on welfare have never been employed; another quarter have been employed only in unskilled jobs.[32]

The main factor influencing whether or not welfare mothers are employed is the ratio of benefits to wages. Welfare mothers are probably as likely to work as other women when there are jobs available with adequate wages. In the six major guaranteed income experiments conducted in the 1970s, it was found that even the presence of a guaranteed income reduced the amount of employment of female heads of households by only 14 percent, and of married men by only 6 percent.[33] In most cases, if welfare mothers are not working, it is more because of their poor job prospects than the disincentives of welfare itself. For uneducated women with several pre-school children requiring costly child care, it is particularly irrational to seek employment.[34]

Given the bleakness of their job prospects, welfare mothers have adapted to their situation of low income and non-standard families. (Ninety percent of AFDC mothers do not have a husband at home: most of these are divorced or separated; almost half of their children were born out of wedlock.[35]) Their main adaptation has been to develop an elaborate network of mostly female kin and friends who offer each other vitally needed goods, services, and emotional support.[36] This adaptation is what makes their lives bearable, if not exactly pleasant. Unless they could feel that this adaptation represented an acceptable way of life, it is hard to imagine that they could develop the self-esteem and confidence so crucial to the psychology of responsibility needed to break out of the welfare system.

The adaptation to their circumstances made by welfare mothers is a source of paradox. Stack illustrates this paradox when she shows that the network of kin and friends works well — so well, in fact, that a woman who wants to attempt a stable traditional marriage must almost always move out of the neighborhood where her network lives.[37] Otherwise, the network and the man would compete for her resources and services, while at the same time his female kin would compete with her for his resources and services.

The network thus serves analogous functions to traditional marriage. Moreover, adaptation to a life centered around the welfare system and the network is analogous to the adaptation that traditional women have made to male-dominated families. Since it is their source of both material support and emotional satisfaction, both groups of women are reluctant to give it up. At the same time, the very strength of the adaptation blocks them from expanding possibilities for their own lives and from being strong models and guides for their children.

In both groups of women — welfare mothers and traditional homemakers — the adaptation involves acceptance of traditional sex roles, in which women devote their lives to raising children while men play only marginal roles in family life because they are occupied with more "masculine" pursuits. This aspect of the adaptation is particularly hard for feminists to accept as a legitimate choice.

As with welfare mothers' involvement in a network, traditional sex roles are a barrier to upward mobility. Research has shown that the sons and daughters of upwardly mobile welfare mothers are precisely those who do not conform to traditional sex roles. The ones who escape from the slums focus on their studies rather than on either the girls' culture of romance and domesticity or the boys' culture of physical prowess and daring.[38]

If sex roles are the part of the adaptation most difficult for feminists to accept, then the part most difficult for traditionalists to accept is the non-standard structure of welfare families. Much of the public's hostility toward welfare is focused on high rates of out-of-wedlock births,[39] amounting to almost half of the AFDC child population.

The ideal traditionalist solution is for the welfare mother to attract a husband capable of supporting her and her children, or failing that, at least to force the father of her children to contribute to their support. Traditionalists and others fear that the welfare system itself drives away the men by usurping their role as breadwinner. In fact, there is some evidence that AFDC may encourage or facilitate the breakup of marriages in the high-grant states and that it may decrease pressure on a woman to marry or remarry.[40]

Public policy has taken two approaches to this problem: to refrain from penalizing fathers who stay at home, and to force deserting fathers to contribute financially. Since 1961, the federal government has permitted the states to pay benefits to families in which an unemployed father is present. At that time, the states changed the name of the program from Aid to Dependent Children (ADC) to Aid to Families with Dependent Children (AFDC), reflecting its concern with the preservation of families. About half the states have adopted rules permitting unemployed fathers in the home, a variation known as Aid to Families with Dependent Children — Unemployed Father or AFDC-U. The results of this change in policy have been disappointing. During the period 1961–67, in nine of the 19 states with AFDC-U the amount of desertion by fathers increased; and in 22 of the 29 non-AFDC-U states during that time, the incidence of desertion by fathers declined. In other words, the non-AFDC-U states had a better trend with respect to paternal desertion than the AFDC-U states.[41]

A second approach, which has been greatly intensified since the 1970s, has been to increase efforts to track down absent fathers and force them to reimburse the government for welfare payments to their wives and children. This would presumably discourage an employed or employable father from deserting in order to shirk his financial responsibilities. The government can now garnishee his Social Security checks, tax refunds, and wages. State governments are required to establish an administrative unit for this purpose. This program has saved the government some money, but there is no evidence that it has had any impact on the rate of desertion.[42]

The probable reason for the failure of such efforts is that the welfare system is not the primary cause of the difficulty in establishing or maintaining traditional families. The primary cause is the inability of lower-class men to obtain steady employment and to fulfill the traditional breadwinner role combined with the reluctance of many lower-class women to have non-earning men in their households.

Some excerpts from a conversation among lower-class Black schoolgirls help explain this reluctance.[43]

> *Cassandra*: My grandmother don't want me gettin married. She say it just too sad. The men be drunk; they be courtin other ladies right after they choose you. . . . When you be married, the man takes and [beats] you.

Cassandra then says that her "uncle" had beaten her aunt even though they were not married.

> My mother say to him . . . "You show me that license if you think you can bang her like that." And the blood popped all over, and my mother had to put a rag on her head . . . and the ambulance came.
>
> *Josie*: Even if I don't know my arithmetic, I still ain't gettin married. The mens just wants to give you babies.

For such girls, the female-centered network described by Stack is obviously a much better adaptation than marriage. Traditional marriage becomes a realistic choice only after the economic situation has changed, and of course not always then: the divorce rate is powerful testimony to the non-adaptiveness of traditional marriage even for many middle-class people.

The great fear of much of the taxpaying public is that welfare mothers' adaptation will become so comfortable that there will be little motivation to break out of welfare dependency by seeking employment. Much of the widespread public concern about cheating is not so much a fear that rules are being broken (many widely publicized studies indicate that only about one percent of all welfare cases involve fraud in this sense[44]), but that welfare mothers are taking advantage of the fact that government policy cannot simply require that all mothers hold jobs, even though it is appropriate for many mothers to do so. However, as the general norm in favor of maternal employment has grown stronger in the 1970s and '80s, government pressure on welfare mothers to take jobs has intensified.

But how can a woman get off welfare if there are no jobs available to her that pay more than welfare? She would have to take a hard look at which of her disadvantages in the labor market were permanent and/or beyond her control and which were not, and begin removing those that were within her control. Having several small children at home is beyond her control, but not necessarily permanent, if she controls her fertility. Research has found that having some sense of the possibility of controlling one's own destiny is a prerequisite to the successful use of birth control techniques.[46] It should be noted that most welfare mothers appear to have already achieved this state. Seventy-four percent of AFDC families contain one or two children; about 90 percent have three or fewer children.[47] The widespread belief (50 percent of the public in one survey) that welfare mothers have one "illegitimate" child after another in order to increase the size of their check is not backed up by research evidence.[48]

Just as the presence of small children is temporary, so too can be the absence of skills and education. It would be absurd to expect any large percentage of welfare mothers simply to go out and get a well-paid job tomorrow. What would not be absurd is to expect a great many of them to begin the long process of acquiring skills and education needed to make their labor-force participation rewarding, both financially and personally. Once the psychology of victimization is shaken off, this could become a realistic goal.

Public policy should help the welfare mother in every way possible, not so much by providing special job training programs, which have a poor track record of actually placing people in jobs, as by providing backup services (child care, counseling, public transportation, and so on) so that she can utilize available high school equivalency courses, community college courses, union apprenticeship programs, employer-sponsored training programs and whatever other training resources exist in her community.

Even after she is trained, the welfare mother faces some permanent disadvantages in the job market: she is a woman and in many cases a person of color in a world that discriminates against both. If she is to deal with the realities of sexism and racism, she must first recognize their existence in all their forms and then free her own mind of them so that they cannot undercut her personal strength.[49] She must at the same time be careful that her recognition of the realities does not merely reinforce the psychology of victimization that keeps her down. It is easier for some women and minority people to spend their lives raging about the trap they are in than to do what needs to be done to break out. On the other hand, people often seem to deny the existence of sexism and racism in order to avoid falling into the psychology of victimization. By this denial they make their lives harder because they are blind to real forces that affect them and unable to unite with others similarly affected to combat these forces.

THE ROLE OF PUBLIC POLICY

What is the role of public policy in all this? Public policy cannot do much to transform a psychology of victimization into one of responsibility. It can, however, do two things: refrain from reinforcing the psychology of victimization or from standing in the way of women who are becoming responsible, and focus on changing those obstacles that are largely beyond the control of individual women. In the first category would be policies that demean and invalidate mothers on welfare, thus making them feel like victims, such as rudeness, long waits and arbitrary actions at the welfare office, workfare at below the minimum wage, unwarranted interference in the mother's personal life, and rhetoric by politicians that encourages the public to see welfare mothers as a pack of lazy cheaters. Reduction of the stigma attached to welfare does not necessarily undermine the motivation to seek employment; on the contrary, lower-class welfare recipients with the longest employment records are the least likely to feel welfare is scorned.[50]

An important victory was won in this area when the Supreme Court ruled that midnight visits by welfare workers (to find out if an unreported man was in residence) were unconstitutional.[51] Since then, however, pressure of all kinds on welfare mothers — to take jobs, to help track down their children's fathers, to work off their benefits — has increased.

The second category of assistance involves positive forms of help, such as family planning services, child care, and other backup services for mothers who are employed, in school, or in training programs, and the vigorous enforcement of laws against discrimination on the basis of sex and race. Unfortunately, in almost all these areas, the Reagan administration is cutting back rather than enhancing efforts. This means welfare mothers must rely more on their own resources and those of their communities and their states.

SUMMARY

The key to the lifting of the pall over welfare is to assist the welfare mother in overcoming the psychology of victimization that her situation and public attitudes reinforce. Only in this way can she do a good job of raising her children, both by teaching them a sense of responsibility for their own destiny and by being a model for them of the possibilities open to a person who has taken responsibility for her own life — which in most cases will mean obtaining the training and education needed for employment that will move her permanently off the welfare rolls. If she is seen as doing a good job of raising her children, the public will not resent the temporary subsidies she needs.[52] Her position will be seen as similar to that of the

middle-class   homemaker   who   is   supported — far   more   gene-
rously — while she is raising her children.

Just as not all middle-class women will be employed, it is unreasonable
to expect that all welfare mothers will eventually be employed. Some
portion of them might choose to stay out of the labor market because of
large numbers of children at home; special needs of some of their children;
their own disability or chronically poor physical or mental health; very low
intelligence; or the fact that they are performing valuable unpaid services
for their network or community, ranging from child care to community
leadership. Although long-term non-employment and a psychology of
victimization probably tend to go together, they need not in every case.
Because of their understandable concern about costs and work disincentives, policymakers have tried to specify exactly who should and should not
be expected to seek employment. But each welfare mother, if she is to
have a sense of autonomy, must retain some discretion, some freedom to
strike her own balance between the inward and outward pull.

A final question remains: What will enable large numbers of welfare
mothers to move toward a psychology of responsibility? It is almost
impossible for a welfare mother to do this alone, especially if she is
surrounded by other people who see themselves as victims. What is needed
is a new welfare movement stressing the potential power of welfare
mothers over their own lives. This movement could emerge from or be
allied with civil rights organizations, women's groups, unions, churches,
and so on. Its thrust would be highly congruent with both feminism, which
stresses the importance of women taking command of their own lives, and
traditionalism, which stresses a woman's responsibility for raising her
children to be independent. Such a movement could play a vital role in
lifting the pall that still hangs over AFDC after two decades of welfare
reform.

This new welfare movement could also lay the groundwork for a shift in
the U.S. political system's approach to public assistance. That system has
set up a program to assist poor children that is only available to non-
standard families, that is, families without a wage-earning father or, in
many states, without any father present at all. Yet the system then
stigmatizes recipients of benefits under the program in large part *because*
they live in non-standard families. At the same time, the system suffers
from the accusation that it creates or perpetuates these non-standard
families.[53]

The only way to escape from this perverse policy is to assist all families
with children. The United States has only one such across-the-board
program and that is the federal income tax exemption (really, a deduction
from taxable income) for each dependent child. In 1986, it was $1080;
under the new tax law it will rise in 1989 to $2000 and after 1990 it will be

indexed for inflation. However, this program, in another perverse twist of policy, fails to benefit the poorest families since they do not pay income tax, or benefits them less because they pay less total tax than the amount of the exemption.

Many other countries offer programs that benefit all families with children and therefore are totally free from stigma. They also have far lower administrative costs (for determining eligibility) and fewer unintended consequences, such as encouraging births out of wedlock. These programs include family allowances (a monthly payment for each child) paid in every country in Europe, Canada, Australia and New Zealand, plus about two dozen Asian and African countries. The amount paid varies a great deal, from Canada's nominal $10 a month to about a fifth of their income for poorer families in France.[54] There is no evidence that such allowances increase the birthrate.[55] Some countries, such as Sweden, further subsidize families with children by giving them housing allowances and a range of social services, including child care centers.

All European countries have a national health plan that pays the medical expenses of the whole population, including children. All European countries offer a legal minimum of 3 months' maternity leave, usually with full or nearly full pay provided by the government, plus in most countries about a year of unpaid leave with no loss of job rights. Sweden offers 9 months of paid leave, usable by the mother or the father.[56] Hungary and Czechoslovakia go even further, permitting all previously employed mothers of children under age 3 to stay at home, with a large percentage of their salaries paid by the government. Far more low-paid than high-paid workers take advantage of these child-care grants.[57]

Given current concern about the size of the federal budget deficit, it seems most unlikely that a major new categorical program like family allowances will be adopted in the near future. The United States lacks the low birthrates that motivate these policies in Europe and the democratic socialist traditions that validate them. What could happen in the United States, though, is that public attitudes about AFDC could come to resemble European attitudes about assisting families with children. AFDC could be thought of as a legitimate subsidy for raising children in difficult economic circumstances; it could be presumed that most parent recipients were doing their best to contribute to their children's well-being. Shifts in public attitudes, public policy, the attitudes of welfare recipients, and the approaches of their organizations would all reinforce each other. AFDC recipients and policymakers could then make decisions about both broad policies and individual cases in an atmosphere of clarity and responsibility rather than mutual blame, despair, and anger.

NOTES AND REFERENCES

1. *Statistical Abstract of the United States, 1985* (Washington, D.C.: Bureau of the Census), p. 45.

2. Ibid., p. 379.

3. Martin Anderson, *Welfare: The Political Economy of Welfare Reform in the United States* (Stanford, CA: Hoover Institution Press, 1978), p. 24.

4. Betty Reid Mandell, *Welfare in America: Controlling the "Dangerous Classes"* (Englewood Cliffs, NJ: Prentice-Hall, 1975), *passim.*

5. Harvey D. Shapiro, "Welfare Reform Revisited," in Lester M. Salamon, *Welfare: The Elusive Consensus* (New York: Praeger, 1978), p. 194.

6. Christopher Leman, *The Collapse of Welfare Reform: Political Institutions, Policy and the Poor in Canada and the United States* (Cambridge: MIT Press, 1980), p. 85.

7. Ibid., pp. 217–219.

8. Henry L. Allen, "A Radical Critique of Federal Work and Manpower Programs, 1933–1974," pp. 37–38, in Mandell, *Welfare in America.*

9. Sar A. Levitan, *Programs in Aid of the Poor for the 1980s* (Baltimore: Johns Hopkins University Press, 1980), p. 35.

10. *Statistical Abstract*, p. 382.

11. Ibid., p. 382.

12. Ibid., p. 356.

13. Ibid., p. 379.

14. Natalie Jaffe, "A Review of Public Opinion Surveys 1935–1976," in Salamon, *Welfare*, p. 226–7.

15. Gilbert Y. Steiner, *The State of Welfare* (Washington: Brookings Institution, 1971), p. 175.

16. Stephen M. Rose, *The Betrayal of the Poor: The Transformation of Community Action* (Cambridge: Schenkman, 1972), p. 60.

17. Elliot Liebow, *Tally's Corner: A Study of Negro Streetcorner Men* (Boston: Little, Brown, 1967), pp. 210–211.

18. James S. Coleman et al., *Equality of Educational Opportunity* (Washington, D.C.: U.S. Department of Health, Education and Welfare, Office of Education, 1966), pp. 288–289.

19. For a description of the psychological meaning of "victim," see Muriel James and Dorothy Jongeward, *Born to Win: Transactional Analysis with Gestalt Experiments* (Reading, MA: Addison-Wesley, 1971), pp. 85–89.

20. Edward C. Banfield, *The Unheavenly City Revisited* (Boston: Little, Brown, 1974), pp. 53–54 *passim.*

21. Milwaukee County Welfare Rights Organization, *Welfare Mothers Speak Out: We Ain't Gonna Shuffle Anymore* (New York: W. W. Norton, 1972), *passim.*

22. Mandell, *Welfare in America*; Frances Fox Piven and Richard A. Cloward, *Regulating the Poor* (New York: Pantheon, 1971), pp. 4–8.

23. Milwaukee, *Welfare Mothers Speak Out*, p. 137.

24. *King v. Smith*, 392 U.S. 309, 1968, and *Shapiro v. Thompson*, 394 U.S. 618, 1969.

25. Piven and Cloward, *Regulating the Poor*, pp. 124–25. The figure on the cost of AFDC comes from the *Statistical Abstract 1986*, p. 357.

26. Leman, *Collapse of Welfare Reform*, p. 181.

27. Anderson, *Welfare*, p. 83.

28. *Statistical Abstract 1985*, p. 382.

29. Leman, *Collapse of Welfare Reform*, p. 57.

30. *Statistical Abstract*, p. 358.

31. *1979 Recipient Characteristics Study, Part 1, Demographic and Program Statistics*, Doc. # HE 3.65:979. (Washington: Office of Research and Statistics, Social Security Administration, DHHS, 1982), p. 25.

32. Levitan, *Programs in Aid*, pp. 33–34.

33. Anderson, *Welfare*, p. 124. Anderson explains, pp. 105–117, that factors unique to these experiments may have made the work reduction artificially low.

34. Steiner, 1971, *The State of Welfare*, pp. 51, 70.

35. *Statistical Abstract 1985*, p. 382.

36. Carol Stack, *All Our Kin* (New York: Harper & Row, 1974), *passim*.

37. Ibid., pp. 113–114.

38. Jagna Wojcicka Sharff, "Free Enterprise and the Ghetto Family," *Psychology Today*, March 1981, pp. 47–48. This research is particularly persuasive because it was not focused around the question of sex roles but rather around the roles of poor children in the family; the finding about sex roles was a surprise to the researcher.

39. Steiner, *The State of Welfare*, p. 53; Jaffe, "A Review of Public Opinion," pp. 225–6.

40. Sheila B. Kamerman and Alfred J. Kahn, *Family Policy: Government and Families in Fourteen Countries* (New York: Columbia University Press, 1978), p. 447.

41. Steiner, *The State of Welfare*, p. 84.

42. Leman, *Collapse of Welfare Reform*, pp. 210–212.

43. Both excerpts are from Mary Frances Greene and Orletta Ryan, "Girls at Noon," in Gregory Armstrong (ed.) *Life at the Bottom* (New York: Bantam, 1971), pp. 106–107.

44. Leman, *Collapse of Welfare Reform*, p. 208.

45. Ibid., p. 31.

46. Frances Moore Lappe and Joseph Collins, *Food First: Beyond the Myth of Scarcity* (Boston: Houghton Mifflin, 1977), p. 67.

47. *Statistical Abstract 1985*, p. 382.

48. Jaffe, "A Review of Public Opinion," p. 22; Kamerman and Kahn, *Family Policy*, p. 447.

49. Elizabeth Janeway, *Powers of the Weak* (New York: Alfred A. Knopf, 1980), *passim*.

50. Mildred Rein, *Work or Welfare? Factors in the Choice for AFDC Mothers* (New York: Praeger, 1974), p. 56.

51. *Wyman v. James* 400 U.S. 309, 1971.

52. Jaffe, "A Review of Public Opinion," p. 225.

53. For a full discussion of this point, see Emily Stoper, "Welfare as Family Policy," paper presented at the Western Political Science Association meetings, Seattle, 1983.

54. James C. Vadakin, *Children, Poverty and Family Allowances* (New York: Basic Books, 1968), p. 10.

55. Eveline M. Burns, *Children's Allowances and the Economic Welfare of Children: Report of a Conference* (New York: Citizens' Committee for Children of New York, 1968), pp. 126–127; Vadakin, *Children, Poverty*, pp. 95–101.

56. Sheila B. Kamerman, *Parenting in an Unresponsive Society: Managing Work and Family Life* (New York: Macmillan, 1980), pp. 164–165.

57. Susan Ferge, "The Development of the Protection of Mothers and Children in Hungary after 1945," in Pamela Roby, *Child Care: Who Cares?* (New York: Basic Books, 1973), pp. 353–357.

11
Divorce and the Transition to the Single-parent Family

Emily Stoper and Ellen Boneparth

Contemporary analysis of the evolving nuclear family tends to focus on the ever-increasing divorce rate and the ensuing problems of the single-parent family. Less attention has been given to the transitional stage from the decision to divorce to the reconstitution of the family. Yet it is in this stage of family evolution in particular that patterns are established that often affect the viability of the family after divorce. Policies on child custody, child support, and family support systems are undergoing change, but these changes are not well understood by the public and the policymakers, in part because they are occurring at the individual or local level, and in part because they are clouded by myths and misrepresentation arising from the emotional context of divorce. This chapter examines some of the emerging trends in U.S. public policy and practice surrounding divorce, with special emphasis on the transition to the single-parent, overwhelmingly female-headed, family. These policies and practices are then contrasted with the very different way of dealing with the same problem on the Israeli kibbutz.

Each year over a million marriages in the United States end in divorce. The percentage of divorced women in the U.S. population tripled from almost 3 percent in 1960 to almost 9 percent in 1984.[1] If present trends continue, more than 40 percent of people who marry in the 1980s can expect to be divorced, and by the 1990s only 56 percent of American children will spend their entire childhood with both natural parents.[2]

Divorced mothers have severe difficulty in providing adequate care for their children while supporting them financially. If the mother has custody (and about 90 percent of divorced mothers do), her standard of living is likely to fall precipitously after divorce, especially if her husband had a fairly high income.[3] This means that the children's standard of living also falls sharply and that her economic worries and her struggle to earn more money may cause her to be less available to them.

POLICY ON CHILD CUSTODY IN THE UNITED STATES

Why is it that about 90 percent of divorced mothers have custody of their children, thus creating a situation in which the parent with the heaviest financial responsibilities usually has the least economic resources? In most cases, the mother, being the primary parent, wanted custody and the father did not. When the father wants custody, he has a good chance of getting it. Recent studies of custody battles in court have found that fathers are winning in 45 to 63 percent of such cases.[4]

This is a very recent trend. From the 1920s through the mid-1970s, mothers who wanted custody were virtually assured of receiving it in all 50 states, though the law never stated that they were favored. What the law did say and still says is that the main consideration in awarding custody must be "the best interests of the child." Until recently judges followed the opinion that at least during the child's "tender years," this was presumed to mean that the mother should have custody unless she was obviously incompetent or immoral. This presumption reversed the previous practice of almost always granting custody to the father, who before the middle of the nineteenth century, was seen as having a proprietary right to his children (who were often an economic asset).

Today two-thirds of the states have rejected the tender years doctrine and the remaining one-third have weakened the doctrine considerably. An examination of recent court decisions indicates that the tender-years doctrine is no longer being accepted as a basis for granting custody. In a number of recent cases fathers have won custody because of their greater financial ability to provide what judges regard as a "good home."[5] A few states now explicitly permit the father's better financial position to influence awards in his favor.[6]

Both courts and legislatures appear to be moving toward a sex-neutral standard. This seems fair on the face of it, but just what does "sex neutral" mean? In weighing the "best interests of the child," how does one weight financial solvency (which a father is more likely to have) against being the primary nurturer (more likely the mother)? The concept of primary nurturer or primary caretaker is difficult to define. In one recent court case it was defined in terms of a series of tasks performed for the child[7]; yet surely a better definition should focus on the nature of the emotional relationship. Another court decision states that the tender years doctrine, which explicitly favored the mother, should be replaced with a primary-parent doctrine, which would favor the mother only in those cases (the vast majority) in which she was indeed the primary parent.[8] Such a doctrine would still require clarifying legislation and litigation to develop an acceptable definition of primary parent. For example, it must be established that employment does not weaken a mother's claim to be the primary parent and that a father's new wife is not an automatic equivalent to a child's mother, even if the mother is employed and the new wife is not.[9]

POLICY ON CHILD SUPPORT

The non-custodial parent (usually the father) is generally expected to pay child support to the custodial parent until the child comes of age, usually at 18. The amount depends in part on the non-custodial parent's ability to pay. Judges almost never require fathers to pay more than about a third of their net income to child support and spousal support (or alimony) combined.[10] The average amount of child support when one parent has sole custody is only 26 percent of the other parent's income. In Los Angeles in 1977 the average monthly amount of child support was $126 per child. This amount, which is fairly typical, did not come close to covering half the actual expenses of raising the child.[11]

POLICY CONFLICTS

In the area of public policy on child custody and support, conflict occurs not so much between advocates of traditionalism and feminism (both of whom, if they are women, tend to favor strong maternal rights to custody and generous child support and spousal support) as between mothers and fathers. The two perspectives are very much at variance and the feelings are often intense and bitter.

The Mothers' Perspective

Divorced mothers usually think that the laws and practices governing child support and spousal support are inequitable because they so often leave the mother and children impoverished. The traditionalist view of custody is that the mother is the primary parent and therefore should almost always be granted custody. Some feminist writers, on the other hand, explicitly reject the assumption that the mother is by nature the primary parent and have even seen equal sharing of parenting as the key to the liberation of women.[12] Yet most feminists also favor a presumption that mothers will receive custody, because they know that in fact, if not by nature, the mother is still usually the primary parent.

Feminist mothers in particular view with great concern any weakening of their legal rights to custody and support. The threat of losing their children is used against mothers by men, for example, by judges wishing to punish mothers for liberated lifestyles or strong job commitments.[13] Moreover, feminists are particularly reluctant to give up the legal presumption of maternal custody just when that presumption is finally being extended, at least in a few cases, to lesbian mothers.[14] Husbands hoping for a more favorable financial settlement or trying to prevent their wives from leaving a marriage in which they were battered or otherwise mistreated are placed in a stronger position since those women have greater reason to fear losing custody of their children. Thus, mothers may be willing to bargain away adequate child support in exchange for the assurance of custody. This is called the "Solomon Syndrome" after the mother in the Bible who was willing to give up her child to another woman rather than having him cut in half.[15]

Both feminists and traditionalists oppose a sex-neutral standard because it would lead to more contested custody cases, in which fathers generally have the financial advantage. Thus, they agree on the great importance of preserving the judicial practice that presumes mothers will be awarded custody.

There is similar agreement on the question of support. The traditionalist view is that when a man marries he undertakes a financial obligation to his wife throughout her lifetime and to any offspring of the marriage while they are minors. This obligation is crucial to the structure of complementary roles within marriage. It is what makes possible the wife's renunciation of paid work in favor of devoting herself to husband and children. While feminist writers reject this whole philosophy of marriage, which is based on sharply divergent masculine and feminine sex roles, they see generous child support and spousal support as a matter of equity, as long as women continue to be at an enormous disadvantage in the labor market.[16] Both feminist and traditionalist leaders, concerned about the problem of non-compliance with court-ordered child support awards, often favor laws providing wage deductions or attachments. Thus, two different roads lead to the same destination: advocacy of generous child and spousal support.

The Fathers' Perspective

The reason for the erosion of the presumption that mothers will obtain custody is that increasing numbers of fathers regard the resulting situation as unfair and are challenging it in a rising number of custody fights. Likewise, there has been a proliferation of men's groups, such as Equal Rights for Fathers, which advocate that a presumption of joint (shared) custody be written into law. Joint custody is a legal arrangement under which each parent is granted equal rights in making decision regarding the children, though overwhelmingly the children live with their mothers.[17] Sometimes the children in joint custody spend about an equal amount of time with each parent, alternating half-weeks, weeks, months, even years. This is an atypical practice but one which receives much attention in publications advocating joint custody.[18]

Ironically, fathers often cite feminists advocacy of equal sharing between parents and of women's workforce participation in support of their right to joint custody or to a sex-neutral standard for granting sole custody.[19] They also cite the many studies that show the pain and trouble caused by divorce with maternal custody: children's loss of a close relationship with their fathers, fathers' loss of a close relationship with their children, and mothers' harried and difficult lives.[20] Other studies show that fathers with custody do not have unusual difficulty in raising their children.[21]

Many fathers regard child support as inherently unjust. Deprived of the companionship of their children except during rigidly specified visitation periods, they feel that they are paying for a benefit they do not enjoy. "My ex-wife took me to the cleaners" is a common fatherly refrain after a divorce. It refers to the division of property (now usually roughly equal in the community property states like California and becoming more equal in other states), as well as to child support and spousal support. In the community property states many fathers have never truly accepted the legal doctrine that states that their wives contribute equally to the accumulation of marital property through their services in the home or their often meager earnings. Nor do they really believe that they have an obligation to support wives or children with whom they no longer have a shared household. They are particularly indignant that there are increasingly stiff federal laws to help the states enforce child support awards without comparable enforcement of visitation rights.[22] (It should be noted that interference with visitation is actually very rare.[23])

Fathers rebel in three main ways against a situation they consider unfair.

1. *Non-payment of child support.* In 1978 a Census Bureau study found that only about half the women awarded child support received it as ordered. Not one study has found a state or county in which more than half of the fathers fully comply with court orders. About half the non-compliers pay too little or too late; the other half pay nothing.[24]

2. *Organizing to push for joint custody* as a presumption in the law and for a sex neutral standard in custody awards, or

3. *Stealing the children* that is, simply transporting them to another state and obtaining legal custody there, often before the custody decision has even been made by the court in the children's home state. This is done either as a means of gaining permanent custody or in order to coerce the wife into relinquishing her right to child support or accepting an unfavorable divorce settlement. The government estimates there are some 25,000 child stealings or "snatchings" a year; private groups say 100,000.

In summary, for mothers, custody of the children, although usually desired, is often experienced as a heavy burden for which they need and deserve much more financial assistance than they are now receiving; for fathers, custody is often experienced as a privilege of which they have been deprived while they are still expected to pay dearly for the support of their children.

Toward Solutions: Joint Custody?

Both mothers and fathers have worked to change the law in recent years, but in opposite directions. Fathers have worked toward tilting the law away from sole custody for the mother and toward joint custody. Some 27 states now have laws that encourage courts to ensure that children have "close and continuing contact" with both parents whenever possible, effectively creating a legal presumption of joint custody.[26] Such a presumption clearly weakens the position of mothers in divorce, since mothers until recently have had the best chance to obtain sole custody in contested cases.

Research shows that joint custody is likely to be successful only for those divorcing couples who have a fairly amicable relationship and an existing pattern of shared parenting. In cases where these conditions do not exist, joint custody may result in a continuation of the fighting that led to the divorce, much to the detriment of the children as well as the parents. Or one parent, usually the father, reneges on his responsibilities to care for and pay the expenses of the children with the result that the mother actually has full care of the children, without financial assistance that she would have had if she had been granted sole custody. Or in some extreme cases, a pattern of wife abuse is renewed. (Some states, such as Florida and Arizona, have passed laws against the granting of joint custody when there is a history of wife abuse.[27])

Joint custody, furthermore, does not solve the financial problems created by divorce. In those cases where joint custody involves children living at least some of the time with each parent, it is expensive, requiring space and also often clothing and equipment for the children in each parent's home. Yet in many instances joint residential custody is interpreted by the court to relieve a father of his child support obligation. Child support is awarded in only 38 percent of those cases, plus 9 percent of cases that receive support for part of the year only.[28] Joint custody may also result in mothers' loss of tax exemptions for the children and in reduction of AFDC payments.

Relatively few divorcing couples have the amicable relations, affluence, and shared parenting patterns that would make them good candidates for joint custody. Therefore, preferable to a presumption written into law would be case-by-case decisions, with each case decided by the judge on the basis of the best interests of the child. One problem, however, with leaving this much discretion in the hands of judges is that it could increase the number of custody battles (because of the uncertainty of the outcome) and could create a feeling among both fathers and mothers that the law was arbitrary. All this might have the effect of increasing the number of child stealings.

Thus, there is no change in the custody rules on which mothers and fathers are likely to agree. Moreover, in view of mothers' feelings that they are unfairly impoverished by divorce and fathers' feeling that they are unfairly deprived of money they earn, it is hard to see how to resolve the impasse over support in a manner satisfactory to both.

Government Assistance

One obvious solution would seem to be government assistance. In some European countries, such as Norway, divorce is automatically followed by an increase in the family allowance paid to the mother and a lowering of her tax rate.[28] But such assistance would be regarded in this country as an incentive to divorce. In any case, we do not have a family allowance and the partial repeal of the "marriage tax" (a higher tax rate for some married couples) has been one of the most widely popular legislative changes in recent years.

Government assistance might be less controversial if it took the form of education and training programs to help divorced women earn a better living. Displaced homemaker programs, providing training, counseling, and referral services to divorced or widowed women, offer one way of doing this. Without fundamental changes in the kinds of job available to women, however, such reforms will not make much difference.

The direction that reform has taken most recently is a tightening of the laws enforcing collection of child-support payments, a reform that generally pleases mothers, not fathers. The Federal Child Support Enforcement Amendments of 1984 passed Congress unanimously. Liberals and feminists liked them because they assisted women who were impoverished and unfairly treated. Conservatives and traditionalists liked them because they rested on the view that fathers should support their own children rather than having them rely on government assistance. The much-touted "gender gap" during the 1984 elections undoubtedly also made politicians of every hue eager to support a measure that would be popular with women voters.

The amendments to Title IV-D of the Social Security Act require each state to run a child support enforcement program that locates absent parents and to enforce child support awards for AFDC and non-AFDC recipients alike. Previously, many states had concentrated their efforts on absent fathers of AFDC recipients. The strongest new provision in the law is the one requiring every state to adopt a procedure, either judicial or administrative, for automatically withholding wages if a parent is one month in arrears. (The legislation originally proposed would have automatically withheld wages from all parents who were ordered to pay child support, thus eliminating any stigma associating with such withholdings. This concept was withdrawn, however, because it was viewed as involving too much state interference in people's lives.) States may also apply withholding orders to other sources of income (even lottery winnings!) and may begin withholding even sooner than one month. Some states, even before the law passed, had begun experimenting with jailing recalcitrant fathers for brief periods, a remarkably effective technique in securing enforcement of support awards.

It must be pointed out that even this tough legislation does not fully solve the mothers' problems, because it does not deal with the issue of the amount of child support awards, except by requiring the establishment of guidelines to be used by the courts. The majority of divorced mothers will still receive grossly inadequate payments. Moreover, by shutting off one avenue of rebellion by fathers, it may result in increased pressure for joint custody and an increase in child stealings, the other two avenues of rebellion. In view of the power of men in the political and judicial systems, it is unlikely that child support payments in the aggregate will ever be substantially increased.

Ultimately, the problem is unresolvable as long as the mother role leaves women economically dependent on their husbands and the marriage bond is so often broken. The woman who enters the work force but earns far less than her husband may be increasing her probability of divorce (the research on this question is inconclusive) while not really making herself economically self-sufficient. But the causes of divorce are more fundamental than female employment. They include the most basic American values: independence, individualism, materialism, and the pursuit of happiness. Given the prevalence of these values, the woman who stays at home is not insured against divorce and will be even worse off if it comes than her employed sister.

When all is said and done, there are probably only three ways that our society can protect mothers from vulnerability to sharp declines in their standard of living. One way is for the community to take substantial responsibility for the costs of raising all children, including support of the mother while she is out of the work force. The second way is for fathers and mothers to redefine their roles to share equally the job of parenting, thus removing the economic disadvantage from mothers. The third way is a restoration of the old norm that divorce is socially unacceptable. Changes moving in any of these directions would increase the economic security of mothers, but none of them seem likely to occur to a significant degree in the near future.

WPP—H*

THE ISRAELI KIBBUTZ

What can Americans learn by looking at an institution in which the community is far more deeply involved in family life than in the United States? And how does such an institution assist family members in coping with divorce?

The Israeli kibbutz, perhaps the longest-surviving twentieth century communal institution to challenge the nuclear family, originated as a small agricultural collective based on the goals of egalitarianism and communalism. In the early years of the kibbutz movement, family issues were insignificant since kibbutzniks were typically unmarried young people, immersed in a struggle for economic survival. Their secular and revolutionary values in many cases made them view the institution of marriage with disdain. As the kibbutzim became established, kibbutzniks set about creating institutions that would foster sexual equality. While much of the literature of the kibbutz applauds the successes of the pioneers in breaking down sex roles, there is also considerable evidence from the writings of the pioneer women that they experienced sex discrimination in work assignments, self-defense and military activities, and leadership roles. What is evident is that as the kibbutz developed, a sexual division of labor emerged in which men assumed the major responsibility for production and economic and political decisionmaking, while women were concentrated in services, serving only minor roles in the decision-making structures of the community.

Today, the kibbutz has evolved from agriculture to include industrial production and services such as guesthouses. Around 3 percent of the Israeli population lives on approximately 300 kibbutzim, ranging in size from roughly 100 to 1,000 families. While economic egalitarianism is still the rule with equal sharing of the resources of the kibbutz, many kibbutzim have evolved, amidst considerable debate, from communal practices such as children's houses for child-rearing and exclusively communal dining, to a more individualized and home-centered lifestyle, with children sleeping at home and some meals prepared and taken in the household. The reasons for this promotion of the traditional nuclear family on the kibbutz are many: the growing economic prosperity and interaction of the kibbutz with the larger family-oriented Israeli society, the failure of the kibbutz to overcome the sexual division of labor, and, for some kibbutzim, the revival of Jewish tradition against which the pioneers rebelled.

While the divorce rate on the kibbutz, and in Israel generally, is low relative to that in the United States, divorce occurs and is slowly increasing. How does the single-parent family fare on the kibbutz? The great proportion of single-parent families are headed by women. The most unequivocal benefit of kibbutz life for these women and their children is economic security, with not only the necessities of life, but also the opportunities for personal development—educationally, socially, and culturally— provided by the kibbutz community. In fact, single mothers seeking to advance themselves with study or activities off the kibbutz, or requesting new housing, often get preferential treatment.

The economic benefits extend beyond security to a situation of economic equality in which the standard of living of single-parent families on the kibbutz is no different from that of two-parent families. Women who experience widowhood or divorce suffer none of the decline in their standard of living that typically accompanies a similar change in marital status in modern Western society. On some kibbutzim, support for single parents even extends to agreement by the kibbutz to pay the alimony or child-support payments of separated or divorced male members whose ex-wives and children live off the kibbutz. Because the kibbutz is organized to provide an integration of family and work roles by relieving women of individual responsibility for child care and many domestic chores, the single mother does not experience conflict between her work and family roles to anywhere near the degree of the single parent elsewhere managing a job and an individual home. As one single mother said in an interview:

> The two biggest advantages go hand in hand. One is guaranteed, high level, no-cost child care and the other is job security and flexibility with a guaranteed median income.

The kibbutz also provides the single parent with a social network—a community—which takes an interest in her/his children and provides children with a wide range of adults to serve as role models. Thus, the kibbutz protects single-parent families from social isolation and, in the best situations, provides social support. For the divorced or separated mother on the kibbutz, if her former spouse remains on the kibbutz, there is the advantage of close contact between the offspring and their father, but also the disadvantage for the mother of continuing contact with her ex-spouse. As one kibbutz mother described the situation:

> Kibbutz life is really advantageous for my son because there is no conflict with being with either parent—he can choose where he wants to be at any point. He's in a much freer situation while we (the parents) are in a confined situation because we have to see each other all the time.

If the former spouse lives off the kibbutz, the divorced mother experiences less social strain, but still has to deal with the fact that she is not part of a couple and may, in some cases, be perceived as a threat to the stability of other couples.

Structurally, the kibbutz provides an enviable solution to the problems of the single parent, as family economic needs are underwritten by the community and role strain between work and family is greatly reduced. What may be missing in the kibbutz environment is some form of organized psychological support for single parents, who have emotional, as well as physical, needs that must be addressed. The widow or divorcee receives considerable emotional support for finding a new mate, but far less for adapting to her aloneness and establishing a rewarding set of social interactions with other adult members.

Despite its evolution to a more traditional family structure, the kibbutz presents an alternative social setting where single mothers experience neither the low social and economic status nor the dependency on government support commonly found in most industrialized countries. While the kibbutz lifestyle clearly lacks appeal not only to non-Israelis, but also to the vast majority of Israelis, it does stand as a significant example of a community in which membership for the single parent and her/his children means equal opportunities for economic and social participation. Perhaps the most important message to be gleaned from the kibbutz experience is that unlike some advanced social welfare states where the family has been redefined to incorporate single parenting, the kibbutz promotes traditional family structures as well as enormous institutional support for single parenting, which remains a viable, if atypical, lifestyle.

IMPLICATIONS FOR THE UNITED STATES

The kibbutz experience makes clear the need in the United States and elsewhere for a community role that goes beyond economic assistance in aiding families, socially and psychologically, in adjusting to divorce. Prevailing U.S. values about divorce are that it is a private matter between the parents, with state intervention primarily through the legal system. Still, even today, the divorced parent often becomes a sort of social pariah, perceived as threatening the stability of intact marriages. Likewise, the children, while pitied, often also become isolated, alienated from the noncustodial parent and thus deprived of an adult role model of the male (or occasionally female) gender. What little community support exists for families making the transition from divorce to single parenting consists of social groups for divorced parents to find new mates and limited amounts for assistance to non-employed mothers in finding their way into the work force.

With divorce an increasingly common occurrence, there clearly needs to be a transformation of values to promote attitudes consonant with reality, as well as efforts to integrate all kinds of families into the community. The mass media are slowly beginning to portray the single-parent family as a viable institution, but they have a long way to go. Social programs are desperately needed to bring single-parent families out of isolation and into contact with each other and with other types of families, so that the stresses of child rearing are relieved and even shared, and so that children have role models of both sexes. Counseling for divorced parents and their children should be widely available on both an individual and group basis, through the school system and other community services. While divorce in urban America may have become common, it has not become normal, that is to say, nonstigmatized, and public policy continues to treat divorce as an individual rather than a community concern.

NOTES AND REFERENCES

1. *Statistical Abstract of the United States* (Washington, DC: Bureau of the Census, 1986), p. 35.

2. Lenore J. Weitzman, "The Economics of Divorce: Social and Economic Consequences of Property, Alimony and Child Support Awards," *UCLA Law Review, Vol. 28* (August 1981), p. 1183.

3. Ibid., p. 1184.

4. Nancy D. Polikoff, "Gender and Child Custody Determinations: Exploding the Myths," in Irene Diamond (ed.) *Families, Politics and Public Policy* (New York and London: Longman, 1983), p. 184–5.

5. Ibid., p. 187–92.

6. Ellen Max, "Custody Criteria, Visitation and Child Support," *The Women's Advocate*, (Sept. 1985), pp. 2, 4.

7. Polikoff, "Gender and Child Custody," p. 187.

8. *Garska v. McCoy*, 278 S.E. 2d 357, West Virginia, 1981.

9. Polikoff, "Gender and Child Custody," p. 190.

10. Weitzman, "The Economics of Divorce," p. 1234.

11. Ibid., p. 1233, 1240.

12. Nancy Chodorow, *The Reproduction of Mothering: Psychoanalysis and the Sociology of Gender* (Berkeley: University of California Press, 1978); Dorothy Dinnerstein, *The Mermaid and the Minotaur: Sexual Arrangements and the Human Malaise* (New York: Harper Colophon, 1977).

13. See *Jarrett v. Jarrett* and *Milovich v. Milovich*, both Illinois Supreme Court, 1980, both reported in *In These Times*, Nov. 12–18, 1980, p. 4.

14. *Bezio v. Patenaude*, Mass. Supreme Judicial Court, reported in *National NOW Times*, Dec.–Jan. 1980–81, p. 14; *Belmont v. Belmont*, New Jersey Supreme Court, 1980, *National NOW Times*, Sept. 1980, p. 10.

15. Max, "Custody Criteria," p. 1.

16. Weitzman, "The Economics of Divorce," p. 1240.

17. Polikoff, "Gender and Child Custody," p. 192.

18. Melvin Roman and William Haddad, *The Disposable Parent: The Case for Joint Custody* (New York: Holt, Rinehart and Winston, 1978).

19. Ibid., p. 24–40.

20. Ibid., p. 48–83.

21. Karen W. Bartz and W. C. Witcher, "When Father Gets Custody," *Child Today*, September 1978, p. 4.

22. John Edward Gill, *Stolen Children: Why and How Parents Kidnap their Kids* (New York: Seaview Books, 1981), p. 47.

23. Max, "Custody Criteria," p. 2.

24. Weitzman, "The Economics of Divorce," p. 1253–4.

25. Gill, *Stolen Children*, p. 15.

26. *Oakland Tribune*, August 17, 1984, p. A2.

27. Eleanor E. Maccoby, Robert H. Mnookin and Charles E. Depner, "Post-Divorce Families: Custodial Arrangements Compared," Paper delivered at American Association for the Advancement of Science meetings, Philadelphia, May 1986. On the state laws on battery and custody, see *The Women's Advocate*, Vol. 7, Number 4, July 1986.

28. Weitzman, "The Economics of Divorce," p. 1267.

PART IV

COMPARATIVE PERSPECTIVES

Introduction

In the past decade, the globalization of feminism has been realized in many different arenas, ranging from the highly formal to informal and including international and regional organizations; coalitions of feminist groups; nongovernmental organizations; research, educational and publishing networks; issue groups; professional associations; and the contacts and exchanges of individual feminist travelers. There is no single impetus for this expanding movement across borders and continents. At the official level, the U.N. Decade for Women (1975–85), which was structured around international conferences in Mexico City, Copenhagen and Nairobi involving hundreds of international agencies and nongovernmental organizations and thousands of women, provided a critical framework for feminist collaboration on the decade's themes of equality, development and peace. At less official levels, the knowledge explosion in women's studies, the communications revolution and the growing consciousness of global interdependence have impelled feminists to reach beyond their own local and national communities to find the causes, solutions and support systems for their common concerns.

The path to global sisterhood has not been easy. International meetings of women have often been disrupted by national and regional antagonisms, permitting the media to belittle the notion of sisterhood as no more realistic than international brotherhood. Likewise, feminists, although consciously struggling against their class divisions, have often been unsuccessful in their attempts to expand participation beyond an elite. Finally, despite a determination to avoid cultural imperialism and a commitment to listening and learning, feminists have continually come up against the hard reality of their own conflicting ideologies and values.

The chapters in this section illustrate the necessity, as well as the complexity, of uniting around global feminism. In Chapter 12, Diane Schaffer outlines the commonalities of the feminization of poverty. The dual burden of work and family and the lack of access to the tools of advancement place many women in both developed and less developed countries at the bottom of their societies. Schaffer examines different social policy models, influenced by varying social ideologies, and finds that whatever their particular approach, they all fail, to some degree, to address the needs of the single female head of household.

Ideology confronting reality is well-illustrated in the case study of women in Greece, a country which faces serious economic problems (lack of resources, huge external debt, large military budget) and which has a strong patriarchal tradition that relegates women to peripheral roles in the development process. As Eleni Stamiris shows in chapter 13, in the last 5 years of socialist government, Greece has embarked on a "top-down" program of gender equality that has brought about potentially revolutionary change in public policy but has, as yet, been unable to alter dramatically women's social reality. She concludes that real change will require economic development and a transformation of both infrastructure and attitudes.

Considering these issues from a foreign policy perspective, Kathleen Staudt and Jane Jaquette in chapter 14 provide an in-depth analysis of U.S. government and international efforts to reorient development programs to eliminate gender bias. The Women in Development Office in the U.S. Agency for International Development has faced a decade of bureaucratic resistance. Likewise, the national machinery to deal with women's concerns put into place in many countries as a result of the mandate of the U.N. Decade for Women has yet to dislodge male prejudice and privilege in economic development programs. While some small progress has been made, it is primarily in "special treatment" programs rather than in woman-centered policy approaches.

Kathleen L. Barry demonstrates in chapter 15 the power of an informal feminist network to put a highly controversial and consistently ignored issue, female sexual slavery, on the international agenda. Once again, the U.N. Decade for Women provided the framework for raising this issue, long avoided by the relevant international agencies. Using their ingenuity, feminists succeeded in defining the issue in human rights terms, thereby making international prostitution a crime against women and, it is hoped, providing a basis for its prosecution through international and national policy development. Equally importantly, feminists have insisted on a global definition of female sexual slavery which links Western and third world women in their struggle against sexual exploitation.

While it is necessary to question, as all these chapters do, the extent of national and international commitment to the advancement of women, it is also necessary to step back and appreciate the strides that have been made during the U.N. Decade for Women. Over the past 10 years, there has been a raising of international consciousness, a great deal of networking, and an expansion of feminist activities in areas from equality to development to peace. While cultural and national differences among women will always persist, an understanding of the commonalities of gender is bringing closer, in Adrienne Rich's eloquent phrase, the "dream of a common language."

12

The Feminization of Poverty: Prospects for an International Feminist Agenda

Diane M. Schaffer

One of the most important outcomes of the United Nations' Decade for Women (1975–1985) is a wealth of data on the status of women throughout the world. The earliest analysis of the U.N.'s worldwide survey, prepared for the 1980 "Mid-Decade" Conference in Copenhagen, gave final credibility to generations of feminists who had asserted that the economic and social oppression of women was a universal phenomenon. While allowing that cultural variations in the legal, economic, social, and political status of women are significant, the Programme of Action produced by the 1980 United Nations conference states:

> Women suffer dual oppression of sex and class within and outside the family. The effects are strikingly apparent in the present world profile of women. While women represent 50% of the world's population, they perform nearly two thirds of all working hours, receive only 1/10th of the world income and own less than 1% of world property.[1]

The inequality women face worldwide places them at the bottom of the economic ladder in every society. As a result, the poorest of the poor, and the majority of the poor, are women. In addition, the proportion of poor who are women has been growing rapidly in the last decade, and the dynamics that have brought increasing numbers of women into poverty show no signs of abating.

The feminization of poverty has presented Western feminists with a challenge yet to be answered. What comprehensive set of policy instruments can be recommended to remedy the feminization of poverty? In recessionary times, even during modest economic growth, any policy agenda that would effectively halt the feminization of poverty would be

...so across race,

profoundly redistributive, not ... presented by the feminization of
class, and national bound...nt mechanisms of redistribution is profound.
In the United S...tions that have formed the core of U.S. public
poverty to p... much of the twentieth century: the nuclear family as the ideal
It chall... structure for social production, the right of male workers to a "family
wage," the husbands' obligation for support of wife and children, and
individual versus collective responsibility. It also brings into question the
legitimacy of the extreme economic privilege enjoyed by Western industrialized nations in comparison to third world nations and raises the
question of the role of the United States in maintaining that disparity.

This chapter will discuss the dynamics of the feminization of poverty as
an international phenomenon and examine the policy implications of
differing approaches to remediation. It is written from the perspective of
the feminist movement in the United States. The central question addressed is: What policy agenda can be defined as the American feminists'
response to the feminization of poverty, within the United States and in the
third world?

I describe the feminization of poverty in the United States—its extent
and its causes, both in demographics and in policy. Then, after a brief look
at the feminization of poverty in other industrialized nations, I turn to
Scandinavia to examine the success and limitations there of policies being
recommended for the United States. The third world and the forces that
lead to feminization of poverty in rural and in newly industrialized regions
are examined. The links between third world feminization of poverty and
policy in the United States are then considered. Finally, some implications
of the international feminization of poverty for feminist political thought
are discussed.

WOMEN AND POVERTY IN THE UNITED STATES

Which Women are Poor?

In the United States, two out of three poor adults are women. Most of
these women are either single mothers or older women living alone. Of
senior women, one-fifth of all women over 60 years of age are poor. A
senior woman is twice as likely to be living in poverty as a senior man.[2] In
1985, although female-headed families comprised less than one-fifth of all
families with children, they accounted for *half* of all families in poverty.[3]

The increase since 1969 in the proportion of the United States' poverty
population who are women is primarily attributable to an increase in the
number of female householders.[4] Forty-five percent of the 3.2 million

increase in family households between 1980 and 1985 consisted of families maintained by women.[5] The President's National Advisory Council on Economic Opportunity, reporting in 1981, emphasized the accelerating growth of the poverty population of single-mother families by pointing out:

> All other things being equal, if the proportion of poor in female-householder families were to continue to increase at the same rate as it did from 1967 to 1978, the poverty population would be composed solely of women and their children before the year 2000.[6]

Although the increase in numbers of women supporting families as single mothers accounts for much of the increase in the feminization of poverty, conditions for single mothers have deteriorated over the same period of time. For example, in 1970 the median income for single mothers was 48 percent of the median for male householders, but in 1981 it had declined to 44 percent.[7] During the first Reagan administration the poorest one-fifth of families in the United States lost almost a tenth of their disposable income, while the richest one-fifth stayed nearly constant (with a loss of only .5 percent). In addition, the poorest of the poor were hit particularly hard during those four years, as welfare and food stamp benefits declined an average of 14 percent of the 1979 level.[8]

Racial Differences

The burden of female poverty is not spread equally across U.S. racial and ethnic groups. In 1982, in comparison to the overall poverty rate of one in five for all senior women, the rate for Black seniors was two in five—*four in five* for Black senior women living alone![9]

Both the proportion of all families which are female-headed and the proportion of those female householders who are in poverty is larger for Blacks and Hispanics than for anglos.* During the 1970s, the proportion of female householders in the black population rose from 30.5 percent to 47.5 percent, in the Hispanic population from 16.9 to 21.8 percent, and in the anglo population from 7.8 to 14.7 percent.[10] In 1984, women maintained more than 73 percent of poor Black families, about 49 percent of poor Hispanic families, and 38 percent of poor white families.

---

* The term "anglo" is used to refer to the non-Hispanic, white majority as counted by the United States census.

Why has the Number of Single-mother Families Increased?

One major cause of the increase in female householders is an increase in the divorce rate. From 1970 to 1984 the divorce rate more than doubled, and it is predicted that half of all marriages of the 1980s will end in divorce.*

A second major cause of the increase in female-headed households is an increase in out-of-wedlock births. In the period 1957 to 1984, the birth rate for single women in the United States doubled.[12] Although this increase is popularly attributed to increased teenage sexual activity, in point of fact, the birth rate among teenage girls has actually decreased since 1957, from 96 births to 51 births per 1,000 girls. However, since fewer pregnant teens now marry, the statistics show a dramatic rise in the number of unwed teens giving birth.[13]

How do Social Policies in the United States Leave Single Mothers at High Risk for Poverty?

Single mothers are at risk for poverty to the extent that the societies in which they live utilize their reproductive labor without directly compensating them. Analysis of the economic position of mothers under U.S. social policies exposes the absence of any coherent family policy, much less one which accepts the reality of a society in which the majority of mothers—married and single—are in the work force or acknowledges the substantial investment of labor and additional resources required to raise children. Three policy areas come immediately to mind when the status of single mothers is evaluated: divorce law, child-care provisions, and welfare systems. In addition, housing policy and the broad domains of employment and health and education policy have contributed to the feminization of poverty in the United States.

Earlier chapters in this book provide in-depth discussions of divorce law, welfare, child care, and employment policy in the United States. The net result of these policies is the creation of a marginal, exploitable pool of female labor, working primarily in the service sector or in the lowest rungs of industry, often part-time because of the necessity of providing care for

---

* It is interesting to note that this is not exclusively an American phenomenon. Divorce rates are rising through most of the developed world. For example, in the Soviet Union one-third of all marriages now end in divorce, and in her urban centers the rate has risen to half, equivalent to the rate in the United States. (See Joel Moses "The Soviet Union in the Women's Decade, 1975–1985" in Lynne Iglitzin and Ruth Ross (eds.) *Women in the World: 1975–1985, The Women's Decade*. Santa Barbara, CA: ABC-CLIO Press, pp. 385–414.) Since 1960 the divorce rate has at least doubled in most European countries.

children and dependent elders, and working without benefits such as health insurance or pensions, or union representation, or opportunity for advancement.

Housing

When choosing housing for her family, a single mother will be looking for a rental unit which will accept children. Assuming she finds one she can afford, she will pay a higher proportion of her income for housing (57 percent) than do single men (30 percent) or married couples (22 percent).[14]

Health care

It is remarkable that health care policy has received relatively little direct attention in discussions of a feminist policy agenda. Perhaps because the issue of birth control has been so very controversial and required so much attention from feminists, the broader issue of health care as a potential entitlement may have seemed less pressing. It is undeniable, however, that the cost of health care in the privatized U.S. system is a strong contributor to the feminization of poverty. In their study of the women who were cut off from welfare benefits under the Omnibus Budget Reduction Act legislation of 1981 (because they were employed, although for very low wages), Zinn and Sarri found that one in seven single mothers had a serious chronic illness, for example, cancer, diabetes, or sickle cell anemia. Yet nearly one-third had no health insurance coverage for themselves, and an even higher proportion had no health insurance coverage for their children. Thus, it is not surprising to find that the need for medical care was the single strongest predictor of reapplication for welfare.[15] We may conclude fairly that many women who would prefer employment to welfare but are employed at poverty-level wages find themselves forced to relinquish employment in order to obtain medical care for themselves or for their families.

Education

Education policy interacts with the labor market in its impact on women. Education does not counteract the impact of discrimination and segregation in the labor force; on the average, a woman with a 4-year college education earns as much as a man with an eighth-grade education.[16] But education policy could be changed to counteract rather than reinforce the inequities in the labor market by abolishing gender-stereotyped materials, and establishing programs that encourage female students to prepare for employment in traditionally male fields. Specifically, it is well established that under current conditions, female students are less likely than males to pursue maths and science courses that prepare them for better-paying employment opportunities. While debate on the extent to which biological factors contribute to this gender division of academic interests continues, ample evidence of the contribution of sex-stereotyped curricular materials and differential treatment by teachers already exists. In their study of the feminization of poverty, the United States Commission on Civil Rights concluded:

> [Occupational segregation is] often not a consequence of personal choice. Many women are led to believe that certain jobs or occupations are the only ones available. Further, their education and training do not always prepare them adequately for other jobs or occupations. Sex stereotyping . . . is at the root of this phenomenon. . . . The evidence suggests that teachers frequently reinforce sex-stereotyped attitudes and behavior. . . . Studies have found sexism is prevalent in educational materials and practices and even in teacher education textbooks. . . . Counselors seldom encourage young women to explore nontraditional courses. . . . Sex-segregated enrollment is also found in vocational education. . . . In conclusion, sex-stereotyping and segregation in education lead females to low-wage occupations and males to highly paid ones, and . . . this is a major source of income disparity between men and women.[17]

Women, therefore, are not rewarded with the same level of economic opportunities as men with equivalent educations, and low educational attainment increases the probability of a woman living in poverty.

> Among female-headed households . . . the poverty rate in 1981 was 48.8 percent for those with less than 8 years of education, 27.8 percent for high school graduates, and 16.6 percent for those with 1 or more years of college. A comparison of all families and female-headed families clearly suggests that low educational attainment leads to a greater risk of being in poverty for female householders than for male householders.[18]

It is crucial, then, that education systems offer programs enabling teenage mothers to continue their educations. Teenage mothers are more likely to drop out of school than their non-pregnant classmates, yet are more likely to bear the major burden of supporting themselves and their children. Teenage childbearing, whether in or out of marriage, is correlated with the probability of dependence on public assistance. The magnitude of the cost to society of its neglect of this population is suggested in the estimate that as much as half the total federal expenditure on AFDC goes to teenage mothers.[19]

POLICY RESPONSE TO THE FEMINIZATION OF POVERTY IN THE UNITED STATES

Consideration of the possible responses to the feminization of poverty renews all of the questions regarding the causes of poverty that were raised during President Johnson's War on Poverty in the 1960s and the subsequent debates over the success or failure of that "war." Women's poverty is substantially different from men's poverty in at least two ways. First, its roots lie in the responsibilities women continue to shoulder within the home—child care, care of the elderly, and homemaking.[20] Second, it is reinforced by a gender-segregated employment market and gender-based socialization in the education system and in the media.

As with any social problem, the prospective solutions to feminization of poverty are tied to the definition of the problem, and any definition is grounded in the political ideology of the analyst. As feminists define their policy agenda in the United States, it will be helpful to delineate the underlying assumptions of the conservative, liberal, and social-democratic perspectives. These assumptions include beliefs regarding the nature of the human family, the function of economic inequality, and the ideal relationship between family and state.

Within conservative ideology it is assumed that poverty is the result of individual failure to compete successfully in the labor market; there will always be a proportion of poor in society, and they should be assisted only in ways which do not erode the incentive to work. The poverty of single mothers in particular is viewed somewhat differently, for the presumption is that the woman and her children ought to be supported by a male wage-earner. The problem, therefore, is defined as the "breakdown of the nuclear family," and the suggested causes, again located within the individual, are selfishness and lack of responsibility (divorce), and sexual promiscuity (teen pregnancy). The conservative thus views the welfare system as encouraging the breakdown of the family by providing support for female family heads. In its 1986 report, President Reagan's Commission on the Family clearly expounded this view, blatantly ignoring research inconsistent with its assumptions. Policy recommendations that emanate from conservative ideology include making divorce more difficult to obtain, making teenage mothers ineligible for welfare (forcing them to rely upon their own families for support and so, presumably, discouraging them from becoming pregnant), and requiring those who receive welfare payments to work in government-designated jobs.

Within liberal ideology also, poverty is viewed as resulting from individual failure to compete in the labor market. Liberals, however, value equality of opportunity to compete and see the government as having a legitimate role in counteracting existing inequality. They readily support, therefore, government intervention in the form of programs to enhance opportunities for the disadvantaged, for example, educational programs for children from poor families. But the larger phenomenon of the feminization of poverty has presented a paradoxical problem for liberal ideology, for liberals have no clear position on the family. Are female-headed households pathological, unhealthy environments for the socialization of children? Or do the problems attributed to broken homes really stem from the stress of financial deprivation, a stress which can be alleviated through public or private assistance? Is mothering an essential contribution to the common welfare of society that should be supported by the state, or is it a private decision in which the state has no legitimate interest? Until a definition of family and articulation of government's proper relation to it can be reformulated, liberal ideology cannot resolve the paradox of women as citizens, workers, *and mothers*. Motherhood is performed in the private realm of the family, yet the obligations of motherhood impair participation in the public sphere.[21] Thus far, liberals have felt most comfortable supporting policies that enhance women's ability to compete in the public sphere as though they were men: affirmative action in hiring, limited moves to eradicate gender stereotyping in educational materials, educational programs for teen mothers, and job training for welfare recipients.

In contrast to conservatives and liberals, social democrats view the state as having an obligation to meet the basic needs of all citizens. The welfare of all citizens is valued more highly than non-interference in the market; therefore, the state should be the employer of last resort and should provide adequate income for those unable to work. Although a view of the family is not explicit in the ideology, social democratic proponents, in practice, have accepted non-nuclear family forms by upholding the right of every child born into a society to have the economic and social support necessary to mature into a healthy, productive citizen. Policies such as state-supported child care, children's allowances, and even social assistance to single mothers are supported, although they originate more from a concern for child welfare than for the welfare of women.

OTHER INDUSTRIALIZED NATIONS

In no other industrialized nation are female householders at so great a risk for poverty as in the United States. Every other industrialized nation (67 countries) provides a family allowance, that is, a non-income tested benefit extended to each family with children in an amount determined by the number of children to be supported. According to Sheila Kamerman, these allowances play a significant role in supporting female-headed families, providing up to a quarter of the family income for both employed and unemployed single mothers.[22]

This is not to say that female householders in other countries are not at a significant economic disadvantage when compared to husband–wife production worker's wage. In a study of eight of the wealthiest industrialized nations, including the United States, Kamerman and her associates found that a working single mother who managed to earn half of an average production worker's salary would not, after all benefits were added, have a year-end income equivalent to three-quarters of that average production worker's wage—and child-care expenses must still come out of that income which she finally receives. If the single mother is not employed, the family income drops to 50–55 percent of the average production worker's wage in Israel, the United Kingdom, Australia and Canada. France and the Federal Republic of Germany are significantly more generous, but only in Sweden does the single-mother family receive sufficient support to bring it close to the average production worker's wage.[23]

Scandinavia: A Feminist Policy Experiment?

Sweden appears to have implemented an exemplary set of pro-woman family policies. Many of the policies implemented there are being considered by American feminists as recommended responses to the feminization of poverty within the United States. Swedish policies directly affecting single parents include (a) a reliable system of child support, (b) child allowances, (c) housing allowances, (d) subsidized child care and (e) social assistance programs. The child allowance is a non-income-tested, standard payment to parents; the amount is determined by the number of children. In contrast, housing allowances, child-care subsidies and social assistance payments are income-tested benefits. Child-support payments are guaranteed by the government through a program titled Advance Payment of Maintenance Allowance. Under this system children are protected from the adverse impact of irregular payment by divorced parents; the custodial parent receives support payments at predetermined levels regardless of the presence or absence of legal judgment against the other parent. Half of all Swedish children in single-mother families received these payments in 1979. The Swedish government expects to recover 50 percent of the cost of this program from payments by absent parents.[24]

The joint effect of these five policies is the creation of a social and economic context in which single mothers and their children do not experience poverty. If she is not employed, a Swedish single mother receives social assistance in addition to child support payments. These two sources comprise two-thirds of her income. In addition, she receives a standard child allowance and an income-tested housing allowance. In total, her disposable income equals 93.8 percent of the average production worker's wage (APWW) in Sweden. By comparison, an unemployed single mother in the United States receives approximately 44 percent of APWW, the amount depending upon the state in which she lives.[25] If she works outside the home—and 86 percent of Swedish single mothers do so—she loses only social assistance. She has access to state-subsidized child care, and, if she earns half the average production worker's wage (APWW), she will have a total disposable income equal to 123 percent of the APWW.[26] A comparable employed mother in the United States will have a disposable year-end income equal to 69–75 percent of the APWW, depending upon the level of child support payments she receives from the children's father.

The comparative advantage for Swedish single mothers is even larger than the AWPP comparison reveals for at least two reasons. First, child-support payments are, in effect, insured by the state; payments are received on time and in full, regardless of the behavior or ability of the non-custodial parent. Secondly, medical needs are met through a system of nationalized health care, so little of the mother's disposable income is jeopardized by illness.

Are Swedish policies an ideal toward which United States feminists should strive? Before answering in the affirmative we should consider the critique emerging from some Scandinavian feminists' analyses. The central argument against these policies is women's continuing lack of power to govern their welfare. While Swedish mothers have been released from dependence upon individual men for economic support, they have been tightly bound to the welfare state and find themselves in a threefold position of public dependence: they are the major recipients of cash and in-kind benefits, they are the majority of service clients, and they are the majority of the employees of the service bureaucracies. They remain in a relatively powerless position because they do not occupy the top decision-making positions in the bureaucracies, nor do they exercise sufficient political clout to successfully combat reduction of services and benefits during times of economic recession. Consequently, even in well-established welfare states like Sweden and Denmark, women suffered disproportionately during the economic recession of the late 1970s and early 1980s. Helga Hernes describes the Scandinavian welfare states as a "tutelary state for women" because women have had a minimal role in the actual decision-making process concerning the distribution of power.[27] Thus, the welfare state, as currently implemented in Scandinavia, has freed women from private dependence and provided protection against the threat of poverty derived from their disadvantaged status in the labor market, but has not significantly altered the political balance of power in gender relations.

WOMEN AND POVERTY IN THE DEVELOPING WORLD

Three-quarters of the world's population lives in the third world. With the exception of some of the oil-rich nations and newly industrializing nations in the Far East and Latin America, third world nations have grown little in per capita GNP since 1960. The poorest countries have actually shown a negative growth rate since the worldwide recession of 1983. Analyzed by population, rather than by country, world growth from 1960 to 1980 left the poorest one-fifth controlling even less of the world's GNP in 1980 than in 1960. In other words, in both relative and absolute terms, conditions have not improved for most of the world's poorest residents, and for some they have actually worsened since 1960.[28]

> Overall, the disparity in income between developing and developed countries continued to widen and there was virtually no change in the distribution of income between the richest and poorest countries of the world. . . . In the low-income countries where population pressures were especially strong, the expansion of the modern industrial sector was unable to absorb the large increments in the labor force. There was an increasing number of unemployed and underemployed among both women and men of working ages. At poverty levels, women were a growing majority.[29]

The impoverishment of third world women is an ongoing dynamic in both urban and rural areas. As in developed countries, the majority of these women are household heads. International data on household structure significantly undercounts female-headed households; male household heads are reported in many cultures in which no male is present or contributing to the family income. Even so, it is estimated that one-fourth to one-third of all families in the world have only a female breadwinner.[30] It is important to beware of western bias in interpreting the economic significance of female householder status in other cultures; the mothers' male relatives, and/or the fathers' male relatives, may contribute resources in the fathers' absence. Yet even in countries with cultural traditions of extended-kin economic units and different, complex patterns of male responsibility, the poorest of the poor are households headed by women.[31]

A major demographic factor that contributes to the increase in single-mother households in the third world is an increasing number of out-of-wedlock births, as the cultural traditions that would previously have tied the father of the child to the mother break down. Two other factors, male migration and war fatalities, are also important contributors to the increasing proportion of single mothers.[32]

In the third world there are few social programs to help a single mother support her children. She is on her own, with help from kin if she is unusually fortunate, shouldering a double burden of home and child care as well as agricultural labor or wage labor.

Industrializing areas

Most of the factors that bind women to poverty in industrializing areas of the third world are analogous to those in the West. Although more than 90 nations now have laws requiring payment of equal wages to women and men performing the same work, this has had little impact on women's wages in the developing world because, as in the West, women usually do unskilled work and are likely to be at the bottom of the wage ladder. Specifically, women are more likely to be employed in the service sector: low-wage jobs without benefits or opportunities for advancement. In Latin America and the Caribbean, it is estimated that four times as many women as men are employed in the service sector, whereas only one-third as many women as men are employed in industry. The burden of housework and child care, often added to the labor required to grow subsistence crops, places women in disadvantaged positions in competition for jobs in industry. As in the West, they are more likely to seek part-time employment and/or intermittent employment, with the attendant disadvantages in salary, job security, lack of union representation, and lack of fringe benefits discussed above.[33]

Three additional industry-related advantages for women are more commonly found in the third world than in the West. The first stems from the need to relocate to an urban center where industry is being developed in order to compete for employment. Although there are regional differences, women, for the most part, have been left to tend subsistence crops and care for children in rural areas while men form the first wave of urban migration for wage employment. Second, although overt gender discrimination in hiring still exists worldwide, fewer third world countries have legislation making such discrimination illegal, and almost none have adequate enforcement. Third, and of rapidly growing importance, is the creation of "free trade zones." In order to attract investment for industrial development, many poor nations, particularly in Asia, have set up geographic areas in which special laws govern financial arrangements and labor relations. The multinational companies that manufacture in these zones are exempted from currency controls and taxed at special low rates. No minimum wage laws apply, and there is seldom enforcement of any health and safety regulations. Union organizing is illegal. Governments seek to draw corporations to their zones through marketing strategies that stress the dexterity and compliance of a readily available work force of young women, a pool that is easily exploitable in that there are few, if any, competing options for employment. Moreover, the continuing renewal of a compliant, low-wage-employee pool is assured, since women in these regions traditionally leave full-time employment when they have children to care for, and thus do not stay long enough to require compensation as senior, experienced employees or to organize.

Asian governments have provided such an attractive package for mult. national development that the employment of young women in free trade zones is the fastest growing employment source in the world.[34] Thus far, electronics and textile industries have been the major industries to take advantage of free trade zones. American, Japanese, and European corporations now employ young women in Hong Kong, Taiwan, South Korea, Singapore, Malaysia, Thailand, Philippines, Indonesia and Mexico under conditions likened to those of nineteenth-century factories in the West: shift sleeping in dormitories owned by the company, working 12- to 14-hour days with breaks too short to eat a meal, severely limited toilet privileges, and daily exposure to toxic chemicals.[35]

Rural Women's Poverty

For third world women in rural areas, inequality translates into poverty through land tenancy laws, land use, and the misdirection of technical assistance. In many areas of the world, a woman has traditionally had access to land only through kinship ties or marriage to a male with land rights. For example, in most of Asia inheritance and divorce laws have left women landless. In other cultures women may own land, but their rights are far more limited than those of men. Under Islamic law, daughters inherit half as much as sons, and a widow inherits only one-eighth of her husband's property if she has children.[36] In areas where women have traditionally held land, land reform implemented under colonial or new national governments has generally established male ownership of land. Even revolutionary governments, while claiming high priority for land reform, have ignored women while redistributing land rights. In Honduras, for instance, a cooperative of women who applied for land were denied "simply because they were women."[37]

The conversion of land use from subsistence to cash crops has brought additional difficulties for women and children in the third world. Because the most fertile and productive land is usually selected for growing cash crops, women, who do most or all of the agricultural labor, must work harder to produce needed subsistence crops on poor land. In addition, their burden of agricultural labor is increased by the demands of the cash crop. For women whose husbands migrate, the entire burden may be theirs. Yet income from the cash crop is almost universally controlled by men, and any benefit to their families is, too often, negligible.[38]

Lack of understanding of the role of women in third world agriculture has resulted in tragic misdirection of western technical assistance. The FAO has attributed much of the decline in per capita food production in Africa over the past two decades to the combination of cash crop development and the concentration of technical assistance on men's rather than on women's agricultural activities.

> Despite the well-documented, crucial role that women play in food production in this region, agricultural modernization efforts have excluded them, leading to negative consequences for food production and the perpetuation of rural poverty.[39]

The above-quoted United Nations report cites diverse examples of the impact of patriarchal control of technical assistance. In Gambia women grow 84 percent of the country's rice harvest but receive only 1/26th of their government's spending on rice-related agricultural projects. A particularly revealing example comes from a study of the comparative success of a new hybrid maize seed in Tanzania and Zimbabwe. In Tanzania, where women do most of the field work, men were given the new seed plus fertilizer and pesticide; the new crop languished. Yet in neighboring Zimbabwe, under the same ecological conditions, the new maize seed was given to women, and the crop flourished. Research identified the crucial difference: in Tanzania women had given the maize crop low priority because the money from it would go to their husbands rather than to them, whereas in Zimbabwe the women could use the cash from the crop to benefit their families.[40]

The same U.N. report exposes another cost of misdirected assistance. When women are household heads, whether their husbands have deserted, migrated, or died, the amount of manual labor required to produce enough food for their children may exceed their physical capabilities. In Africa, for example, the amount harvested may depend upon the amount of work a woman can fit into daylight hours rather than the potential yield of her land.[41]

American citizens are linked to the plight of third world women in at least two important ways. First U.S. foreign policy governs the way foreign aid projects are defined, assigned priority, and implemented. Staudt and Jaquette's analysis in chapter 14 of the U.S. A.I.D. office's response to a congressional mandate for the inclusion of women in planning and developing aid projects suggests that U.S. aid will continue to suffer misdirection.

Second, U.S. foreign policy governs conditions of direct foreign aid and the participation of the United States in the World Bank and other fiscal entities that provide loans to third world countries. The United States is a major lender to third world nations and heavily influences the economic policies of those countries through the conditions attached to its loans. When, for example, a third world country is required to show its "good faith" effort to repay a loan by converting much of its fertile land from subsistence crops to cash crops, conditions for women and children in that country are often eroded.

In fact, third world feminists are currently questioning many of the assumptions regarding the nature of social and economic development in the third world which are at the core of the U.S. approach to foreign aid. In a coherent and thoughtful philosophical tract presented to the United Nations' 1985 End-Decade Conference, an organization of development scholars from nonaligned nations stated:

> In many of the discussions and actions generated throughout the Decade it has been implicit that women's main problem in the Third World has been insufficient participation in an otherwise benevolent process of growth and development. Increasing women's participation and improving their shares in resources, land, employment and income relative to men were seen as both necessary and sufficient to effect dramatic changes in their economic and social position. Our experiences now lead us to challenge this belief. . . . We can no longer assume that the development process as it has evolved in most third world countries is inherently benign to people living there.[42]

AN INTERNATIONAL FEMINIST POLICY AGENDA

Having surveyed the extent of the feminization of poverty worldwide, we can now ask whether an international policy agenda might be drafted, and if so, whether it would elicit support from feminists in the United States.

The FLS

The 1985 concluding conference of the U.N. Decade for Women produced a comprehensive statement of an international policy agenda for women. This statement, titled *Forward Looking Strategies for the Advancement of Women to the Year 2000* (hereafter referred to as the FLS), was constructed and signed by all U.N. member nations, including the United States, the U.S.S.R., all other industrialized nations and most of the third world. Despite widely differing cultural, economic, and political traditions, member nations agreed to a document of 272 paragraphs, which defines goals for improving the status of women and outlines strategies, both general and specific, for meeting these goals. All the policy domains relating to the feminization of poverty are addressed: employment, education, health, child care, housing, social services, rural development, and legal contexts for divorce, inheritance, land rights, and access to credit. The title of the document signifies the U.N.'s intention to reconvene a world conference on the status of women in the year 2000 and to repeat the process, employed in 1980 and 1985, of requiring all member nations to report on their progress toward the goals upon which they have agreed.[43]

The FLS is a remarkable document in that its recommendations represent common agreement among nations with capitalist and centrally planned economies, nations influenced by every cultural tradition and every major world religion. With respect to the feminization of poverty, five characteristics of the FLS are of immediate importance. First, the FLS takes an unequivocal stand on the need to change all laws and traditional customs standing in the way of social, economic and political equality for women. It calls for ratification of the 1981 Convention on the Elimination of All Forms of Discrimination Against Women by all member nations who have not yet agreed to it. The convention, adopted by the U.N. General Assembly in 1979, contains 30 articles that delineate areas in which governments must take action to assure equal rights for women, including civil rights, such as rights to own and inherit property; political rights, such as the right to vote and hold office; marriage rights, including the rights to choose a spouse, to decide on number and spacing of children, to choose a family name and occupation, and the same rights and responsibilities as a husband in marriage and parenting. Other areas covered by the convention include education and health concerns. Employment rights include equal pay for work of equal value, and social services that permit parents to combine family obligations with work.[44] As of January 1984, only 54 nations had ratified the convention, although nearly 100 had signed it. Most of Western Europe, Scandinavia, many of the Eastern European countries, and the U.S.S.R. have already ratified the convention, but the United States has not.[45]

Second, the FLS specifically recognizes the significance of the population of single-mother families in the world, and, third, it explicates the link between single-motherhood and poverty:

> Recent studies have shown that the number of families in which women are the sole supporters is on the increase. Owing to the particular difficulties (social, economic and legal) which they face, many such women are among the poorest people concentrated in urban informal labor markets and they constitute large numbers of the rural unemployed and marginally employed. Those with very little social and moral support face serious difficulties in bringing up their children alone. This has serious repercussions for society in terms of the quality, character, productivity and human-resource capabilities of its future citizenry.[46]

Fourth, while it does not specify a level or kind of direct government involvement, the FLS does charge governments with the ultimate responsibility for assuring equality for women. Specifically with respect to single-mother families, the FLS states:

> Governments are urged to ensure that women with sole responsibility for their families receive a level of income and social support sufficient to enable them to attain or maintain economic independence and to participate effectively in society. . . . Special attention should be given to assisting those women in discharging their domestic responsibilities and to enabling them to participate in and benefit from education, training programmes and employment.[47]

For the most part, the FLS stance could be characterized as consistent with either a modified liberal or a social democratic ideology. Although governments are held accountable for changing the conditions that have resulted in gender inequality, and these conditions are identified across the spectrum of public policy areas, the recommendations for remedying injustice remain in the public domain and focus upon increasing women's ability to compete in the economic domain outside the home.

On the other hand, even though it is approached indirectly, the private sphere of the family is addressed in so far as the burden of childcare and housework is unequally apportioned. A strong theme throughout the FLS is the need to alter gender socialization in the education system and in the media so that future generations of men will expect to participate equally in child-rearing and housekeeping responsibilities:

> . . . governments and non-governmental organizations should mobilize the mass media and other means of communication to ensure public consensus on the need for men and society as a whole to share with women the responsibilities of producing and rearing children. . . . [48]

Similarly, the importance of development of childcare is acknowledged repeatedly, and governmental interest is firmly established; however, responsibility, when delineated in the Strategies sections, does not necessarily extend beyond incentives to private employers:

> . . . [governments should] give priority to the development of social infrastructure, such as adequate care and education for the children of working parents, whether such work is carried out at home, in the fields or factories, to reduce the "double burden" of working women in both urban and rural areas. [Governments] should offer incentives to employers to provide childcare services and to allow either parent to work flexible hours in order to share the responsibilities of child care.*[49]

Fifth, the FLS pays particular attention to the plight of rural women. It emphasizes the need to guarantee women's access to land and "control [over] the products of their labour and their income."[50] The FLS calls for all agricultural technical assistance and training to be restructured to match the reality of women's role in all phases of agricultural work. With respect to the planning and implementation of development projects, the FLS calls for the integration of women both as planners and managers, and for the reevaluation of all projects and procedures to identify and eliminate

---

* In the FLS, U.N. member nations took the symbolic step of recognizing women's unpaid labor in the home by altering the computation of each nation's gross national product (GNP) to include the economic value of that labor. It is estimated that the world's GNP will increase by one-third when household labor is added.

biases grounded in the presumption of male leadership and family responsibility.[51]

Implementation of the recommendations of the FLS would clearly result in a national redistribution of resources. Less apparent is the extent to which implementation of the FLS recommendations would be redistributive across class. To the extent that costs of nurturing a new generation are assumed communally, through child allowances, child-care tax credits, etc., there would be moderate redistribution resulting from an increase in taxation to fund increased services. Similarly, implementation of the recommendations on health care entitlements could result in some across-class redistribution. Equal pay for work of equal value, if implemented, could also compress the economic class hierarchy.

Although the FLS leaves open the degree of communal responsibility governments' internal policies should assume, and thus appears compatible with liberal capitalist values, it clearly adopts a "new world economic order" perspective on relations between first and third worlds. It states that the improvement of conditions for women in the third world is predicated upon general improvement of economic circumstances, and that such general improvement is not possible until first world nations accept a "restructuring of international economic relations on a just and democratic basis" (paragraph 98). The United States voted against all paragraphs of the FLS that express this point of view, as it has voted against the previous U.N. resolutions that called for a new world economic order.[52] Among the issues involved are forgiveness of third world debt, increased aid in the form of grants (rather than loans) from first world to third world countries, and lowering of trade barriers to increase the competitiveness of products from third world countries.

Prospects for Support

As with all United Nations resolutions, the FLS has no legal standing in the United States, although a resolution in support of the FLS would indicate congressional intention to move the U.S. laws and policies to conform with the FLS standards. President Reagan, whose daughter headed the U.S. delegation to the 1985 World Conference, has not requested that Congress consider the document, nor has any congressional committee taken the initiative to introduce it.** Meanwhile, academic and non-governmental

---

** Members of the staff of the House Foreign Relations Committee attended the conference and provided the committee with a full report, which includes the FLS.

organizations that were represented at the World Conference (most notably, the American Association of University Women), have undertaken the task of educating women in the United States about the standards for equality, development, and peace explicated in the FLS. Without leadership from within the governmental power structure, the bottom-up education process will proceed slowly, but the very existence of an international standard, to which the United States does not currently conform and to which the current federal government is unresponsive, may eventually make a significant contribution to mobilizing elite, educated women.

Will the international feminization of poverty promote a worldwide feminist movement? Will the agenda outlined in the FLS be perceived as policy in the interests of all women? Will we see new coalitions of women, coalitions that bridge economic class and national boundaries, growing out of a consciousness of common interests?

Evaluating the prospects for support of an international feminist agenda from a feminist movement within the United States revolves around three sets of issues, which I identify as the mother/citizen dilemma, the class/gender dilemma, and the world economy dilemma.*

The mother/citizen dilemma. The conceptual problems presented by separation of private and public spheres, and adherence to individual over collective responsibility for nurturing children, were mentioned above in the discussion of liberal ideology. There is, among feminist theorists in the United States, lack of consensus on the desirable level and kind of governmental partnership with families. To the extent that women form a partnership with the state and are supported by social programs in their work as mothers, they will have a common interest in the support of those social programs. Several writers have begun to explore the possible shift in political consciousness that could result from women's increasing experience of *client* relationships to the state. Noting that women comprise the majority of recipients of benefits from social insurance and welfare programs, Barbara Nelson suggests that women may indeed become increasingly identifiable as a political interest group. Nelson cites three trends that bear on this issue: (a) women are now voting in equal proportion to men, and, since women outlive men, they net a larger total number of votes; (b) there is an increasing rate of improverishment of

---

* I have chosen to frame the dilemmas in the vocabulary of liberal ideology. The socialist feminist in the United States does not have the same conceptual difficulties with the FLS (although there are others instead), but since liberal ideology dominates the feminist movement in the United States, all feminists must consider its potential strengths and weaknesses when evaluating the future of the movement in the United States.

women (the feminization of poverty), with a consequent increase in their participation as clients of social service programs; and (c) there is evidence of a gender gap in voting behavior, with women showing significantly lower approval of military expenditures and significantly higher approval of expenditures for social programs than men do.[53] Unfortunately, there is to date little research upon which to base a prediction of the ultimate impact of women's client relationship upon their voting behavior. Thus far we know that poor women are more likely to vote than poor men; on the other hand, the poorest women, those on welfare, are somewhat less likely to vote. In the short term, it appears that the extent to which the feminization of poverty mobilizes women as a voting block will largely depend on the extent to which working-poor and middle-class women perceive a common interest in preserving and/or expanding social services and entitlements that diminish their economic vulnerability as mothers.

The Gender/Class Dilemma

The alternative paths available to remedy the impoverishment of single mothers have potentially differing impacts upon the development of solidarity among women in the United States. While it is currently accurate to say "poverty is just a divorce away" for middle class mothers, their vulnerability could be dramatically reduced through policies that would have little impact on their working class and low-income sisters. For example, changes in divorce law to tie a larger portion of a divorced father's wages to maintenance of his children and ex-wife could remove the threat of poverty for middle class mothers, provide some assistance to working class wives, and have virtually no impact on women whose children's fathers are unemployed or absent. Such a policy would strengthen women's ties to men of their economic class, and diminish the probability of a strong, across-class women's movement. Similarly, child-care policy proposals based on allowances from taxable income may meet the needs of middle class mothers, while low income women will require a subsidy. In contrast, approaches to halting the feminization of poverty through a revaluing of nurturing expressed through entitlements for parents would, as long as women continue to perform most reproductive labor, strengthen the perception of common economic interests for women.

There are currently efforts to educate women about the feminization of poverty and to build coalitions across class lines to support changes in family law, employment practices, and health care policy. Two examples are Women for Economic Justice in Massachusetts, an advocacy project that is building a coalition of social service and union organizations[54], and the Women's Economic Justice Project in Oakland, California, which has worked since 1982 to educate women about the feminization of poverty, calling open hearings in urban and rural areas throughout the state.[55]

Attempts to form cross-class coalitions in the women's movement are not new, although the phenomenon of single parenting, with its substantial economic risks, have added a new dimension to this old problem. In the highly conservative political climate of the 1980s, the feminization of poverty may not lead to clearly recognized coalitions across classes. However, as indicated by the gender gap, a significant link may already have formed, based on awareness of trade-offs between military expenditures and social program budgets. Traditionally middle class peace advocacy groups and political associations of low income women, particularly service employees' unions, can join to oppose military spending without developing agreement on a domestic family policy agenda.[56]

The World Economy Dilemma

Thus far, awareness of links between U.S. international development policy and the impoverishment of third world women has been limited to academic circles and core feminist networks. Similarly, labor conditions for women workers in free trade zones have received relatively little attention in the United States, even though the U.N. Decade conferences of 1980 and 1985 provided ample data on the problem. We may, however, see interest in international economic issues develop across a broader spectrum of women's organizations if awareness of personal economic linkages grows. For example, unemployed garment and electronics workers in the United States (almost all women) have a common economic interest with the women in free trade zones. Wives of bankrupt soy bean farmers in Iowa may discover a common interest with wives of subsistence farmers in Brazil.

While general awareness of global economic links builds, feminist theorists in the United States will be grappling with the challenge presented by third world feminists throughout the decade. Policy fronts largely ignored by western liberal feminists, for example, trade protectionism, regulation of international businesses, and the loan policies of nations and of institutions like the World Bank, are acknowledged as crucial contributors to women's poverty in the developing world.[57] Thus, a truly international response to the feminization of poverty will require a shared understanding of the West's responsibility toward developing nations and a shared theory of the dynamics of desirable regional development.

NOTES AND REFERENCES

1. United Nations, *Programme of Action*, 1980.

2. Karen Stallard, Barbara Ehrenreich, and Holly Sklar, *Poverty and the American Dream: Women and Children First* (New York: Institute for New Communications, South End Press, 1983).

3. United States Department of Labor, Women's Bureau, *Facts on Women Workers*, Fact Sheet No. 86, 1986, p. 3.

4. Victor Fuchs, *The Feminization of Poverty?* Working paper 1934, National Bureau of Economic Research, Inc., Stanford, Ca., May 1986.

5. U.S. Department of Labor, *Women Workers*, p. 3.

6. Cited in Stallard et al., *Poverty and the American Dream*, p. 7.

7. Ibid., p. 6.

8. Frank Levy and Richard Michel, "Redistributing Income—the Wrong Way," *Dissent, 31* (Spring 1984), pp. 174–5.

9. Stallard et al., *Poverty and the American Dream*, p. 7.

10. U.S. Department of Labor, *Women Workers*, p. 5.

11. Ibid., p. 3.

12. *Statistical Abstract of the U.S.*, U.S. Census Bureau, 1986, p. 35.

13. U.S. Bureau of Census, cited by Richard Cohen, "Teenage Pregnancy: A Dilemma Dialogue Won't Solve," in the *San Jose Mercury News*, October 28, 1986, p. E6.

14. Ellen Boneparth, "Women and Public Policies: Comparative Perspectives on Welfare Mothers" in Harrell Rodgers (Ed.) *Public Policy and Social Institutions* (Greenwich, CT: JAI Press, 1984), p. 134.

15. Forty percent of the women who reapplied for welfare cited health insurance as the reason. For further detail, see D. K. Zinn and R. C. Sarri, "Turning Back the Clock on Public Welfare" in *Signs, 10* (2), 1984.

16. U.S. Department of Commerce, Bureau of the Census Public Information Office, *We the American Women*, 1985, p. 11.

17. U.S. Commission on Civil Rights, *A Growing Crisis: Disadvantaged Women and their Children*, May 1983, pp. 37–39.

18. Ibid., p. 36.

19. Ibid., p. 11.

20. Ruth Sidel, *Women and Children Last: The Plight of Poor Women in Affluent America* (New York: Viking Press, 1986).

21. For examinations of the stance of liberal political theorists toward women and toward the family see Carole Pateman, "Feminism and Democracy" in Graeme Duncan (ed.) *Democratic Theory and Practice* (Cambridge: Cambridge University Press, 1983); Barbara Nelson, "Women's Poverty and Women's Citizenship: Some Political Consequences of Economic Marginality" in *Signs, 10* (2), 1984; and Zillah Eisenstein, *The Radical Future of Liberal Feminism* (New York: Longman, 1981).

22. Sheila Kamerman, "Women, Children, and Poverty: Public Policies and Female-headed Families in Industrialized Countries" in *Signs, 10* (2), 1984, pp. 36–46.

23. Ibid.

24. Ibid.

25. Kamerman computed this figure for conditions in Pennsylvania, a state in which AFDC benefits were more generous than two-thirds of the other states.

26. Ibid., pp. 38, 46.

27. Helga Hernes' work is cited by Birgit Siim in "Women and the Welfare

State—Between Private and Public Dependence," Working paper, Institute for Development and Planning, University of Aalborg, Fibigirshcede II, 9100 Aalborg, Denmark.

28. Ruth L. Sivard, *Women . . . a World Survey* (Washington, DC: International Center for Research on Women, 1985).

29. Ibid., p. 9.

30. Ibid., p. 11.

31. See, for example, Mari Clark, "Woman-headed Households and Poverty: Insights from Kenya" in *Signs, 10* (2), 1984.

32. Sivard, *Women . . . A World Survey*, p. 10.

33. United Nations, *The Status of the World's Women 1985* (Oxford, England: New Internationalist Publications, 1985).

34. Ibid., p. 74.

35. See Annette Fuentes and Barbara Ehrenreich, *The Global Factory* (new York: Institute for New Communications, 1983). Also Marilee Karl, "Integrating Women into Multinational Development?" in *Women and Development* (Geneva: ISIS, 1983).

36. United Nations, *Programme of Action*, p. 71.

37. Ibid., p. 71.

38. Ibid., pp. 69–70.

39. Ibid., p. 71.

40. Ibid.

41. Ibid.

42. Gita Sen, *Development, Crisis, and Alternative Visions: Third World Women's Perspectives* DAWN, Institute of Social Studies Trust, New Delhi, India, 1985.

43. *Forward Looking Strategies for the Advancement of Women to the Year 2000*, resolution adopted by consensus at the 1985 World Conference to Review and Appraise the Achievements of the United Nations Decade for Women: Equality, Development and Peace, Nairobi, Kenya, July 15–26, 1985. A complete copy of this resolution is contained in the report of the Congressional Staff Advisors to the Nairobi Conference to the Committee on Foreign Affairs of the U.S. House of Representatives, January 1986, (U.S. Government Printing Office Document 55-756 0), titled *U.N. Conference to Review and Appraise the U.N. Decade for Women, July 15-26, 1985*.

44. United Nations, *Convention on the Elimination of all Forms of Discrimination Against Women*, adopted by the General Assembly on December 18, 1979. Fully reprinted in an excellent resource on outcomes of the first half of the U.N. Decade for Women titled *Looking to the Future: Equal Partnership between Women and Men in the 21st Century*, published by the Women, Public Policy and Development Project, Humphrey Institute of Public Affairs, University of Minnesota, 909 Social Sciences, 267-19th Avenue S., Minneapolis, MN. 55455.

45. Sivard, *Women . . . A World Survey*, pp. 30–31.

46. *Forward Looking Strategies . . . ,* paragraph 294.

47. Ibid., paragraph 295.

48. Ibid., paragraph 228.

49. Ibid., paragraph 228.

50. Ibid., paragraph 62. The Convention Against Discrimination Against Women covers many of the key legal issues for rural women as well.

51. Ibid., paragraphs 174–188.

52. See the Declaration and the Program of Action on the Establishment of a

New International Economic Order (General Assembly resolutions 3201 (S-VI) and 3202 (S-VI), respectively).

53. Barbara Nelson, "Women's Poverty and Women's Citizenship," p. 92.

54. Women for Economic Justice, 59 Temple Place, Room 612, Boston, MA 02111.

55. Elaine Zimmerman, "California Hearings on the Feminization of Poverty" in *Signs, 10* (2), 1984, pp. 394–410.

56. In 1983 world military expenditures exceeded $700 billion, more than all governments spent for the protection of their citizens against disease, accident, and ill-health. See Sivard, *Women . . . A World Survey*, p. 56.

57. Gita Sen, *Development, Crisis*, pp. 16–30, 52–59.

13
The Women's Movement in Greece

Eleni Stamiris

Although feminism, like democracy or socialism, appeals to a universalistic solidarity, the character of particular women's movements is still shaped by profoundly national contexts of history and socio-economic progress. The uneven trajectories of contemporary capitalist development and of under-development have imparted to the national contingents of the interna-tional women's movement varying demands, priorities, structures and orientations.

In each case the form of the emergence of modern feminism has been directly influenced by changes in the role of women in the national productive system. For example, the women's movements in the advanced industrial countries have been influenced by the increasing integration of women into the wage economy and by the partial socialization of reproduc-tion to help meet the demand for female labor-power. In contrast, the economic position of women in many developing countries has greatly deteriorated over the recent years. The education gap between the sexes has widened, domestic activities have been devalued, and frequently women have become marginalized within the wage economy.

Greece is an intriguing case precisely because its socio-economic pattern displays many of the features and contradictions of both advanced and less developed countries. The classic 'semi-peripheral' economy, Greece com-bines a significant 'off-shore' commercial and shipping complex with a patriarchal agricultural economy and a weak manufacturing base. Al-though women's role in the Greek economy has been greatly transformed over the last thirty years, women have not increased their presence within the wage sector. At the same time post-war Greek history has been dominated by civil war, counter-revolution and the struggle against military dictatorship. Thus the contemporary women's movement has been particularly influenced by the roles of women within democratic and class struggles. Most recently the efforts of the socialist PASOK government to implement gender equality from the "top-down" have raised important questions about the relationship between the autonomous mobilization of women and the parties of the Left. In the survey that follows, beginning with a brief evocation of the origins of feminism in Greece, I have tried to elucidate the peculiarities of historical and social development insofar as they have influenced a distinctive women's movement.

WOMEN IN MODERN GREEK HISTORY

Like all great popular struggles, the long Greek War of Independence in the early nineteenth century drew upon the stamina and courage of women. For much of the period, while men were in the mountains fighting the Ottoman armies, women were the mainstay of the agricultural economy. After most of the peninsula won freedom in 1821, some upper-class women who had been involved in the national movement began to voice the demand for girls' schools and female literacy as first steps in raising the status of women. However, since parts of Greece remained under Turkish occupation, the "women question" continued to be overshadowed by war efforts, and the energies of upper-class women were redirected towards charitable work with the poor, war orphans and refugees.

What can be properly called the first wave of the Greek women's movement emerged after 1856 with the initial flowering of capitalist development. The spectacular growth of commerce and the merchant fleet, coupled with the efforts between 1874 and 1885 to modernize the economic and administrative structures, contributed to the emergence of a definite bourgeoisie with a modern outlook. It was middle-class women of this ascendant stratum who now took the lead in voicing the more radical liberal demand for the vote as well as for the abolition of infamous laws barring women from the professions, business and government. In 1870 the pioneering women's periodical *Eurydice* was published, calling for more equal treatment at work and in education, and incorporating feminist ideas from Western Europe. In 1872, the Ladies' Association for the Education of women was founded, and in 1879, the Union of Greek Women. In 1887 the *Newspaper for Ladies* began its 30-year history, while in 1908 the first woman student was admitted to the University of Athens. Under the shadow of national bankruptcy in 1883, however, the liberal optimism of the middle classes was shattered. Mass emigration to North America provided the main outlet for idle male hands, while women stayed behind to care for children and tend the land. However, continuous economic crisis together with war, or the threat of war, made it almost impossible for women's demands to be heard. Middle-class women's groups reverted to conservative charitable work until the end of the First World War.

The post-war crisis, including the expulsion of 1.5 million Greeks from Asia Minor, led to the disappearance of the last remnants of *tsiflikia*, the

Greek form of feudal holdings, as all large estates, clerical and private, were appropriated in 1923 and redistributed to the male peasantry. This epochal transformation—which cast the countryside in its present mould of myriad family-based small farms—consolidated the patriarchal structure and cultural conservatism of Greek rural society. The transformation of the propertyless male peasant into a smallholder was mirrored inside the family by the enhanced authority of husband and father. Although the interwar years witnessed a small-scale industrial boom in the towns, the urban economy remained dominated by artisan units and almost half the male work force was in crafts or services. A small female proletariat existed in the textile mills and tobacco plants, but women as a whole were still overwhelmingly and disproportionately confined to agriculture. While men were able to take advantage of new opportunities resulting from urbanization, the women were left behind as unpaid custodians of a subsistence agricultural system, a pattern that has tended to persist to the present day.

In this interwar period middle-class women were able to recover confidence and renew the struggle for women's rights. They demanded better educational and vocational training, improved working conditions, social benefits for working women, and a range of other social reforms. Greek organizations became affiliated with international associations ranging from the YWCA to the International Women's Union. Most importantly a preliminary campaign was organized for women's suffrage, culminating in the concession of municipal franchise in 1934. This second wave of intense activity, led by the militant League for Women's Rights, was brought to an end by the repressive dictatorship of Metaxas in 1936, followed by the long cycle of war, occupation and civil war.

During the anti-fascist resistance and the Civil War, Greek women played unprecedented roles. As previously in Greek history, they kept the farms and fed the children, while nursing the wounded, knitting the uniforms and transporting the food and ammunition. But they also participated in mass rallies and strikes, assumed high positions of leadership and responsibility, fought side by side with men in the underground and in the mountains, and received equal treatment from torturers and executioners. They also formed their own resistance organization, The Free Young Women, affiliated with the National Patriotic Youth Organization (EPON) in the larger structure of the National Liberation Front. It was during the German occupation, moreover, that Greek women were for the first time able to enjoy full rights in the liberated zones established throughout the country. The "mountain government" proclaimed that "all Greeks, men and women, have equal political and civil rights" and implemented this principle in the social institutions of Free Greece. Referring to the election of representatives to its National Council, it stipulated that "all men and women over eighteen may participate." It also established "equal pay for equal work." During this momentous period of modern Greek history, women lived as equal citizens in their own country.

WOMEN IN THE POST-WAR ECONOMY

Post-war economic growth in Greece was purchased at a relatively high price: sharpened income inequalities, persistent unemployment, massive flight to the cities, foreign emigration and increased dependence on the United States of America and Western Europe. When popular forces in the 1960s challenged the repressive model of economic development that the victorious counter-revolution had installed in 1949, the colonels took power and stamped out democracy between 1967 and 1974. With the overthrow of the junta in 1974, the worsening economic climate tilted popular support toward the left and brought a Socialist government into power in 1981, promising to elaborate a new political and developmental alternative.

For Greek women, in sharp contrast to the general trend in North America and Western Europe, the period since 1960 has seen various forms of economic *marginalization*. Over the last half-century women's formal participation in the labor force has increased by barely 5 percent from (26.2 percent in 1928 to 31.9 percent in 1981) and the ratio actually declined from 1961 to 1981. This dramatic exclusion of women from the formal workforce and their ghettoization in the informal sector has been accompanied by a strengthening of family values and of the ruling ideology that keeps them in their "natural" roles of childcare and home-management. The "good housekeeping" role of women has become a fetish especially among the middle classes, leading to obsessions with extreme household cleanliness and the overindulgence of children.

By the middle of the 1960s, uneven internal development, backward technology, a surplus rural population and a system of exploitation of peasant producers by a wide range of middle men and by state price controls had created an unprecedented flight of workers from the countryside to towns and foreign lands, where immigration served the needs of expanding Western economies.

For those who were not swept away in the tide and remained on the land, survival of the small family-farm has depended upon the *unpaid* labor of women family members in the transition from a primarily subsistence to an overwhelmingly cash-crop system. Greek agriculture has few instances of capitalist farming using wage labor. Small-holders exploit family labour, which has lowered the subsistence level of the producers and allowed surplus to be transferred from agriculture to the capitalist sectors. Men's direct control over women within the structure of the patriarchal rural household has assured a degree of super-exploitation necessary to offset the low prices of farm products. The axis of gender exploitation was superimposed on that of class exploitation. As imported inputs like fertilizers continually pushed up production costs, against a background of depressed agricultural prices, the only variable factor of production that the small proprietor was able to control and manipulate was the labor of his wife and himself.

Throughout the 1960s the increased commercialization and mechanization of agriculture produced new sexual divisions of labor. Production for the market came under men's control, displacing the traditional subsistence economy that was the responsibility of both men and women. Expanded mechanization and improved methods of cultivation benefited men directly by the application of machines to what had become men's work, as well as, indirectly, by releasing male hands to undertake a wide range of off-farm activities. On the other hand, with mechanization, the displacement of female labor from the fields shifted women's work back toward the home and to labor-intensive women's tasks in food production for the family: management of farm animals, cultivation of kitchen gardens, and so on. Thus men's labor took on wage forms in the new situation while women's work both on farm and in the household remained unpaid.[1]

More significantly, female labor under the new conditions of cash-crop production became a *supplementary labor reserve* for peak work periods. Given the rural exodus, the severe shortage of male labor and the high cost of hired hands, the availability of women's labor throughout the year became a strategic stop-gap without which the small family-farm system could not have survived. At the same time, withdrawal from full-time cash-crop production not only deprived women of formal recognition as producers in their own right, but also denied them access to land, machines, credit, training, participation in cooperatives, pensions and other social benefits. As unpaid family help (the legal category) and without monetary value attached to their labor, rural women became economically and socially marginalized despite the absence of any reduction in their workloads (the rural woman's working day is currently estimated at 14–16 hours).

THE POLITICS OF DOMESTICATION

Like the capitals of other developing nations, Athens has had to absorb the major influx of migrants from the countryside. But swelling urbanization has not been accompanied by extensive industrialization. Despite new enclaves of multinational manufacturing investment, the overwhelming orientation of Greek capital remains toward commerce and shipping. This

combination of tremendous population in-migration without industrialization has had adverse effects on all segments of the working classes, but the
impact on women has been most severe. While the male migrant
population settled into petty commerce, crafts and various parasitic
activities, women moving to towns remained in the home or were
marginalized in the informal economy.[2] In Athens, which by 1972 had
absorbed about two-thirds of the active population not engaged in agriculture, the employment ratio of women dropped from 21.4 percent in 1961 to
19.45 percent in 1971. Over the next decade there was only a small
improvement as women's participation in the Athenian work force increased to 23 percent in 1981.

The economic alternative for many women in towns became participation in an informal economy that was a direct extension of housework:
live-in domestics, house-cleaners, seamstresses, pieceworkers, and so on.
Although these income-generating activities were crucial to a large number
of households, they left women without basic social benefits, union
protection, opportunities for training or social recognition. At the same
time, women were effectively blocked from entrance into petty commerce.
Until 1982 married women could not legally establish a business without
their husband's consent.[3]

This domestic marginalization of large segments of the female population in the midst of rapid urbanization allowed the substitution of women's
unpaid labour for state welfare expenditure. Women provided essential
services in lieu of the social infrastructure that the state refused to create.
This structural relationship was reinforced by strongly patriarchal cultural
prescriptions which emphasized women's traditional roles, and by a form
of machismo that was perhaps more virulent than anywhere else in the
Mediterranean.[4] The military junta codified chauvinist values in its slogan
"Fatherland, Family, Religion." The honor of the family continued to be
represented by female chastity, which was entrusted to the vigilance of
fathers and brothers against the corruptibility of women's nature.
Women's work outside the home—or, for that matter, participation in any
larger extra-familiar role (public life, community affairs, etc.)—was seen as
a serious threat to this system of male honor and family status. The total
domestication of women became in effect an express symbol of petty-
bourgeois prestige.

Locked in their reproductive roles, and with less social or monetary
value attached to their work than on the farms, women in towns experienced a decline in their family and social status. The adaptation of the
traditional dowry of land in the new urban situation clearly reflected this
deterioration of women's position. In agrarian society, the view of females
as inherently inferior and a burden to the family is widespread, but women
still perform too many essential productive functions to be entirely

marginalized. In the urban setting, however, women were confined to what is considered unproductive domestic work, even if, in reality, they were also contributing to family income through episodic work in the informal sector. As housewives supposedly dependent on their husband's income, urban women were obliged to compensate for their liability by providing larger dowries. As part of the dowry men began to demand an apartment in the city—a radical departure from the village custom which held men responsible for building the patrilocal home. The rapid inflation of dowries placed unbearable pressures on the bride's family to accumulate dowries of real estate, cash, furniture, and so on. It is not surprising that in the face of such exorbitant new demands, many Greek women turned to emigration as a matrimonial frontier. In the large post-war tide of emigration, reaching almost a million by the early 1970s, the proportion of women increased from one-third to almost half of the flow. For many women, emigration became a means to acquire dowries for marriage at home, or to find foreign husbands for whom dowries were not necessary. For men, by the same logic, migrant labor of seafaring became the principal source of financing dowries for their daughters or sisters.

At the same time, education became a crucial element in the dowry package, especially for women who sought urban marriages of higher social standing, so that between 1961 and 1981 the education gap between girls and boys gradually decreased.[5] In the villages the limited resources of the family were devoted to education of the most promising male children, while girls made do with household training for domestic roles. In the urban context, however, education together with an apartment dowry became a woman's ticket to higher social status, not in her own right but through the position of her husband. In the long run, the new value given to women's education, even within the context of a reactionary dowry system, was to play a decisive role in nurturing a new women's movement.

THE NEW WAVE OF GREEK FEMINISM

By the end of the Civil War in 1949 all progressive movements in Greece had been crushed. The women's mass organizations that had developed at the end of the German occupation, addressing for the first time the needs and problems of all women, were dissolved.[6] Their records were confiscated and destroyed, and many of their members took the road to exile or were locked up for years in concentration camps. (The camp at Trikeri alone held 5,000 women.) The few organizations that did survive, such as the Panhellenic Union of Housewives, the YWCA, or the League of Business and Professional Women, developed by inclination or force of circumstance in a fundamentally conservative direction. It was not until the

1960s, in the period before the colonels' coup, that a militant women's movement reemerged as a wing of the popular struggle for radical social change. Of the new groups formed in this period, the most important was the reconstituted Panhellenic Union of Greek Women (PEG). After its foundation in 1964, the PEG displayed a remarkable dynamism but was suppressed by the dictatorship in 1967. Again all progressive organizations were liquidated, and many feminists were sent to prison or interned. Large numbers were subsequently arrested, tortured and condemned to lengthy imprisonment for activities against the dictatorship. As in the past, women were asked to put aside their own special demands in order to support a fresh struggle for freedom and democracy.

Thus while Western feminism was undergoing a great renaissance in the late 1960s and early 1970s, with vigorous debates over ideologies and goals, the discussion of feminist theory in Greece was almost entirely stifled by a dictatorship resting on the cult of the family. When the colonels finally fell in 1974, the women's movement which reemerged was integrally connected with the wider context of progressive politics. Indeed, the first women's groups were initiated by political women belonging to parties of the Left, who simultaneously held in view strong political, social and feminist goals. "There can be no women's liberation without social liberation, no social liberation without women's liberation" became the slogan of an increasing number of feminists.

The primacy of safeguarding democracy underpinned all feminist concerns in this early period of transition back to a parliamentary system. Greek feminists not only demanded equal rights with men but they also protested against the capitalist structures and alienating productive processes into which they were by no means eager to be integrated. Their challenge was to the very class structure of a society that exploited and oppressed them.

One of the first major collaborative efforts of the new women's groups was the campaign against that epitome of patriarchy, the Greek Family Law, itself based on Byzantine tradition. A Co-ordinating Committee of Representatives of Women's Organizations (SEGES)[7], formed in 1976, helped to organize extensive mobilization against the law, and an expert committee appointed by the government incorporated some of the women's demands in the so-called Ghazis reform bill. When the bill failed to pass through parliament, however it became clear to feminists that the Conservative government was only paying lip-service to equality and had no intention of rectifying even the most blatant forms of discrimination. Despite this temporary defeat, feminists extended their struggle to other areas of women's oppression—above all, their general marginalization in wage employment. As women's dependence and domestication were at the heart of their inferior position, feminists demanded equal access to employment until this was achieved. A related and equally important demand concerned the abolition of occupational sex segregation (full access to all occupations and equal opportunities for promotion) as well as equal wages for work of equal value and extensive social protection, including for unpaid family helpers, piece-workers in cottage industry and the informal sector of the economy. Pensions, medical care and maternity allowances were particularly vital for rural women, the most exploited sector of the Greek labor force.

At the same time, women's groups presented a compelling analysis of the state's failure to socialize the costs of reproduction. Pointing to the necessity of sharing domestic work between men and women, and to the state's obligation to undertake the social function of providing services for the workforce, they demanded the provision of such services as day care, paid parental leave, extended school hours for children of working parents, inexpensive public cafeterias, public washing and ironing facilities, and so on. They further addressed the underlying problem of children's socialization into traditional gender roles, proposing the democratization of the school system and the rewriting of sexist textbooks. They also demanded free and legal abortion on demand, the establishment of family planning centres, and an effective government department to promote policies for women. As we shall see, the principal fruit of this agitation was the platform of women's emancipation that the new Socialist government brought with it in 1981.

BUILDING A GRASSROOTS MOVEMENT

After the fall of the Colonels, the new women's movement modelled itself on more familiar forms of organization: a constitution, centralized and hierarchical leadership, work in committees, an electoral system and a spreading network of branches. In the initial stages, some of the budding women's groups also leaned heavily on the established parties of the Left. The first important umbrella organization, formed immediately after the collapse of the junta in 1974, was the Democratic Women's Movement (KDG), which rallied around it many of the progressive women of the Left. In 1976, with the establishment of the party of the Panhellenic Socialist Movement (PASOK) and the consolidation of the communist split between the KKE and KKE-Interior, two other major organizations developed: the Union of Greek Women and the Federation of Greek Women, ideologically oriented to PASOK and the KKE respectively. These organizations drew some of their membership from the KDG, which subsequently aligned itself with the KKE-Interior. Party affiliation thus often provided the broader male legitimation needed for the women to mobilize throughout the country, since male party members or sympathizers found it difficult to oppose the recruitment of their wives and daughters into what they considered as the party's women's group. Given the still marginal position of most Greek women in production and the difficulties of organizing them, the support of popular political movements was an effective means of spreading feminist ideas.

Of course, dual allegiance to a party and a women's organization did not come without problems for most female activists, particularly since the different instances competed for time and energy. Moreover, feminists within the parties of the Left inevitably came into conflict with persistent male biases and androcentric thinking. From the very beginning, some male party members had resented the autonomy and exclusiveness of the women's groups, which seemed a *terra incognita* beyond the reach of the party. Others would not accept in their theoretical framework any rationale for the separate organization of women since the party was supposed to espouse uniform goals.[8] The primacy given to women's questions by the more militant women's groups was infrequently shared by party comrades, who often accused women of unreasonable extremism, so that the initial system of mutually reinforcing relationships gave way to uneasy alliances. Other women's groups that emerged during this period enjoyed a considerably smaller membership, and Western radical feminism then appealed only to a small number of young middle-class students and intellectuals, often educated abroad, and was generally perceived by both women and men as yet another import of 'decadent' cultural imperialism.

Within the women's movement itself multiple strains obtained, as sisterhood could not readily smooth out the rough edges of competitive party politics. The dynamics of fission and fusion between women's organizations along party ideology prevented the full empowerment of women in a common feminist front. Divergent ideologies between women's groups and tendencies within them furthered the divisiveness, and as the movement developed and matured, a full spectrum of feminist responses to the women's question was elaborated by the end of the 1970s.

First, the older, liberal tradition changed little in its basically individualist and egalitarian approach. The women's struggle was still conceived as focused on "equal rights, equal obligation" and opposition to open discrimination in economic and public life. Women's full integration in society on an equal basis with men was considered the final goal. On the other side, the traditional socialist position submerged the whole women's question within a larger critique of capitalist society, claiming that Greek women's low status derived from their position in the structure of production as a reserve army of labor. In this view, women's struggle was an integral part of the broader working-class struggle against imperialism, and women's employment conditions became the main practical focus. The solution to the woman question was the transition to socialism and peace.

As the struggle for socialism had primacy for women, both women and men operated from an identical paradigm that did not create antithetical interests or conflict between women's organization and the party.

A third strain, the socialist-feminist orientation, was also strongly represented in the women's movement by such organizations and centers as the Union of Greek Women (EGE), the Democratic Women's Movement (KDG), the Mediterranean Women's Studies Institute (KEGME) and others. The EGE and the KDG both had an important grassroots organization spread over Greece, in towns, villages and islands. The socialist-feminists were in partial agreement with the traditional equation of women's oppression with capitalism, but they argued that, since it also derived from patriarchy, it would not magically disappear with socialist transformation, as the actually existing socialist societies demonstrated. The feminist struggle was thus a difficult and profoundly revolutionary challenge to the very fabric of society, from the micro-level of the family to the macro-level of world male culture.

Finally, as socialist-feminists tried to maintain a balance between the commitments to socialism and feminism, the more radical fringes of the movement began dropping out of the formal women's organizations to create their own autonomous network. Like the radical feminists of Western Europe, they rejected all existing authoritarian structures, relationships and processes, including participation in the political parties that were seen as absorbing and colonizing the women's movement. Their main target was not capitalism but male power and supremacy per se, against which they counterposed feminism as a new humanist ideology and practice that would create the foundations of a new society. However, the fluid and unstable enclaves of radical feminism in Athens and Salonika had little success in proselytizing among women in general—the price to be paid for feminist autonomy in a society dominated by partisan politics.

THE PASOK EXPERIENCE

In October 1981 the PASOK Socialist government came to power bearing gifts for Greek women. Leaping out of the dark ages of cultural conservatism, Greece suddenly became an international forerunner in progressive public policy for women. In this transformation the Union of Greek Women (EGE) led by Margaret Papandreou, the wife of the prime minister, played a key role in formulating policies and pressuring the government for their adoption. The PASOK government eventually took up most of the suggestions of the EGE and other women's groups, albeit in a diluted form. First the perennial demand for reform of the infamous Family Law was granted as a goodwill gesture towards women, who had been highly instrumental in PASOK's margin of victory. The new family provisions abolished the old patriarchal categories and replaced them with the family founded on equality. The husband was no longer the head and arbiter of children's destiny, and family decisions were made the joint responsibility of both spouses. Children's upbringing had to be conducted without gender discrimination, and children born out of wedlock became equal before the law. In the civil code, divorce by mutual consent—another traditional demand of the women's movement—was legalized and the humiliating dowry institution was formally abolished.

Female equality was institutionalized by an official decree that established special national machinery to promote much-needed legislation and to monitor its implementation, including a Prime Minister's Council for Sex Equality, upgraded in 1985 to a General Secretariat, and a network of Equality Bureaus in every prefecture to assist in the decentralization of the drive to advance the position of women. A specific government program for women was incorporated in the national and sectoral plans along with a barrage of new legislative reforms, bringing all national legislation into line with the principles of equality and ratifying Greece's adherence to the UN Convention for the Elimination of All Forms of Discrimination against Women and International Convention No. 103 for the protection of maternity. Pensions and medical coverage were extended to uninsured working women and equality bureaus set up in each labor inspectorate. Assistance to working parents with children was provided through parent leave, which established the father's right to share in the raising of children. Rural women's backward social position was partially ameliorated through abolition of the law which prohibited their participation in agricultural cooperatives, and, more substantively, through the extension of maternity allowances and medical and pharmaceutical benefits.

Within a few years this reform program had revolutionized the statutory framework of Greek society. In addition, school books were rewritten with the help of women's organizations to express the principle of equality, and some family planning services were introduced for the first time in town and countryside. A rudimentary social infrastructure came into being, including hundreds of new day-care centers. Job cooperatives were initiated to increase women's employment, and some opportunities opened up in non-traditional occupations such as bus-driving. In effect the PASOK government succeeded in implementing much of the reform agenda that the women's organizations had been demanding since the fall of the junta.

WHAT REMAINS TO BE DONE

Despite the Socialist government's top-down efforts to alter women's legal and civil status, equality is still nowhere near to being achieved, and the old patriarchal assumptions are still firmly rooted in Greek society. Legal changes and government programs were like drops in a sea of discrimination. Opportunities for wage employment continued to be scarce in almost zero-growth conditions, and unemployment was hitting women twice as hard as men, especially in the younger age brackets. Those women employed outside the home were still situated at the bottom of the occupational and salary scale, as a largely unskilled, underemployed and underpaid labour force. Women with higher education and skills faced gender hierarchies that still concentrated men at the top, especially in the fields of science and technology. It was becoming apparent to feminists that reforms of a mainly statutory nature were only the first step in a long process in which only major restructuring could create the conditions for equality between women and men.

Since women's struggles had for so long been waged at the level of equal rights and opportunities, the government's thorough reformulation of laws and policies based on the principle of equality eliminated for a while the militant cutting-edge once characteristic of the movement. Women's organizations took a back seat to the government drive for equality. Abandoning its vigorous confrontation tactics, the movement was now pushing into other areas and levels of activity, as well as attempting to expand its grassroots base. Small consciousness-raising groups of the autonomous kind emerged in the cities, going in and out of existence according to their more or less temporary goals.[9] Alongside members' homes or special meeting-places, women's bookshops served as new center of information and theoretical development. Research and documentation centers, such as the Mediterranean Women's Studies Institute and the Center for Documentation and Study of Women's Problems, also provided library facilities and an elementary information base on the international women's movement. Women anthropologists, sociologists, agronomists, economists, psychologists and political scientists opened up new areas to investigation—field work in village communities being of particular importance in the Greek context. Women's studies programs were informally introduced at Salonika University by feminist teachers and students, as well as on the island of Spetses through a two-week KEGME summer program for women from the whole Mediterranean region. Distinctive women's art, film and theatre began to make its appearance, and a whole range of magazines circulated in Athens and the provinces—from commercal weeklies, through magazines primarily addressed to the membership of women's organizations, to theoretical journals attuned to the latest debates of Western feminism.[10]

By the mid-1980s the women's movement was reopening with new fervor the old controversy about abortion, birth control and sexuality, declaring women's basic right to control their own bodies and functions as the fundamental goal in the struggle for equality. For years Greek feminists had been campaigning for free and legal abortion, as women were daily risking their lives and health in the estimated 250,000 to 300,000 abortions performed on them annually—terminations which, though illegal, were widely tolerated in an Orthodox culture markedly different from Mediterranean Catholicism. By the end of 1985 a bill was before Parliament that would leave women free to decide on abortion up to the twelfth week of pregnancy or the twenty-fourth week in the case of fetal abnormality, after which individual cases would be examined by a special committee. No restrictions whatever would apply in cases of rape or incest, or of danger to the mother's health. The cost of the operation would be covered by the national health insurance scheme. In addition, feminists continued to argue for sex and contraceptive education in schools, for a nationwide system of child care, family planning and public health, and the provision of strong incentives for families having children.

Another major issue in the agenda was the tenacity of traditional values and perceptions of women's roles, and the stereotypical image of women in the mass media. Women's organizations were pressing for the clean-up to begin with the state-controlled radio and television. With regard to the exploitation of the female body in advertising, the government was preparing a bill that would partly meet the demands of women. Feminists were again taking up the issue of violence against women, urging that refuges for battered wives should be set up in the large cities. For the first time the government itself was taking some steps, as the General Secretariat for Equality launched a training program for professionals involved with battered women and drew up plans for a protection center in Athens.

It remains obvious that political marginalization was a powerful factor in keeping women powerless and perpetuating their inferior social and economic status. Trade unions, political parties, parliamentary bodies and government itself had a sorry record of failing to integrate women not only in executive office but even within their rank and file. The Socialist government's move towards some decentralization had benefited a few women who were elected to prefectural or local councils. By and large, however, only a few token women were to be found in central and higher instances, with little power or voice to make a notable impact on women's behalf. In 1985 the Greek Parliament had 13 women among a total of 300 deputies. This marked a significant but very small increase since 1956, when two women occupied seats in Parliament. Women accounted for 9 out of 55 nomarchs, 4 out of 276 mayors, 22 out of 5,751 community presidents. There were two women presidents of public organizations, one minister (of culture and science), three deputy ministers (of health and welfare, social security and industry), and three heads of general secretariats (health and welfare, Greeks Abroad, equality).

Greek women's organizations were also seriously engaged in forging links of international solidarity, especially with the third world. Through the workshops they organized and the interventions they made in Nairobi, Greek feminists had a strong presence at the United Nations World Conference on Women in July 1985. International political issues, such as the struggle for disarmament and demilitarized zones in the Mediterranean and elsewhere, were being actively take up by feminists, who countered male aggression by raising their own voices loud and clear: "No to military bases and nuclear weapons in Greece!"; "No to poverty and starvation in the Third World!"; "No to Star Wars!"; "Yes to Peace, Friendship and Solidarity with all women and peoples of the world!"

The first years of PASOK government did succeed in opening for women a window to reform, although fundamental changes could only come about on the basis of other developments. Feminists all over the world are already posing alternative development strategies for the benefit of women, men, families and societies as a whole. In this respect, they stand in the vanguard of national and international struggles for "real" development for all. Moreover, recent interest in the restructuring of sex roles, as well as in women's studies and the critique of mainstream knowledge and science, is helping to bring about a conceptual reassessment of and new perspectives on the notions of work and non-work, power, development, equality, and so on—a process that is beginning to inform and empower the Greek women's movement. At the end of the UN Decade of Women, there is an imperative need for a broad feminist alliance in Greece, for an autonomous women's movement that will struggle for an alternative development in which people matter and will advance its own feminist values and radical vision of a new humanist society. The future of the Greek women's movement is wide open.

NOTES AND REFERENCES

1. As recently as 1981, only about 40 percent of all active women were remunerated for their work.

2. Whereas in Britain, for example, 90 percent of the net increase in the working population between 1950 and 1971 was accounted for by women, "housewifeization" after marriage became an entrenched institution in Greece, with only a fifth of married women, as against three-quarters of unmarried women, going out to work in 1971.

3. In general, post-war economic growth occurred in areas employing a high proportion of male workers. For example, the spectacular boom in the construction industry provided employment to 255,000 in 1971 (10.7 percent of the male work force and 0.2 percent of the female work force). The modernization of transportation–communications absorbed 8.4 percent of the male and 1.5 percent of the

female work force. Shipping was exclusively male-dominated (73,151 in 1971), providing a major opportunity for the unemployed and underemployed male rural population. Employment in industry in general benefited men more than women (30 percent to 16 percent of their respective work-force totals in 1971). Only the tertiary sector has given an advantage to women in recent years (employing 16.5 percent of the female labor force in 1961, 20 percent in 1971, and 40.2 percent in 1981).

4. It should be mentioned, though, that Greek emigrant women abroad entered the labor force on a massive scale, surpassing the rate of their non-emigrating sisters. Weak demand for paid labor in Greece was thus the basic factor underlying the persistence of the housewife syndrome.

5. Whereas in 1961 only 36.6 percent of women (and 50.3 percent of men) received primary education, the gap had decreased to 51.6 percent of women and 60.9 percent of men by 1981. University graduates comprised 0.9 percent of women and 2.9 percent of men in 1961, while the corresponding figures for 1981 were 3.5 percent of women and 6.8 percent of men.

6. Some of the best known were the Women's Rights Organization of Pireaeus and the Athens-based Panhellenic Union of Women (PEG), which became a founding member of the International Democratic Federation of Women, formed in Paris in 1945, and went on to publish a journal, *Greek Women*. In 1946 the PEG organized a national conference at which a permanent coordinating body—the Panhellenic Federation of Women (POG)—was constituted. The Women's Union of Salonika was just one of the dense network of urban women's groups that was set up in the same period.

7. In the next few years SEGES brought under its umbrella the Democratic Union of Young Women, the Union of Greek Women Lawyers, the Union of Greek Women, the Democratic Women's Movement, the Movement of Women in the Resistance, the Federation of Greek Women, the Panhellenic Union of Housewives, the Progressive Union of Greek Mothers, the Association of Greek Secretaries, the Association of Greek Housewives, the Association of Women University Graduates and the Coordinating Committee of Working Women.

8. In terms of official party policy, the exception in this regard is the KKE-Interior, which recently recognized the need for an autonomous movement on the grounds that women are the ones best suited to articulate their own problems and to direct their own struggle for liberation.

9. The autonomous movement included such groups as the Anarchofeminist Women's Group, various self-help and self-awareness collectives, the Autonomous Movement of Women and many others. See *Women's Agenda*, Utopia Publishers, Athens 1986.

10. Among the major periodicals are: *Women's Struggle* (Published by the League for Women's Rights), *Open Window* (EGE), *Contemporary Woman* (OGE), *The Bulletin* (KDG), *New Horizons* (YWCA), *Women of Europe* (Commission of European Communities), *Earth* (Salonika Women's Group), *Women's Whisper* (newsletter of the Greek Housewives), *Mousidora* (Women and Film), *Out* (Multicultural Women's Liberation Group), *City of Women* and *Hypatia*.

14

Women's Programs, Bureaucratic Resistance and Feminist Organizations

Kathleen Staudt and Jane Jaquette

While women represent 60 percent of the world population, they perform nearly two thirds of all working hours, receive only one tenth of the world income and own less than one percent of world property.[1]

By now, this dramatic statement from the Program of Action from the Mid-Decade Conference has become a near-cliché within the women-and-development community. After a whole decade of attention among United Nations affiliates and international feminist communities, official programs for women's advancement have been established in 90 percent of national governments; progressive laws and policies are in place for women[2]; and women's organizational growth has flourished. Yet barely a dent has been made in redistributing resources and values among men and women.

In the first edition of this book we argued that women's programs faced a profound bureaucratic resistance to what is essentially a redistributive and thus conflict-laden issue. Program politics are played out in less visible, bureaucratic settings. Apparent policy victories at the legislative or executive levels are often caught in a bureaucratic mire of inaction, avoidance, and distortion.[3]

As that argument was developed, gender redistribution presents a threat, not only to collective male power, but also to the prospective redistribution of power within individual families and households. As women gain more economic resources, their potential leverage and autonomy within households increase as well. For this reason, programs to enhance women's economic integration and redistribute opportunities and resources by gender pose a special threat to male bureaucratic decision makers, a threat with which they can easily identify and stymie in myriad ways.[4] Eventually, though, women's economic integration will prove efficient and effective, thereby *serving* bureaucratic interests. Unless grounded in a women-centered approach that includes women's reproductive as well as productive interests, bureaucracies can easily exploit women and constrain them in new ways. Therefore, only autonomous international feminist movements provide the necessary challenge to technical bureaucratic discourse and actions.[5]

In this chapter, we examine the Women in Development (WID) Office in the U.S. Agency for International Development (AID) during the United Nations Decade. In particular, we assess bureaucratic politics in the pursuit of internal strategies, and the nurturance of external constituencies and their effects on agency performance. The WID Office faces obstacles similar to those faced by women's bureaus elsewhere in the world, constrained by their governments. We then explore women's programs in the context of the United Nations Decade for Women.

AID'S WOMEN IN DEVELOPMENT OFFICE[6]

In the early 1970s, the U.S. Agency for International Development underwent significant policy changes, as mandated by Congress. This large bilateral development assistance organization, with AID field missions in more than 60 countries, was to pursue new directions. This was a policy change mandated by Congress to encourage growth with equity and basic human needs approaches to reach the rural poor majority in developing countries. One of the new congressional mandates called for women's integration into development programs. Numerous "women's issues" in Southern Hemisphere countries, such as heavy physical labor and high rates of maternal mortality, can be attributed to the slim resource base on which those economies rest. Nevertheless, none of these mandates, nor any thereafter, legitimized the redistribution of wealth among countries, primarily between North and South, such as expressed in calls for the New International Economic Order (NIEO). Nor has inattention to NIEO prevented a growing transnational awareness of the feminization of poverty in the international order among women-and-development activists.

Redistributive claims with*in* a polity offer a formidable challenge. Had it not been for a small group of women, knowledgeable about both the personalities and procedures associated with amending the U.S. Foreign Assistance Act, a Women in Development amendment would have fallen through the cracks of a reconceptualized development program in 1973. Washington professionals such as Virginia Allen, Arvonne Fraser, Mildred Marcy, and Irene Tinker testified at congressional hearings, drafted language, and contacted friends and colleagues to push for the amendment's inclusion. Preparations for the 1975 International Women's Year Conference in Mexico City heightened the visibility of women, as did the U.N. move to extend the year into a decade.[7]

The Percy amendment, named after its Senate sponsor, Charles Percy, prompted AID to establish a planning committee and eventually an office in the policy branch of the agency. Initially, though, the WID coordinator's office was attached to the AID administrator, the chief political appointee in the agency. She doubled as the Equal Employment Opportunity officer, which initially confused the issue of women in development with affirmative action efforts within the agency. Her WID task was to reorient agency programming in ways that would direct project resources to women in the many AID-assisted countries.

AID projects in the past had focused on women as mothers or on what some agency documents described as "at-risk" reproducers in family planning programs. Recognition of women's existing and possible productive economic work was virtually absent. At that time, gender-differentiated impact was nonproblematic to decision makers, whose normative vision perceived men as economic providers and women as domestic dependents in nuclear families, however much that image departed from reality. Home economics programs in Africa in the 1960s, for example, called for men to bear more responsibilities for agriculture so that women could better care for the home and children.

Scholarly studies, most notably beginning with those of Ester Boserup in 1970, highlighted the negative impacts of development on women.[8] Women farmers and traders were bypassed in the allocation of land, resources, training, and credit. Girls' education lagged behind that for boys. Nor did technology spread in gender-neutral ways. Consequently, men were the main beneficiaries of the development process, augmenting their power collectively and individually. These differential impacts occurred largely in market economies. If state bureaucracies intervened, they appeared to institutionalize and aggravate existing practices. AID had, until 1973, represented the mainstream of capital-intensive, growth-oriented development approaches, which channeled resources almost exclusively to men. Initial WID strategy sought a fairer, more equitable distribution of resources that was cognizant of women's actual and potential economic activity. The task seemed clear: make the AID bureaucracy work in a gender-neutral fashion that nevertheless encouraged development according to the buzzwords of the time—"with equity" and toward meeting "basic human needs."

To reorient a complex agency like AID, both at headquarters and in its many field offices, was an enormous task for the WID office, made ever so much more so by its limited budget, hovering around $1 million in a $

billion agency,[9] and with few staff amidst thousands, not including numerous contractors.[10] Aggravating these difficulties further was the ideological resistance that WID staff faced. WID staff were often greeted with remarks suggesting they were exporting "women's lib," and destroying traditional values and families at home and abroad. Mainstream AID staff would sometimes trivialize and personalize their reactions to discussions of women's income-earning or agricultural activities with reference to their own wives. Jokes about "developing a woman" or the lack of a men's development program bordered on outright hostility. WID advocates' personal appearance and personality characteristics were utilized by mainstream staff in making evaluation judgments.

WID Office strategy aimed to dilute this ideological resistance through its support of scholarly studies on women heads of household, women's work in water and fuel collection, agriculture, markets, and other topics, which largely paralleled AID's sectoral concerns. Consistent with WID's mandate to highlight the differential impacts of development was work with the Bureau of the Census to supply and publicize extensive gender-differentiated data.

The WID Office's proselytizing role lacked sufficient resources and, unlike other internal AID offices, lacked authority to halt or delay projects potentially destructive to women. As Judith Tendler pointed out in her classic study, the main task of mid-level and AID mission staff was to move money, that is, to spend what Congress allocated through designing and funding projects.[11] WID staff were given the authority to participate in project review committees, but in WID's initial years, WID staffers' questions at review committee meetings were sometimes greeted with laughter and most often ignored. Gradually, WID comments were taken more seriously, but the office lacked veto power and increasingly had to make its case on economic and efficiency grounds.

WID's limited resources and authority provided little leverage for its advocacy activities inside AID. Female empowerment goals gradually augmented the WID Office's heretofore ineffective internal approaches. In 1977, the position of coordinator was rotated from a careerist insider to a political appointee from the outside. Arvonne Fraser brought certain advantages to this role. She had been involved in the behind-the-scenes maneuvering to create the Percy amendment in 1973 and was a leading feminist activist, a recognized figure in Washington and beyond. In addition, she had participated in the 1975 International Women's Year Conference in Mexico City. Her approach linked the WID Office and its concerns with outside constituencies that could lobby AID and Congress to fulfill the WID mandate in ways the WID office alone could not.[12]

These constituencies had ripple effects beyond the WID Office and AID. However, supporting the constituencies consumed energy and resources that proved difficult to balance with the Office's internal mission. As constituencies became differentiated, they sometimes competed over the availability of the WID Office's limited funds in ways that strained commitment to feminist process. Moreover, mainstream AID seemed to view women's politics with a special annoyance, even though political linkages in other areas are the norm for the agency.

Fraser helped stimulate a WID Correspondent's Group in the Organization of Economic Cooperation and Development/Development Assistance Committee (her counterparts in Europe). She tried to disassociate women's economic roles from their reproductive roles, since AID had a family planning bureaucracy.[13] And she supported projects that women's organizations elsewhere in the world could implement. Her vision was that government programming alone was not enough, that women's political empowerment, both at the grassroots and elite levels, was necessary to transform projects and policies.

The WID Office was actively involved in U.N. international conferences through sponsoring studies to be circulated at meetings, briefing U.S. delegates, and funding travel for some international participants. Unfortunately, for several years, U.S. contributions to the U.N. Voluntary Fund for Women pulled the WID Office into a cumbersome and sometimes controversial review process of U.N. projects.

Eventually, the U.S. constituencies stabilized in organizational form, the most important of which was the Association for Women in Development (AWID), created in 1982. Whether the association was viable was another matter. AWID, based on the idea of "trialogue" among academics, policymakers, and practitioners, joins people of different discourses, world views, and fields of work. Some of its members are even hostile to the idea of foreign assistance. AWID has sponsored several dynamic conferences, but it has not developed into a political force.

At the same time, WID staffers tried bureaucratic approaches to penetrate AID's procedures, plans, and budgets in order to work from within. Woman-Impact Statements were required, but were often recycled from project to project. The 1978 WID hearings in Congress produced a temporary consensus between members of Congress and WID staff over earmarking $10 million for women in development spending in AID.[14] AID's general counsel, however, interpreted congressional intent to mean that AID merely had to verify in reports to Congress that at least $10 million was being spent annually on women in development. Consequently, a massive tracking system was devised in the WID Office to monitor and report on agency activity. The office depended upon reports from AID field missions and geographic bureaus that both exaggerated and underestimated activity, generally due to prevailing ignorance about what constituted women in development.

Among the WID Office's few early allies were WID field officers in AID's geographic bureaus and field missions. Typically selected without WID Office consultation, some WID officers lacked expertise or even interest in the issue, and were assigned this responsibility in addition to many others. Yet, WID Office staffers attempted to build alliances with other internal offices that share interests in promoting their own responsibilities and programs involving women.

The bureaucratic approach took firm hold after Fraser left. An experienced development administrator, Paula Goddard, took the helm in 1980, followed by political appointee Sarah Tinsely, a Republican party activist with strong ties to the AID administrator. Staff training took on new importance as a way to influence knowledge and values. The WID training effort expanded from an optional speaker on WID to AID's 3-month staff training program in 1977 to include training for staff and senior personnel with case studies in conjunction with the Harvard Institute of International Development. Consultants with WID expertise were available to AID field missions. In the early 1980s, Women in Development peaked in the agency in terms of funding, staff, and respect. In contrast to the earlier emphasis on equity, WID's 1982 *Policy Paper* made an economic and efficiency case for women in development, the latter of which was persuasive to a greater number of people. Equity approaches were out of favor in Washington at the time. The stage was set for institutionalization when Tinsley and Goddard went on to better jobs in the agency. Though data broken down by gender are required in internal agency reports, project evaluations often contain little people-oriented data to break down.

All this activity made some dents in AID performance. The percentage of women in AID-supported training rose from 4.5 in 1973 to 13.3 in 1978 and 18 percent in 1984.[15] However, in the core development sector of agriculture, fewer than 10 percent of all project descriptions for the late 1970s and project projections in AID's 1980 *Congressional Presentation* even mentioned women. When they did, it was in ways featuring an old-style home economics approach rather than one treating women as economic producers.[16] By 1980, the WID Office's *Reports to Congress* concluded that 2 percent of AID funding was directed to women in development; this doubled to 4 percent in 1982. The fact that the 1985 *Report* contains too many blank categories from regional bureaus to make a percentage determination[17] indicates that the WID Office lost even its minimal capacity to make missions and regional bureaus report their activity. The current percentage of overall funding, always a potential embarrassment to AID, goes unreported.

A secure existence for the WID Office has always been in doubt. Only a few years after the first U.N. conference in Mexico City, rumblings were heard against WID on the grounds that a separate office was unnecessary. Some disgruntled mainstream AID staff looked toward the end of the U.N. Decade on Women as the end of justification for a WID office. From its early budget of approximately $.3 million to a high point of over $2 million in 1982 and 1983, WID's budget dropped to $.75 million in 1985. In the late 1970s and early 1980s, two or three social scientists complemented the career and political appointees on staff; today WID is left with a skeleton staff and political appointees from inside the agency with no social science support. It is likely that such a situation will raise questions about competency of the office and further reduce its impact while justifying additional budget cuts.

Politically, the WID Office can be useful to an ever-unpopular agency like AID. Beyond that, though, the promise of a successful WID for the development process has sparked special interest from Peter McPherson, a former Peace Corps Volunteer and AID administrator under Reagan. McPherson speaks out in favor of more emphasis on women in development, in marked contrast to earlier administrators who were lukewarm, silent, or even maligned the office. However, political appointees like McPherson are invariably pulled in diverse directions, leading to possible erosion from within key constituencies. (At AWID's 1984 conference, for example, his remarks at the opening dinner, harshly criticizing the lack of democracy in Nicaragua, led to boos, hisses, and a partial walkout among members of the audience. His actions were prompted by a series of Washington newspaper articles criticizing his moderate political views and even his attendance at the AWID meeting where a "known communist," the wife of the Nicaraguan ambassador, was a scheduled discussion speaker at a roundtable luncheon. Although he survived politically, McPherson's appointee status restricts his ability to maneuver and automatically limits his term of office.) Subsequent appointees may take a different attitude toward WID altogether. A major setback occurred in 1984 when Charles Percy lost his Senate seat, though supportive staffers remain at the Senate Committee on Foreign Affairs.

The WID Office, meanwhile, has become increasingly incorporated into an agency that has adopted the philosophical approach of the Reagan administration. Nowhere is this better illustrated than in the office's centerpiece for the End-of-the-Decade Conference in Nairobi, a monograph entitled *Paths to the Future*. Contracted to the Sequoia Institute and authored by persons without previous WID experience, it aims at the analysis of macro-economic policy. *Paths* makes the long overdue critique of heavy-handed statist approaches to development and the useful point that governments can learn from women in informal sectors about how to unleash productive forces. Yet it comes close to arguing that only a free market economy can integrate women. Lead author Jerry Jenkins points to

Malawi as an example of an integrated economy, though women in Malawi face similar circumstances to women elsewhere in Africa, where their usually unpaid labor relieves men and the state of social responsibility and even subsidizes other development sectors. Jenkins' surprise at the number of women farmers, a majority of all farmers, merely reflects the Malawian government's comprehensive enumeration techniques, rather than women surging forward to benefit from agricultural opportunity.

If the market were free of discrimination and historical legacies that institutionalize male control of female procreation, sexuality, and work, the market approach would have possibilities. However, it ignores WID scholarship that documents the differential impact of development benefits on men and women in market economies and the consequent marginalization of women. The market approach even calls into question the validity of continuing WID offices and AID-like agencies for development.

THE DECADE CONTEXT

Ironically, the declining influence of the WID Office at AID has been accompanied by a growing consensus on a WID agenda at the international level, partly a result of the diffusion and diversification of feminist issues and perspectives during the U.N.-sponsored Decade for Women. This section addresses the role of the decade in raising women's issues and forging an international agenda, the importance of linkages among bureaucracies and between bureaucracies and women's organizations at all levels, and tensions within the international feminist movement that challenge the WID approach—substantively and organizationally.

The decade was structured around three U.N. conferences (Mexico City, 1975; Copenhagen, 1980; and Nairobi, 1985) that served as quasi-legislative processes to debate and legitimize a set of demands, and to set procedures to implement the desired changes. The often restrictive forms of interest aggregation and articulation performed by representatives of member governments in the official meetings were in contrast to the open political arena of the non-governmental organization meetings: the Tribune of 1975 and the Forums of 1980 and 1985.

The documents that emerged from these conferences (the *Plan of Action* in 1975, the *Programme of Action* in 1980, and *Forward Looking Strategies* in 1985) are in part directed to popular constituencies (such as world public opinion, attentive publics in the member countries, and women's organizations), but they are primarily written and conceived of as guidance to bureaucracies. The decade mobilized the active involvement of existing U.N. agencies (e.g., WHO, FAO, ILO, and the Secretariat); it established new ones (such as the Voluntary Fund for Women, now UNIFEM, and the International Research and Training Institute for the Advancement of

Women, or INSTRAW). Member governments were asked to adhere to international standards of legal equality and greater resource access for women and obliged, through the conference process itself, to report publicly on progress made in these areas. A succinct summary of reports from 121 governments to U.N. agencies appraising achievements of the decade presents little "good news," save a lessening of the gender gap in education, a slight change in wage disparities between men and women, and the existence of more laws calling for equality.[18]

The decade was also very successful in mobilizing women's organizations through networking, change by example, and the process of "representation" at the forum itself as a political trigger and backup for the pressures on bureaucracies—local, national, and international. It encouraged the formation of "national machineries"—women's bureaus and offices within the structure of existing national bureaucracies, to monitor progress and to prompt and implement new policies and programs.[19]

Through a decade of dialogue and often acrimonious debate, this multifaceted process succeeded in creating a remarkably high degree of consensus about what should be done about the condition of women. An important part of that consensus is support for a WID agenda per se, that is, support for the recognition, remuneration, and enhancement of women's productive roles, increased access to economic and educational resources, and acceptance of the proposition that other concerns—women's health status, political participation, role as mothers—should be furthered in ways that foster women's access to economic resources rather than increase their "domestication" or dependence on male providers.

By any standards, the demands that crystallized during the decade are redistributive. The documents call for the reallocation of current and future resources between men and women, just as the NIEO (New International Economic Order) calls for a redistribution of resources between rich and poor countries. Yet, unlike much of the U.N. language of the NIEO, the decade demands are couched in incremental policymaking terms rather than in the rhetoric of conflict. It is worth reviewing the process to understand how this came about and why it represents a political strategy for bureaucratically led change.

There is a strong continuity between the issues and priorities of the 1975 *Plan of Action* and *Forward Looking Strategies*[20] passed by consensus in Nairobi a decade later. Both begin with issues of legal equality and the legal basis for women's political participation. Both focus sharply on women's undervalued role in agricultural production and underrepresentation in modern sector economic activities, though the list of problems has grown longer and the list of potential solutions more specific as the decade progressed. Problems and solutions in women's health care are identified and women's differential access to education at all levels is criticized. Both point out the potential of women's values and women's organizations in promoting disarmament, and the linkages that exist between equality—between men and women, rich and poor—and peace.

Between 1975 and 1985, there were also some important changes that reflect an expanding "feminist" definition of the issues. Violence against women, at the heart of male/female power relations, was not a salient concern in 1975, but it is the explicit focus of seven paragraphs, some quite detailed, of *Forward Looking Strategies*. Abused women have been added to the list of elderly women, migrant women, refugees, and other deserving special attention. The *Plan of Action* expressed concern about prostitution; *Forward Looking Strategies* condemns pornography and has expanded its analysis of women's image in the media to include its portrayal of women as victims. It defines and condemns sexual harassment and notes that domestic servants as well as women working in factories and offices are vulnerable to this form of abuse.

That men should share domestic responsibilities is barely hinted at in the *Plan of Action*, but stressed at various points in *Forward Looking Strategies* where, for better or worse, it receives much more attention than the provision of state-sponsored services, such as child care. The concepts of comparable worth (which provoked U.S. reservations to these paragraphs, as U.S. policy is "equal pay for equal work"), remuneration for housewives, and the inclusion of family workers in social security programs, were also endorsed, and the argument was made that women should not only have increased access to resources that will increase their incomes, but that for income strategies to be effective, women must retain *control* over what they earn.

The decade claims for women are occasionally promoted in terms of the special responsibilities women have to children, and there is strong support for women's organizations and, implicitly, women's solidarity. But the foundation for women's claims is egalitarian (not women's special characteristics) and individualistic rather than communal. In Copenhagen, the *Programme of Action* interpreted equality to mean not only "the elimination of de jure discrimination, but also equality of rights, responsibilities and opportunities for the participation of women in development, both as beneficiaries and active agents" (Paragraph 10). In *Forward Looking Strategies*, equality is defined as:

> both a goal and a means whereby individuals are accorded equal treatment under the law and equal opportunities to enjoy their rights and to develop their potential talents and skills. . . . For women, in particular, equality means the realization of rights that have been denied as a result of cultural, institutional, behavioral, and attitudinal discrimination. (Paragraph 11)

In some instances, particularly with regard to women's reproductive roles, equality is not assumed to mean equal treatment but equal result: the fact that women bear, nurse, and still take most of the responsibility for raising young children requires special treatment to ensure that women will be able to participate in the work force and society as fully as men.[21] In rare instances, the decade documents resort to "efficiency" as opposed to "equality" justification for women's claims; *Forward Looking Strategies* observes that women-in-development programs have too often been viewed as "welfare" efforts, as costs rather than as contributions. In the anti-statist and post-civil rights atmosphere of Washington, efficiency arguments have displaced equity arguments for WID interests at AID, but the decade commitment to equality as a goal in itself is generally clear and presented without apology.

The United Nations itself operates on the principle that equality is a self-evident goal; witness the U.N.'s role as the arbiter between the global "haves" and the "have-nots." The decade documents thus draw on a tradition of rights language in the U.N., and a broader context of international public opinion that still accepts such language as legitimate. Discrimination against women is bad because all discrimination against the weak is bad; women's marginalization is repugnant because the battle against political and economic marginalization is at the heart of the U.N.'s conception of its role.

Egalitarianism is also fully congruent with the fundamental norms of modern bureaucracies, the main audience toward which the *Plan*, the *Programme*, and *Forward Looking Strategies*, we argue, are directed primarily. As Max Weber observed, "bureaucratic organization has usually come into power on the basis of a leveling of economic and social differences."[22] Bureaucracies don't make revolutions by themselves, but require specific goals, concrete tasks, and measurable results. The *Plan*, the *Programme*, and *Forward Looking Strategies* provide not only an egalitarian rationale for women's claims, but an operative framework for reformist bureaucratic action.

Once the bureaucratic function of these documents is recognized, it is striking to note the number of paragraphs prescribing a strategy of what might be called *bureaucratic realpolitik*. Fully 193 paragraphs of *Forward Looking Strategies* stipulate the responsibilities of various governmental and international agencies, which are called upon to collect and analyze data; to distribute their resources more equitably, using delivery mechanisms that have been shown to reach women more effectively (e.g., female agricultural extension agencies, and training programs that fit women's over-burdened schedules); and to collect sex-differentiated data on the impact of all these efforts. These are concrete tasks that bureaucracies can perform. Much of the decade's attempt to change traditional values also has a bureaucratic focus: women can be hired, old-line managers can be retired, and national bureaucracies can use their regulatory powers (over media content, or textbooks and educational curricula) to promote change, while excising rules and regulations that may have been part of standard operating procedures in the past, but which experience has shown to be discriminatory or exclusionary.[23]

The *Plan of Action* recognized the importance of formal political participation as a means to promote women's issues; both the *Programme of Action* and *Forward Looking Strategies* recognize and build on the burgeoning growth and activity of women's organizations, which have been the hallmark of the decade. Two decades ago, Theodore Lowi identified a bureaucratic triangle of linkages between interest groups, politicians, and bureaucrats, which, when mobilized, was very powerful in legislating and implementing policies according to shared interests.[24] Recognizing implicitly that the political leg of this triangle may be nonexistent (as in miltiary-dominated governments) or attenuated (due to the lack of women in office or to weak feminist orientations on the part of women who are elected), the decade documents "walk on two legs" of Lowi's triangle: women's organizations and sympathetic bureaucratic activists. The document calls on governments to promote and support both of these (Paragraph 126).

We are witnessing currently the growth, increasing organizational capacity, and visible involvement of women's organizations from the village to the international level. At the international level alone, an impressive array of transnational groups seeks to carve out a niche or special function from self-help to political advocacy. This is in contrast to international women's organizations of the past, which tended to be international federations of national service organizations, such as the YWCA or the association of university women. Groups like the International Women's Tribune Center or the New International Publications Cooperative specialize in networking and information sharing among groups; others, like DAWN,[25] are seeking new political agendas and explicitly reinforcing the development of international feminist alternatives based on third world perceptions and interests. There are groups devoted to the exchange of scholarly information and development-related studies; to supporting the ratification of the Convention Against All Forms of Discrimination Against Women (passed by the U.N. in 1980); and to seeking international cooperation on disarmament and peace. In different ways and in different constituencies, these groups can mobilize public opinion, channel intellectual and financial resources, and lobby governments and agencies. As the U.N. withdraws from its role of providing an arena for setting agendas and mobilizing support (and as AID pulls back from any leadership role), the prospect for continued awareness, implementation, and agitation will increasingly fall to women's organizations.

During the decade, an important obstacle to achieving consensus and broad support came from ignorance and resistance outside the international women's movement—by women as well as men—and from those who saw the conferences as a platform to argue issues that many feminists thought tangential to the women's agenda. The issue of politicization of the decade conferences has been much discussed in the news media and elsewhere[26] and a full analysis is beyond the scope of this discussion. However, *Forward Looking Strategies* was passed by consensus, and we have come to the end of the U.N.-sponsored "decade process." The growth of the international women's movement and the blossoming of many varieties of international feminism have gained visibility for women's issues and the WID agenda in the international policy arena, a partially institutionalized place on bureaucratic dockets, both domestic and international, and a great deal of political support and public awareness. A healthy pluralism is present in feminist discussions. It is perhaps not premature to predict that the most important future challenges to the decade consensus will come from within the international women's movement itself, from competing visions of feminist futures and conflicting views on how to implement them.

A significant potential weakness we see in the current consensus is its individualistic bias. The concepts of individual fulfillment and freedom, inspiring to many, are at the core of liberal internationalism. However, they are vulnerable from a number of different directions, and a major challenge from any one of them could undermine the decade consensus. First, individualism is vulnerable to a resurgence of fundamentalist religious values, which may be a major source of women's activism in the future. The national, religious, and even family loyalties that have marked the modern resurgence of fundamentalism can be deployed in ways that make improvements in women's economic status or overt exercise of power seem selfish, anti-family or unpatriotic. From the opposite direction, changes within feminist thinking may increasingly favor communal justifications for women's rights (as seen in women's spirituality, in ecological feminism, and in separatist feminism). Finally, the new trends in feminist theory, which see women as responding to an ethic of caring or as acting (whether properly or inevitably) primarily in the context of relations to others (particularly family others[27]) may begin to undermine claims that women make as individuals *for themselves*.

A second, very important division among modern feminists that affects both the legitimacy of the decade agenda and the consensus, exists between committed socialist feminists and those who might be classified either as "agnostics" or "non-believers" with respect to socialism. Many feminists worldwide first were active in leftist politics and are likely to be sympathetic to socialist goals, even if they are critical of existing socialist governments and opposed to violent revolution to force change. There is a crucial difference between those who actively support changing women's access to resources ignoring the issue of whether such changes increase the chances that capitalism will fall sooner rather than later, and those who preserve a "critical distance" because such efforts assume a capitalist economy, and if successful, might give capitalism a longer lease on life. Unlike support for the NIEO—a spectrum of demands each of which could be met by a greater or lesser response—the demand for a socialist system remains dichotomous: a system is either socialist or not, despite all the intellectual difficulties with such determinations. As a result, few (if any) countries qualify as truly socialist. Within each country and internationally, incrementalist and reformist solutions of the sort outlined in the decade consensus are vulnerable to radical criticism, and may not command full support among many educated and activist women who are their logical supporters.

The third important split within international feminism, one that contrasts with many of the optimistic arguments of this chapter, is the growing articulation of those feminists opposed to bureaucracy. Inspired by radical feminists of the late 1960s and by Michel Foucault, and argued most clearly by Kathy Ferguson,[28] the feminist opposition to bureaucracy is based on the incompatibility between bureaucratic norms of hierarchy, top-down communication, and objectivity, and feminist values of egalitarianism, participation, and connectedness. These critics have predicted that bureaucrats would use their technical expertise to isolate themselves and create a new kind of elite, and that bureaucracies, especially "service" bureaucracies, are self-perpetuating and difficult to control and change.

Adele Mueller has applied Kathy Ferguson's critique precisely to the question of the creation of WID knowledge and the legitimacy of a WID bureacracy: "Liberal feminist scholarship elaborating and accomplishing the work of articulating women's issues and state bureaucracies is bound to the reproduction of existing ruling relations."[29] Like Ferguson's, Mueller's anti-bureaucratic critique eventually merges with her critique of capitalism, but not without doing considerable damage to bureaucratic solutions along the way. As Ferguson concludes,

> Bureaucratic opposition of necessity is aimed at limited personnel or policy reforms, not at the transformation of the social setting within which the bureaucracy is situated . . . [such oppositions] leave the order intact. In light of this conclusion, liberal feminist hopes that organizations will be rendered humane, less oppressive, and more conducive to genuine personal growth by the inclusion of women are revealed to be naive and pious hopes.[30]

And, as Foucault reminds us, those who set themselves up as progressive bureaucrats are hardly trustworthy: however appealing their goals, following the inner logic of bureaucratic structure and their own motivations to succeed, they will become the new elite once the new goals are institutionalized.[31]

On the other hand, it is not obvious that the anti-bureaucratic approach will necessarily be wedded to support for socialism, a system characterized, even in the best of cases, by rock-solid, expanding bureaucracy and by persistent denial of the elitism such bureaucracies create. It is equally plausible to link the anti-bureaucratic critique to conservative pro-market policies, and few would argue that the attack on the welfare state has meant gains for women. The insight that women do not fare well in the marketplace is the starting place for the women-in-development approach, and subsequent studies have not altered the foundations laid by Ester Boserup over a decade and a half ago.[32]

CONCLUSIONS AND IMPLICATIONS

Near the beginning of the decade, a Women in Development Office pursued strategies to reduce or eliminate gender bias in the bureaucratic operations of the Agency for International Development, including its projects in developing countries. Limited initially by its bureaucratic approach, the WID Office went on to adopt a more political approach, stressing female empowerment and encompassing feminist constituencies in the United States and elsewhere. Always controversial, this political approach gave way to a renewed and increasingly effective bureaucratic approach, couched in economic and efficiency arguments. Amidst new leadership and a changed political context, AID chipped away at the WID Office's staff and resources; today, total demise of the WID Office is quite possible. For a decade's worth of effort, overall AID progress toward integrating women in development was meager. Bureaucratic resistance, on the whole, still characterizes the response to this women's program.

Conferences during the international women's decade produced an expanding feminist agenda and a flourishing set of diverse women's organizations. Final conference documents from Nairobi resemble neither a lengthy and polished press release nor a utopian wish list, but rather an operational guide set largely within a national bureaucratic framework. That sort of strategy complements the egalitarian norms that are supposed to characterize bureaucratic principles. Left untouched, though, are questions on both elitist national bureaucracies and on international inequities that more radical development advocates address.

What are the prospects for success of bureaucratic approaches? The data that governments provided to assess change over the decade show minimal progress. "Women's machinery," now in a vast majority of countries, fares as well or as poorly as the WID Office in AID, stymied as such offices all are by inadequate resources, insufficient staff, ideological inertia, and the dogged expected resistance to gender-redistributive threats.

Meanwhile, women's organizations have grown and feminist agendas have expanded to include a wide array of the so-called public and private issues. Growing female empowerment may make some impression on political representatives and bureaucratic staff who are part of a triangle of those who make and implement policy, a triangle that assumes at least some degree of pluralist politics and bureaucratic accountability to the public.

The post-decade activities that will occur in both national and international arenas raise several questions. To what extent will bureaucracies—largely "manned" by those who absorb the gender prejudices of their own societies—yield to feminist pressures? On what grounds will they yield, with what effects for women? What internal bureaucratic changes are necessary to facilitate real institutionalization such as more women policymakers, women's programs integrated into, rather than peripheral to, development policy, and performance evaluations that reward progress toward feminist ends? Will differentiation among feminists spur creative administrative approaches, or serve as an excuse to stall any action at all? Will governments report gender-differentiated data publicly, even without the stimulus of international conferences? Can individualistic, egalitarian grounds be reconciled with collective or "special treatment" claims in states that historically have assumed and depended on women's unpaid labor to fulfill their economic and national goals?

Although it would be a mistake to assume widespread political pluralism, the state may be a far more formidable obstacle than the lack of pluralism. The slow creep of bureaucratic progress over the decade was not simply the result of a lack of data, inept or uninspired management, temporary irrationality, or momentary departures from the norms of egalitarianism. Rather, the slowness is grounded in male privilege itself. We wonder whether practical, forward-looking strategies are any match for the deep institutionalization of male interests found in states of all ideological beliefs. Indeed, bureaucratic strategies are often state-strengthening strategies. Yet without gender redistribution, an expanded state perpetuates gender gaps.

At the same time, decade-oriented conceptions of gender are a far cry from the ideological baggage carried and embedded in existing laws, policies, and programs of various states. We need female empowerment to transform states and bureaucracies so that a woman-centered approach, rather than special treatment, becomes the norm. Women's development needs and status have been identified and articulated; the next stage must be a concentrated effort to transform both national and international bureaucracies to respond to those needs.

NOTES AND REFERENCES

1. *Report of the World Conference of the United Nations Decade for Women,* Copenhagen 1980, A/CONF.94/35. The statement would be difficult to document, given the only recent and somewhat sparse attention to disaggregating data by sex in government reports and scholarly studies.

2. *The State of the World's Women 1985,* World Conference to Review and Appraise the Achievements of the United Nations Decade for Women, Nairobi, Kenya, July 15-26, 1985, as reprinted in the *U.N. Conference to Review and Appraise the U.N. Decade for Women,* Report of Congressional Staff Advisors to the Nairobi Conference to the Committee on Foreign Affairs, U.S. House of Representatives, January 1986, p. 80.

3. Kathleen Staudt, "Bureaucratic Resistance to Women's Programs: The Case of Women in Development," *Women, Power and Policy,* Ellen Boneparth (ed.) (New York: Pergamon, 1982), pp. 263–281.

4. Kathleen Staudt, *Women, Foreign Assistance and Advocacy Administration* (New York: Praeger, 1985).

5. Jane S. Jaquette and Kathleen A. Staudt, "Women as 'At Risk' Reproducers: Biology, Science, and Population in U.S. Foreign Policy," *Women, Biology, and Public Policy,* Virginia Sapiro (ed.) (Beverly Hills, CA: Sage, 1985), pp. 235–268.

6. This section summarizes part of Staudt, *Women, Foreign Assistance and Advocacy.* We have both worked in AID/WID under the Intergovernmental Personnel Act—Staudt as Social Science Analyst and Jaquette as Policy Analyst.

7. Irene Tinker, "Women in Development," in Irene Tinker (ed.) *Women in Washington: Advocates for Public Policy* (Beverly Hills, CA: Sage, 1983), pp. 227–237.

8. For example, see Ester Boserup, *Woman's Role in Economic Development* (New York: St. Martin's Press, 1970); Irene Tinker, "The Adverse Impact of Development on Women," in *Women and World Development,* Irene Tinker and Michele Bo Bramson (eds.) (New York: Praeger, 1976).

9. Funding levels change yearly. More than half the approximately $4 billion is allocated to what was referred to in the late 1970s as Security Supporting Assistance, rather than developmental grounds.

10. Once over 17,000 in the late 1960s, with a Vietnam Bureau, AID staff had fallen to fewer than 6,000 a decade later. With ever-increasing concerns to "do more with less" as the internal campaign referred to in 1979, agency work is contracted out and we know of no counts available for the many consultants and contractors semi-attached to AID.

11. Judith Tendler, *Inside Foreign Aid* (Baltimore: The Johns Hopkins University Press, 1975).

12. As Tendler argues, AID's constituencies serve as surrogates for the ultimate users of AID programs elsewhere in the world who, as outsiders, lack political leverage. Those constituencies, of course, may also benefit materially from contracts from AID.

13. See note 5. This bureaucracy was not always concerned with income generation and rarely with empowerment.

14. U.S. Congress, Committee on International Relations, Subcommittee on International Organizations and on International Development, "International Women's Issues," Hearings and briefing, 95th Congress, March 8 and 22, 1978.

15. The first two and fourth figures are from Staudt, 1985, p. 95, while the third is from "Women in Development: Looking to the Future," Hearing before the

Committee on Foreign Relations, U.S. Senate, June 7, 1984, p. 25.

16. Staudt, *Women, Foreign Assistance*, pp. 99–101.

17. Women in Development Report to the Committee on Foreign Relations, U.S. Senate, and the Committee on Foreign Affairs, U.S. House of Representatives, 1978, 1980, 1982. Also see *Women in Development: The First Decade 1975–1984*, A Report to Congress by the Agency for International Development, 1985.

18. See note 2.

19. There has been substantial criticism of women's bureaus and women's sections for creating a "ghetto" or preventing women's issues from being fully integrated into the work of the government or international agencies to which they are attached. We would argue that the issue has been wrongly construed as one of either/or: either a women's section *or* "true" integration. Obviously, the ideal is full integration but the problem is how to make that happen. Women's sectors and bureaus are a means, but not the only means, to the inclusion of women's issues in agency policy and programming. Strategies that propose to do without such institutionalized interest representation are likely to produce bureaucratic rhetoric but not sustained action, innovative programs, or acceptable levels of monitoring. The problem for the specialized women's sections and bureaus is to avoid isolating themselves from the rest of the agency and from their natural constituencies, and understandable but bureaucratically self-destructive response to agencies' attempts to defend themselves against intrusive competitors for scarce resources.

20. *Forward Looking Strategies* was published along with a summary of conference preparations; a brief analysis of conference issues, proceedings and outcomes, and a list of delegates, by the House Foreign Affairs Committee. See U.N. Conference (Note 2).

21. In this the United States is the odd culture. Fear that acceptance of difference will lead to the treatment meted out to blacks under the "separate but equal" doctrine, aware that "protective" legislation has been used to bar women from high-paying jobs and that maternity leave has been used as an excuse for not employing women, the women's movement in the United States has been particularly leery of any argument for women's rights that distinguishes women from men on the grounds of their reproductive responsibilities. However, in legal theory, the principle that different people must be treated differently to produce ultimate equality (as in the progressive income tax) is still well within the liberal egalitarian tradition. See Frances E. Olsen, "The Family and the Market: A Study of Ideology and Legal Reform," *Harvard Law Review*, 96, (May 1983), 1497–1578. We seem to run into psychological, political, and economic barriers in applying the principle to women here in the United States that are not encountered in Europe or the Third World. There, the state's role in family life—both strengthening it and regulating it—is not controversial. For an excellent discussion of the changing politics of the public/private distinction, see Janet Siltanen and Michele Stanworth, "The Politics of Public Man and Private Woman," in Siltanen and Stanworth (eds.), *Women and the Public Sphere: A Critique of Sociology and Politics* (New York: St. Martin's Press, 1984), pp. 185–209.

22. "From Bureaucracy," in H. H. Gerth and C. Wright Mills, eds. and translators, *From Max Weber: Essays in Sociology* (New York: Oxford University Press, 1958), p. 224.

23. In the rapidly growing field of "women in development," the Non-Governmental Organization Forums that have run parallel to the official U.N. meetings have been an important part of the feedback loop.

24. Theodore Lowi, "American Business, Public Policy Case Studies, and Political Theory," *World Politics, 16* (July 1964).

25. DAWN is the acronym for Development Alternatives with Women for a New Era, a group of "activists, researchers, and policy makers who are concerned with developing alternative frameworks and methods to attain our goals of economic and social justice, peace, and development free of all forms of oppression by gender, class, race, and nation." DAWN collaborators include the African Association of Women for Research and Development, Dakar, Senegal; the WAND Unit of the University of the West Indies, Barbados; the Asian and Pacific Development Center, Malaysia; and the Chr. Michelson Institute, Norway. They have a secretariat in New Delhi, an office in Rio de Janeiro, and have published and distributed *Development, Crisis, and Alternative Visions: Third World Women's Perspectives*, available through DAWN, Institute of Social Studies Trust, SMM Theatre Crafts Building, 5 Deen Dayal Upadhyay Narg, New Delhi 110 002, India.

26. See Margaret E. Galey, "The Nairobi Conference: The Powerless Majority," *P.S., 19*, (Spring 1986), 255–265, and the Staff Report to the House Foreign Affairs Committee, *op. cit.*

27. See, for example, Carol Gilligan, *In a Different Voice* (Cambridge: Harvard University Press, 1983) and Jean Elshtain, *Public Man, Private Woman* (Princeton, NJ: Princeton University Press, 1981).

28. Kathy E. Ferguson, *The Feminist Case Against Bureaucracy* (Philadelphia: Temple University Press, 1984). See particularly Michel Foucault, *Power/Knowledge: Selected Interviews and Other Writings* (New York: Pantheon Books, 1972).

29. Ferguson, quoted in Adele Mueller, "The Bureaucratization of Feminist Knowledge: The Case of Women in Development," *Resources for Feminist Research* (Canada), *15*, (March 1985), 36–38.

30. Ferguson, *The Feminist Case Against Bureaucracy*, 1984, p. 121.

31. DAWN's position shows an awareness of this problem and strongly favors decentralization, local self-reliance and empowerment. For a criticism of population policy and programming control, see Jaquette and Staudt, 1985, "Women as 'At Risk' Reproducers."

32. But see David L. Kirp and Mark G. Yudof, *Gender Justice* (Chicago: University of Chicago Press, 1986).

15
Female Sexual Slavery: The Problem, Policies and Cause for Feminist Action

Kathleen L. Barry

THE PROBLEM

These stories were recounted in *Female Sexual Slavery*[1] to convey the range of situations which enslave women today:

> A young girl, now a prostitute, was sexually molested and raped by her stepfather regularly for 4 years. He threatened that if she told her mother he would leave them homeless and penniless. . . .

> Two runaway girls from Pennsylvania get off a bus in Sacramento. They are kidnapped, raped, and forced into prostitution. . . .

> A prostitute decides to leave her pimp, and when he hunts her down at her aunt's house, he takes her away with him. As a warning against future escapes, he beats her with the base of a car jack until he fractures her skull. . . .

> A wife gathers up her 5-year-old twin daughters and leaves home. She is hunted down by her husband, and when he finds her he beats her and fires his shotgun within an inch of her head as a warning in case she tries to run away again. . . .

> Several thousand teenage girls disappear from Paris every year. The police know but cannot prove that many are destined for Arab harems. An eyewitness reports that auctions have been held in Zanzibar, where European women were sold to Arab customers. . . .

> In one year, 2,000 girls were reported missing from a rural area of India where procurers had been posing as labor contractors. . . .

These women and girls are victims of female sexual slavery. Some have escaped; others have not. When it is organized, female sexual slavery is a highly profitable business that merchandises women's bodies to brothels and harems around the world. Practiced individually, without an organizational network, it is carried out by pimps whose lifestyle and expensive habits are supported by one or more women whom they brutally force to sell their bodies for their profit. The private practice of female sexual slavery is also carried out by husbands and fathers who use battery and sexual abuse as a personal measure of their power over their wives and/or daughters. *Female sexual slavery is present in all situations where women or girls cannot change the immediate conditions of their existence; where regardless of how they got into those conditions they cannot get out; and where they are subject to sexual violence and exploitation.* Sexual slavery, whether it is carried out by international gangs, or individual pimps, is a highly criminal and clandestine activity; the slavery carried out by fathers and husbands is kept secret and is socially tolerated as well. Its setting may be an Arab harem, a German eros center, an American pimp pad, or a suburban home. Wherever it is located, it brings both monetary gain and personal satisfaction to its perpetrators.

Female sexual slavery is not an illusive condition; the word *slavery* is not merely rhetorical. It is not some condition in which a woman's or child's need for love allows her to fall into psychological patterns that make it possible for her to accept abuse with love or to feel joy in pain. This slavery, an objective social condition of sexual exploitation and violence, is not limited to international traffic; it is pervasive throughout patriarchal societies.

As long as a woman or girl is held in sexual slavery, sexual intercourse is, by definition, rape. If one is not free to consent or reject, one is forced; and forced sexual intercourse, whether physically brutal or seductively subtle, is rape. The fact of rape is determined by its objective conditions. If those are conditions which a woman or girl cannot leave or alter, then they are conditions of slavery.

Rape is the primordial core of female sexual slavery, extending from the most public international traffic in women for prostitution to the most private slavery in a suburban home, city tenement, or rural cottage.

It is a political crime of violence against women, an act of power and domination. Kate Millett coined the term *sexual politics*. Sexual slavery is the very essence of sexual politics in its most extreme and ugly form.[2]

THE POLICIES[3]

About 20 years ago the United Nations, Interpol and various international human rights organizations buried their previous investigations, resolutions and other work on forced prostitution and traffic in women. They accepted the popular misconception that most prostitution is voluntary work and therefore does not constitute a fundamental violation of women's human rights. This was the international situation when I began to research and investigate traffic in women and to interview women who had been enslaved in prostitution. At the time I was motivated not only to uncover the abuses that the international human rights community chose to forget, but also to understand the relationship of the force, coercion and violence in prostitution to the violence in all women's lives around the world, in wife battery, rape, incest, bride-burning, excision, and pornography. Such an analysis meant recognizing that all of these crimes against women, including prostitution, are not isolated tragedies but, rather, are carefully woven into the structure and content of patriarchal power and male domination around the globe.

The more deeply I became involved in studying the problem and in recognizing the resistance of international agencies to confront it, the more fully aware I was that there will be no effective strategy against female sexual slavery until feminists organize in concert, beyond all the patriarchal boundaries that divide us—just as we have against such practices as wife battery and sex tourism. The first impetus for the meeting convened in Rotterdam in 1983 to form an international feminist network against female sexual slavery came from the recognition that feminists, along with the officials and the organizations that often participate in hiding them and shrouding them with silence, must take the responsibility for confronting the practices that enslave women. Until feminists organize to demand that these practices, in their specific incidence and in their powerful institutional base, constitute a violation of women's human rights, there will be no genuine international concern for the victims nor any opportunity to confront the private as well as political and economic interests that promote prostitution and the traffic in women.

The first major opportunity for feminists to discuss these issues on an international basis came with the United Nations Mid-Decade Conference on Women in Copenhagen in 1980. Despite the fact that UNESCO had reported on the torture of women in prostitution at the International Women's Year Conference in Mexico City in 1975, which adopted resolutions calling for action, and although *Female Sexual Slavery* had been published in 1979 and provided the documentation of this traffic, it was impossible to get the planning commissions for the Copenhagen meeting to place the issue on the agenda of either the governmental or nongovernmental conference (NGO Forum). It was only at the last minute, a few weeks before the Copenhagen meeting opened, that several feminist delegates were able to pressure the planning committee of the NGO Forum to schedule a workshop on female sexual slavery. During these workshops on female sexual slavery and sex tourism, feminists discussed the problems with representatives in the governmental conference. Feminist determination to address these issues led to a resolution against the traffic in women, which was adopted in World Plan of Action for Women.

The consensus from these workshops and meetings was that we needed to create a means for feminists to organize against female sexual slavery on a global basis. Through the very spirited discussions in these sessions, it became clear that while national politics, cultural practices, and languages separate us, the violation of women in female sexual slavery is both global and international: global because it affects women in all conditions in most nations and cultures, and international because it often involves trafficking women from one country to another. We defined female sexual slavery more broadly than do the United Nations or its agencies concerned with the traffic in women. We include in our concerns any situation from which a woman cannot escape and if in that situation she is physically abused and sexually exploited. In these meetings we realized that as we defined female sexual slavery, it applied to women who are the victims of sex tourism, the victims of gangs that traffic in women from South America to Europe, women who are sexually tortured and enslaved as political prisoners in totalitarian dictatorships, and women enslaved in their own homes.

We left Copenhapen in the summer of 1980 with an international advisory committee in place and a plan to organize an international network of feminists. We then began to look for the women in each world region who were attempting to address these problems within their own cultural and political contexts.

Before considering the kind of concerns feminists must bring to the international confrontation of these practices, a brief history of the human rights community is necessary to understand both the advantages and the limitations of the work that has been done previously.

The United Nations and the Human Rights Community

In 1949 the United Nations ratified the Convention on the Traffic in Persons and the Exploitation of the Prostitution of Others. Since then, except for a few efforts from some individuals and non-governmental organizations, the United Nations has virtually abandoned the problem, allowing the traffic in women to become invisible once again. In 1974 a Working Group on Slavery was organized primarily through the efforts of Patrick Montgomery, formerly of the London-based Anti-Slavery Society. This Working Group meets once a year to report on slavery practices around the world to a subcommittee of the United Nations Human Rights Commission. Given the inattention of the United Nations bureaucratic machinery, most cases (of the few that are ever reported) never find their way to international public attention.

Consequently, many feminists who have been working on issues of traffic in women hoped that the United Nations Status of Women

Commission would be more responsive to this problem. The Convention to Eliminate All Forms of Discrimination was ratified in Copenhagen in 1980; it provided women with an international instrument they could utilize to insist that nations address and confront practices of female sexual slavery. For that reason we wanted to involve the United Nations Status of Women Commission in our meetings. We invited the director of its Branch for the Advancement of Women, Centre for Social Development and Humanitarian Affairs, to join us for a few days in Rotterdam in 1983. In response to our invitation the director informed us that "Branch for the Advancement of Women has no budgetary funds to attend such meetings. In addition, the staff member who is working in this special field has been on sick leave for three months." This kind of bureaucratic evasion has consistently been employed by international officials to avoid the issues of female sexual slavery. Without international feminist presence and pressure, even the Status of Women Commission will allow patriarchal interest to bury the issue. Nevertheless, many women associated with the Status of Women Commission have worked energetically for the adoption of resolutions against traffic in women and to insist that the Economic and Social Council investigate the problem and recommend actions against it.

As a result of this feminist-initiated pressure and of the Copenhagen Conference's 1980 resolution against traffic in women, which requested that the United Nations conduct a systematic international study of the problem, in 1982 the Economic and Social Council asked the secretary general to appoint a special rapporteur to make a "synthesis of the surveys and studies on the traffic in persons and the exploitation of the prostitution of others that have been or are being carried out within the appropriate agencies of the United Nations system or outside the system," and to propose measures to prevent and to suppress the practices "that are contrary to the fundamental rights of the human being." Jean Fernand Laurent, of the French Ministry of Exterior Relations, was appointed special rapporteur and began his investigation. In March 1983, he presented his report to the United Nations which, with the resolutions that resulted from it, constitute the most far-reaching action of the United Nations on this problem to date. The report stated:

Like slavery in the usual sense, prostitution has an economic aspect. While being a cultural phenomenon rooted in the masculine and feminine images given currency by society, it is a market and indeed a very lucrative one. The merchandise involved is men's pleasure, or their image of pleasure. This merchandise is unfortunately supplied by physical intimacy with women or children. Thus, the alienation of the person is here more far-reaching than in slavery in its usual sense, where what is alienated is working strength, not intimacy.

Likewise, in the past few years, some human rights organizations have begun to renew their energies against the traffic in women. The newly organized Defense for Children covers a large area of children's rights including exploitation of prostitution. The English-based Anti-Slavery Society for several years addressed the issue of forced prostitution and traffic in women when Patrick Montgomery was their secretary. However, since Montgomery retired, the society has refocused its concerns and recently stated that the traffic in adult women and female sexual slavery are not within its mandate. Focusing their efforts on child labor and slavery of children, they do, however, consider child prostitution and pornography to be particular problems. Regrettably, separating child from adult female prostitution has been part of the tradition of silence that has cloaked female sexual slavery in invisibility.

At the same time, groups such as the World Council of Churches and other similar international organizations have become concerned with sex tourism in Asia. Yet we fail to find similar concern for women in prostitution in other parts of the world. Separating child from adult female prostitution, or exploitation of Asian women used in sex tours from the rest of Asian prostitutes and from other women in the world continues to confuse the issue. It reveals that a different set of standards is employed to determine what is exploitative for different groups. It introduces benevolence toward particular groups such as children or some third world women, instead of applying a human rights standard to each individual subjected to degrading, dehumanizing and/or exploitative practices in female sexual slavery. Consequently, the structure of male domination and the power of economic interests remains masked behind benevolent efforts.

Within the international human rights community the only organization that continues to be concerned with the traffic in women or the sexual enslavement of adult women is the International Abolitionist Federation, working through its French branch, the Union Against Traffic in Human Beings, and its English counterpart, the Josephine Butler Society.

Human Rights and Feminist Perspectives on Prostitution

Organizations such as the International Abolitionist Federation argue that laws should be abolished which either prohibit or regulate prostitution. The abolitionist position favors strengthening laws against pimping and procuring, and presses for their vigorous enforcement because it is through pimps and procurers that women are forced into prostitution and prevented from escaping it. According to the abolitionist position, any condition of prostitution that is coerced and forced is a violation of a woman's human rights. Abolitionists do not want the state's intervention to regulate prostitution since they recognize that the main advantage of legalization is for the male customer and not the woman. Instead, the abolitionists believe that it is the duty of the state to press for more vigorous prosecution of pimps and their gangs rather than to formulate regulations and thereby legitimize prostitution. They argue that when the state regulates or "legalizes" prostitution, it is in a position to conveniently ignore the traffic in women because it sanctions prostitution as a legitimate form of work and an accepted social institution, and therefore does not concern itself with whether or not women are trafficked or coerced.

Regarding the individual woman involved in prostitution, the abolitionist position is that as long as a woman freely enters prostitution and can leave freely (in other words, as long as she is in control of her prostitution), the state should not interfere. While the abolitionist position is careful to protect individual women from moralistic condemnation, it consistently refuses to address the institutional basis of prostitution. The abolitionist concern with the free will of individual women ignores an institution that is both coercive and misogynist.

A feminist analysis can accept the abolitionist position for individuals but feminism requires that in exposing patriarchal power we must separate the individual from the institution of prostitution as a product of male domination, sexual violence, and enslavement. Acceptance of prostitution as an inevitable social institution is lodged in the assumption that sex is a male right, whether it is bought, sold, seized as in rape, or more subtly coerced as in sexual harassment.

Theoretically, if sex is a male right, then sex, according to the institution of prostitution, is and should be packaged and sold as a commodity. Further, sex and woman's bodies are commodities that can and should be sold by women themselves, or through pimps and procurers, to customers. In other words, the institution of prostitution, regardless of whether individual women are voluntarily entering or are forced and coerced into it, requires that we accept that sex is and should be a commodity, and that women's bodies (as well as those of children) are the vehicles through which sex is transformed into a commodity.

A Feminist Critique of Prostitution

The fact that sex and women's bodies are commodities to be sold in prostitution, and the meaning for all women that men take the acquisition of this commodity as their right, is a central issue for feminists. The assumptions that form the institutional base of prostitution have rarely been analyzed because prostitution has traditionally been seen as synonymous with prostitutes. Traditionally, patriarchy does not distinguish between the individual (women in prostitution), and the institution, the commodity-based market of prostitution. The women become the institution, and the commodity—the pimps, the market and particularly the practices of procuring, seasoning, and prostituting—are invisible. By collapsing distinctions between the individual and the institution, prostitution becomes inevitable. This leaves the validity of its existence unquestioned.

Meanwhile, women in prostitution face the hypocritical male sexual morality requiring that they be socially condemned for being prostitutes and explicitly available on the market. Feminists are becoming sensitive to the issue of women in prostitution, but within the women's movement, there is still hesitancy to question the institution for fear that they will appear to be condemning the women themselves. We as feminists are acutely conscious of not wanting to judge the women in prostitution even as the male-dominated societies previously have.

As we begin to question the inevitability of the institution of prostitution, it becomes necessary for us to examine several tacit assumptions. What does it mean for a woman to choose to be in prostitution? When we say that a woman or girl chooses prostitution, we are implying that this is free choice. I would like to suggest several issues which the "choice" of prostitution raises for feminists.

1. Many young girls and women in prostitution have been victims of prior sexual abuse, particularly incest in the home. Is not their free choice already determined by these prior conditions?
2. Many young girls and women have turned to prostitution because in the face of extreme poverty, they have found no other alternative. Why is prostitution so often the only apparent choice in the face of starvation? And most important, when a woman or girl is faced with either severe poverty or rendering herself as a commodity for prostitution, can this be considered a choice at all?
3. Liberal Western sexual ideology uses this poor women's alternative as a validation of prostitution for women who are not caught in poverty. If poor women can choose prostitution, then women who are not poverty-stricken but are underpaid in the labor force can logically choose prostitution as a means of earning better wages.
4. Western sexual ideology states that a woman should not continue to be exploited as a secretary earning low wages when she could earn more money in less time as a prostitute. It does not raise questions about the actual experience of prostitution, therefore eliminating the concern for the effects of this "work" on the woman.
5. When the question of choice is taken beyond how it is determined—whether by previous sexual exploitation or by poverty—it brings us to an examination of the validity of the institution from the standpoint of

WPP—L

individual responsibility. We do an injustice to our sex if we do not ask women to be socially responsible for their own free choices. When prostitution is accepted as a logical choice for the underpaid woman, it is then argued (again according to Western liberal ideology) that in comparison to married women, prostitutes at least sell sex and do not give it away. This misogynist assumption places Western liberal feminists who employ it in a position of having to accept and validate sex and women's bodies as market commodities.

6. Patriarchal ideology reaches its logical conclusion from the above arguments when it is asserted that "all women are whores." This was the headline of the Copenhagen newspapers during the Mid-Decade of Women meeting from an interview with members of prostitute collectives organized under the umbrella of the English-based Wages for Housework.

Even though many of these ideas are voiced by some women in prostitution, they represent the ideology of male domination. Viewing prostitution as woman's choice is a way to reduce all women to the lowest and most contemptible status of women in any male-dominated society.

It is in these attitudes toward a woman's choice that we find the justification of prostitution as a form of work for women. It is argued that most of women's labor is exploited, and this is only another form of women's work. But if we accept prostitution as a form of women's work, then we must accept sex and women's bodies as commodities, an idea that is at the core of so much sexual exploitation and violation. Undoubtedly, this ideology has different expressions in various parts of the world. Exposing ideology is important to developing strategies against any oppressive institution; therefore, these diverse expressions should be explored and identified.

Prostitution is intricately interrelated with the exploitation and oppression of all women. Sexual violence and sexual slavery are the most obvious connections. But, if prostitution is considered a valid form of work, we logically should be expanding our energies to make it an opportunity for all women. In approaching the issue of women in prostitution from a feminist perspective, it is important that we use the same understanding and basis of judgments for them as for any other woman. For example, it is a fundamental principle and practice of feminists that the root of our understanding of the conditions of women's lives comes from women telling their own story, exposing their own situations. But we do not assume that each woman's story constitutes the entire objective truth of the situation. We realize, for example, that many women who are victimized in their home will continue to defend their home, cover up for their husbands who are beating them, and idealize marriage, until they are able to recognize that they are unjustly abused. In analyzing prostitution, we run the risk of idealizing sisterhood and objectifying women in prostitution, if we do not assume that at least some of the same problem exists for them. We must continue to listen to women's stories, but as feminists, we can do this only with an approach that does not tolerate any patriarchal institution that serves men through the exploitation and subordination of women.

Analysis of Prostitute Organizations

Many of these issues have caused problems in relationships between women's groups and prostitute organizations. There is a wide diversity of orientations and strategies employed by various prostitute organizations. I have categorized the orientations of prostitute organization in an attempt to clarify their politics and their work (obviously some of these categories overlap with each other).

1. There are organizations like SOS Prostitutes in France and several others in Southeast Asia that provide shelter and refuge for women getting out of prostitution, as well as advice and encouragement to those thinking of leaving prostitution.
2. There are organizations that focus on the police harassment of women in prostitution, and also seek to change laws punitive to women in prostitution.
3. Relying on the assumption that prostitution is a legitimate form of work for women, some organizations are campaigning to have prostitution accepted as a valid profession for women and as a vanguard of free, sexual expression.
4. There are prostitute organizations that fight police fines of prostitutes, accept prostitution as a legitimate form of work, and argue that pimps are actually boyfriends, lovers or husbands; therefore, laws against pimping should be relaxed or modified so as not to interfere with women's private lives. Many of the organizations articulating there demands are supported financially by pimps; some are directed by them.
5. Finally, there are organizations that publicly identify with the above demands for prostitutes, but are covertly working toward their own political ends while co-opting and exploiting prostitute organizations.

In examining the relationship between the feminist movement and prostitute organizations, we face the serious question of how to support and work with individual women in prostitution without supporting the institution, something that places us in opposition to the prostitute organizations supporting the institution. Feminist work against the traffic in women is obviously incompatible with pimps' support of prostitute organizations. To analyze some of the assumptions of prostitute organizations, we must examine them separately from their social context, and ask new questions in order to seriously confront the practices of traffic in women and female sexual slavery.

Prostitution Redefines Woman: Child Versus Adult Prostitution

Most people agree that child pornography and child prostitution are human rights violations. Customers continue to demand younger and younger children to serve them sexually. Trafficking children in prostitution and providing them for pornography is a highly profitable market for pimps and procurers.

Let us examine briefly the kinds of problems that result when child prostitution and pornography are separated from the issue of sexual exploitation of women. Ultimately, the invisibility surrounding the violation of women serves to perpetuate the exploitation of children. Is child prostitution considered a serious crime because it is assumed that children should not be sexually active? Undoubtedly that is part of the reason, but we assume also that the sexual use of young childen by adult men can be psychologically as well as physically damaging. Campaigns against child pornography and child prostitution are based on the belief that we must protect our children from sadistic abuse and perverted behavior. Yet our patriarchal but benevolent organizations enter into some dangerous inconsistencies when they assume that it is a crime for men to buy sexual perversion and to employ sadistic behavior on children, but that it is a form of work and an expression of sex for women.

One of the legal problems that results from a different standard of exploitation for children is that many countries are trying to define children as adults and, by doing so, are making more younger female bodies available to customers. Various countries have introduced legislation lowering the age of consent, something that assists pimps and procurers in their traffic of women and children. Pimps and procurers are more legally vulnerable when they are trafficking 12-, 13-, and 14-year-old girls who are still considered as children or minors by law. In the United States today, the scandals that surface periodically exposing child prostitution and child pornography have to do only with very small children because 12-, 13- and 14-year-old girls are considered socially to be adults. Young girls of this age are being bought on the streets as if they were adult women. Our social redefinition of woman as a 12- or 13-year-old exploitable object lays the groundwork for their legal redefinition.

There are special considerations we must make when we discuss child prostitution and pornography. The physical and psychological effects of sexual exploitation in prostitution and pornography on the young may well be more severe than the effects of such practices on women. Nevertheless, an act intended to degrade, humiliate and exploit is a violation of the human being, whatever her (or his) age, culture, race or condition. Forced prostitution, female sexual slavery, and the related practices of rape, wife abuse, sexual harassment and pornography constitute violations of the human being in whatever context and against whatever age they occur.

The designation of some groups of people as "other" is the foundation of racist and imperialistic exploitation. Sex tourism is based on the racist myths that Asian women are particularly submissive and passive. Fortunately there are now groups in Europe and Asia concerned with exposing the men who travel to Asia for sex tours. Another example is found in an agency advertisement in Florida, which has been marketing Colombian girls to American men utilizing racial myths and stereotypes as part of their appeal.

But it is not enough for Western women to become concerned only with the exploitation of women in other parts of the world. I summarized the problems this situation produces in my book, *Female Sexual Slavery*:

> Feminists from Western nations have often been guilty of approaching women in Third World countries with an air of superiority which assumes that they will bring liberation to the less fortunate and enlightened. Besides the racism this attitude implies, it also reflects the extent to which Western feminists have not been able to recognize the severity of their own oppression.[4]

For example, as an American feminist I cannot afford to lose track of the fact that when the United States decides to exploit resources in any other part of the world, women are among the commodities it purchases, particularly through its military. But, in responding to the sexist dimensions of imperialism, I must also become concerned with the fact that similar to every imperialist nation, what the United States does in subjecting women of other countries has been practiced first on its own women. American imperialism is built upon racist and sexist exploitation at home, just as the European men who avail themselves of Asian sex tours have already learned and practiced sexual domination of their own women in marriage and in prostitution.

What this means is that Western women must be as concerned with the exploitation and enslavement of women in their own countries and cultures as they are with that of women in other parts of the world. It is only with this understanding that feminists can begin to work toward a full definition of women's human rights beginning with the self, and extending into international work through concern for all women as individuals. It is there that the authenticity of international feminist work is established.

THE ACTION

Since spring 1983 when 25 women from almost as many countries first came together in Rotterdam to form an International Feminist Network against Female Sexual Slavery, we have worked on organizing against this problem in our own communities, countries, and regions, and reported to each other and to the international community (as occurred at the 1985 UN Conference on Women in Nairobi, Kenya). This network has given a new, feminist presence to this issue in the international community. Evidence of its effectiveness is the new research on female sexual slavery and a UNESCO meeting in Madrid in March 1985, which called together experts on the causes of prostitution, including several of the feminists active in networks in different world regions.

As a result of the new discussion and debate on this issue in the international community, I proposed to the UNESCO experts the formulation of a new international instrument, which would require nation-states to redefine their approaches to and their laws against prostitution. (This proposal is a reformulation of the abolitionist position which I had originally endorsed in 1979 in *Female Sexual Slavery*.) It rejects the distinction proponents of decriminalized prostitution make between forced and voluntary prostitution and instead recognizes all "commoditization" of women's bodies for sexual exchange as a violation of human dignity and therefore of human rights. It requires that:

1. All laws penalizing the prostitute (victim) must be decriminalized;
2. Pimping must be redefined from the crime of "living off the earnings of women in prostitution" to being a coercive system that not only puts women in prostitution, but prevents them from leaving it while requiring that their bodies be rendered into commodities for sexual-economic exchange;
3. That clients or customers of prostitutes be criminally prosecuted for participating in the commodity exchange of women's bodies;
4. That the state be made responsible for establishing women's training and health programs as well as employment opportunities (the absence of which causes additional coercion of women into prostitution).

When the Madrid meeting agreed to accept this proposal as part of their recommendation, as rapporteur, I wrote the following summary, which was adopted by the group of experts and incorporated into the UNESCO report:

> In finding the causes of prostitution we have opened a new discourse which will break the silence surrounding the exploitation of women in prostitution. Therefore we depart from the traditional understanding of prostitution, by refusing to make a distinction between forced and voluntary prostitution.

Consequently, we refuse to recognize prostitution as a profession. Instead, we understand that prostitution constitutes a commodity exchange of the woman's body in which there is a profound objectification of women. The "sex" that the customer purchases requires that the body of the woman becomes an instrument for men to use. We recognize in the new discourse that this constitutes an assault against the dignity of women and a form of sexual violence.

We find that the commodity of the woman's body causes a severe problem in the breakdown of the woman's identity and a destruction of her sense of self-worth. This phenomenon has its roots in the social structure where it has been made invisible by several factors. First is violence in the family, particularly sexual assault of children, which is only now beginning to be uncovered by the new research motivated by the feminist movement. From this research in the United States we find that high percentages (60%–85%) of women in prostitution have been victims of incest, assault or rape. This has been found to be the first step in the breakdown of woman's identity, which is necessary to render the human body into a sexual commodity for economic exchange. Secondly, governmental institutions and social services often implicitly accept prostitution as being natural for some women, an economic alternative, a form of work, an exchange where the health of the body of the woman should be protected so as to not endanger the customer through contagion of venereal disease, AIDS, etc. Thirdly, other social-economic structures which dominate human beings establish a pretext for prostitution. For example, where there is the alienation of labor, the displacement of refugee persons, male immigration which separates men from their families, or the debilitation of men fighting in war, then the "sexuality of prostitution" becomes for men in these conditions an amelioration of their social circumstances. These factors, which have been kept invisible, actually form a promotional system for prostitution.

Prostitution is promoted through sexualization. By "the sexuality of prostitution" we mean a form of male sexuality which, as a product of the dominant, traditional discourse considers prostitution as sex and pornography as eroticism. By reducing sexuality to this objectified and instrumental purpose, not only are women objectified but men are manipulated to believe that this sexuality of prostitution is the solution to their problems from work, war, refugee and immigrant conditions. If we follow the traditional, dominant discourse on prostitution where prostitution is considered sex and pornography is considered to be eroticism, we are led to solutions which either are repressive to the society and punitive to the women in prostitution or validate prostitution as sex and a profession. But we find that this sexuality of prostitution does not constitute a sexual experience for the commoditized woman's body. By finding the causes of prostitution in this meeting and through the new work in the feminist movement, we open a new discourse which considers prostitution as a form of sex discrimination, sexual violence and the violation of human dignity.

Prostitution, an extreme case in the exploitation of women, requires a radical feminist analysis if we are to develop public policies and programs to effectively respond to the conditions of women's lives. Through studying the objective conditions of women cross-culturally, we have found that prostitution is another of the aspects of oppression that women have in common despite their diverse cultures. This has led us to realize that only by adopting an international human rights perspective that considers the protection of human dignity as central to human rights will we be able to respond to this issue.

Consequently, we have found that international agencies (such as the United Nations) concerned with human rights often are sometimes more receptive to this analysis and policy response than are many local and national governments. By developing international policy aimed at treating prostitution as a crime against women, we are beginning to find the basis for influencing policy and promoting legal change at the national and local levels. Meanwhile, this work has established another link between third world and Western women in our mutual efforts to promote international feminism and claim the full range of our human rights.

NOTES AND REFERENCES

1. Much of this section is taken from Kathleen Barry, *Female Sexual Slavery* (New York: New York University Press, 1979).

2. For this reason, prostitution is considered here as distinct and separate from male (adult) prostitution. Male prostitution is differentiated from female prostitution and sexual slavery by the power relations between men; generally men in prostitution do not enter into the same dependency relations with their pimps or customers. Second, male prostitution is a continuation of a wider range of objectified and sometimes violent male sexuality evident in many forms of men's sexual practices in both the homosexual and heterosexual worlds.

3. Much of this section is taken from Kathleen Barry, "The Opening Paper: International Politics of Female Sexual Slavery," in *International Feminism: Organizing Against Female Sexual Slavery*. (New York, 1984).

4. Barry, *Female Sexual Slavery*, p. 203.

16
Conclusion: Toward the Year 2000

The women's movement emerged in the late 1960s from the shadows of American politics, where it had been languishing since the achievement of women's suffrage in 1920. The movement presented new grievances, new issues, new solutions, and a new vision for the future. At first, the movement was a cry of outrage against the blatant injustice and, yes, cruelty, of the ways women were treated, not just in the job market but in a thousand ways that were unconscious or invisible to the public eye: the battering of wives, the demeaning media stereotypes, the backroom abortions, the smugly accepted quotas in education and the professions, the dreary low-paid "women's" jobs.

The movement transformed the way people think about women and in the process won a series of smashing policy victories. Yet by 1980 it was apparent that these changes had not had the desired consequences. Women in ever-increasing numbers had moved into the work force during the 1970s and 1980s (from 43 percent in 1970 to 54 percent in 1985).[1] As they moved in, they broke into many occupations in which women had been either rare or entirely unheard of: firefighters, corporate vice presidents, telephone line workers, lawyers, doctors, police officers, even astronauts. A woman was elected prime minister of Great Britain and, perhaps even more surprisingly, mayor of Chicago.

And yet by 1980 it had begun to seem that the more things changed, the more they remained the same. The wage gap between women and men had not decreased during the 1970s. At the beginning of the decade, full-time working women had been earning 59 percent of what full-time working men earned; by the end of the decade the gap was exactly the same. How could this be? It seemed that most of the new female arrivals to the work force had found jobs in the lowest paying occupations as office, sales and service workers. Often they experienced their entry into the work force not as liberation but as a burden, since their paid work was simply added to the unpaid work they performed at home.

Another victory won by the early women's movement was the Supreme Court decision legalizing abortion in the famous 1973 case of *Roe v. Wade*. With legal abortion backing up contraception, women presumably would

WPP—L*

297

be freed to have babies only when they really wanted them and were able to give them the best care without undue sacrifice of their own identity. Yet the 1970s saw rapidly rising birthrates among unwed and/or teenage mothers.

Deep-seated public attitudes were slow to change. Quite early, the women's movement had taken gay rights, particularly for lesbians, as one of its causes. During the 1970s a great deal of the heterosexual public accepted the idea that it was wrong to discriminate against homosexuals (though in the 1980s the AIDS scare has caused a return of much homophobia). A few heterosexuals even saw that the homosexual movement carried an important benefit from them, too: if they gave up their fear and loathing of homosexuals, they would be better able to accept their own masculine (for women) or feminine (for men) side, and thus could be more complete, secure, and productive human beings. Yet in an important sense nothing changed in this area either. Many women continued to build their own sense of self-worth and identity around their partnership with a man or their aspiration for such a partnership.

In short, the women's movement by 1980 had found that the path to the fulfillment of its vision was longer and rockier than had been imagined 10 years earlier. One significant barrier was that a few highly vocal women began to advocate turning back, restoring the kind of family in which father ruled the roost while mother baked the cookies. Yet even the anti-feminists' greatest victory, the defeat of the Equal Rights Amendment, was caused largely by the inherent difficulty of ratification of any constitutional amendment rather than by a loss of public support for the amendment.

In fact, in some ways attitudes really had changed in the direction hoped for by feminists. By 1980, homemakers found themselves apologizing for not being in the work force, whereas 10 years earlier, employed women had been on the defensive for not being at home raising children. Public opinion polls found near-universal opposition to any form of discrimination in education or employment. Even Phyllis Schlafly, the outspoken leader of the anti-ERA forces, when explaining why the United States was a great country for women, gave as one of her two main reasons the existence of anti-discrimination legislation! (The other reason was the availability of household labor-saving devices, presumably desirable because they could release women from household drudgery so that they could follow her example and lead political movements.)[2]

Even men supported the women's movement to an extraordinary degree. Public opinion polls found men's support to be almost as strong as women's for anti-discrimination laws, legal abortion, and the Equal Rights Amendment.[3] *The Hearts of Men*, published in 1983, made a plausible case that men had been wanting a change from traditional sex roles beginning in the 1950s, even before there was a highly visible women's movement.[4] Many men had begun to see that working long hours as the sole breadwinner often left them exhausted, emotionally empty and estranged from the very wives and children whom they were supporting.

Moreover, for most poor women, including many Black women, the traditional Dad-at-work/Mom-at-home family had never existed. For them legal abortion, subsidized child care, battered women's shelters, laws against pregnancy discrimination and so on, were even more indispensable than for middle class women. Any attempt to restore the mythical Golden Age that the anti-feminists envisioned was unthinkable for them.

The women's movement in 1980 was proud of its string of legislative and judicial victories: enforcement machinery (including affirmative action) for the Equal Pay Act of 1963 and Title VII of the Civil Rights Act of 1964 ban on employment discrimination, an equal credit law, a law against pregnancy discrimination, Title IX of the Education Amendments of 1972 forbidding sex discrimination in education, legal abortion, the reform of many police and court practices relating to rape and the treatment of battered women, and many more. Yet it was clear that far more needed to be done if these reforms were to have their full impact on women's lives.

Feminists asked themselves what direction should be taken by the women's movement in the 1980s. The answer was not clear. Women's political energies were dispersed in many different directions during the Reagan era. The early policy achievements had been mostly of a regulatory nature, to refer back to Lowi's famous typology (see pp. 15–16). Prospects did not seem good for distributive policy (subsidies) during an era of massive budget cutting in domestic government spending. Redistributive policy change seemed an even more distant dream.

One obvious possibility was to continue pressing for regulatory reform. In the 1980s the liberal feminist lobbying groups were able to add another to the series of anti-discrimination laws for which they had fought when Congress passed the Retirement Equity Act of 1984, which brought about significant pension reform. In 1986, NOW announced plans to push for reintroduction of the Equal Rights Amendment in Congress. However, neither of these efforts could be described as an exciting new direction for the women's movement.

Other approaches seemed more promising. The 1980s saw a new emphasis on the issue of violence against women, particularly in a heterosexual context. Sexual harassment of women tenants, marital rape, date rape, "granny bashing," father–daughter incest were all newly emerging issues. In addition, in the 1980s for the first time feminists began to press the issue of pornography that portrayed violence against women as a presumed underlying cause of rape, wife battering, and the more recently spotlighted forms of violence against women. The new focus on violence has a great deal of gut-level appeal to large numbers of women, including those who might not otherwise identify with the women's movement. The injustices in this area are palpable and serious, and are capable of being at least partially remedied by regulatory reforms, such as legislation against marital rape.

The emphasis on pornography, however, may be a dead end, for several reasons. Pornography's causal relationship to violence against women has not been clearly shown, as even the 1986 Meese Commission (in the Report of the U.S. Attorney General's Commission on Pornography) conceded, though at the same time recommending stern measures against pornography. The issue is also divisive for feminists, some of whom feel that the attack on pornography undermines both sexual freedom (including that of women) and the First Amendment. The Supreme Court agreed with them on the latter point when in 1986 it struck down an Indianapolis anti-porn ordinance based on model legislation written by feminists. Some argue that the issue of pornography will probably fade away, as it becomes increasingly apparent that even if porn is a significant cause of violence against women (which is not at all clear), there is not a great deal that can be done about it. On the other hand, a focus on the issue of violence against women itself is likely to continue to produce both new awareness (about the incidence and types of violence) and new changes in public policy.

Many women are beginning to organize around another form of violence: war. The 1980s saw a revival of concern about the danger of nuclear war and the wasteful spiraling of the nuclear arms race. Women played an exceptionally prominent role as peace activists. Dr. Helen Caldicott founded the very active and effective anti-nuclear-war group, Physicians for Social Responsibility (although she was eventually pushed out of its leadership by a mostly male group of physicians). Petra Kelly became an international spokesperson for the Green party of West Germany. Women's peace groups founded in earlier eras such as Women Strike for Peace, Another Mother for Peace, and the Women's International League for Peace and Freedom were revitalized. And millions of women marched in demonstrations, lobbied for a nuclear freeze, organized teach-ins, and even lived in all-female peace camps outside the walls of nuclear installations in the United States and Britain. The peace movement seemed an ideal outlet for women's newfound political empowerment.

Yet for many women the peace movement was an alternative to the women's movement rather than an extension of feminism into a new area. To some women, peace work even seemed to be an extension of traditional roles, particularly the mother role. Helen Caldicott expresses the view that as the nurturers of life, mothers have a special responsibility to assure its future preservation. This seems to imply that since men's major role is not the nurturance of life, they should feel free to leave the question of its preservation up to women, thus perpetuating a particularly unfortunate form of the division of labor between the sexes: women work for peace, men make war.

Others have argued that women's work in the peace movement tends to cast them in the role of outsiders, contending against the ones in power but not seeking to share that power, and therefore not being taken seriously by the powerful. Sheila Tobias and Shelah Leader argued in 1982 that women must free themselves of this outsider's mentality and educate themselves about the details of weapons systems and strategic doctrines; Tobias wrote a book to help them do so.[5] Judith Stiehm, in the first edition of *Women, Power and Policy*, made the further point that when women leave the business of war to men, they put themselves in a "protected" category of people—passive, dependent, unfree, ultimately treated as children.[6]

All of this is not to suggest that women should give up peace activism and join the Marines. It does suggest, however, that feminists' participation in peace work should be informed by an awareness of the dangers of disempowerment inherent in such work if it is pursued without an accompanying feminist consciousness. Perhaps every woman peace activist should draw up her own realistic and detailed weapons policy, in anticipation of the day she is appointed secretary of defense. Every woman working in an all-women peace group should ask herself why her group does not include men. And every woman working in a mixed peace group should ask herself if she has the same leadership opportunities as the men in her group do.

Peace work, as well as a wide range of other political issues, could become areas in which feminism potentially extends its range and influence. After all, the women's movement will not have achieved its goal until women are as effective and influential as men in every area of life. For the remainder of the century, not only peace but basic survival issues are a logical area in which to extend a feminist perspective. (As this book has amply documented, women are far more likely to live in poverty than men.)

For the U.S. women's movement, a new emphasis on poverty issues would bring a number of benefits. First, it would be a way of reaching out to elderly women and women of color and of laying the basis for much stronger coalitions. It would also be a basis for linkage to unions, liberal churches, civil rights groups, and other organizations that have traditionally been concerned with government policies toward the poor. Finally, it would make possible a much stronger international outreach, both to the third world and to social change groups in Europe and elsewhere.

The U.S. women's movement has been widely perceived, in this country and abroad, as white and middle class in its emphasis and style. This has resulted in a certain amount of isolation and a good deal of breast-beating. A greater emphasis on poverty issues would correct this problem. It would be exciting to see a feminist approach to welfare, teen pregnancy, homelessness, the poverty and loneliness of many older women, inadequate health care, hunger, and the struggles of new immigrants. All of these are significant problems of American women not yet cohesively addressed by the women's movement.

In addition, the women's movement must tackle the issue of the family much more directly than it has done in recent years. This is a difficult issue, because any criticism of the existing institution of the family tends to be seen as an attack on the family as such, rather than on some ideological vision of the family. It is also difficult in practical terms because many feminists have abandoned the nuclear family—choosing to remain single or to divorce; to focus their energies on their careers; to bond with other women in lesbian relationships, friendship networks, or support groups; to live far away from their families of origin; to cohabit with a series of different men; to exercise their option not to have children; or to have children using artificial insemination. These are all perfectly legitimate choices. Yet the women who make these choices are to some degree out of touch with the roughly three-quarters of U.S. women who do live in nuclear families.

When Betty Friedan wrote in 1981 that the second stage for the women's movement was to reconcile women's family lives with their new status in the rest of society, she was roundly attacked by many feminists.[7] Yet Friedan's essential point was correct. Further advances in women's employment are likely to be blocked by the lack of consideration for or adequate assistance to employed women in their family roles. Violence against women is likely to continue at high rates as long as women have no alternative to remaining within the nuclear family. Women will continue to be grossly underrepresented in positions of leadership and in the ranks of those who make major achievements as long as the major energies of most women are taken up by family responsibilities.

Even women who choose not to live in families or not to be mothers are negatively affected by the fact that others expect them to become mothers and discriminate against them accordingly. Feminists need to come to grips with the fact that without significant changes in the relationship of the family to society, women will always be second-class citizens. Feminists also must begin to explore what form these changes might take.

It is highly suggestive that in European countries, which offer a far wider range of subsidies and services to families than are available in the United States, the wage gap between women and men is much lower than in the United States. These countries offer such benefits as state-run child care centers or pre-schools for a significant percentage of children under 5; paid maternity (and sometimes paternity) leaves for all workers for anywhere from 3 to 9 months, followed by unpaid leaves for even longer periods, with guaranteed rights to return to the job without loss of seniority; a national health plan providing free or nearly free medical care to the whole population, including children and pregnant women; children's allowances and housing allowances for all families with children; state collection of child support payments, with the risk of non-collection borne by the state, not the mother; and so on.[8] All of these benefits are offered in the context of social attitudes that see procreation as a contribution to the society, in contrast to the common American view of procreation as a selfish personal choice and sole responsibility of women.

But why look outside the family at all? If mothers are handicapped in everything they do, is not the obvious solution to get fathers to shoulder their share of the burden of childrearing? Obvious perhaps, but not easy. Countries such as China and Cuba have policies of urging husbands to do their share of housework and child care—policies that have little perceptible impact. Still, some combination of paid parental leave and the use of social institutions—public schools, the media, the churches and synagogues, appealing role models and (not least) rock music—could begin to make a difference. Parental or maternity leave is now offered by some 37 percent of American businesses.[9] The Family and Medical Leave bill, which would require up to 18 weeks of unpaid leave for care of newborn, newly adopted or seriously ill children, as well as leave for workers with serious health conditions, has been introduced in both houses of Congress (its House sponsor is Rep. Patricia Schroeder) and appears to have a good chance of passage. The role of government in resocialization would occur not so much through new legislation or court decisions as through the rhetoric of popular and effective leaders.

Yet it is doubtful that men will play a significant role in raising children unless there is a major change in social values, in the direction of deemphasizing the traditionally masculine goals of money and power, and increasing the emphasis on the traditionally feminine values of nurturance and emotional commitment. In the 1980s, millions of young women have begun to prepare themselves in a more serious way than ever for the pursuit of money and power. Perhaps in the 1990s, millions of men, disgusted and disillusioned by the loneliness of lives filled with hostile take-over bids, negative campaigning, plant closings, heart attacks and repeated divorces, will decide to devote more of their energies to their families. Ideally, as Diane Franklin and Joan Sweeney suggest in chapter 3, women and men together will seek to develop styles of both working and living that are less stressful, alienating, and isolating, which will help heal the split between home and work that is at the heart of both women's powerlessness and men's loneliness.

Until now, the women's movement has expressed itself politically mostly through conventional lobbying, litigation, and coalition-building. Most women who run for political office have been careful not to be publicly identified as feminists. The much-discussed gender gap of the 1980 and 1984 elections largely fizzled—not surprisingly, since women could hardly be expected to vote along the lines of a distinct women's perspective if neither candidates nor political parties were expressing such a perspective and delineating what it might mean in terms of policy. By staying within the bounds of conventional two-party politics, the women's movement did succeed in winning a number of real victories. But this approach made it utterly impossible to articulate and promote the alternative value system discussed above; it may be that women's status cannot really change without such a transformation of values.

Until now, radically alternative feminist values have been expressed only through a decentralized network of bookstores, small publications, presses, record companies, self-health clinics, and so forth. This network has no effective channel of communication to or through the political system, the corporations, the media, or the educational system, and thus its influence is necessarily very limited.

But suppose a distinctively women's point of view were expressed through a new political party. The sense of unity and new direction that the party would arouse would draw larger numbers of women into political activism. Since such a party would probably not have the funding or power base to elect many candidates, its main function would be to serve as a voice for articulating a women's point of view, perhaps a broader one than the one that has been called feminist. If the party were able to attract a significant number, say even 5 or 6 percent, of the vote (and the potential is there, since women voters outnumber men voters and the number is growing all the time), it could influence the positions of both major parties—as, for example, George Wallace's third party in 1968 and Eugene V. Debs's Socialist Party in 1912 and 1920 succeeded in doing. In addition to articulating a distinctively female point of view, a women's party would put pressure on the major parties to run more women candidates and on those candidates to help expound that point of view. In Norway, the existence of a small women's party has encouraged the rise of women's influence in the major parties, thus helping to elect a woman prime minister. In Iceland the feminist party now holds the balance of power in national politics. An American women's party could use rallies as a way of creating emotional solidarity around its causes, as well as media images of women uniting to express their political commitment. It need not run candidates in every race around the country, but could target, for example, officeholders whose votes and actions harmed women, children, or families.

Feminists of the 1980s should not be discouraged by the lack of success of Alice Paul's earlier Women's Party, which was in large part due to the fact that its emphasis on the Equal Rights Amendment during the 1920s through 1950s put it at odds with almost all progressive women leaders of that period. This particular moment in history may be ideal for the launching of such a third party, since both the major parties seem divided and directionless, groping for some sort of vision for the future. The women's party could offer such a vision and thus perhaps help bring about the long-overdue realignment of American political parties.

Of course, there are serious barriers to the development of a women's party. In order to achieve maximum effect, it would have to draw the energies and the funds of most of the women now working through interest groups, major parties, and grass-roots women's movement organizations. And it may be that their diverse approaches are more effective than the high-risk strategy of creating a women's party would be. A women's party would greatly complicate the task of reaching out to male-dominated or mixed-gender organizations like liberal churches and labor unions, which would be important allies in almost all policy areas of special concern to women. Finally, in order to be successful in attracting voters and activists, a women's party would have to have charismatic leaders who were acceptable to nearly all the disparate groups and individuals who make up the women's movement. Such women are not yet visible on the horizon.

Perhaps, many of the goals and strategies discussed above as advantages of a women's party could instead be carried out by women's interest groups and caucuses within the major parties—such as articulating a women's point of view in American politics, organizing rallies, and targeting particularly objectionable anti-women officeholders. It is clear that women are still not fully included in U.S. party politics and that their distinct attitudes and interests on a wide range of issues are rarely recognized.

Underlying any new political strategy is the necessity to revitalize the women's movement. While the movement is clearly not in its death throes, as some had predicted a few years ago, it is in search of new life and energy. The path to revitalization stretches ahead, with new broader issues to work toward such as ending poverty and violence, winning public support for family issues like child care and child support, and achieving a non-nuclear peace. Broader coalitions, nationally and internationally, are being formed to attain these ends. The outlook in 1988 is certainly more positive than at the beginning of the 1980s, as the struggle gains new momentum. After several millenia of patriarchal politics, and after only two decades of women's rapidly changing consciousness, it no longer seems utopian to believe that women as a political group will come into their own by the year 2000.

NOTES AND REFERENCES

1. *Statistical Abstract of the United States, 1986* (Washington, DC: Bureau of the Census), p. 391.

2. Phyllis Schlafly, *The Power of the Positive Woman*, (New York: Jove, 1981).

3. *Gallup Poll* (Wilmington, Del.: Scholarly Resources, Inc., 1984), abortion attitudes on p. 240, job discrimination attitudes on p. 195, ERA attitudes on p. 138.

4. Barbara Ehrenreich, *The Hearts of Men: American Dreams and the Flight from Commitment* (Garden City, NY: Doubleday, 1983), passim.

5. "An Intelligent Woman's Guide to the Military Mind: What Kinds of Guns are They Buying for Your Butter?" by Sheila Tobias and Shelah Leader, *Ms.*, Vol. 11, July-August 1982. The book referred to is Sheila Tobias and Peter Goudinoff, *What Kinds of Guns are They Buying for Your Butter? A Beginner's Guide to Defense, Weaponry and Military Spending* (New York: Morrow, 1982).

6. Judith Hicks Stiehm, "Women, Men and Military Service: Is Protection Necessarily a Racket?" in Ellen Boneparth (ed.), *Women, Power and Policy* (New York: Pergamon, 1982), pp. 282–293.

7. Betty Friedan, *The Second Stage* (New York: Summit Books, 1981).

8. Kahn, Alfred J. and Sheila B. Kamerman, *Not for the Poor Alone: European Social Services* (Philadelphia: Temple University Press, 1975), passim. The salaries of full-time women workers average about 80 percent of men's in Europe, compared with 64 percent in the United States.

9. Sherry Buchanan, "Baby Leave: The Hard Part is Getting Dads to Take It," *International Herald Tribune*, July 23, 1986, p. 8. Not all fathers will choose to spend significantly more time with their children, and the ones who do so will find themselves at a competitive disadvantage in the world of work. Interestingly, 41 percent of the companies that offer unpaid paternity leave to men do not think that fathers should take the leave! Presumably, they view taking paternity leave as displaying an unmanly lack of ambition and job commitment.

Index

About the Editors and Contributors

ELLEN BONEPARTH is a Foreign Service Officer serving at the U.S Embassy, Athens, Greece Formerly, she was a professor of political science, specializing in American government, public policy and women's studies. She was the editor of *Women, Power and Policy* (Pergamon Press, 1982).

EMILY STOPER is Professor of Political Science and Co-Director of Women's Studies at California State University, Hayward. She is the author of numerous articles about women and politics and public policy on the family, as well as an article about the Student Nonviolent Coordinating Committee. She also teaches courses on Soviet government and Soviet foreign policy. She was recently elected vice president, program chair and president-elect of the Northern California Political Science Association. In her spare time, she enjoys folk dancing and cross-country skiing.

KATHLEEN BARRY teaches feminist theory at Brandeis University. She is the author of *Female Sexual Slavery* and a forthcoming biography of Susan B. Anthony. She has organized an International Feminist Network Against Female Sexual Slavery.

ANNE N. COSTAIN is an associate professor of political science at the University of Colorado, Boulder. She has studied Washington-based lobbying by women's organizations over the past decade with support from the Center for the American Woman and Politics at Rutgers University, the Brookings Institution in Washington, and the Mary I. Bunting Institute at Radcliffe. Her current research focuses on congressional responsiveness to women's issues.

IRENE DIAMOND is an associate professor of political science at the University of Oregon. She has published on women's politics, family policy and feminist theory and is currently working on a book on feminism and ecology, *Women and Fertility: The Political and Spiritual Promise of Ecofeminism*.

DIANE W. FRANKLIN, Ph.D., is a social psychologist who is currently on the faculty of the College of Business at Northeastern University. Previously she wrote labor and human resource management cases at the Harvard Business School. Her research interests include women and work, "new forms" of work such as part-time work and telecommuting, and training programs in multinational corporations. She is also a consultant to a project on non-traditional jobs for women.

PATRICIA HUCKLE is an associate professor at San Diego State University where she teaches courses on women and the law, the women's movement and international feminism in the Women's Studies Department. Dr. Huckle has published articles on affirmative action, utopianism, Title IX and athletics, and is currently completing an authorized biography of activist Tish Sommers. She lives on a sailboat in San Diego bay.

JILL NORGREN is associate professor of government at John Jay College of Criminal Justice of the City University of New York. She writes on public policy, especially questions of family policy and sub-cultures. Her articles have appeared in *Western Political Quarterly, Howard Law Journal, The Nation* and the *New York Times*. Her forthcoming book is *American Cultural Pluralism and the Law* (Praeger).

MARGARITA PAPANDREOU is the President of the Women's Union of Greece and International Liaison of Women for a Meaningful Summit. She is married to Andreas Papandreou, Prime Minister of Greece, and has four children.

SARA E. RIX, holds a Ph.D. in Sociology from the University of Virginia, and is Director of Research at the Women's Research and Education Institution (WREI), the nonpartisan research arm of the bipartisan Congressional Caucus for Women's Issues. At WREI she specializes in social, policy, and comparative research and analysis. Her primary research interests are employment policy, retirement policy, and the economics of aging.

DIANE SCHAFFER is associate professor of social work and coordinator of women's studies at San José State University in California. Her research focuses on the viability of single-mother families in different cultural contexts. In 1985 she designed the curriculum for and taught in the African/American Institute on Women in Development held in conjunction with the United Nations Decade Conference on Women.

ELENI STAMIRIS is an anthropologist who, since 1982, has been director of the Mediterranean Women's Studies Institute, Athens, Greece. From 1984 to 1986, she served on the Board of Trustees of the United Nations International Research and Training Institute for the Advancement of Women (INSTRAW) and in 1986 she served as president. She is married and has a daughter.

KATHLEEN STAUDT is associate professor of political science and assistant dean, College of Liberal Arts, at the University of Texas at El Paso. She has published articles about women's politics and Kenyan agricultural policy in *Comparative Politics, Journal of Politics, Journal of Developing Areas* and *Development and Change*, among others. She is currently working on an edited collection, *Women, Development and the State*, with Sue Ellen Charlton and Jana Everett.

JOAN L. SWEENEY, Ph.D., is an organizational psychologist who is currently working as director of enterprise development with Metasystems Design Group, Inc. Her pioneering research on women in the Committee of 200 is the basis of Something Ventured, Something Gained, a training program on risk taking and business growth. She is also a research associate for entrepreneurship and economic development at the Stone Center, Wellesley College.

LOUISE A. WILLIAMS, a principal consultant with the California Legislature, Assembly Office of Research, researches policy on biotechnology and other high technology issues. Formerly, she was a project director and senior analyst at the U.S. Congress, Office of Technology Assessment. She received her Ph.D. in physical anthropology from UCLA.